NIGERIAN CHIEFS

ROCHESTER STUDIES in AFRICAN HISTORY and the DIASPORA

(ISSN: 1092-5228)

NIGERIAN CHIEFS

Traditional Power in Modern Politics, 1890s–1990s

Olufemi Vaughan

UNIVERSITY OF ROCHESTER PRESS

First published 2000.
Softcover edition published 2006.

University of Rochester Press
668 Mt. Hope Avenue, Rochester, NY 14620, USA
www.urpress.com
and Boydell & Brewer Limited
PO Box 9, Woodbridge, Suffolk IP12 3DF, UK
www.boydellandbrewer.com

ISBN: 1–58046–040–2 (Hardcover)
ISBN: 1–58046–249–9 (Softcover)
ISSN: 1092–5228

Library of Congress Cataloging-in-Publication Data
Vaughan, Olufemi.
    Nigerian chiefs: traditional power in modern politics, 1890s–1990s / Olufemi Vaughan.
        p. cm. — (Rochester studies in African history and the diaspora, ISSN 1092–5228; v. 7)
    Includes bibliographical references and index.
    ISBN 1–58046–040–2 (alk. paper)
    1. Yoruba (African people)—Politics and government. 2. Yoruba (African people)—Kings and rulers. 3. Yoruba (African people)—Government relations. 4. Chiefdoms—Nigeria—History. 5. Power (Social sciences)—Nigeria. 6. Nigeria—Politics and government. I. Title. II. Series.
DT515.45.Y67 V38 2000
320.9669—dc21
                                                                99–088099

A catalogue record for this title is available from the British Library.

Designed and typeset by ISIS-1 Corporation.
This publication is printed on acid-free paper.
Printed in the United States of America.

CONTENTS

MAPS

TABLES

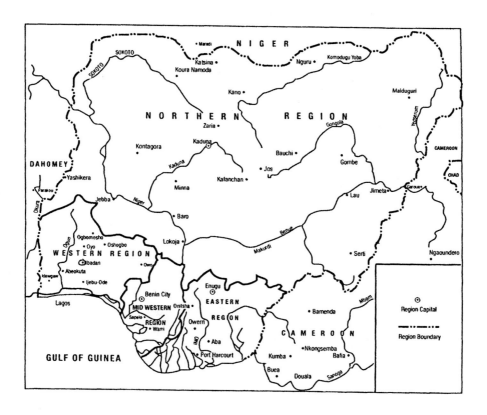

Nigeria

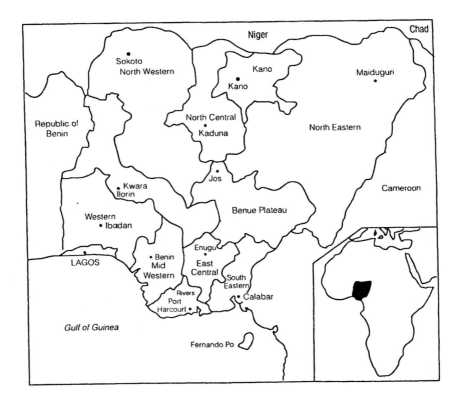

The Twelve States of Nigeria (1967–1976)

Yorubaland Towns and Sub-Groups

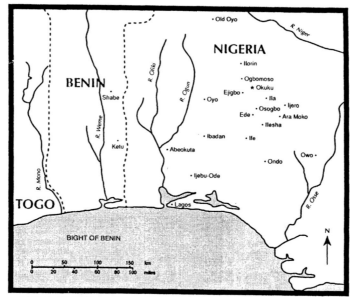

Yoruba and Their Neighbors in the Nineteenth Century

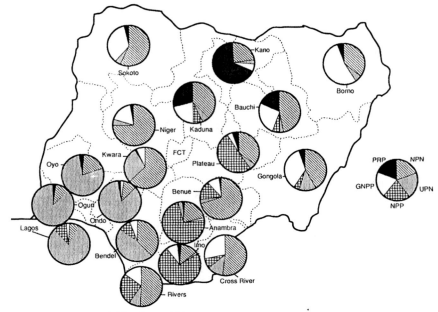

Nigerian Senatorial Election 1979

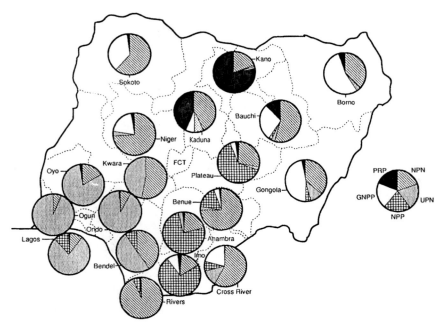

Nigerian Gubernatorial Election 1979

To My Mother, Aduke

ACKNOWLEDGMENTS

This book benefitted from the contributions of many friends and colleagues. I owe a considerable intellectual debt to three eminent Africanists: A. H. M. Kirk-Greene, Terence Ranger and Gavin Williams. As dedicated teachers and mentors, they offered essential guidance and critiques during the initial stages of this study. Their steadfast support over the years is an important source of inspiration. Less directly, I am grateful to a number of scholars for their pioneering work on grassroots politics in Nigeria. While my citations will reveal the extent of my intellectual debts, I would like to pay particular tribute here to Roland Abiodun, Ladipo Adamolekun, A. G. Afigbo, J. A. Atanda, Toyin Falola, Julius Ihonvbere, George Jenkins, P. C. Lloyd, J. D. Y. Peel, Kenneth Post, Richard Sklar and C. S. Whitaker.

Special thanks to Funso Afolayan, Toyin Falola, Julius Ihonvbere, Herman Lebovics, Ann O'Hear, Barbara Weinstein, and the late Lajla Lund for reading draft chapters and offering thoughtful suggestions. I simply cannot find appropriate words to thank Katharine Moseley for her signal contribution to the finished work. A meticulous, generous and patient critic, she closely read the entire manuscript, providing critical intellectual insight and editorial expertise.

For professional solidarity during the years this book was in the making, I owe heartfelt thanks to Tajudeen Abdul Raheem, Awe Abiodun, A. G. Adebayo, Adesoji Adelaja, Okon Akiba, Anthony Akinola, Claire Alexander, Kayode Fayemi, Kelechi Kalu, Foluso Ladehinde, F. H. I. Oditah, J. K. Olupona, Femi Taiwo and John Wiseman. And to Jide Eniola, Mercy Erike, Neil Joseph, Data and Dawari Longjohn, Barbara and Ira Margolies, Kolade Oke, Esther Traub and Diane West, for "some perspective," support and unfailing good sense of humor during the critical final stages of the manuscript. I should also acknowledge the support of my colleagues at Stony Brook, particularly: Bill Arens, Amiri Baraka, Donna Di Donato, Barbara Frank, Aisha Khan, Ira Livingstone, Iona Man-Cheong, Gary Marker, William McAdoo, Ernest McNealey, Frank Myers, Leslie Owens, Joel Rosenthal, Michael Schwartz, S. N. Shridar and John Williams.

The series editor, Toyin Falola, and two senior officials of the University of Rochester Press, Louise Goldberg and Timothy Madigan, had the temerity to believe in the manuscript—a leap of faith I trust they will not regret. I am grateful to them for their strategic combination of support, encouragement and professional expertise. I would also like to thank the Ford Foundation for supporting my research on indigenous political structures and state formation in Africa.

Finally, and most important, my loving gratitude to my wife, Rosemary, our children, Moni, Ayo and Olu, and the "clan" in Ibadan. This book is a token of my appreciation for their love and support.

I would like to acknowledge the following publications which served as models from which the maps were derived: *Geography of Nigeria in Focus* (Lagos: Government Printer, 1980) [maps 1, 2 and 3]; Ulli Beier, *Yoruba Beaded Crowns* (London: Ethnographica, in association with the National Museum, 1982) [map 4]; and *The Nigerian 1979 Elections* (Lagos: Government Printer, 1979) [maps 5 and 6, also the four tables].

1

INTRODUCTION

The idea that indigenous structures are dynamic entities, capable of imaginative agency, has once again gained currency in Africanist scholarship. In a context of emerging civil society and a crisis of state legitimacy, this renewed preoccupation with grassroots structures is gaining prominence at a time when African states are confronting an extraordinary degree of global marginality. And just as this complex issue of "structures of societies" has serious ramifications for processes of state formation,[1] so does it have important implications for Africanist social science itself. Through a detailed historical study of the impact of chieftaincy politics on social relations in western Nigeria (the region of the Yoruba people), this book explores the creative response of indigenous political structures to the problems of modernization and governance that have engulfed the African continent during the past century. The analysis suggests that while indigenous structures have become part and parcel of contemporary stratification and politics, they have had equivocal consequences for the legitimation of the Nigerian state. At the same time, I argue that the postcolonial state project requires—indeed, cannot avoid—an imaginative integration of antecedent structures with the agencies of the modern state.

The Yoruba experience exemplifies the dynamism of chieftaincy structures in modern Nigerian politics. Since the imposition of colonial rule in the late nineteenth century, these structures have demonstrated remarkable adaptability as important institutions of governance. Chieftaincy structures are continuously regenerated in rapidly shifting sociopolitical and economic contexts. Nigerian communities with centralized political institutions

1

persist in promoting the status of their traditional rulers and chiefs as veritable expressions of communal aspirations. Indeed, those with relatively diffused leadership systems have adopted imaginative strategies to create chieftaincy positions and to enhance their prestige. In the case of the Yoruba, elaborate kingship and chieftaincy institutions have served as the centerpiece for the construction of a pan-ethnic identity in the colonial and postcolonial period. Thus, engulfed in the historical processes of Nigerian state formation, Yoruba chieftaincy structures have retained their importance as critical mediums of class formation, intergroup competition and communal aspirations.

The resilience of chieftaincy structures is thus not unconnected to the crisis of the Nigerian state itself; this is most apparent in the ways in which dominant ethno-regional commercial and bureaucratic elites have struggled for state power over the past four decades. Postwar Nigerian history is replete with civilian and military regimes that have emerged and disappeared in quick and baffling succession. The custodians of chieftaincy, however, remain a permanent feature of local communities. This phenomenon has serious implications for the stability and legitimacy of the contemporary state.

This book centers on the interplay of chieftaincy politics, elite formation, communal identities and the struggle for state power in colonial and postcolonial Nigeria. We will map out the conflicting ideologies and multiple levels of authority that have sustained the power base of Yoruba political elites since the imposition of colonial rule in the late nineteenth century. At the core of this analysis are the changing fortunes of Yoruba obas and chiefs in the unfolding drama of power politics in the twentieth century. The central actors in the study are, then, those traditional rulers, *obas* (as well as their counterparts in other regions: *emirs, obis, obongs,* etc.), and subordinate *baales,* chiefs and village heads who, until the demise of colonial rule, were the repositories of local political authority. Our focus will shift between the local, regional and national levels, scrutinizing official policies towards traditional rulers, chiefs, and local government institutions, on the one hand; on the other, the active role of chiefly rulers and other grassroots elements in local politics and governance. The study is organized around the following major themes: colonial rule, chieftaincy and the struggle for legitimation in Yoruba communities; chieftaincy politics, ethno-regionalism and elite formation during decolonization; and chieftaincy structures, ethno-regionalism and the struggle for state power in postcolonial Nigeria. Such an analysis must underscore interactions among obas, chiefs, colonial functionaries, local councillors, politicians and so on.

The detailed case studies that sustain these themes are drawn from Oyo Province, an amorphous collection of kingdoms and chiefdoms which was forged into the largest administrative jurisdiction in colonial southern Nigeria. As it was organized in the 1930s, the region consisted of Ibadan Division, Oyo Division, the Northern District of Oshun and the Central District of Binukonu. As a consequence of the decolonization process, when three regional governments were created, it emerged as a critical section of the Western Region. In 1976, when a military regime carved the Western State (the Yoruba region) into three units, the area became known as Oyo State. Significantly, it contains three pivotal regional towns of Ibadan, Oyo and Ife, where chieftaincy structures have experienced considerable stress since the early nineteenth century.

Theoretical Perspectives

Postwar analyses of chieftaincy structures were initially dominated by the now largely discredited mid-century modernization paradigm. Premised on positivist and evolutionary assumptions, these earlier studies of the nation state project predicted the imminent demise of chieftaincy structures in African politics. Analyzed in the context of third world decolonization, the cold war and global capitalism,[2] modernization theorists emphasized the erosion of chiefly power in the postcolonial African state. For example, Marion Levy contended that, with the advance of modernization, indigenous structures and practices would rapidly wither away.[3] Similarly, the Ugandan ethnographic studies of social anthropologist Lloyd Fallers concluded that the incompatible values of modernization and traditionalism would marginalize chiefly power in African states.[4] These dominant postwar social science perspectives drew heavily from Max Weber's notion that power is legitimate only when the political community expresses voluntary consent.[5] This conceptualization is based on the assumption that rational human behavior is best mediated by the agencies of the modern state and civil society. Thus, since indigenous African structures were widely held to be dysfunctional in this postwar political context, modernization theorists contend that their marginalization is an essential precondition for the socio-political and economic development of African states. Given the resilience of indigenous political structures and the colossal failure of the Nigerian state, it is essential to re-open the discussion on the role of chieftaincy in colonial and postcolonial Nigerian politics. Indeed, by emphasizing the normative and utilitarian attributes of indigenous institutions in the structural transformation of Asian and African states, some notable revisions in the modernization paradigm have anticipated the adaptability of these structures to modern political development.[6]

This perspective, which underscores the dynamic interplay between "traditional" and "modern" structures, has a distinguished intellectual record in an Africanist social science scholarship that predates the modernization paradigm itself. Social anthropologists such as K. A. Busia, Lucy A. Mair and P. C. W. Gutkind provided the initial systematic studies of chieftaincy institutions in mid-twentieth century African communities engulfed by rapid social change. Busia's pioneering study on the political transformation of Ashanti political structures showed how chiefly authority was steadily challenged by the encroaching forces of modernization—most profoundly expressed through Christian values and shifting colonial imperatives—in the late colonial period.[7] Nevertheless, Ashanti "paramount chiefs" thrived because they imaginatively applied the legitimating ideologies of chieftaincy to the unfolding structures of colonial governance. Similarly, Mair argued that while modern local government and parliamentary structures undermined indigenous political institutions during decolonization, chiefly rulers still managed to retain political significance by projecting themselves as the custodian of cherished local values amidst rapid social change.[8] Drawing examples from several communities, Gutkind went on to demonstrate that, despite their loss of power to a new Western-educated elite, chiefs remained influential even in urban areas, because they reflected critical linkages between "indigenous" values and the destabilizing forces of social change.[9]

A number of other essays by African, American and European scholars written in the 1960s dealt with the changing status of West African chiefs during colonial rule and decolonization. These still provide the most comprehensive analyses of chieftaincy politics in anglophone and francophone Africa.[10] They highlighted the paradox—that the pivotal role of chieftaincy structures was sustained by the calculations of the holders of state power, the colonial administrators, followed by the indigenous educated elites, who sought to co-opt the chiefs for legitimation and mobilization purposes within the evolving colonial and postcolonial dispensations. The critical insight of these studies, however, was limited by their teleological preoccupations which obscured the dialectical interactions between chieftaincy and state structures in colonial and postcolonial Africa.

The dependency paradigm, which gained currency as a radical alternative to modernization theory, was equally short-sighted. Preoccupied with the advance of global capitalism, the marginality of third world economies, and the role of "comprador" classes in the economies of new states, dependency theorists underestimated the critical role that indigenous structures—most notably chieftaincy institutions—might play in the transformation of African states.[11] In short, while modernization analyses dismissed indigenous structures as dysfunctional to a Western-style developmental process, the dependency paradigm reduced these institutions to mere reflections of social class. Thus, the dependency paradigm's instrumentalist Marxist preoccupations ignored the continuing relevance of indigenous structures as modern expressions of communal and class interests.

The limitations of these perspectives, coupled with the rapid disintegration of the African state in the 1980s, prompted analysts to embrace a new approach, this time emphasizing the interaction between state and society as the critical element in the (il)legitimacy of the African state. But despite the new emphasis on "civic values" and "associational life"[12] as critical variables of analysis, this paradigm still reifies a Western notion of civil society as the critical building block for modern institutions of governance.

Three noteworthy African examples explains this tendency to either incorporate chieftaincy into—or marginalize it from—an evolving "public" sphere. In Botswana, where chieftaincy structures were integrated into what has become a relatively viable liberal democratic system, powerful chiefs, as representatives of local communities, continue to exert influence in the electoral system, and are critical in the implementation of state policies, especially at the local level.[13] This role, however, has created a gulf between local chiefs and the holders of state power. Conversely, in Uganda, where the Kabaka and powerful "paramount chiefs" were granted legislative and executive authority in the colonial and early postcolonial period, a commission of inquiry, chaired by renowned political scientist Mahmood Mamdani, called on President Yoweri Museveni's government to replace chieftaincy structures with elected "resistance" committees.[14] Finally, by granting powerful chiefs official advisory and executive roles, South Africa's post-apartheid Federal Constitution of 1993 incorporated chieftaincy institutions into the structures of the state and civil society. South African chiefs were accorded ex-officio functions in their local government councils, and were granted the power to exercise specific functions in the adjudication of indigenous law. And in provincial legislatures, "houses of chiefs" were granted advisory powers in customary matters. Finally, the constitution gave a national council of chiefs the power to advise the national government on local and national issues.[15] These extensive constitutional powers in the late twentieth century are indications of the continuing significance of chieftaincy in South Africa's complex society.[16]

The case studies of chieftaincy politics analyzed here reveal that the crisis of the postcolonial Nigerian state is intimately connected to the massive gap between state agencies and diverse local communities.[17] This crisis of state legitimacy necessitates a critical inquiry into the significance of indigenous political structures in Nigerian politics.

Following Jean-François Bayart's imaginative attempt to historicize the postcolonial African state,[18] I argue that chieftaincy structures are critical elements in the complex history of state formation in twentieth-century Nigeria. These indigenous institutions are significant not simply for their ideological content, but more so because they are a key arena for the dynamic interplay between state and communal structures. Bayart's historical sociology of the African state drew its inspiration from Fernand Braudel's notion of the *longue duree*.[19] Insisting on a distinctive interdisciplinary approach, Braudel's magnificent contribution to social science rests on the integration of "events" to their broad historical context. This methodological approach[20] emphasizes the persistence of structures, rather than radical breaks with the past. By focusing mainly on "government" or "high" historical events, the conventional political historian not only ignores the complexities of communal existence, but, more importantly, presents mere symptoms as fundamental historical shifts. This perspective encourages the integration of the conventional historical method of collecting archival materials and analyzing them chronologically or thematically with the sociological methodology of induction and generalization. Furthermore, Braudel's insistence on a sociological approach to historical inquiry calls for multiple methods of analyses as a strategy of articulating how evolving structures interact with changing societies. For Braudel, the *longue duree* is characterized by hierarchies, currents and movements of social forces, conditioned by geography and demography.[21] While this perspective revealed the durability of medieval European social institutions and patterns of daily life (as expressed through family structures, diet, communication, clothing, housing, etc.), their persistence was less apparent with the advent of industrial capitalism.

The notion of the *longue duree* opens up analysis of the fluid incorporation of indigenous African structures into modern processes of social change.[22] Despite a Eurocentric tendency that underscore Europe's long and turbulent process of state formation, this perspective is still a profitable way of analyzing the incorporation of African societies into a colonially derived modern state. Confronted with the rapid pace of social change since the mid nineteenth century, African political actors were consumed with subjective interpretations of a past in which chieftaincy structures play a pre-eminent role. Thus, mindful of the limitations of an orthodox Braudelian approach, this book will show how chieftaincy structures survived the rapid social change that engulfed the Yoruba region in the twentieth century. Furthermore, this perspective is useful because it will allow us to historicize exogenous and endogenous forces as dialectical expressions through which Yoruba communal identities were reconstructed in a colonial and postcolonial context. These processes of communal regeneration must show how political actors utilize indigenous structures to reinforce contemporary political realities. Thus, Bayart contends that "the structures of political arenas cannot be isolated from their articulation with related arenas, and that internal and external explanations are inexplicably linked. . . . Extraversion and the cultural schisms it causes have been common currency of the past. They constitute viable modalities of politics."[23]

It follows that an integration of the comparative political analyses of African states and the historical studies of Nigerian state formation will provide a deeper understanding of the critical role of indigenous political structures in the postcolonial African state. An analysis of modern Yoruba politics drawn from studies in social history and comparative politics, colonial archives, local historical accounts, official documents and newspapers reveals the complex interactions between Yoruba chieftaincy structures and Nigerian state agencies in the twentieth century. Starting with the indirect rule system, which drew heavily from conflicting interpretations of precolonial Yoruba political relations, British administrators, obas, baales, chiefs, educated elites and elders deployed traditional accounts through which local communities contested power during colonial rule. The most enduring legacy of these colonial practices is apparent in contentious notions of chieftaincy rules and customary laws.[24] Indirect rule in the Yoruba region in many ways resembles what the eminent historian, Terence Ranger, observed in the Zimbabwean archives:

> What I found in the files was a tragi-comedy, often verging on farce. I found that after 60 years of destructive colonial rule the administrators had discovered the sovereign virtues of "custom" and "tradition". I found the files full of desperate attempts by district commissioners to defend what "custom" and "tradition" meant, and even more desperate attempts to carry them out in practice.[25]

These themes have been brought sharply into focus by two important studies—by J. D. Y. Peel and David Laitin, respectively—on the historical sociology of Yoruba communities and the evolution of the Nigerian state. In an authoritative sociological exploration of Yoruba politics, Peel shows how colonial rule, the political economy of the postcolonial state, and the exigencies of regionalism transformed collective political consciousness and action among a major Yoruba subgroup, the Ijesha, in the course of the twentieth century.[26] Similarly, Laitin's imaginative application of Gramsci's theory of hegemony to colonial and postcolonial Yoruba politics suggests that the major feature of Yoruba collective political action involves a consistent exploitation of Yoruba ancestral city state fissures.[27] Laitin concludes that—despite the more recent influence of Christianity and Islam on Yoruba social relations—collective political action in the region is still dominated by the grassroots structures of "hometown ideologies." Co-opted by the British, this adherence of the Yoruba to hometown ideologies provided the framework on which the colonial system of indirect rule was subsequently institutionalized. And since hometown consciousness is a formidable platform for the construction of hegemonic ideologies, the new men of power skillfully utilized this medium as a crucial political resource, mobilizing political followings along communal lines. Laitin's study captures a critical aspect of the Yoruba past which has retained political significance throughout the twentieth century. Yet, while ancestral hometown fissures remain vital in modern Yoruba politics, local elites have nevertheless demonstrated considerable flexibility since the imposition of colonial rule.[28] It follows that in order to define new strategies of collective action—whether drawn from hometown loyalties or other social boundaries—myths, traditions, rituals and social memory would assume considerable significance in the modern construction of communal identities.[29]

This analysis thus contends that communal identities based on the reconstructed traditions of hometown allegiances must incorporate important historical trends of the nineteenth century, such as the consequences of the Yoruba wars, and the impact of world religions on local communities. Both Christian missions and Islamic influences were to shape social relations in the Oyo Province of the twentieth century. And the nativist sentiments from which chiefs, elders and charismatic leaders would construct an ancestral hometown political consciousness would draw on populist religious sentiments.

The driving engine of this complex process has been the modernizing elites, especially politicians and state functionaries, who utilized communal structures and ideologies as mediums for political mobilization during the decolonization process.[30] The paradox of the Yoruba nationalists thus lies in their embrace of communal and traditional doctrines that extol the corporate character of local groups, while simultaneously claiming that modern development requires the expertise of the intelligentsia.[31] In this sense, the ideologies that sustained elite power were inextricably linked to the ideology of imperial legitimation itself. The renowned Nigerian political theorist Peter Ekeh, perceptively notes:

> Anti-colonialism did not in fact mean opposition to the perceived ideals and principles of Western institutions. On the contrary a great deal of anti-colonialism was predicated on the manifest acceptance of these ideals and principles, accompanied by the insistence that conformity with them indicated a level of achievement that ought to earn the new educated Africans the right to the leadership of their country.[32]

Indeed, twentieth-century concepts of development and enlightenment among the Yoruba, as elsewhere in West Africa, were derived from the imbrication of external and internal sources; the former are associated with the advent of world religions, Western education, imperialism, long-distance trade and travel.[33] Although integral to the colonial enterprise, these developments were products of great political transitions in which competing elites had much to gain from the reorganization of societies and in which the uncertainties of rapid social mobilization induced local people to reaffirm their commitment to communal ideologies.[34] This critical historical moment in colonial Nigeria was the period of decolonization. As the major transitional phase in twentieth-century Africa, the politics of decolonization unleashed competing communal doctrines that were grafted on substantive, but highly contentious notions of traditional authority. This development would have serious implications for the postcolonial Nigerian state.

In a subtle analysis of the twentieth-century nation-state project, A. D. Smith provides a useful theoretical perspective through which I explore the significance of chieftaincy politics in the evolution of the Nigerian state. His critique of Eric Hobsbawm and Terence Ranger's "invention of tradition" thesis[35] is a constructive way of interrogating the political usage of chieftaincy structures—and their "traditional" ideologies—in the process of state formation in Nigeria. In his introduction to the *Invention of Tradition*, Hobsbawm had concluded that it "is clear that plenty of political institutions, ideological movements and groups—not least in nationalism—were so unprecedented that even historic continuity had to be invented, for example, by creating an ancient past beyond *effective historical continuity . . .* "[36] Smith's own summary of Hobsbawm's basic assumption is worth quoting here:

There is also an overriding need, in such destabilizing circumstances, to mask the radicalism of social change with a veil of tradition and continuity with an assumed past, usually a national one. Certainly, it is in the interest of ruling classes or sub-elites to foster such a sense of continuity, in order to resocialize uprooted populations and inculcate new values of order and hierarchy. Only by these means can the ruling classes reassert their control over the dangerous and dislocating processes of rapid industrialization and political mobilization which threatened to overturn the existing class order. It follows that the "superstructure", in the form of "invented traditions", plays an unexpectedly crucial part in the creation and stabilization of modern societies and regimes.[37]

Smith first questions the analytic concept of "invented traditions," an idea he claims is derived from the "retrospective judgment of the historian." This "retrospective judgment," Smith claims, obscures the complex character of traditional themes in nation-state projects. He then contends that a broader analytical concept which seeks to appropriate interpretations of the past for contemporary political usage should encompass the variety of traditional and historical possibilities such as the "rediscovery," "revival," or "reconstruction" of pre-existing themes.[38] Furthermore, Smith claims that the notion of "tradition" itself is a conceptually elusive term. Indeed, his apprehensions were anticipated by earlier critiques of modernization theory, among which C. S. Whitaker's monumental studies of northern Nigeria are exemplary. Focusing on the processes of institutional transformation during decolonization, Whitaker contends that politicians and emirs in the North neither clung to a strict pattern of "traditional" government nor accepted "modern" elements indiscriminately. Political development did not entail a straightforward and unilinear movement from a "traditional" Islamic aristocracy to a more modern pattern of constitutional democracy. Rather, it was a complex imbrication of both elements.[39] In fact, Whitaker rejected the dichotomous conceptualization of the process of institutional change, especially the problematic categories of "modern" and "traditional." Instead, he coined the term "dysrhythmic" as a way of explaining the "interdependence" inherent in complex processes of change.[40] In short, the complex political interactions between the forces of "tradition" and "modernity," as S. J. Tambiah reminds us, must be seen as "constituting dialectical tensions" rather than "age-sanctified rules."[41]

Finally, Smith cautions against Hobsbawm's preoccupation with nationalist elites as deliberate "inventors" and "designers" of the modern nation state, an approach he sees as reflecting a limited Marxist perspective. For Smith, political classes are effective defenders of tradition only if "invented traditions," along with reconstructed histories, resonate in the collective imagination of local communities.[42] The construction of political ethnicity, though varied and multidimensional, as Morris Szeftel notes, must reflect the sociopolitical realities of the local community:

> A variety of forces, historical and social, will shape the form of the appeal made to subjects, the way in which group membership is defined, the program of action proposed, and the way in which some elements of the group 'history' are selected for inclusion, others are excluded and many remain contested within the group.[43]

Stephanie Lawson, similarly, has noted that "the myth of cultural homogeneity" constructed by Fijian elites in reaction to their perceived political vulnerability *vis-à-vis* other groups was firmly rooted in historical imagination and modern sociopolitical developments.[44] Smith's Pakistani illustration is particularly apt: "without the historical memories, heroic myths and ethno-religious ties to the Muslim population, no amount of conscious manipulation or invented traditions could have brought the state of Pakistan into existence, or set it onto the tortuous road of national formation."[45]

The local, national and global context in which Yoruba political elites constructed a pan-ethnic identity in the terminal years of colonial rule is thus crucial to the analysis of chieftaincy politics and social relations in Nigeria. Elite "reconstruction," "recombination," and the embrace of "myths, symbols, memories, and tradition"[46] are not novel ideas; precolonial Yoruba societies, like most others in Africa, have regularly embarked on such an enterprise. What made this process of traditional regeneration critical for Yoruba communities during this period was the global context of third-world decolonization, nationalism, global capitalism and the cold war. These global forces were certainly compounded by particular regional and national conditions.

The implications of conflicting interpretations of the past thus cannot be underestimated, either for elite consolidation or for the viability of the postcolonial state. Critical analyses of the ideological expressions inherent in chieftaincy structures must account for both what is "left *in* and *out*" of local discourses. This is particularly relevant since resistance ideologies of the "masses," as Michel-Rolph Trouillot notes, often seek to "bring back" marginalized themes as alternative narratives of progressive change.[47] And with regards to Yoruba conflicts, local historical accounts, firmly rooted in chieftaincy structures, are seldom committed to accurate historical analyses, but rather defend particular group and communal interests. Despite deep communal commitments, the masses of the Yoruba rural and urban poor, like most marginalized communities, have imaginatively constructed alternative narratives (often within indigenous structures) as oppositional traditions, doctrines, and a folklore of "infrapolitics" resistant to elite domination.[48] With traditional rulers and chiefs assuming new roles as intermediaries between their local communities and the holders of state power, popular resistance of the masses has had serious implications for the legitimacy of chieftaincy structures in colonial and postcolonial politics.

A critical theoretical dimension of the application of local historical accounts to modern Yoruba collective action was poignantly analyzed by J. D. Y. Peel, in an article on the role of the Ijesha past in twentieth-century Nigerian politics.[49] This contribution was offered as a critique of the "presentist" perspective of Yoruba oral traditions in which local historians rigidly interpreted the past as a prelude to the rapidly changing conditions of the twentieth century.[50] For Peel, the basic element of Yoruba local histories, whether oral or written, can be summed up as one in which the making of history

> is really a single process with two strands: the practice of fashioning a future social order entails a constant re-evaluation of the past. Consequently the historical—supposedly factual accounts of what has happened—can never be entirely separated from the mythical, persuasive elaborations of what exists externally and what might be.[51]

Despite these subtle analyses, straightforward instrumentalist perspectives which link unproblematic ethnic groups to the struggle for state resources still dominate the social science analysis of Nigerian communal identities and the nation state project. The earlier book of the eminent political scientist Richard Sklar, *Nigerian Political Parties*, remains an exception as the authoritative Africanist analysis of how communal-based elites define collective political action as struggles for scarce resources of wealth, status, and power.[52] While the material base of communal relations is critical, Sklar argues that state formation in Nigeria during decolonization entailed strategies of mobilization which integrated antecedent structures and modern political parties. Rajni Kothari's observation over three decades ago, that the key challenge confronting the contemporary Asian and African state lies in the effective reconciliation of a wide array of indigenous and modern forces within a viable system of compromise and accommodation,[53] is even more valid today. The crisis of political legitimacy confronting the Nigerian state is intimately linked to the ambiguous nature of the public sphere and the absence of viable national institutions capable of unifying a deeply fragmented nation state. The narratives of local politics that are the focus of our analysis here will be viewed in the context of a process of state formation that rests on a tenuous interaction between ambiguous "traditional" structures and modern bureaucratic institutions. The main concern of regional political classes has been to protect their interests by seeking refuge behind traditional structures, themes and symbols that are summoned to validate local aspirations.[54] In this context, state structures are hardly used as effective institutions of administration and governance. Rather, they function largely as mechanisms for allocating patronage and ensuring political domination.[55] Thus, chieftaincy structures—as communal and ethnic-based institutions—partly reinforce a rentier state dominated by ethno-regional commercial and bureaucratic classes.

In this book, I have interwoven the themes of chieftaincy, communal identity, elite formation and the struggle for state power in the twentieth century with the tumultuous nineteenth-century political antecedents on which colonial and postcolonial Yoruba politics have been grafted.[56] I treat the nineteenth century not simply as another prelude to the history of Nigeria. Rather it is integral to the conflicting meaning of tradition today, not only making the twentieth century intelligible, but, more importantly, shaping the very course of political change. In the next study, some overview of earlier history and Braudelian politico-economic, and demographic context would be desirable.

A Turbulent Nineteenth Century

Despite their social, cultural and religious similarities, major Yoruba subgroups such as the Oyo, Ekiti, Egba, Ijebu and Ijesha evolved distinctive political structures in the course of the nineteenth century. These variations were in large measure the result of the old Oyo Empire's precipitous decline and the Fulani invasion in the northern Yoruba region earlier in the century.[57] Besides the disruption of many Oyo Yoruba communities, the crisis resulted in the fall of the old Oyo Empire (with its capital in Oyo-Ile), which for several centuries had served as the epicenter of the Yoruba region.[58] To chart the dynamics of Yoruba power relations in the nineteenth century, I adopt J. D. Y. Peel's schema of the "hierarchy of political power," in which he presents Ijesha politics in "the context of its external relations to a hierarchy of communities."[59] These relations are shaped by the ability of the indigenous political elites to command such important resources as slaves and tribute. Peel's "hierarchy of communities" emerged ' through three primary axes of conflict in Ijesha society. First, power relations were expressed through competition between powerful constituents (of "in-groups" and "out-groups" of chiefs and elders) and the Ijesha crown in the capital of Ilesha. A second axis of conflict was centered on local tensions, principally between elders and youths; a third, on Ijesha elite struggles to extract resources from provincial communities. This fluid structure was sustained by pressures from subordinate groups

> to increase their pull at the center or to try to break away from its domination altogether. But though the categories might be aligned, they tended to adopt different strategies. . . . Membership in these categories was not permanent: youths became elders and the roundabout of chiefly fortunes was likely to turn. The subordinate towns, however, at least to the extent that their people were sociologically distinct from Ilesha, . . . sought to break out of the capital's domination, to enter the regional hierarchy as independent units.[60]

In the typical Yoruba town, power relations were dominated by the competition between a divine king called the *oba* (*ekeji lehin orisa*—second only to the gods), and a council of chiefs. Obas were typically chosen from candidates presented to a council of kingmakers by eligible segments of royal lineages. In nineteenth-century Oyo town, for instance, eligible candidates for the obaship (the *Alaafin*) were selected by elders of royal lineages and then presented to the *Oyomesi*, the council of kingmakers, who reserved the right to sanction or reject the selection.[61] As is often the case with divine kingship, Yoruba obas were far from absolute monarchs. Important political decisions undertaken by civil and military chiefs, and sanctioned by heads of powerful lineages, age groups and local priests, were proclaimed in the oba's name by the council of chiefs. The council, both in practice and theory, reflected the interest of powerful lineages in its decisions, which dealt with such matters as public projects, lineage conflicts and military campaigns. In the important Ekiti town of Ado, for example, decisions were made by the senior *Olori marun* chiefs and the junior *Ijoye* chiefs in the oba's name. In Egba kingdom, where the obas' power was equally limited, political and commercial functions were discharged by the *Ogboni*, the civil chiefs; the *Olorogun*, the war chiefs; and the *Parakoyi*, the guild of traders.[62] And in Ondo, Ijesha and Akoko, where obas enjoyed extensive powers, charges of arbitrary rule were occasionally reflected in popular insurrections instigated by disgruntled chiefs and lineage heads.[63]

These limitations on his authority, however, should not be taken to mean that the Yoruba oba was simply subjected to the whims and caprices of local chiefs and other leaders. Besides the sacred attributes of kingship institution itself, the oba embodied local aspirations and communal ideals. Furthermore, the Yoruba oba enjoyed considerable influence with other political leaders, who were still obliged to solicit his approval and promulgate important decisions in his name. The oba's authority was also enhanced by his great wealth and his elaborate palace retinue of courtiers and messengers. Indeed, the well-known Yoruba tradition of reserving portions of tribute, tolls and war booty for the oba survived the turbulent nineteenth century.[64] In addition, the oba's exclusive control over important chieftaincy titles gave him influence among powerful lineage heads and chiefs who still required titles as a source of political legitimacy. Thus, despite his limited role in public affairs, the nineteenth-century oba, like his predecessors, drew considerable influence from the "mystic aura" and exalted position of kingship,[65] of which the most important symbol was the beaded crown.

Political legitimacy was ultimately based on community consent. Nineteenth-century Yoruba towns were generally divided into wards (*adugbo*), under the leadership of lineage heads. These wards consisted of patrilineal descent groups organized in extended family compounds known as *agbo-ile*. These units, each with its own corporate identity, were the most basic unit of Yoruba social organization. Community interests and opinion were transmitted through lineage heads to the main locus of power, the oba's council of chiefs. Conversely, political decisions taken by the council of chiefs were disseminated through these channels to townspeople. As the main link between local groups and the axes of power, lineage heads were engrossed in the economic, social and political affairs of their respective constituencies.

Yoruba politics in the nineteenth century, however, involved more than the internal administration of the major towns. As headquarters of preeminent obas and chiefs, "metropolitan" centers had suzerainty over semi-autonomous provincial hamlets, villages and minor towns. Ruled by councils of chiefs, under the leadership of head chiefs known as *baales* in Oyo or *oloja* in Ondo, these communities were obliged to pay regular tribute and levies to the capital. The interests of "metropolitan" rulers were represented through special envoys called *babakekere* or *ilari* in Oyo. As the critical intermediary with provincial communities, the babakekere, as described by O'Hear, "was a patron who interceded on his clients' behalf with a higher authority or government functionary."[66] In return for their loyalty, provincial communities were offered some protection from the many conflicts of the period by patrons who had much to gain in maintaining such control.

This fluid system of power relations gave rise to the reconstitution of old polities in the course of the nineteenth century. This was reflected in the rejuvenated Oyo kingdom, which drew on the prestige of its imperial past; the relatively peaceful Ijebu kingdoms, which displayed remarkable continuity with tradition; the loose federation of Egba towns;[67] and, finally, Ife, a centralized kingdom with satellite provinces. In addition, new Yoruba polities such as the Oyo-dominated town of Ibadan, the new Oyo Kingdom at Ago Oja, the Egba town of Abeokuta, the Ekiti town of Aiyede and the Modakeke community in Ife emerged during this period. The power struggles that ensued failed to produce a dominant state that could mediate the tensions endemic to the "hierarchy of communities." Thus, unlike old Oyo, which for more than two centuries had retained effective control over much of the region, as well as influence over non-Yoruba states such as Dahomey, Nupe and Ibariba, none of the new military states was able to assert such hegemonic power. In the new dispensation, command over military resources took precedence over the stable political traditions of preceding centuries.

These political innovations had far-reaching implications for colonial governance in the subsequent era of British rule. Their impact was immediately apparent in the critical northern section of the Yoruba region—the area which became known as Oyo Province, including such towns as Ibadan, Oyo, Ife, Ilesha, Iseyin, Iwo, Ede, Ogbomosho, Ejigbo, Oshogbo, Ikirun, Eruwa, Ikire and Okeiho-Iganna. Of these, the new state of Ibadan, analyzed extensively in subsequent chapters, emerged as the centerpiece of power relations in the nineteenth century.

Initially a military settlement for Oyo, Ife, Egba and Ijebu soldiers and refugees, Ibadan played a leading role in resisting the Fulani jihadists who had destabilized the northern Yoruba region and had occupied the Oyo Yoruba town of Ilorin.[68] The military dynamic of the region was initially completed by Ijaye—another dominant military state—which protected the western Yoruba region from Dahomey attack. Finally, regional stabilization was encouraged by the revival of the Alaafin's court at Ago Oja, a new town eighty miles south of the old Oyo capital of Oyo-Ile. Still with some moral authority over Oyo-Yoruba towns, Alaafin Atiba gave Ibadan's ruler, Oluyole, the title of *Bashorun* (chief councillor of Oyo); similarly, he gave Kurumi, ruler of Ijaye, the title of *Are-Ona-Kakanfo* (generalissimo of the realm). This gave Ibadan and Ijaye at least a patina of legitimacy as guardians of a disintegrated realm. But in reality these emerging power blocs consisted of no more than a "triumvirate of warlords" whose claims, whenever the opportunity arose, were repudiated by provincial towns.[69] Nevertheless, Ibadan, by far the most formidable of the nineteenth-century states, marched forward in defeating the Fulani at Oshogbo in 1840, checked Fulani incursions into Ekiti in the 1850s, and under the able military strategist, Ogunmola, defeated its arch rival, Ijaye. During the rule of Are Latosisa, it moved towards military domination of most of the Yoruba region in the 1870s, embarking on an ambitious program of expansion, and raiding eastward into Ekiti, Akoko and Igbomina for slaves. It took an alliance of Ekiti and Ijesha forces and the sixteen-year Kiriji war to finally stem Ibadan's aggression in 1879. Southward, Ibadan menaced the formidable Ijebu and Egba who controlled the trade routes to European goods and firearms on the coast.

As a military state that depended on war for its economic viability, Ibadan's political organization differed significantly from older Yoruba kingdoms, relying heavily on large numbers of fighting men.[70] As the pre-eminent military state in the Yoruba region, unfree labor—derived from slavery and pawnship, deployed in farming and warfare—became an important calculus of power. Renowned Nigerian historian Toyin Falola succinctly describes its significance for the economy of the military states:

> Evidence of large-scale production and trade by military elites and wealthy personages inevitably meant that slaves were used to maintain production and distribution and to uphold the lifestyle of the elite. Without a single exception, all the great names of the nineteenth century built large households with considerable numbers of slaves, and almost certainly pawns as well. It is possible to construct a multiple model of political economy that includes two modes of production, with a slave mode as the dominant one in the military states, next to a lineage mode in other areas.[71]

As an important source of palm oil, Ibadan also grew rapidly into a major commercial center. Its population grew as well, due to migration from other Yoruba communities as well as the flow of slaves. These developments, along with Ibadan's political and military ascent, called for a more effective system of administration.

In its early days, Ibadan was organized into relatively small semi-autonomous military camps, based on Yoruba subgroups whose warlords combined military duties with local administration.[72] With the military triumph of the more numerous Oyo, Ibadan rapidly became a more culturally cohesive Oyo Yoruba town. Under Bashorun Oluyole, the able Oyo military leader who ruled in the 1830s, Ibadan's diffused system of warlordism took a more centralized structure. Three chieftaincy hierarchies were created. The *baale* (*baba ile*, father of the land) and his chiefs were largely responsible for the civil administration of the town, coordinating decisions with lineage heads, priests, and leaders of other important local groups such as artisans, trade guilds, and age grades. Led by the *Balogun* (the *babaogun*, the war general), the second chieftaincy line consisted of the most influential heads of lineages who, through military campaigns, had acquired what P. C. Lloyd has referred to as "free-floating resources"[73] in slaves, tribute, and tolls. And finally, a category of junior war chiefs, known as *seriki*, complemented the military leadership of the *balogun* chiefs. The baale, balogun, and seriki, heading the three respective chieftaincy lines, were followed by the subordinate ranks of *otun* (second-in-command), *osi* (third-in-command), and so on. Finally, a fourth chieftaincy line of women chiefs, with a similar ranking pattern, was created later in the century. But the significance of military activities to the consolidation of elite interests[74] gave the balogun category preeminence over other centers of power. The eminent Oyo local historian, Samuel Johnson, noted the relative weakness of the baale in this respect:

> The baale is always chosen from old retired war chiefs, always at sufferance of the balogun, who had equal authority and more real power. But when the balogun has become old and has won all his laurels, he is expected to be the next baale. A young balogun with his future to make yielded the mayoralty to an older chief, usually an otun-baale.[75]

Not surprisingly, the relations between Ibadan rulers and provincial communities reflected the prevailing politico-military emphasis of the period. In this environment, so profoundly shaped by military power, the success of individual chiefs depended on their access to the fighting men of Ibadan and provincial communities. As Ibadan's military exploits advanced, with the conquest of Ekiti, Ijesha, Akoko, Igbomina and other Oyo communities, its rulers became patrons (babakekere) of these provincial towns and villages.[76] Fashioned after the ilari system of the old Oyo Empire, the control of the babakekere was expressed mainly through the regular payment of tribute, ensured in turn by the *ajele*, who collected tribute and provided vital information to Ibadan chiefs. S. A. Akintoye has noted that the popular perspective, which dismisses the ajele as rapacious sycophants, is not altogether accurate.[77] This view, he contends, obscures the complex conditions under which Ibadan's ajeles discharged their admittedly exploitative duties. Akintoye observes two major variations in the relationship between Ibadan's ajeles and the Ijesha and Ekiti communities they controlled. On the one hand, a minority of ajeles discharged their duties with considerable constraint, and in these cases were even cautiously embraced by provincial authorities. On the other hand, ajeles abused the provincial population, in keeping with their *raison d' etre* as agents of extraction and even occasional plunder for Ibadan chiefs.

Ibadan's domination of the Yoruba region, however, was short-lived. There was growing resistance to its expansionism, coupled with the opposition of Christian missionaries and British colonial authorities in Lagos to the Yoruba wars. By the end of the century, this had encouraged the displacement of Ibadan's war-driven chieftaincy structure by a more stable system of government. Heads of established lineages, known as *mogaji*, were now recruited into junior chieftaincy positions on the basis of their personal accomplishments, the influence of their lineage and their seniority. Chiefs and mogajis presided over group meetings, mediated conflicts, and allocated resources and responsibilities among their members. They also represented the interest of their lineages in the baale's councils. Since only a few of the lineages in the town could acquire chieftaincy titles at any given time, the interests of non-chiefly lineages were represented by a patron chief called the *Babaogun*.[78] Thus, Ibadan developed a fluid chieftaincy structure which, by the end of the nineteenth century, provided cohesion within the town, as well as a measure of control over provincial towns and villages. While Ibadan's politico-military state led to fairly stable economic activities in trade, agriculture, arts, and crafts, its initiative in statecraft required peace to flourish. Its persistent military exploits, with their attendant sociopolitical dislocations, engendered intermittent discontinuity in the economic development of the Yoruba region in the second half of the nineteenth century.[79]

Structure and Objectives

Drawing from an interpretive history of colonial Ibadan's relations with its neighbors in Oyo Province, the next chapter—chapter 2—contends that it was the struggle of obas, chiefs, educated elites and elders for power, privilege and status that lent new meaning to traditional authority and communal identities in the early colonial period. The case studies analyzed here suggest that reconstructed histories, myths, traditions, social memory and symbols were critical to the consolidation of elite interests in Yoruba towns. These representations, propagated by Yoruba elites and further distorted by colonial authorities, provided the ideological platform on which much of twentieth-century Yoruba collective political action was later grafted.

Set in the context of postwar colonial reforms, chapter 3 both underscores the deep incongruity between local social structures and the agencies of the modern state, and also shows how communal, regional and class interests intensified the political ferment of decolonization. While the decolonization process was marked by elite claims to various notions of "Western enlightenment" and "indigenous development," Yoruba nationalists nevertheless forged alliances with obas, chiefs and elders in their struggle to gain access to state power. Thus, while recognizing the significance of postwar constitutional reforms, chapter 3 contends that it was not only rapid social change, but the construction of conflicting communal ideologies—from myths, traditions and local histories, centered on chieftaincy institutions, ancestral hometowns and kinship groups—that fed the process of elite formation at the time. These developments, moreover, occurred in a new context of political reorganization along regional lines. The centrifugal forces generated by communal and ethno-regional tensions thus were especially significant, tending to delegitimate the fragile Nigerian federation created in 1947. The consequences of these developments are further explored in chapter 4. On the one hand, radical reforms formally marginalized chiefly authority with respect to the newly established state structures. On the other hand, the politics of decolonization entailed the incorporation of obas and chiefs—despite the waning of their political fortunes—into new democratic institutions of regional power. To mobilize mass support, regional politicians also turned to the obas and chiefs, constructing a new pan-Yoruba communal identity in the process.

Chapter 5 turns to the broader political arena of the post independence period from 1960–1966. In the initial years of constitutional democracy, acrimonious competition of elites for state power put considerable strain on chieftaincy structures. Nigeria's politics of federalism further intensified the clash of communal, ethno-regional and class interests during this tumultuous period. The solidification of ethno-regional power configurations by military strategies of governance is the theme of chapters 6 and 7. Case studies for this period show how chieftaincy structures continue to serve as ideological expressions and organizational nodes for various interests. They also reveal, however, the limitations of various versions of the military's neotraditional strategies of governance (whether the pre-Civil War policies of Generals Ironsi and Gowon or the attempt to "rationalize" local and chieftaincy structures in Oyo State under the Mohammed/Obasanjo regime). Chapter 8 analyzes the familiar pattern of electoral politics in which Yoruba elite interests are sustained through the propagation of reconstructed communal histories and neotraditional ideologies from

1979–1983. Chieftaincy politics thus reinforced the prevailing ethno-regional power structure, local power configurations and political alignments which had resulted from the turbulent years of parliamentary democracy. Finally, chapter 9 examines the lingering significance of chieftaincy structures in a second military era, following the demise of the Second Republic in 1983. Within the context of the deepening social contradictions of the 1980s and the 1990s, especially the economic crisis of the time and the politicization and fragmentation of the military, the chapter underscores the implications of chieftaincy structures for elite consolidation within local, regional and national configurations of power.

2

COLONIAL DISTORTIONS: INDIRECT RULE IN OYO PROVINCE

British colonialism in Nigeria was based, of course, on the indirect rule system, an adaptation of indigenous political structures to the needs of local administration. Questions of local governance were typically shaped by prevailing colonial policies, perspectives of British administrators and the complex character of the new administrative jurisdictions themselves; complex local structures were adapted to general statement of colonial policy. This chapter will show how the interaction between colonial objectives and rapidly changing sociopolitical conditions transformed chiefly power in Oyo Province. As the provincial epicenter, Ibadan provides a critical medium for the analysis of power relations among contending communities and interests in the region. Reinforced by contending claims of indigenous authorities, this history of colonial Ibadan's relations with its neighbors in Oyo Province examines how elite power—through the alliance of obas, chiefs, elders and local leaders—transformed city politics during the colonial period. As new administrative rules transformed ideas of "traditional authority" in Yoruba communities, they engendered recurring controversies among elites who claimed to represent competing local interests. Drawing on the support and opposition of obas, title-holders and local elders, these interests were most profoundly expressed through an emerging class of educated Christians who dominated the hometown-centered "progressive" unions that had emerged in many communities by the early 1920s.

By embracing monarchical structures as the legitimate form of Yoruba political authority, British colonialism used the mythical concept of the Yoruba crowns as a rationale of indirect rule. This historical reconstruction had serious implications for the relations between major towns of the province, notably Ibadan, Oyo, Ife, Ilesha, Iseyin, Iwo, Ede, Ogbomosho, Oshogbo, Ikirun, Ejigbo, Eruwa and Okeiho-Iganna. As "quasi-metropoles," smaller rural communities were linked to these towns by history, custom, politics and spatial economic relations. And despite the conflicts of the nineteenth century, British colonial policies envisioned neat hierarchies of power among local rulers. In this rigidly structured system, "metropolitan" city-states such as Ibadan, Oyo, Ife and Ilesha assumed greater political significance in the years following colonial rule. The metropolitan status of Ife and Oyo was simply rationalized by their traditional significance in Yoruba history, while Ibadan's political prominence was due to its military exploits during the nineteenth-century Yoruba wars.[1] For these reasons, the colonial treaties signed between the British and the rulers of northern Yoruba towns conceded suzerainty to these states. It was clear that it was the Alaafin of Oyo who stood to gain the most from this hierarchical order. Because of Oyo's political significance (based in large part on its politico-military supremacy in the seventeenth and eighteenth centuries),[2] several colonial treaties gave the Alaafin formal sovereignty over most other Yoruba obas.[3] Furthermore, against the background of the Yoruba wars and a new cultural awakening prompted by missionary education, a new class of Western-educated elites emerged as the custodians of communal aspirations. These factors influenced the meaning of Yoruba indigenous political authority under the colonial dispensation.[4] When indirect rule was eventually imposed, the Alaafin's "historic" status provided a convenient organizing principle.[5] This notion of a supreme Yoruba crown—reflecting a selective embrace of traditional themes and administrative priorities of indirect rule—thus emerged as the central institution through which competing constituencies both projected and resisted the colonial enterprise. Correlatively, rulers of newer city-states, lacking such mythical pedigrees, saw their power base decline.

Ibadan is the critical case in point. Lacking the myths and traditions of the ancestral centers of Oyo, Ile-Ife and Ilesha, Ibadan's rulers were forced to concede considerable powers to the Alaafin, despite the city's real socio-political and economic importance. We now turn to a detailed analysis of how historical reinterpretations of traditional authority transformed the status of Ibadan, within the provincial jurisdiction of Oyo, after the imposition of colonial rule.

The process started with the appointment of Gilbert T. Carter, former administrator of the Gambia, as Governor of Lagos in 1890. Carter's main task was to open the Yoruba hinterland to British trade and political influence. After signing treaties with the Alake of Abeokuta, the Alaafin of Oyo, and other Yoruba obas, he arrived in Ibadan on 26 March, 1893, with the hope of a similar political breakthrough. Unfortunately for Carter, Ibadan's chiefs, led by the Balogun,[6] proved relatively less compromising. They declined Carter's treaty because their control over land ownership and domestic slaves would be adversely affected.[7] Undeterred, the British increased their pressure, assuring the chiefs that the colonial government would respect their authority. Immediately after his installation on 23 June, Baale Fijabi accepted the original terms of the agreement, signing a treaty with the Acting Governor of Lagos, George C. Denton on 15 August. When Carter (who had gone on leave) returned, he appointed R. L. Bower, a captain in the British army, as the first British resident of Ibadan. Captain Bower's arrival in Ibadan, with about one hundred Hausa infantrymen, formally brought Ibadan under British rule, and ended its system of civil-military government.[8]

British colonial rule was grafted on the prevailing power relations, where Ibadan enjoyed considerable power in the nineteenth century. In the new political dispensation, colonial rule was centered on important "metropolitan" city-states, particularly Ibadan (because of its military preeminence), and Oyo town (long the epicenter of Yoruba politics).[9] Under colonial rule, however, the principal instrument of political control (in Oyo Province) was the council of chiefs, presided over by the British resident. The first council, established in Ibadan in 1897, consisted of the resident, the baale, the otun baale, the osi baale, the balogun, and other senior chiefs. This council had jurisdiction over both Ibadan and Ife-Ilesha Divisions. In 1898, the British administration created a similar council in Oyo town. This native authority (NA) council, which had jurisdiction over Oyo Division, consisted of the Alaafin and seven of his most senior chiefs, in addition to the resident. Ibadan, however, lacked established historical claims to authority both over the northern district towns of Ogbomosho, Iwo, Ejigbo and Ede, and over Ife-Ilesha Division. Thus, its supremacy in the early years of colonial rule was short-lived. As British authorities confronted conflicting political claims by obas, baales, chiefs and other elites in the Division, they sought a more reliable traditional foundation on which to construct indirect rule.[10]

Despite their initial commitment to the pre-existing arrangement as the basis of indirect rule,[11] British administrators increasingly found it expedient to alter these sometimes ambiguous structures. The indirect rule system had in fact been introduced by colonial governor Sir Fredrick Lugard (later Lord Lugard) as a strategy of local administration in the vast northern emirates, following its conquest between 1897 and 1903.[12] The system, which adapted "indigenous" political institutions to British colonial control, was subsequently imposed on the southern provinces in the early 1900s. Given the diverse political structures in the Nigerian region, this strategy of local administration and control met with varying degrees of success in different parts of the northern and southern provinces. For instance, while it achieved relative success in the north and southwest (the Yoruba region) where centralized monarchical structures were critical components of indigenous sociopolitical formations, it met with utter failure in the southeastern provinces where British policy had imposed a rigid hierarchical chiefly system—the "warrant system"—on diffused and decentralized indigenous political traditions. "Novel in degree and territorial scope," as A. G. Afigbo notes, the indirect rule system proved a colossal failure in these colonial jurisdictions.[13] And even in the Yoruba region where the system achieved some success, its excessive hierarchical structure soon disrupted the evolving balance of power between political actors and local constituencies throughout the colonial era. The most notable case in Oyo Province was the celebrated rivalry between the Alaafin of Oyo and the Ibadan chiefs. There was a noticeable shift in power towards the Alaafin in 1897, when—under Sir Henry E. McCallum as Governor of Lagos, and F. C. Fuller, former district commissioner in Lagos, as resident of Ibadan—the Alaafin's territorial jurisdiction was expanded considerably, at Ibadan's expense. This significantly increased the prestige of the Alaafin among provincial elites.[14]

The plight of Ibadan's chiefs became even more acute under McCallum's successor, Sir William MacGregor, Governor of Lagos from 1899 to 1904. Through the Native Council Ordinance of 1901, MacGregor reduced the role of the residents in the NA councils from an executive to an advisory capacity, and then appointed "paramount rulers and chiefs" executive president in their place. Since provincial and divisional councils exercised extensive authority over all aspect of local administration within their jurisdictions, the new ordinance established an hierarchical structure of local administration under the authority of a traditional ruler—the Alaafin, in the Oyo case. In a province of this size and complexity, this required a rigid interpretation of traditional political relationships, not only between those defined as paramount rulers, such as the Alaafin of Oyo, the Ooni of Ife, the Owa of Ilesha and the Orangun of Ila, but also among those chiefs designated as "non-royal" rulers, such as the baales of Ibadan, Ogbomosho and Iwo. Moreover, by establishing a centralized system of local administration under traditional potentates, MacGregor's ordinance enhanced the power and prestige of historically important monarchs such as the Alaafin and the Ooni, while eroding the previous authority of Ibadan's chiefs in many northern Yoruba towns. The Nigerian historian, J. A. Atanda, notes the historical re-interpretation that occurred in this context:

> Since, at least by tradition, one paramount chief was "more paramount" than the other, the idea soon arose that the "most paramount" chief should also be most powerful. And in the area under study (Oyo Province), that most paramount chief was none other than the Alaafin, "the head of Yorubaland". It is largely this type of thinking that led to the policy of "reviving the ancient powers and glory of the Alaafin", creating, as it were, a new Oyo empire.[15]

MacGregor's policy also increased the paramount rulers' jurisdiction in legal matters. For instance, when the colonial government decided to extend the supreme court's jurisdiction over Ibadan in 1904, it was the Alaafin who approved the provision.[16] And amidst the steady erosion of the authority of Ibadan chiefs, both Residents Fuller and Elgee, confronted with the demands of a large and expanding city, instituted modest municipal improvement schemes which utilized the expertise of educated elites.[17]

The policy initiated by Governors McCallum and MacGregor was consolidated during the legendary "reign" of Captain William A. Ross, Resident[18] of Oyo Province from 1914 to 1931. A former district commissioner of Oyo Division, Ross worked ceaselessly to advance the authority and prestige of the Alaafin, whom he considered the legitimate ruler of the Yoruba. And he worked just as hard to undermine the influence of other Yoruba rulers, most especially Ibadan baales, who had acquired considerable regional power in the more recent past. His long service in Oyo town, and his friendship with Alaafin Siyanbola Ladigbolu I, were critical factors here. With Ross as resident, the Alaafin's control was extended throughout the province—over a total area of 14,831 square miles, making it the largest province of colonial southern Nigeria.[19] Although the British authorities initially assumed that the Alaafin's supreme status would legitimate colonial objectives in the region, this novel interpretation of Yoruba political authority in fact contradicted the relationship between Yoruba rulers that had prevailed in the nineteenth century.[20]

Captain Ross's interpretation of indirect rule in Oyo Province was based on a restoration of precolonial traditions that had been the subject of controversy among local Yoruba historians. In the excessively authoritarian regime constituted by the twin rulership of Captain Ross and Alaafin Ladigbolu, the Alaafin acquired both *de facto* and *de jure* suzerainty over other major rulers. From the perspective of the Ibadan chiefs, Ross had not only usurped their political powers, but had overturned existing power relations among northern Yoruba communities. The ceremonial homage which Ibadan chiefs had paid to the Alaafin as "spiritual father" was conveniently interpreted by Ross as *de facto* suzerainty of Oyo over Ibadan.[21] To impose this authoritarian structure, both Ross and Alaafin Ladigbolu summoned "traditional" themes of the grandeur of the "old Oyo empire," along with its myth of the Alaafin's seniority *vis-à-vis* other Yoruba rulers. This obscured what in fact had been a shifting nineteenth century political environment in which the Alaafin's authority had been very much in doubt, and in which the status of Ibadan as the pre-eminent military power had been undisputed.[22] In short, Ross ignored the political dislocations of this previous era, and the extent to which the rise of new towns—such as Ibadan, Ijaye and Abeokuta, with their war-based economies—had effectively undermined Oyo's influence.

It was at best naive to assume that this reconstructed myth of traditional authority could create political order among competing obas and hometown elites. A neotraditional structure that embraced the Alaafin as the fulcrum of power among Yoruba rulers in the province in fact distorted pre-existing political arrangements and routinized new forms of political relationships throughout the province. To legitimate the Alaafin's "traditional" preeminence, the colonial regime invested considerable resources in historically intelligible, but highly contentious interpretations of traditional African monarchs as royal potentates. This in turn required constant intrigue, and arbitrary use of colonial state power.[23]

It is worth exploring why Ross instituted this problematic strategy of indirect rule in a province as complex as Oyo. Although arbitrary in style and scope, Ross's policy in Oyo Province was a logical reflection of the administrative system that was evolving throughout colonial Nigeria. As mentioned earlier, the policy which had been embraced by Ross's predecessors, Elgee and Fuller, reached its zenith when the former Governor of Northern Nigeria, Sir Frederick Lugard, was appointed Governor-General of the recently amalgamated northern and southern provinces in 1914. Convinced that previous British policies in the Yoruba region had encouraged political disintegration, Lugard thought that the British could most expediently consolidate their authority by projecting the Alaafin's "traditional" pre-eminence as supreme "paramount ruler" of Yorubaland. Since

British residents and district officers enjoyed considerable latitude in the implementation of general policy, Ross, an avowed Lugardian, carried this sentiment to its logical conclusion.

Given the inconsistencies between the new colonial order and the previous political relationship among provincial towns, indirect rule failed to construct a stable mechanism for mediating conflict; rather, it relied heavily on authoritarian measures and manipulation of local interests. Within Oyo town itself, colonial rule undermined the fluid power relations between the Alaafin and the Oyomesi, the powerful council of traditional kingmakers. In fact, the Alaafin was freed from their authority, under Captain Ross's residency. Atanda notes the implications of this development:

> . . . [D]uring the colonial period, the Oyomesi neither ruled with the Alaafin nor had the chance to act as a check on his power. Instead, members of the Oyomesi had to curry the favor of the Alaafin in order to be able to get remunerative posts as Babakekere (sublords) or as native court judges.[24]

As far as Ibadan's chiefs were concerned, Captain Ross's tenure brought little more than persistent humiliation. Succession to major Ibadan chieftaincy titles came under the Alaafin's authority, as did all decisions of significance to local administration that had previously been made by the baale and the chiefs. Tight political control of Ibadan chiefs and district towns was ensured through the Resident's heavy-handed messengers and clerks, and through Ross's removal of uncooperative baales and chiefs. In the first two decades of his residency, three Ibadan baales—Irefin, Shitu and Ola, who in various ways questioned the legitimacy of the provincial NA structure—were deposed. Their sudden dismissal had little to do with substantive issues of governance. Rather, Ross and the Alaafin simply suspected that they were disloyal.[25] Moreover, Ross affirmed the Alaafin's authority by bringing most communities in the province under his judicial control. For example, despite the reservations of British officials in Lagos, the Resident pushed through a measure which gave the Oyo Court of Appeal (with the Alaafin as president) appellate powers over the Appeals' Court in Ibadan, and over all other appeals courts (including Ife Division) in the province.[26] Indeed, in an attempt to fully cement the political hegemony of the Alaafin in the provincial NA, Ross moved the administrative headquarters from Ibadan to Oyo. At least on matters of local administration, Captain Ross's version of indirect rule in Ibadan was, as George Jenkins imaginatively puts it, "a matter of very direct control mitigated only by intrigue."[27] Ross was less concerned with establishing an efficient local government

structure, responsive to pressing problems of local administration and development, than he was with erecting an authoritarian system under the
undisputed control of the Alaafin. Embracing the Alaafin as the source of
legitimate traditional authority throughout the province, local government
was reduced to tax assessment, simple mechanisms of chieftaincy succession and the adjudication of native law; it ignored the idea of local government as an expression of communal aspirations.[28] Thus, the era of Captain
Ross, as Jenkins notes, was "a political one, concerned mainly with the
influence among men but devoid of consideration for effective local administration."[29] His residency was known in Ibadan as the era of *Gbamileti
fi mi han*—"slap his face and show him who I am" (the Resident's messengers were known to inflict instant punishment on those considered impertinent). It was a period when all important political decisions hitherto taken
by the baale and the chiefs were placed under the Alaafin's control.[30]

Not only did Ross's reign in Ibadan subject the chiefs to scorn and
ridicule, but it marginalized the city's small class of wealthy Muslim traders
and Western-educated elites. In fact, for Captain Ross and Alaafin Ladigbolu,
indirect rule in Ibadan meant the total exclusion of the rising Christian
elite, who, because of their education, became increasingly vocal about urban affairs. They formed new social groups that raised questions about the
provision of municipal services and the subordination of Ibadan to the
Alaafin. On these issues, both Christian and Muslim elites collaborated
with the traditional chiefs to challenge Ross's policies. As early as 1914, the
Egbe Agba O'tan (organization of local elders) was founded to defend Ibadan
against the policies of the colonial authorities. In fact, it was formed secretly, shortly after Baale Irefin was deposed, by such prominent Christians
as I. B. Akinyele, and E. H. Oke (the latter a former secretary of the Ibadan
NA), and by wealthy Muslim traders, such as Salami Agbaje, the subject of
a major conflict in the late colonial period.[31] The organization broadened
its political base by appointing the Ooni of Ife as patron in 1923; in March
1928 it made the educated crown prince of Ife, Adesoji Aderemi, (who
succeeded as Ooni two years later), an honorary member. Ife was the mythical
cradle of Yoruba civilization, itself subjugated to the Alaafin; by embracing
Ife royals, the Egbe sought at least a symbolic counterweight to the political
supremacy of the Alaafin. Moreover, with the support of prominent members of the Egbe, a newspaper called the *Yoruba News* was founded in January 1924 to express the views of the educated elite. In addition, the newspaper advanced the concerns of prominent Muslim traders such as Salami
Agbaje, Adebisi Giwa and Folarin Solaja, representatives of what was becoming a competitive and free-wheeling commercial sector.[32] In 1921, the

cooperation between wealthy Muslim traders and Christian elites led to the formation of another local organization, the Ibadan Native Aboriginal Society (INAS). It was, not until 1922, however, with its transformation into the Ilupeju Society (society for the unity of the town), that the organization, with Agbaje as its president, committed itself to a policy that would eventually restore Ibadan's independence from the Alaafin. The renowned political sociologist Gavin Williams in his short biography of a prominent local leader, Akinpelu Obisesan, notes that the educated men of the time

> sought to advance their interest and secure recognition of their status within the colonial order. Their political concerns were distinctly parochial; their main objections to colonial administration was to the subjection of Ibadan to the arbitrary rule of the Alaafin of Oyo and his messengers, and Ross' evident contempt for educated Africans.[33]

Despite the plight of Ibadan's chiefs during the era of Captain Ross, the collaboration between the chiefs and the educated elite resulted in several significant accomplishments during the 1920s. These achievements, which had little support from the resident, nevertheless led to a modest improvement in Ibadan's municipal development. Starting in 1924, chiefs and community leaders mounted a sustained campaign for pipe-borne water; this pressure eventually led to the installation of Ibadan's first modern water system in 1943.[34] Earlier collaborations between the new intelligentsia and the chiefs, coupled with Ibadan's important status as the Yoruba region's most important city, had forced the colonial authorities to open the first modern hospital in the southern provinces in the Adeoyo section of the city in 1927.[35] Significantly, in the early 1930s, the government instructed NA Engineer Robert A. Jones to rehabilitate Ibadan's primitive roads; in addition, Jones supervised the construction of the historic Mapo Hall, at a total cost of twenty-four thousand pounds.[36] These accomplishments were all made despite Ross's emphatic endorsement of Ibadan's subordinate status within the "traditional" hierarchy of rulers and towns. Within Ibadan itself, chiefs, community leaders and the "new men" were well aware that the Lugardian concept of indirect rule not only violated the spirit and letter of the colonial treaty of June 1893, which had ceded Ibadan to the British, but was also a flagrant distortion of the politico-military realities of the nineteenth century. Given their old age, Ibadan chiefs clearly had a good knowledge of the pre-existing political relations among Yoruba communities; they knew that the previous arrangement favored Ibadan, and not other towns. Baale Shitu's alleged impertinence towards the Alaafin, for example, was not unconnected to Shitu's own pedigree in Ibadan's relatively short political history. The "obstinate" Baale, as Atanda rightly noted, was "Shitu Omo Are," son of the famous Ibadan military ruler Are Latosisa of the famed Kiriji war, who ruled the city between 1871 and 1885.[37]

The disparity between the political realities of the nineteenth century and the indirect rule system that followed thus provided a fault line through which competing interests sought to undermine Captain Ross's overrule. In Ibadan, the initial tremors were the reactions of local interests to the Alaafin's suzerainty over the town's chiefs, and the demands of increasingly restless local elites for a more responsive native authority structure. Once Captain Ross retired in 1931, these rumbles became an avalanche.

Reforming the Lugardian Structure

Ross left a legacy Ibadan's people would remember for many decades: an inefficient administrative structure marked by the domination of the Ibadan NA and other districts by the Alaafin. Despite Ross's policies, the early 1930s ushered in a dynamic period, when new social and economic developments would bring rapid social change, precipitated by the interaction of powerful local interest groups such as chiefs, educated Christians, Muslim and women traders, artisan guilds and farmers groups.

Before we examine the implications of these dynamics for chiefly power and communal relations in Oyo Province, we should explain at this stage why it was Ibadan that would experience—as opposed to the prominent provincial centers of Oyo, Ile-Ife and Ilesha—such far-reaching changes. As a result of its extensive size, population, location and diversity, Ibadan had steadily evolved into Yorubaland's pre-eminent commercial and political center. It was a cultural metropolis as well, in which two world religions, Christianity and Islam (major forces in many West African communities by the late nineteenth century) were transforming its social character. Over several decades, the activities of Christian (mainly Protestant) missionaries had prompted the formation of distinctive communities, particularly around Anglican churches in the Kudeti and Aremo sections of the city.

Ibadan's Anglicans owed their origin to a German-Swiss missionary from Schorndof, Reverend David Hinderer, and his English wife, Anna Martin, who had arrived in Ibadan in May 1853 to establish a mission station for the Christian Missionary Society (CMS). I. B. Akinyele, in his local history of Ibadan, *Iwe Itan Ibadan*, first published under the auspices of the *Egbe Agba O'tan* in 1916, suggests that relations between the early Christian minority and the larger communities in the second half of the nineteenth century were generally amicable. In fact, Ibadan's first primary school was started in a house given to Reverend Hinderer by Baale Oyesile Olugbode in the Kudeti section of the city. By the turn of the century, other Christian communities emerged, reflecting the efforts of the Roman Catholic, Methodist, Baptist and independent African churches.[38] The official account of the dedication of St. Peter's Church, Aremo, carried in the annual CMS publication, *The Western Equatorial Africa—Diocesan Magazine*, in 1910, captures the commitment and enthusiasm of one Christian congregation:

> On Trinity Sunday, 1910, the Aremo congregation saw the completion of their labours, when St. Peter's, their parish church, built in memory of Mrs. Aimee L. Harding, was dedicated for divine service by the Rt. Rev. Oluwole, D.D. . . . The members of Aremo church, voluntarily gave free labour, they broke the stones at the quarry and carried them to the site, they also carried sand, earth and cement. . . . The members of other congregations in Ibadan rendered valuable help, and the sister churches in Lagos, Abeokuta, and Ijebu and private friends in these places gave liberal contributions.[39]

As elsewhere in Africa, Christian missionary activities encouraged the advancement of Western education.[40] Fifty years after the modest success of a handful of mission-based schools, the Baale School was established in 1904, specifically devoted to the education of children of chiefs. But since chiefs and mogajis (the heads of powerful lineages) were less inclined to take advantage of this resource, children of Christian "commoners" (as had been the case for other missionary schools) found here another institution through which their distinctive interests and values might be consolidated. As social anthropologist Peter C. Lloyd has argued, education provided an important alternative for segments of the society that lacked access to conventional channels of power. In the case of Ibadan, members of powerful chieftaincy lineages and other influential local groups typically shunned Western and Christian education. Their ambivalence and occasional hostility is understandable, since overt proselytizing often accompanied the education provided by Christian missions, effectively undermining the indigenous religious traditions with which their traditional authority was so closely underpinned. Thus, throughout West Africa, tensions between Christian values and the interests of chiefs and elders initially prompted opposition to the mission schools. Lloyd concludes that: "In contrast, men of low social status, seeing little opportunity to achieve chieftaincies (because of poverty or because their descent group had no title), turned more readily to Christianity and sent their children to school."[41] In Ibadan, chiefs and mogajis were thus slow to see the immediate benefits of a western education. Instead, they focused their attention on chieftaincy and land matters and on their NA responsibilities that not only demanded considerable time, energy and resources, but also provided some reinforcement of their authority.

The increasing influence of Christian elements at the expense of chiefs, mogajis, Muslims and elders, was further enhanced by the establishment of a CMS secondary school, the Ibadan Grammar School in March 1913. Reverend Akinyele, a prominent member of the Egbe and brother of I. B. Akinyele, became the school's first principal, serving until 1931. Despite CMS support, it was the leadership and financial assistance of educated Christians in the *Egbe Agba O'tan* and later the Ibadan Progressive Union (IPU) that sustained this ambitious project in its critical early years.[42] Since the colonial authorities gave little support, the school depended on the generosity of the CMS and of local Ibadan philanthropists such as Samson Okeowo, a wealthy trader of Ijebu descent who provided the building in which the school was housed in its formative years. More than a decade later, in 1929, the colonial government finally established a government secondary school, the Government College. The expansion of schools in Ibadan further increased the weight of the Western-educated elite, and its friction with the chiefs. Despite these tensions—which arose in many Yoruba towns during this period—chiefs were hardly an uncompromising aristocracy blindly devoted to the *status quo*. As J. D. Y. Peel notes:

> It is important not to succumb to a teleology which explains a phenomenon in terms of what it was to become. The first question to be posed is whether the conflict of these rival political elites, the chiefs and the educated, has its basis in an opposition of local class interests. The answer may be anticipated: only very partially so.[43]

Islam, which was deeply engaged with popular local concerns, had an equally profound impact on Ibadan's political, social and commercial life.[44] Significant Muslim presence was already apparent by the second half of the nineteenth century. Starting with the conversion of its famous ruler, Are Latosisa, in the mid nineteenth century, Islam rapidly became an influential force, especially among the powerful chiefly lineages. Islamic influence also grew because of the presence of wealthy Muslims such as Adebisi Giwa, Folarin Solaja and Salami Agbaje. Reinforced by their commercial ties with

European and Lebanese trading companies, they had assumed an important local political role by the 1920s.

Ibadan's leading position also reflected its remarkable economic growth
in the 1930s and 1940s. By 1930, the lucrative cocoa trade had become the
city's main source of wealth,[45] providing traders and farmers with new op-
portunities. It also generated taxes to finance ambitious projects, such as
the installation of paved roads, pipe-borne water and electricity. This improved the living and working conditions of thousands of Ibadan inhabitants. In addition, Ibadan's new position as the political headquarters of the
Western Provinces, dating from 1943, encouraged thousands of Yoruba
and other Nigerian immigrants to flock to the city.

These developments demanded the reorganization of provincial, district and city administration. The highly centralized indirect rule system
erected at the turn of the century by Captain Ross was clearly inadequate to
meet the challenges of an increasingly complex city.[46] Fortunately for Ibadan,
Ross's successor, H. L. Ward-Price, was committed to the creation of a
more efficient system of local government. After years of service as district
officer in Ife and Ibadan, it appears that Ward-Price was uncomfortable
with Ross's system of provincial administration, and was eager to implement progressive change.[47]

This was encouraged by the constitutional reforms introduced by the
colonial government in the early 1930s. It was evident by this time that the
Lugardian structure of indirect rule was no longer sacrosanct, whether for
the "new men" or for progressive British colonial administrators. According to Sir Donald Cameron, Governor of Nigeria from 1931 to 1935, for
instance, "the time was past, when anyone could pretend that indirect rule
was a sacred and mysterious art peculiar to Nigeria and understood by a
chosen few."[48] For indirect rule to continue as a viable system of local administration, it would have to adapt; reformers such as Cameron (and his
predecessor Sir Hugh Clifford, Governor from 1919 to 1925), contended
that it was time that British traditions were drawn upon in this respect.[49]
The 1933 Native Authority Ordinance and Native Court Ordinance expressed the new official attitude. The NA Ordinance required that paramount rulers consult a council of chiefs and elders on all matters affecting
the welfare of the people under their jurisdiction. While they still retained
their executive powers under the supervision of the residents and the district officers, paramount rulers would now have to recognize the councils'
advisory and consultative roles.[50] This historic provision, reflected in the
popular parlance "chiefs and council," was a fundamental departure from
the autocratic sole native authority system favored by Ross and his contem-

poraries. Despite this new ordinance, paramount rulers such as the Alaafin retained considerable political power; in fact, they could override the advice of their council, and take sole action in emergency situations.[51]

Cameron's policies were carefully implemented by his successor, Sir Bernard Bourdillon,[52] governor from 1935 to 1939. Despite its limitations, the NA Ordinance affected two major areas of local politics in Oyo Province. First, for the first time in four decades, colonial authorities had curtailed the centralized power in the hands of obas—classified earlier as traditional Yoruba potentates. Not surprisingly, paramount rulers resisted, ignoring their advisory councils. This widespread opposition prompted Governor Bourdillon, during a keynote speech at the obas' conference in 1939, to caution against the danger of autocracy:

> Any attempt by you to centralize authority unduly in any one person and to ignore your councils and other chiefs is bound to end in disaster. Your surest method of strengthening your own position in the hearts of your people, and of carrying out satisfactorily the difficult and important duties which government has thrust on you, is not to ignore these subordinate authorities, but to make the fullest possible use of them.[53]

Second, the reforms immediately boosted the morale of educated elites, whose increasing rumbles over inefficient and corrupt local administration were becoming a concern to senior colonial officials in Lagos and Enugu. In the specific case of Ibadan, British administrators had by this time lost confidence in the chiefs' ability to effectively manage such a large and complex city. Indeed, colonial memoranda during this period show that Governor Cameron's idea of reform included increasing involvement of educated elements in the daily functions of the NA council.[54] For A. H. M. Kirk-Greene, the eminent scholar of African colonial studies, Cameron's ordinance was historic, promoting

> the free allegiance of a people to a chief without recourse to external measures; the representation of western educated elements in native administrative councils; and the establishment of a formalized councillor rather than an apparent one man rule.[55]

This attempt to include educated elites in the NA system became widely known as the "critical progressive second phase" of indirect rule.[56]

The reforms had a significant political impact. Due to their social cohesion, reflecting their exposure to Western education and missionary ethos, Christian elites in Ibadan, as in other Yoruba towns, were poised to take advantage of reform. In Ibadan, this took the form of a new town-based organization, the Ibadan Progressive Union (IPU), inaugurated by prominent local Christians in June 1930. The group, which emerged as the dominant political force in the city, had its origins in the historical and cultural preservation society, *Egbe Agba O'tan*, founded in 1914. Taking advantage of the new political environment, IPU men openly embraced the political reforms that gave them an initial entree to local politics. Indeed, prominent IPU leaders, such as I. B. Akinyele, D. T. Akinbiyi, J. A. Adetoun and T. L. Oyesina would wield considerable power in Ibadan politics for the next four decades. As men of relatively humble background, with no immediate claims to chieftaincy, the educated Christians were independent of the powerful chiefly lineages. However, despite their religious and educational backgrounds, they initially cooperated with traditional leaders (most of them non-Christian and uneducated) to transform the subordinate status of Ibadan within the provincial NA structure. Ibadan politics in the early 1930s became a matter of power sharing between the principal political actors: the resident, the district officer, the chiefs, community leaders and members of the IPU. Of these groups, it was the IPU men who most effectively articulated Ibadan's interests, mobilizing diverse groups in the city (including the chiefs) against the domination of the Alaafin.[57] As the self-appointed voice of the city, IPU men pressed Resident Ward-Price for the independence of Ibadan Division, the provision of public infrastructure, and the inclusion of educated elites in local administration. Their persistent demands, coupled with the excesses of the Alaafin and his courtiers,[58] and the progressive dispositions of Ward-Price and of senior officials in Lagos, all combined to encourage reforms at various levels of provincial administration. In Ibadan, Ward-Price encouraged local chiefs to nominate two prominent educated Christians, I. B. Akinyele and J. O. Aboderin, as advisers to the council in 1933.[59] Convinced that the efficiency of the divisional NA council would depend on the progressive transformation of Ibadan's chieftaincy institution, Ward-Price, with the support of Christian elites, also encouraged the senior chiefs to install educated men as junior chiefs.[60]

The reforms, however, went much further than this. Thanks to the joint pressure from both chiefs and IPU men, colonial officials authorized the most remarkable constitutional change in Ibadan's colonial history: the subdivision of Oyo Province and the granting of independence to Ibadan in 1934.[61] The new divisional NA Council included nine senior chiefs: four from Ibadan and one each from the northern districts of Ede, Ogbomosho, Oshogbo, Iwo and Ejigbo. As the headquarters of a new independent NA,

Ibadan chiefs now had jurisdiction over legal and financial matters in these major towns. Although the colonial government established sub-treasuries for the district towns in 1940, Ibadan's fiscal authority, due to the centralized tax system, persisted until 1946.[62] Just as Ibadan's elites had opposed the domination of the Alaafin, the chiefs and educated elite of the four district towns now questioned Ibadan's claims to legitimacy as superior traditional authority.[63] No sooner had the ink dried on the document of reorganization than district obas, baales, chiefs and educated leaders began to question this new interpretation of traditional authority, making Ibadan the division's legitimate suzerain. Toyin Falola notes the political implications of this situation for British officials in Lagos and Enugu:

> The problem of subordinating one oba and its people to another was recognized in the 1930s following the ceaseless demands by the other towns in the division for autonomy. Intelligence work had been undertaken to reexamine the constitutions of the various councils and determine whether they accorded with the people's history and customs or were imposed for mere administrative convenience. The desirability of decentralizing administration and reviewing the forms of local government in the large towns was also condemned. The benefits of this intelligence work did not come until the 1940s.[64]

The resistance of Ogbomosho chiefs and elites illustrates how opposition was mobilized against yet another rigid case of indirect rule. As in Ibadan, where the elites of the *Egbe Agba O'tan* and later the IPU used their modern skills to challenge the domination of the Alaafin, Ogbomosho's educated Christians used Western cultural forms to advance their parochial concerns. This was expressed particularly through a proliferation of local historical writings that were popular by the beginning of the twentieth century in most Yoruba towns. Citing cases from Ilesha, Abeokuta and Oyo, Robin Law, a leading historian of the Yoruba, notes the political implications of these hometown historical accounts:

> Abiola, Babafemi and Ataiyero wrote their Ijesha history (1932) at the request of Sierra Leonean repatriates of Ijesha origin resident in Lagos, who were anxious to know of the past of the original home. . . . This sort of use of history in service of a local micro-nationalism was to become very common in the twentieth century, when the Yoruba historiographical tradition became increasingly particularistic.[65]

As for the veracity of these local accounts, Law cites an anonymous Egba observer of 1886 who, reacting to debates on Egba traditions in the annual report of the Abeokuta Patriotic Association, remarked:

With regards to our traditions, folklores, legends, etc., valuable as they are, there must ever be conflicting opinion, each man magnifying himself above the other, each tribe or country wishing to be accounted superior, every private man claiming to be a prince or claiming to be regarded as being blessed with a tinge of royal blood. Thus, it happens that one version of a tradition among the Egbas differs totally from a version of the same tradition among Ibadan and so on.[66]

While Law's concern was primarily with local historiography, his insightful study also points to the political uses of these reconstructed histories, and to the political motives of their authors. The historical preoccupations of Egba and Ijesha elites in the late nineteenth century were in part a reaction to the intruding "gaze" of European missionaries, explorers, adventurers and colonial administrators.[67] In Ogbomosho as in other towns in Oyo Province, the objectives of local historians in the 1930s were even more parochial: mainly to advance hometown and elite interests within the colonial dispensation. As had I. B. Akinyele with *Iwe Itan Ibadan* (the history of Ibadan), N. D. Oyerinde, Ogbomosho's influential Christian,[68] used his book, *Iwe Itan Ogbomosho* (the history of Ogbomosho), to advance the status of his hometown in the NA jurisdiction. Oyerinde's history, published with the support of the Ogbomosho Progressive Union (OPU)[69] in 1934, challenged the traditional assumptions of the colonial NA structure, notably the subordination of Ogbomosho to Ibadan rule. He questioned the veracity of Akinyele's *Iwe Itan Ibadan*, which presented Ogbomosho as having been a vassal of Ibadan in the nineteenth century. In a study of colonial Ogbomosho, Nigerian historian Babatunde Agiri notes the political significance of Oyerinde's book:

> It was partly to refute the colonial administrative set up in Ogbomosho and some heresies that had been committed against the town by other historians and their own published works. . . . It also provided the historical arguments for Ogbomosho politicians during their agitations first for the separation of the Ibadan Division from the autocracy of the Alaafin between 1931–1932 and secondly for the creation of the Oshun Division from the Ibadan Division during 1948–1951. In fact, it is significant that the book was published in 1934 after Ross had left the colonial Service and Sir Donald Cameron, the British Governor of Nigeria (1931–1935) had revised the principles of the Lugardian native authority system in Nigeria.[70]

Oyerinde's *History of Ogbomosho* was a book of important political dimensions that drew selectively from both oral and missionary accounts for colonial consumption. Like Akinyele's *Iwe Itan Ibadan*, it shows how literacy and modern skill, were utilized as instrument for the advancement of political interests.[71]

But it would be wrong to assume that Oyerinde and other Ogbomosho Christian leaders were concerned only with their town's subordination to Ibadan and Oyo. Within the town itself, the Ogbomosho Progressive Union, like its counterparts in Ibadan only a decade before, was concerned with the slow pace of reform and what it generally regarded as the stranglehold of conservative chiefs over the local council. While they articulated hometown doctrine in opposition to Ogbomosho's subordinate status, educated Christians cautiously denounced the NA council, under the control of the baale and the chiefs, as inefficient and corrupt.[72] Despite their spirited opposition, Ogbomosho and other district towns remained subject to Ibadan until the 1940s when the colonial government introduced another comprehensive local government reform.

In the intervening period, however, the NA reform under Ward-Price advanced the status of Ibadan chiefs and elites *vis-à-vis* the chiefs of district towns in the following concrete ways. Yielding to the request of local elites and chiefs in 1936, Ward-Price changed the title of the head chief of Ibadan from baale to the *Olubadan* (oba of Ibadan), a title which for the first time conferred the insignia of a Yoruba oba on Ibadan's baale.[73] This grand change, from baale (head chief) to Olubadan (oba), immediately conferred on the Olubadan the prestige traditionally reserved for historic Yoruba crowns such as those of the Alaafin of Oyo, the Ooni of Ife, or the Owa of Ilesha. An added plum for the city occurred in 1934, when Ward-Price moved his office to Ibadan, citing the administrative advantages of Ibadan over Oyo. He did this without the sanction of senior officials in Lagos and Enugu.[74] The status of Ibadan was further enhanced when it became the headquarters of the chief commissioner of the Western Provinces in 1938. So, after the reforms of 1934, Ibadan's NA consisted of the Olubadan, the senior chiefs, two Ibadan councillors, and the head chiefs of district towns (the Oluwo of Iwo, the Ataoja of Oshogbo, the Baale [later Shoun] of Ogbomosho, the Timi of Ede, and the Elejigbo of Ejigbo). Ibadan's Christian elites scored another victory in their campaign for representation when the colonial government established the NA Advisory Board in 1941.[75] Although drawn from major groups throughout the city (with eight of its members from key communities and four nominated by the Olubadan-in-Council), IPU men used the advisory powers of the board to present their perspectives in council deliberations. Indeed, the long-term objectives of the board were apparent from the beginning, when they unsuccessfully proposed in 1942 the appointment of two more educated men as councillors.[76]

Predictably, the marked improvement in the political fortunes of Ibadan chiefs spelled a radical reduction in the authority of Alaafin Ladigbolu. A man of strong character who had enjoyed more influence than any other ruler in colonial southern Nigeria, the Alaafin resisted the colonial reorganization. He had complained about the increased power of the Ibadan chiefs as early as 1932, only one year after the departure of his friend, Captain Ross. In an initial appeal to Resident Ward-Price, in a minor incident involving the conviction of one of his messengers in Ibadan for theft, Oba Ladigbolu protested that

> you (the Resident) and I ought to sit down and discuss, you are shaming me [*sic*]. Captain Ross did not use to [*sic*] treat me like this, you ought not to take my case to Ibadan, I am not equal to Ibadan people. Captain Ross did not tell me that my case will be going to Ibadan for trial. . . . You are my Resident of Oyo and not Ibadan.[77]

Furious over the more important issue of the transfer of the Resident's office from Oyo to Ibadan, the Alaafin went over Ward-Price's head by directing his anger at higher authorities in Enugu and Lagos. Despite some concern about the rapid pace of reforms,[78] senior British administrators at the provincial headquarters were not favorably disposed to such complaints. However, the Acting Secretary of the Southern Provinces, Captain Buchanan-Smith, advised Ward-Price to

> discourage any attempt by educated Ibadans and others to make capital out of the move (of headquarters to Ibadan) to the disparagement of the Alaafin. There have been signs of late that some of the Ibadans have not been able to resist the temptation to advertise their success.[79]

The Alaafin's problems were a clear indication that IPU activities had achieved their desired effect. In only a decade, the new men, armed with official approval, had instigated the transformation of the Oyo Provincial NA structure. Indeed, within Ibadan itself, educated Christians soon succeeded in expanding chiefly lineages so that educated elite personalities of humble origins could acquire chieftaincy titles. Their long quest for titles, which goes on to this day, eventually succeeded in putting three original members of the IPU, I. B. Akinyele, D. T. Akinbiyi and E. A. Adeyemo, in the position of Olubadan. A first step was the installation of I. B. Akinyele and J. O. Aboderin as junior chiefs, for meritorious service as councillors in the early 1930s. Two more IPU men, D. T. Akinbiyi and J. A. Adetoun, were appointed councillors in 1936, as were Akinpelu Obisesan and J. L.

Lasebikan in 1939. From their influential positions as junior chiefs and councillors, they made inroads into city politics, tilting the balance of power in favor of educated Christians.

Thus, by 1940 the critical question was the degree to which the educated and commercial elite would be involved in the administration of the council, and whether city government would be run by the senior chiefs or by a modernizing elite of Christian professionals, such as Akinyele, Adetoun, Akinbiyi and Obisesan, allied with progressive wealthy Muslim traders like Adebisi Giwa, Folarin Solaja and Salami Agbaje. While the political activities of the 1930s transformed Ibadan's position *vis-à-vis* the Alaafin, by the 1940s administrative reforms in Ibadan were leading to conflicts of their own. These conflicts, which centered on competition for control of the NA council, provoked a sharp response from the senior chiefs, who saw their authority threatened by the new Christian and Muslim elites. Thus, the reform which sought to make local government more representative and efficient sowed the seeds for political conflict in the late 1930s and 1940s. Despite the chiefs' misgivings, the economic and political transformation of Ibadan still forced them to cooperate with IPU men on local issues, including the implementation of important municipal programs that had been formulated in earlier decades. For example, chiefs and educated elites cooperated to complete the city's pipe-borne water and electricity schemes in 1943. In addition, even as chiefs grew leery of the new men, a coalition of Christian elites, Muslim traders and chiefs still worked closely to complete the Ijebu By-Pass, which linked key commercial areas such as Gbagi, Mapo and Molete.[80]

Chiefly ambivalence concerning the rising status of Christians in the NA council was not the only source of political disaffection. Members of local trade and craft guilds, women traders and Muslim leaders were also becoming increasingly resentful of the rise of educated Christians to political prominence. Through close links to the influential CMS, educational institutions and other powerful local organizations, coupled with the consolidation of elite ties through marriage alliances, IPU men wielded considerable influence in Ibadan's cultural and political life. Kristin Mann's important study of Christian marriage and elite formation in colonial Lagos is equally applicable to Ibadan:

> The elite's unique marriage practices created barriers to entry into the group and reinforced exclusivity. They convinced the elites and others of the group's moral and cultural superiority and legitimized its influence and authority in colonial society. Marriage also concentrated education and property within

a similar number of elite families and cemented a dense web of kinship and affinal relations that promoted the economic and political interests of the group and its individual members.[81]

Similarly, in their authoritative political biography of Adegoke Adelabu, charismatic political boss of postwar Ibadan, Post and Jenkins note that Christian elite influence was a "longstanding one in terms of political generation . . . with a self-perpetuating and interlocking (power structure) that controlled NA policies and the lives of non-members."[82]

These developments led to the formation of the Ibadan Patriotic Association (IPA), an umbrella organization of all those who wished to limit the IPU's political influence. The IPA, which took its origin from the *Egbe Omo Ibile*,[83] and rallied mass support, was founded in 1936 by Bello Abasi to support his aging father, the Olubadan, Oba Aleshinloye. Although the IPA projected itself as the defender of chiefly authority and cherished local traditions, the organization in fact was more concerned with how to extend to its members some of the privileges that were increasingly coming under the control of the IPU men. In other words, opposition to the IPU became the vehicle for those who sought access to office, resources and patronage from the NA council.[84] Moreover, IPA leaders demanded representation on the council so that membership would not be the exclusive monopoly of the educated Christians favored by Ward-Price. Finally, they resented the IPU's influence on the grounds that it encouraged a Christian morality that often conflicted with their religious beliefs.

Once set in motion, the momentum for change is often difficult to restrain. As the shift toward a new alignment in Ibadan politics became increasingly apparent, the government introduced the Native Authority Ordinance of 1943. The ordinance established the *oba-in-council* NA structure in which policy decisions had to reflect a broader consensus of council members, eliminating the paramount chief's special status as key decision-maker.[85] Furthermore, for the first time in colonial Nigeria, the ordinance allowed for some democratization of local administration. Under the ordinance, local representatives would be either elected or nominated to serve a term of two years in the NA councils. The paramount ruler now had to comply with the decisions of the majority in all cases before the council except in periods of emergency.[86]

In Ibadan, sixty-two ward representatives were elected from the city and neighboring communities to serve on the advisory committee to the NA council. Of these, fifteen were elected to serve on the sub-committee of the council. The junior chiefs and mogajis, previously excluded from direct participation in the NA, now had two representatives each in the council. Not even the formidable resistance of the chiefs and their supporters could stem the change introduced by the colonial government and eagerly implemented by the Christian elites. These political developments set in motion the radical reforms of the postwar years, and the political backlash articulated in a formidable Ibadan nativist ideology. These local Ibadan concerns were further complicated by the struggle of a pan-ethnic Yoruba elite to mobilize communal (Yoruba) support against other dominant ethnoregional elites, especially the Hausa-Fulani, in the Northern Provinces, and the Igbo, in the Eastern Provinces. These subjects are analyzed in the next chapter.

3

CHIEFTAINCY AND POLITICAL REFORMS IN LATE COLONIALISM

The previous chapter explained how the constitutional reforms of Governors Clifford and Cameron transformed the Lugardian structure of indirect rule that had been established at the turn of the century. In the 1930s, after the residency of Captain Ross, local organizations, especially the IPU, effectively collaborated with the chiefs to transform local politics. After World War II, the colonial government was forced to respond to growing demands for democracy and development. This gradually brought the indirect rule system to an end, as it became clear that control over native administration would have to shift from the chiefs to the Western-educated elites. This new perspective brought Nigeria to another watershed in its constitutional development.

The present chapter analyzes how the postwar colonial policy of a new British Labour government radically altered the the debate over local governance in Nigeria's southwestern provinces (the Yoruba region). The power struggles that ensued further complicated colonial rule at the local, regional and national levels of administration; these political arrangements were most apparent in rapidly emerging ethno-regional political alliances which were sustained by reconstructed local ideologies of power. Though primarily concerned with parochial issues, diverse local elites remained critical agents of political change. Their goals variously converged and conflicted with the objectives of colonial officials and the new regional politicians regarding colonial governance and decolonization. While decolonization encouraged conflicting claims of "western enlightenment" and "traditional rulership," both were crosscut by the new calculus of regional and local power that came to dominate Yoruba politics after the war.

Labour's Local Government Despatch

Many studies of anglophone West Africa have convincingly argued that the victory of the Labour Party in the 1945 British parliamentary elections, the activities of the Fabian Colonial Bureau, and the progressive attitude of Secretary of State for the Colonies Arthur Creech Jones all contributed to the radical shift in British colonial policy after the war.[1] Reluctant to accede to nationalists' demands for independence, Prime Minister Clement Attlee's government formulated policies that responded to the pressures of an emerging national political class, while ensuring imperial interests.[2] Thus, prompted by African nationalist demands and the global struggles for decolonization, the British government and senior Whitehall officials abandoned the previous colonial policy of benign neglect, in favor of a more vigorous pursuit of the political transformation of West Africa. To leading Colonial Office officials, only an authoritative statement of policy could transform the ineffective native authority (NA) structures. The views expressed by G. B. Cartland, a senior official in the African Division of the Colonial Office who had served as District Commissioner in the Gold Coast from 1935 to 1945, reflected the new thinking among Labour politicians and the more progressive elements in Whitehall. In 1946, this veteran Africanist dismissed the NAs as capable only "of dealing with the most primitive problems." His senior colleague, Andrew Cohen, head of the African division in Whitehall, went a step further, asserting that only a modern local government system, based on the leadership of educated elements, could provide a durable framework for colonial development.[3] While in principle embracing this perspective, Secretary of State Creech Jones took a more cautious position: he favored a policy that would be grafted on the aspirations of diverse communities under the leadership of the educated class.[4]

What came of this imperial discussion was the celebrated 1947 *Local Government Despatch*. The historic document, which encapsulated the Labour government's postwar policy towards its African territories, revealed a general disenchantment with the indirect rule system and the chieftaincy structures on which it was based. Emphasizing the rationale for the new policy, Creech Jones noted that the key to success lies in the development of an efficient and democratic system of local government. . . . Local because the system of government must be close to the common people and their problems. Efficient because it must be capable of managing the local services in a way which will help to raise the standard of living, and democratic because it must not only find a place for the growing class of educated men, but at the same time command the respect and support of the mass of the people.[5]

Thus, as far as the secretary of state was concerned, the "modified traditional machinery" that had served the British in West Africa for half a century must now adapt to the demands of a new era.[6] This shift in policy thus spelt the beginning of the end of chiefly power in local administration.

The details of the new policy were hotly debated at a summer school program on African administration organized by the Colonial Office at Queen's College, Cambridge, in August 1947. Attended by senior colonial officials, it provided a forum for the clarification of general policy under the supervision of the Colonial Office.[7] Discussions centered on broad local government issues ranging from finance and taxation to land use and economic development, public infrastructure, politics and race relations. Cohen, who chaired the crucial sessions on local government reforms, considered the fate of traditional title holders: "Taking a long view . . . a time may come when in increasing number of places, chiefs will no longer be in a position to make an effective contribution to the development of local government."[8] In short, by emphasizing the importance of community development, responsive local government, and the participation of educated Africans, Cohen argued that a cardinal aspect of the new policy would be the marginalization of traditional title-holders at all levels of government, not just locally.

Despite its historical significance, the new policy was in fact not as radical as Cohen and his associates had claimed. Emphasizing its limited scope in the case of the Gold Coast, political scientist Richard Crook notes that the despatch represented "the old (indirect rule) wine in a new (local government) bottle"; this new idea of good governance merely substituted "the possession of literacy and democratic community endorsement for traditional entitlement."[9] Nevertheless, the shift from the old guard, the chiefs, to the educated elites is significant, with far-reaching implications for local power relations. With fragile ties to local patronage structures, educated elites in southern Nigeria utilized the legitimacy of traditional rulers and chiefs, whose political fortunes were clearly on the wane. Crook describes the dilemma of the educated in the emerging political dispensation as a group who would be worthy collaborators in government, make government more legitimate, head off criticisms of chieftaincy as anachronistic and despotic, and yet be responsible. Where could such elusive Africans be found? The answer was in local politics, from amongst the ranks of local critics of chieftaincy and its alleged abuses.[10]

The complex implications of Creech Jones's reform policy were reflected in the ensuing confusion that arose in many African local jurisdictions. In fact, evidence from Nigeria suggests that there was no coherent implementation of this policy at the provincial and district levels. Rather than precipitate the reform that eventually took place in Yoruba towns, Creech Jones's policy, as D. A. Low notes, merely encouraged a process that was well under way throughout British colonial Africa.[11] Oyo Province and in particular the Ibadan Divisional NA provide an illuminating example of how these new ideas of reform shaped collective political action in the immediate postwar years.

The Agbaje Affair

The comprehensive local government reform enshrined in the *1947 Despatch* was not implemented until January 1951, when Sir John S. Macpherson, Governor of Nigeria, appointed administrative officer H. L. M. Butcher as sole commissioner to investigate allegations of corruption in the Ibadan NA. Ironically, the investigation that triggered the most comprehensive reform in Ibadan's colonial history was instigated by the chiefs themselves. The focus of Butcher's investigation was the celebrated Agbaje agitation of 1949–1951. The event resulted in a bitter conflict between a progressive senior chief, Salami Agbaje, and his conservative colleagues who dominated the NA council. It exemplified a new political climate, marked by the chiefs' concern that imminent local government reform in southern Nigeria would curtail their local political role.

Salami Agbaje, born in Lagos in 1880, migrated to Ibadan with his parents as a child. By 1904 he had entered the lucrative trade in cocoa, textile and basic consumer items. He added a hauling business to his commercial enterprise and by the early 1920s become Ibadan's most affluent merchant. This rapid rise in economic fortune led to his appointment to the Legislative Council (a national advisory body to the governor) in 1930, and his installation as a junior chief by Baale Okunola Abasi in 1933.[12] Although Agbaje had little formal education, he gave generously to both

Christian and Koranic schools. Skipping eight titles in the Balogun chief-taincy line, he was installed the *Ikolaba Balogun*—the twelfth most senior Balogun title—in 1936. This rapid climb can be attributed to Agbaje's influence among powerful Ibadan personalities. By the early 1940s, Agbaje had become a senior chief, and figured as the most influential man in city politics. In Ibadan, as in most Yoruba communities, a man with Chief Agbaje's wealth was obliged to render favors to an extensive network of clients.[13] By the mid 1940s, many chiefs and mogajis were heavily indebted to him, having borrowed significant amounts of money to finance their titles.

The typical *olaju* (enlightened) elder statesman, as described so viv-idly by J. D. Y. Peel,[14] Agbaje resented the conservatism of other chiefs who dominated the NA and the native courts, including their subordinates, the junior chiefs and mogajis, who in their desire to gain influence in local politics, did the bidding of their superiors at every turn. The progressive Agbaje, who favored administrative reforms, called for the separation of the native courts from the executive branch of the NA council. A member of both the NA and the native court of appeal, Agbaje encountered stiff opposition, and found himself isolated from his colleagues.

In 1948, at the age of 68, Chief Agbaje was installed Otun Balogun, the second highest title in the Balogun line. As one of the four most senior chiefs, Agbaje was now eligible for the title of Olubadan. The likelihood of a self-assured progressive holding the highest chieftaincy title in the land, at a time when prospects of comprehensive reform were in the air, was anathema to the chiefs. Junior chiefs and mogajis (prompted by several senior chiefs) secured the support of Adegoke Adelabu (see chapter 4), the general secretary of the *Egbe Omo Ibile*, to press charges against Chief Agbaje. They submitted a petition to the Olubadan-in-Council demanding the removal of the Otun Balogun in December, 1949. The petition, which was accepted by the Olubadan and senior chiefs, accused Agbaje of "injustice, selfishness, avarice, exploitation, deceit, vindictiveness, machination, ruth-lessness, ambition and tyranny." More specifically, Agbaje was accused of being "merciless" in a lawsuit involving an ex-court clerk called Lawoyin, and having done all in his power to subjugate Ibadan to the Alaafin of Oyo.[15]

Before the Lagos government became involved in the dispute, British administrators in Ibadan sought to prevent an open confrontation between Agbaje and his opponents. N. E. Whiting, the senior district officer (SDO), opposed the junior chiefs and mogajis, referring to them as "interested parties" determined to make political capital out of Agbaje's removal as

Otun Balogun. In January 1950, W. Milliken, the district officer (DO) declared at a NA council meeting that the government had "no axe to grind in the conflict." He advised the Olubadan and the senior chiefs to drop the charges since the dispute would only bring Ibadan's chieftaincy institution into disrepute. As the crisis deepened, the Resident intervened, claiming that the allegations were not supported by concrete evidence. He advised the Olubadan-in-Council to "bury the hatchet."[16] Defeated but not beaten, the junior chiefs drew up a "compromise" settlement which stated that Chief Agbaje could retain his current title only if he renounced his right to become Olubadan. Agbaje, who had maintained his innocence all along, rejected the terms of the settlement. In April, the Olubadan-in-Council defied British administrators and came out in the open by publicly associating themselves with their subordinates, the junior chiefs. They called for the removal of Otun Balogun Agbaje as member of the NA council and as judge in the native court of appeal. A suspension order issued against Chief Agbaje in June by the Olubadan-in-Council was immediately declared *ultra vires* by the colonial government. In response, the senior chiefs boycotted all NA council and judicial court meetings attended by the Otun Balogun.[17] As the crisis intensified, the Governor finally appointed H. L. M. Butcher to investigate the charges.

Influential personalities and organizations featured prominently in what became colonial Ibadan's most spectacular investigation. Predictably, conservative groups and individuals supported the chiefs while progressives favored Agbaje. Pro-Olubadan organizations such as the Maiyegun League, the IPA-*Egbe Omo Ibile*, and many associated groups cooperated with the chiefs and mogajis to bring charges against the Otun Balogun. Though a Muslim, Agbaje had the support of influential IPU leaders; Reverend Akinyele, founder of the Ibadan Grammar School and Anglican Bishop of Ibadan Diocese, spoke highly of Agbaje's reputation, good deeds, and outstanding contribution to the progress of Ibadan.[18] His brother, Chief I. B. Akinyele, who had assumed the title of *Osi Balogun*, and the IPU Councillor, Akinpelu Obisesan, both testified in his favor. The Agbaje dispute soon widened the division between traditionalists, who saw administrative reforms as an attack on their authority, and reformists, who stood to gain under a new political dispensation. As self-appointed custodians of local custom, the chiefs, in a passionate petition to the commissioner, pleaded that Agbaje was

> the wonder of the time. Nobody knows anything about his lineage— how, when and why he managed himself into Ibadan. We challenge him to

publish his genealogical tree. He is not by natural endowment, up-bringing or philosophy of life the right type of man in which to entrust the government of his fellow men.[19]

Not even the intervention of senior obas such as the Ooni of Ife, Oba Aderemi, the Alaafin of Oyo, Oba Adeyemi II, and the Awujale of Ijebu-Ode, Oba Gbelegbuwa II, could bring respite to the dispute. Despite the strong allegations against Agbaje's lineage by his opponents, the obas' testimony to Commissioner Butcher hinted at the real reason behind the conflict:

> Chief Agbaje has been too outspoken and unguarded in his contributions to the discussions at the council and committee meetings, owing to his progressive outlook; and has therefore become unpopular with the majority of Ibadan chiefs who are averse to rapid change.[20]

To say the least, the allegations brought against Agbaje were vague and ambiguous. Charges such as "selfishness, avarice, vindictiveness, and ambition" can hardly be regarded as civil transgressions, serious enough to merit the deposition of a senior chief who retained favor with British administrators. Thus, while clearing Agbaje of all charges, Butcher concluded that "even if we accept the allegations as true, they cannot be legally defined as offenses for which a person can be punished by the state, but as nothing more than defects of character."[21] An additional investigation that focused on alleged maladministration in Ibadan and districts was of greater significance to the chiefs. British administrators charged that the NA was inefficient and corrupt at virtually every level of administration. Specifically, they alleged that local administration was unduly centralized in the hands of a few illiterate old chiefs, who could no longer manage the affairs of southern Nigeria's most complex city.

The issue of effective local administration also included concerns over Ibadan's fiscal condition. In a serious indictment of the NA's financial department, the SDO charged that "shortly after the divisional treasury was divided into autonomous units, the NA faced a financial blizzard." The 1949–1950 estimates had shown a major deficit between ordinary revenue and recurrent expenditure, revealing that social services were being run at a heavy loss.[22] Colonial strategies of tax collection only complicated the crisis. When taxation was introduced to Ibadan in 1918, chiefs and their agents were given the sole responsibility for collection. They resorted to the precolonial politico-military system of the *babaogun*. In the nineteenth-century war-based economy of Ibadan, the success of the babaogun (war chiefs) was measured by the number of *omogun* (warriors) they attracted.

This anachronistic system, on which Ibadan's tax collection was based, actually survived until 1952. Based on the logic of the babaogun system, a chief's influence under colonial rule was in part expressed through the size of his tax list.[23] Thus, in 1924 and 1925, the eleven most powerful senior chiefs collected 6,500 pounds, while their next sixteen junior colleagues collected only 3,500 pounds. As an incentive to encourage aggressive collection, the government allowed the chiefs to retain a small proportion of the proceeds. In 1918, they were allowed 10%; by 1935 their share had fallen to only 5% of the amount collected.[24]

The babaogun system was thus based on a reconstructed notion of traditional authority through which, while retaining portions of the tax proceeds, chiefs and lineage heads reinforced British colonial objectives. Since the British had to raise revenue for municipal programs, and at the same time pacify chiefs who initially resented their loss of economic rewards from military campaigns, the colonial government adapted the old babaogun and *ajele* system of warlordism that had thrived in the previous century. Because of the economic rewards, powerful chiefs and mogajis actively participated in the system, supporting tax increases from time to time.[25] Given the general poverty of the population, many small holders, landless peasants and the mass of urban poor resented their babakekere and babaogun (colonial tax collectors) who were seen as agents of a corrupt NA council. Opposition to the payment of tax was common throughout Ibadan and the districts.[26]

It was evident by the mid1920s that this system of tax collection was grossly inadequate for a city as complex as Ibadan. In 1926 the government proposed a method of direct taxation which would have eliminated the babaogun system. Chiefs and mogajis, who stood to lose from the proposed reforms, successfully mounted a fierce campaign against it. By the early 1930s, however, memoranda from British administrators indicate that tax evasion was a serious problem throughout the province.[27] Commissioner Butcher himself was dismayed to realize, during a meeting of the NA's finance committee, that at least three chiefs were fast asleep and the council bankrupt of any serious ideas. As he later observed, "rather than paying close attention to financial matters, seventeen of twenty three members of the council had their attention fixed on their next chieftaincy title."[28]

To rectify these problems, Butcher recommended the withdrawal of tax collection functions from the chiefs. A new system of territorial collection, based on the new electoral wards, was suggested as an alternative. He argued that this system would both provide the NA with extra revenue, and eliminate the corruption common under the babaogun system.

Butcher's investigation of the native courts also had serious implications for chiefly authority. It will be recalled that one of the main issues that led to Agbaje's disfavor with his colleagues was his call for the separation of the judiciary from the executive branch of the NA. As in the case of the NA and its departments, there were widespread allegations that the native courts were grossly inefficient and corrupt.

The 1914 Native Court Ordinance had placed the courts under the firm control of the chiefs. Each court exercised powers granted by specific colonial warrant. The superior court in a given jurisdiction was a judicial council of senior chiefs presided over by a paramount ruler; the next consisted of a number of high ranking title holders; while the last was made up of junior chiefs and local elders. The power of these courts was vested in the chiefs, who in theory were supervised by the district officer (DO). Although the DO was not a member of these courts, he had access to court proceedings and records, and reserved the right to order a retrial, or to suspend or modify a sentence.[29] Theoretically, the principal objective of the native court system was the administration of justice in a simple and inexpensive way, striking a reasonable balance between "customary" requirements and modern standards. There was, however, a major gap between theory and practice, as corruption was rife in many native courts throughout the Western Provinces. It was therefore not surprising when Butcher recommended a complete separation between the NA executive and judiciary: NA council members would no longer be eligible for appointment to the native court.[30] The thorny issue of native court administration however would persist throughout the 1950s; this will be discussed in greater detail in the next chapter.

Commissioner Butcher also recommended the reorganization of administrative relations between Ibadan and its district towns. Since Ibadan Division generated more revenue than any other province in the region, he argued, and given the repeated demands of district towns for their own NA, Ibadan Division should become a province with three distinct divisions: Ibadan city and its hinterland, the Northern Districts of Oshun, and the Central Districts of Binukonu and Igboora respectively.[31] Such a proposal, if approved, would curtail the control that Ibadan chiefs since 1934 had exercised over district towns and villages. This proposal would result in the immediate loss of about half the territories under the control of Ibadan elites—in favor of the chiefs and politicians of the district towns who had consistently questioned the legitimacy of Ibadan rule.[32]

Butcher also took a radical position on the status of "native settlers"[33] in local administration. As we discussed earlier, rapid urbanization and economic development had attracted thousands of Yoruba and non-Yoruba immigrants to Ibadan in the 1930s and the 1940s. Unlike the Hausa[34] and Lebano-Syrians,[35] Yoruba migrants, for cultural reasons, were generally assertive in political and economic affairs. They were also different from earlier settlers (and their descendants) who had migrated to Ibadan in the second half of the nineteenth century. In the case of the Ijebus, Falola has noted that earlier settlers in Isale-Ijebu had been well integrated into the city by the late colonial period. They settled in Agbokojo, Oke-Ado, and Oke-Bola, traded in Aminigun and Agbeni, and retained strong ties with their hometowns in Ijebuland. These Yoruba communities—like so many successful immigrant mercantile communities elsewhere—were often berated by the Ibadans as a "parasitic class" that infringed on the birthright of natives.[36] Falola perceptively attributes the deep resentment of native Ibadans against Ijebu settlers to the economic imbalance in the colonial economy:

> [I]ndigenes were pushed to the farms while strangers controlled trade. The Ijebu were part of the groups that enjoyed economic dominance. Consequently, they employed indigenes as agents and sold to them on credit.[37]

Following a Yoruba tradition of paternal genealogy as the legitimate basis of hometown claims, as opposed to actual residence, these thriving communities (which included other Yoruba sub-groups, such as Egba, Ijesha, Ekiti and Oyo), were excluded from direct participation in local administration. But by the late 1940s, they had become a formidable political force in Ibadan. Leaders included prominent Yorubas such as Obafemi Awolowo, the Ijebu leader of the newly formed Action Group (AG); S. L. Akintola, the Ogbomosho editor of the *Daily Service*; and prominent AG politicians, Abiodun Akerele, legal partner of Awolowo, and the Egba lawyers, J. O. Craig and Isaac Delano. While native settlers paid taxes and contributed substantially to the economic and sociopolitical vitality of the city, they were deprived representation in the NA council, and, as non-Ibadan natives, they were denied access to land. They were now determined to take advantage of the favorable political climate to press their case. In a memorandum to Commissioner Butcher, the Ibadan Native Settlers Union demanded the removal of the legal barriers affecting them and called for immediate representation in the NA council.[38] Butcher was amazed that such a substantial section of the tax-paying population, including influential professionals, were not only deprived of political representation but were totally ignored.[39]

In short, Commissioner Butcher exonerated Chief Agbaje of all charges. More importantly, he imposed comprehensive reform on the NA council. By suggesting the independence of the northern and central districts from Ibadan chiefs, Butcher had recommended a radical reorganization of Ibadan Division's administrative structure. Within the city itself, he called for the overhaul of the authoritarian system which excluded native settlers from representation in the NA council.

This proposal, if adopted by the colonial authorities, would have irreversibly transformed local administration and the relationship of Ibadan with its districts. Butcher concluded that the problems that had plagued local administration were systematic, rooted in the Ibadan chieftaincy structure and the concentration of power in the hands of "a few aged and senile chiefs who owe their position not to ability or intelligence but to having lived longer than their fellow men."[40] In short, Butcher recommended far-reaching reforms, a new local administration system in which the authority of the Olubadan and senior chiefs would be confined to matters of general policy, and the authority of Ibadan over its northern and central districts would be withdrawn.

No group in the city, not even the IPU, anticipated such radical change. Despite its reformist perspective, the IPU was opposed to the proposal both because of Ibadan's loss of territorial control, and most importantly, because they would be obliged to share economic and political power with the native settlers. Since both policies would entail the advancement of native settler interest in local politics, IPU men cooperated with the chiefs and mogajis to thwart what they considered to be an infringement on Ibadan's traditional prerogatives.

Influential groups such as the conservative IPA-*Egbe Omo Ibile*, the Maiyegun League, and the Ibadan Welfare Committee, all of which had been allied with the chiefs against the IPU in the 1930s, were even more resolute in their attack against the new proposals. With the assistance of a prominent Igbo lawyer, Fred Anyiam, they petitioned the governor that

> the Olubadan and Ibadan NA has not been fairly treated by the Commissioner . . . and the recommendation to divest authority from the Olubadan and Ibadan NA is not conducive to good administration and savors of prejudice, hatred, and other manners of uncharitableness.[41]

So pervasive was Ibadan's opposition to the impending reforms that even Ibadan students in London, through their association, the Ibadan Descendants Union, resolved that Governor Macpherson had encouraged an "obnoxious proposal" and an "ill-fated misuse of power."[42]

The government decided to establish a reform committee to implement Butcher's recommendations. In keeping with the established tradition of agitation against unfavorable colonial policies, the senior chiefs mounted a campaign against the committee and its chairman, SDO John F. Hayley. Ibadan chiefs petitioned the Chief Commissioner:

> We view with disfavor the appointment of Mr. J. F. Hayley as the Chairman, Reform Committee, in view of the rather unfriendly record of Mr. Hayley when he was ADO in Ibadan. We remember with misgivings the past record of Mr. Hayley in Ibadan administrative affairs, as we doubt whether he can exercise his function judiciously and without any trace of unfavorable bias he had for Ibadan.[43]

Curiously, they called on the government to appoint the Olubadan—the embodiment of the discredited political order—to be chairman instead. Organizations representing the interests of the native settlers and the district towns, on the other hand, of course favored Butcher's report. The *Ogbomosho Parapo*, for example, sang its praise, while pouring scorn on Ibadan chiefs:

> [We] wish to express our sincere gratitude to Mr. Butcher for his foresight and impartial report which duly express the deep yearning of our people for separation from the Ibadan NA, the greatest clog in the wheel of progress. . . . [W]e hereby reaffirm our full support for the memorandum, seeking our separation from an administration firmly wedded in nepotism, selfishness and inefficiency.[44]

The members of the Hayley Reform Committee were drawn mainly from the educated elites, such as quarter representatives S. A. Oloko and T. L. Oyesina; leaders of Ibadan Citizen Committee S. A. Akinfenwa and E. A. Sanda; IPU members J. A. Ayorinde and S. O. Lanlehin; and Councillor Akinpelu Obisesan. It also included two reform-minded chiefs: Osi Balogun I. B. Akinyele and Ekarun Olubadan E. A. Akinwale.[45] Conspicuously absent were members of the Egbe Omo Ibile, the Maiyegun League and the *Iyalode* (head of women chiefs), who, having formed an alliance with the majority of the chiefs, would have nothing to do with a proposal that had brought Ibadan's chieftaincy institution and the aged Olubadan into such disgrace.[46]

The Reform Committee transformed the Ibadan and districts NA. With regard to the controversial issue of the central and northern districts, Hayley noted that "there was no doubt concerning the strength and the view of public opinion which categorically insisted on their complete separation from Ibadan at the earliest moment."[47] He further argued that Ibadan's chieftaincy disputes and ineffective local administration had crippled the

progress of these communities. The committee thus called for the independence of the northern and central districts from Ibadan chiefs.[48] The existing NA was divided into two major administrative jurisdictions. The city
of Ibadan and its rural appendages would have a separate NA, while district
communities would now have their own administration.

In Ibadan, ten quarters were added to the existing sixty-five as the
basis of local government representation. Beyond their function of linking
the NA to the various constituencies, quarters now provided the structural
base for an electoral college from which thirty-one new councillors would
be selected to share power with the Olubadan, the ten senior chiefs and the
Iyalode.[49] This landmark decision, which gave elected councillors numerical superiority in the NA council, formally brought the chiefs' exclusive
control of local administration to an end. Another setback was the Reform
Committee's decision to separate the judicial system from the executive
council, as Agbaje had demanded, and to introduce an administrative secretary to coordinate the activities of the executive council and its subordinate departments.[50] The Committee's decision on tax collection also undermined the chiefs. Although committee members called for the
establishment of a special subcommittee to address tax matters, they provided two important guidelines in this area: tax collection should no longer
be the perquisite of chiefs and mogajis; and it should be reorganized on a
territorial basis.[51]

The Hayley Reform Committee had confirmed the worst fears of
Ibadan chiefs and various local elites. Its decisions had radically transformed
chiefly power in three major areas of local administration: the NA, the
native courts and tax collection. For the first time since the imposition of
colonial rule, the dominant position of chiefs in local administration, sustained for more than five decades by a special partnership with British administrators, gave way to a system in which the chiefs would have to share
power with educated politicians.

The consequences of this new administrative arrangement are significant to a study that has the pursuit of power and the construction of
legitimacy doctrine as a central theme. Ibadan chiefs sought to resist reform by emphasizing their own political and social significance, projecting
their collective interests as a reflection of the popular will and presenting
government reform as an unwarranted attack on Ibadan's customary ways.[52]
As in the 1930s, cherished local "traditions" that emphasized the cohesiveness of the Ibadan hometown provided a populist doctrine through which
local elites mounted their opposition to administrative reforms. Controversies over local government provided a focus for political cleavages not

only between competing interests within the city, but also between Ibadan and the district towns. By granting independence to district towns and ensuring the democratic rights of native settlers, Butcher had stirred a hornet's nest. Local leaders presented the gains of these communities as detrimental to the political and economic interests of Ibadan natives. Indeed, the idea of sharing power with the native settlers—especially the enterprising Ijebus, who had strongly campaigned for reforms—was anathema to most. An Ibadan hometown ideology that defined other Yoruba communal groups in adversarial terms provided a focal point through which the grievances of chiefs and local politicians were articulated and rationalized. A communally based political movement, *Mabolaje*, would emerge to give organizational expression to Ibadan's populist opposition to further reform.

Again, however, the political upheaval in Ibadan during this period should not be mistaken for an irreconcilable confrontation between a reactionary traditional aristocracy and a progressive modernizing elite. No doubt confrontations between chiefs and educated elite over administrative reform would be a chronic feature of the decolonization process. It would become even more apparent in the 1950s that political alignments (especially as expressed by the new local and regional political parties) were based on an ongoing shift in colonial policy which gradually reversed the fortunes of chiefly rulers. Since decolonization emphasized the constitutional and structural basis of power relations at the regional level, this shifted the political focus away from the local level, where grassroots struggles over traditional status and official reform had been rooted historically. These political developments, within the context of the new politics of federalism, shaped contending subnational interests and complicated the expression of community-based doctrines. Before analyzing how the creation of a new regional government affected communal politics in Ibadan and Oyo Provinces, it is useful to sketch the constitutional provisions that established the federal framework on which both intra-and inter-regional power relations were based.

The Macpherson Constitution: The Emergence of Regionalism

As political developments unfolded in the immediate postwar years, and with the very future of Nigeria increasingly at stake, the British colonial government, under pressure from southern nationalists, began to gradually transfer power at the regional and national levels. The centerpiece of this process was the Nigerian Constitution of 1951. The deliberations that led to this historic compromise reflect the role of traditional titleholders in the evolution of regional structures of power. The varying levels of involvement of prominent traditional rulers in the constitutional review conference, and the powers consequently granted them under the 1951 Constitution, can be attributed to the political functions they had assumed in the colonial NA system. Provinces where the structures of indirect rule were entrenched emerged as relatively cohesive regions where traditional rulers and title-holders provided a fulcrum for the erection of a new regional political class. Thus, at least in this specific sense, the process of decolonization was a steady progression of colonial policies and ordinances since the imposition of British rule in northern and southern Nigeria in the late nineteenth century. And as we shall see, this would set the stage for the complex interplay between ethno-regional and class interests in the postcolonial period, when traditional rulers and chiefs continue to play a critical role. These contentious issues had severe implications for the viability of Nigeria's new federal structure. Vigorously debated by regional representatives, the constitution gave extensive powers to regional governments through a quasi-federal structure. Known as the Macpherson Constitution (named after Nigeria's Governor, Sir John Macpherson), the constitution took effect after a year of intense deliberations by a constitution-drafting committee and a review conference drawn from major sections of the federation. As a critical part of emerging regional political class, title-holders especially from the Northern and Western Provinces, where chieftaincy structures were entrenched in the indirect rule system, featured prominently among the delegates entrusted with the task of ratifying the new constitution. Thus, despite the initial attempt to democratize local government institutions, chieftaincy would once again serve emerging elites as important legitimating structures during this historic period of constitutional transformation.

The Northern Provinces had the highest representation of "paramount rulers" among its regional delegates. Prominent emirs, a number of whom had served on the Legislative Council, led the Northern delegation to the review conference in Ibadan. A prominent member of the Sokoto ruling house who later emerged as the most influential regional politician, the Sardauna of Sokoto, Mallam Ahmadu Bello, was also in the Northern delegation along with other powerful title holders. These emirs and chiefs collaborated with educated commoners led by Abubakar Tafawa Balewa, who later became Nigeria's first prime minister, to promote the interest of the dominant emirate elite in the Northern Provinces. Northern delegates presented a formidable voice on all major issues in the draft constitution. They not only succeeded in warding off what they perceived to be the onslaught from the more educationally advanced Southern delegates, but also consolidated the relative weight of the socially more cohesive North. In the debates that ensued, the gulf between North and South was immediately apparent: on the issue of revenue allocation, for example, Northern delegates successfully challenged the formula established by the 1947 Constitution[53] instituting a "per capita" system that gave weight to the numerical superiority of the North in terms of population.[54] Similarly, they insisted on a proportional representation system that would guarantee 50% of the seats in the national legislature for the Northern Region.[55] With an eye to entrench chiefly power in the emirates, Northern delegates effectively questioned the merits of a uniform local government reform proposal. Ahmadu Bello was unequivocal on the subject:

> Reforms in local government throughout Nigeria are indeed overdue but it will rather be a pity and suicidal to discard the sound foundations that have already been laid. Everybody in Nigeria is in favor of reforms of local government but such reforms are, I think, the concern and responsibility of individual regions.[56]

Unlike their Southern counterparts, Northern delegates were equally united on the critical debates that dealt with the constitutional role of traditional title-holders in politics. They questioned the wisdom behind the growing trend among Southern elites to grant traditional rulers only a secondary political role.[57] The Wali of Bornu's humorous characterization of the attitude of educated Southerners towards the chiefs typified this gap:

> I see no reason why they should be excluded from participating in all important discussions in important councils. I do not like to see chiefs treated by their people in the same manner as dolls are treated by children. I cannot believe that the chiefs in the West are considered to be too holy to rub shoulders with their subjects in the councils.[58]

In the North, the traditional aristocracy effectively collaborated with educated elements to advance Northern interests in a tripodal regional context. Delegates from the Western Provinces, in contrast, reflected the typical ambivalence of the Yoruba educated elite for traditional rulers in politics. In fact, with only two prominent regional obas present—the Ooni of Ife, Sir Adesoji Aderemi, and the Oba of Benin, Oba Akenzua II (both considered progressives)—the Yoruba political class made it abundantly clear that they were favorable to the diminution of chiefly power. The predominant perspective was expressed by spokesmen such as Michael A. Ajasin, later the political boss of Owo; Bode Thomas, a Lagos representative in the Legislative Council, and future deputy leader of the Action Group; and S. O. Awokoya, an Ijebu politician who would serve as regional minister of education in the 1950s.[59] Obafemi Awolowo, by this time a pre-eminent Yoruba politician, took a similar view. In his *Path to Nigerian Freedom*, completed in 1945, Awolowo criticized indirect rule:

> Quite apart from traditional usage, it is plain common sense that people who attain to political leadership in the way these chiefs do should not be entrusted with too much power. Moreover, in a rapidly developing country like Nigeria the enlightened classes are entitled to a considerable share in the conduct of public affairs. It would appear, however, that having committed egregious blunders, the Nigerian government is reluctant to own up to them. It never stops short at anything to bolster up the prestige of a chief who is accused of incompetence, dishonesty or autocracy.[60]

In response to a proposal of the Wali of Bornu, who advocated an active role for paramount rulers in the national legislature, Bode Thomas elaborated the purported Yoruba view: "it is the wish of chiefs in the Western region," he claimed, "not to sit in the central legislature. It is also the wish of the people that they do not take their seats in the central legislature."[61] Thomas further observed:

> I have already said how much chieftaincy is an admired and acceptable institution—in so far as our chiefs rule us with discretion, in so far as they are not tyrants, we have nothing against them. When we find an institution to be faulty, we are ready to make adjustments and then we would take steps to replace that particular person, but not the institution itself.[62]

The Ooni of Ife, however, distanced himself from Thomas and other "progressives," noting that local communities could only benefit from the wealth of experience that traditional rulers had acquired over the years. He favored the incorporation of chieftaincy, in fact, at all levels of state affairs.[63]

The position taken on the chieftaincy issue by Eastern delegates was even more radical than that of the new men of the West. The Eastern delegation dismissed chieftaincy as a retrogressive institution, capable of looking after only the most mundane social affairs.[64] This position reflected both the relative egalitarianism of Igbo traditional formations, and the dismal performance of the colonial warrant chiefs that the British had imposed.[65] This situation created a political vacuum which the educated Igbo were quick to exploit. Assessing the role of chieftaincy structures in colonial Igboland, Ebere Nwaubani notes:

> By the 1930s, Western education had thrown up "new men," Western-educated elements for whom "native administration," run by corrupt and despotic chiefs who laundered colonialism, was totally obnoxious. These "new men," often urban-based, with their improvement or development unions, were far better placed than the chiefs to mediate social change for the rest of the society. By the 1940s, the new class—expanded by increased access to the schools—had come fully into its own as society's communicators. . . . So by 1950, chieftaincy, which had been knocked off its high pedestal after 1929, was in full retreat. The advent of local government ensured that the chiefs lost their role as the link between the people and the government, and even their functions as administrators and tax collectors.[66]

Despite these divergent regional perspectives, the constitutional conference ratified a tripodal regional system that opened the door to the political pre-eminence of the North.[67] Given its population and size, half (sixty-eight) of the federal legislators were selected from the region. A relatively weak unicameral federal legislature, the House of Representatives, drawn from the three regional houses of assemblies, constituted the national government. Despite the extensive powers of the regions, the constitution granted the federal legislature powers in two important regional matters. First, the national legislature could legislate on all matters pertaining to regional citizens. Second, in some special cases, the federal council of ministers could exercise executive authority over bills enacted in regional legislatures.[68]

With the exception of a unicameral legislature in the East where chiefs were given no special role, the 1951 Constitution provided for bicameral legislatures in the Northern and Western Regions where the NA system had entrenched and preserved chiefly powers. Each of these two regions was given a house of chiefs, the members of which were nominated by the dominant political parties. Yoruba obas, however, lacked the powers of their Northern counterparts; in the Federal House of Representatives, for example, emirs could constitute up to half the Northern Region's representation, but only three obas were allowed. The House of Chiefs in the Western Region, however, like its northern counterpart, had considerable power. With the exception of money bills, which could be introduced only in the House of Assembly, all other bills had to be passed by both regional houses in order to become law.[69]

These constitutional reforms, as well as the major devolution of power that seemed in the offing, prompted the formation of new political parties to contest the forthcoming elections. In the Western Region, a pan-Yoruba sociocultural group, the *Egbe Omo Oduduwa*, provided the foundation on which a formidable regional party, the Action Group (AG), was to be established. Obas, seen as legitimate spokesmen for local aspirations, actively participated in the formation of this organization, which provided an institutional platform for dialogue between the new generation of Yoruba politicians and the chiefs in the 1950s.

The Formation of a Yoruba Political Party

Throughout Nigeria, the early 1950s witnessed the establishment of strong political ties between grassroots political organizations and the new political parties, the latter generally taking an ethno-regional or town-based form. Looking at the postwar Yoruba case, Lloyd has argued that, although local organizations had attempted "to remain above party issues and to keep foremost their loyalty to the towns," they nevertheless "tended to assume party labels, and in time became party branches."[70] Similarly, the most powerful party in the Northern Region, the Northern Peoples Congress (NPC), emerged in 1951 as a political offshoot of the *Jam'iyyar Mutanen Arewa*, a predominantly Hausa-Fulani elite organization rooted in emirate ideology. The NPC, led by the Sardauna of Sokoto, Mallam Ahmadu Bello, was subsequently dominated by an alliance between the *Masu Sarauta*, the Hausa-Fulani emirate structure, and a small group of relatively young senior civil servants and businessmen from the North. In the Eastern Region where indigenous political institutions were relatively marginalized under the indirect rule system, local and regional political parties emerged mainly with the assistance of ethnic unions. The Igbo State Union, a central pan-ethnic organization which provided a rallying point for a cluster of civic associations, contributed significantly to the eventual preeminence of the National Council of Nigeria and the Cameroons (NCNC) in regional politics.[71] The prominent role of the Igbo State Union and other "tribal" groups immediately compromised the progressive reputation of this premier nationalist organization. The NCNC was soon perceived as an instrument of Igbo sectional and elite interests, thus gradually eroding its popularity in Yoruba towns. This in part explains the rationalization for the formation of the *Egbe Omo Oduduwa* in 1948, and the regionally based party, the Action Group (AG), in 1951. Reacting to charges of ethnic particularism,[72]

Obafemi Awolowo, who soon became Yorubaland's most prominent politician, defended the creation of a Yoruba party during this period:

> In 1943 the Igbo Federal Union was launched, and Dr. Azikiwe himself was not only a prominent member of it, but also its president. Both the Ibibio Union (now known as Ibibio State Union) and the Igbo Federal Union (now known as Igbo State Union), arouse among their respective members such enthusiasm and selfless devotion as had never before been known in the country. I welcomed this phenomenon as a worthy means to a great end. If the members of each ethnic group feel happy among themselves; if they are free, within prescribed limits, to order their own lives and advance their culture as they like; and if the solidarity and devotion exhibited within their ranks can be sublimated to the cause of the nation, the federal unity of Nigeria would have been assured. . . . The Yorubas are a highly progressive but badly disunited group. They pay lip-service to a spiritual union and affinity to a common ancestor—Oduduwa. . . . I thought it was in the best interest of Nigeria that the Yorubas should not be reduced to a state of impotence, into which they were fast degenerating. . . . I decided therefore, to do all in my power to infuse solidarity into the disjointed tribes that constitute the Yoruba ethnic group, raise their morale, to rehabilitate their self-confidence, and to imbue them with the confidence that they are an important factor in the forging of the federal unity of Nigeria.[73]

The *Egbe Omo Oduduwa* was in fact initially formed by Awolowo and a group of Yoruba students in London in 1945. Admist the unfolding regional power configuration after the war, it was inaugurated in Nigeria as well, in a well-publicized ceremony attended by obas, chiefs and prominent politicians in the symbolically significant town of Ile-Ife in June 1948.[74] Sir Adeyemo Alakija—a prominent Yoruba barrister who had served variously in the Legislative Council, the Governor's Executive Council, and as president of the Lagos-based Nigerian Youth Movement (NYM)—was elected president of the Egbe; vice presidents were S. A. Akinfenwa, an Ibadan businessman, and Reverend I. O. Ransome-Kuti, the prominent Egba educator. Dr. Kofo A. Abayomi, a Lagos medical doctor, was elected treasurer, while H. O. Davies, and Bode Thomas, both Lagos-based barristers, were elected legal advisers. Awolowo himself was chosen for the pivotal position of secretary-general.

The primary objectives of the Egbe was to foster unity among Yoruba sub-groups, and promote the social welfare of Yorubas through the encouragement of education and economic development. The strong emphasis on ethnic solidarity had led the founders of the organization to appropriate the myth of Oduduwa, the legendary progenitor of the Yoruba, as the Egbe's symbolic focal point. The political realities of decolonization, especially its salient regional dimensions, encouraged Egbe leaders to emphasize cultural themes, even the reconstruction of a mythic past.[75] The conceptions underlying the Egbe thus typify the dilemma of African elites who, despite their liberal training in Western traditions of science and rationality, still were attached to and would profit immensely from narrow ethnic identities, informed by reconstructed notions of local history, mythology and traditional ways.[76] These communal identities, in effect, consolidate elite interests during this period of historic change.

Noting the complexities of this phenomenon in African states during decolonization, Immanuel Wallerstein observes that the holders of state power were

> confronted in the process of (their) incorporation into the capitalist world economy by an intrusive ideology which not only rejected the worth of the gods who had been Africa's, but also was pervasive in that it took on multiple clothing: Christianity, science, democracy, Marxism. This experience was not of course unique to the African continent, nor was the reaction of Africa unique. Cultural resistance everywhere to this intrusive, insistent, newly dominant ideology took ambiguous forms. On the one hand, many Africans accepted the new universalism, seem to learn its secrets, seeking to tame its excesses, seeking to gain its favor. On the other hand, many Africans (often the same ones) rebelled against it.[77]

This was in part the dilemma that confronted Egbe leaders who, in their attempt to legitimate their political claims and increase their popular appeal, embraced traditional structures and their custodians, the obas as well. This notwithstanding, the new men's political objectives, and the rapid social transformation of southern Nigeria since the 1930s, minimized chiefly influence in the political development that ensued.[78] Despite his apparent ambivalence towards chieftaincy institutions, Awolowo had admitted only three years earlier the seemingly contradictory situation of the Yoruba educated elites. He observed that the institution had an

> incalculable value for the masses in Western and Northern Nigeria. This being so, it is imperative, as a matter of practical politics, that we use the most effective means ready at hand for organizing the masses for rapid political advancement.[79]

Although politicians dominated the affairs of the Egbe, important functions were reserved for obas, too. For example, senior obas such as the

Ooni of Ife, Sir Adesoji; the Alaafin of Oyo, Oba Adeyemi II; the Alake of
Egbaland, Oba Ademola II; and the Oba of Lagos, Oba Adele II, were
named patrons of the Egbe.[80] For their part, the obas were enthusiastic
about their new responsibility. An invitation from celebrated sons of
Yorubaland in politics, business and the civil service, now poised to acquire
the mantle of political power, was an offer they hardly could resist. Moreover, most of the obas found the formula of Yoruba unity within a Nigerian
federal framework appealing. Following his appointment as patron, the
Alake of Egbaland wrote an enthusiastic reply to the Egbe's president,
Akinola Maja:

> I am therefore with you heart and soul and shall make it a point of duty to
> give moral as well as financial help at all times which in your judgment is
> necessary to do, so as to win support to the great cause under your personal
> direction.[81]

The obas took their commitment to the Egbe seriously (not surprisingly, since such cultural nationalism gave them a whole new lease on life).
Whenever new branches of the Egbe were established in Yoruba towns, the
obas presided over the inaugural ceremonies.[82] Their dedication to the ideals of the Egbe was such that, in many cases, obas presided over local Egbe
meetings in their own residences and palaces. In many parts of the region,
some obas even became spokesmen and propagandists for the Egbe,[83] while
others made financial contributions to a special endowment fund of the
organization. For example, in 1951 the Ooni and the Awujale of Ijebuland
each contributed 110 pounds, while a relatively minor oba, the Jegun of Ile
Oluji, contributed 25 pounds. In 1952, prominent obas again donated
generously to the Egbe's endowment fund (the Alaafin gave 150 pounds,
and the Ooni and the Osemawe of Ondo contributed 110 pounds respectively).[84]

Obas also reinforced their special ties with the Egbe by conferring
chieftaincy titles on its most prominent leaders. Bode Thomas, a legal advisor to the Egbe, led the way in what soon became a free-for-all chieftaincy
"grab." A year after the official inauguration of the Egbe, he was given the
title of Balogun of Oyo by the Alaafin, Oba Adeyemi II. His colleague in
the Egbe Executive Committee, H. O. Davies, was given the title of Otun
of Efon Alaye in 1951. In April 1952, the Oba of Lagos, Oba Adele II,
honored three prominent Egbe leaders, Adeyemo Alakija, Akani Doherty
and Kofo Abayomi, with the distinguished titles of Baba Eko, Otun, and
Baba Isale respectively. Awolowo was not left out: in 1954 the Alake of

Egbaland made him the Lisa of Ijeun and by December 1956 he had acquired seven honorary and traditional titles.[85] This trend assumed alarming proportions as obas throughout the region began to anoint their illustrious "sons of the soil." So disturbing was the proliferation of honorific titles that at the 1958 gathering of regional obas in Benin, the Ooni deplored the indiscriminate creation of spurious titles and their conferment on undeserving candidates.[86] Despite the obvious political pecuniary and considerations that often accompanied their conferral, these titles also could bestow considerable popular prestige on the regional politicians who acquired them. The obas' monopoly over these highly regarded symbols of influence was a source of material rewards (obas often accepted gifts and money for their conferral), while reinforcing strong ties with politicians. Taking the educated elites' competition for titles as an important anomaly of colonial political economy, Sara Berry notes that social change during decolonization

> reflected processes whereby institutional mechanisms of resource access adjusted to changing circumstances. People sought access to new resources of wealth and power through existing institutional channels and used their newfound wealth and influence in ways which served to restructure old institutions and social relations rather than to destroy them.[87]

Despite these formidable political alliances, the Egbe's agenda was still too parochial to provide the expansive institutional base necessary for the competitive regional framework of Nigerian politics. Yoruba leaders of the Egbe were quick to realize that another political platform organized along the lines of a modern political party was essential to challenge the NCNC. On 26 March 1950, Awolowo and seven Egbe associates convened in his Ibadan residence to inaugurate a new political party, the Action Group (AG). Their primary objective was to gain control of the Western Regional Government in the 1951 election, by mobilizing Yoruba opposed to the prospect of an NCNC government in the West.[88] Given the NCNC earlier influence in southern Nigeria,[89] regional elites insisted that only an ethnic-based party could effectively articulate the real aspirations of Yorubas in the federal context.

Furthermore, as noted earlier, the Igbo State Union had assumed a visible role in the political activities of the NCNC by the late 1940s. The ties between the Union and the NCNC was so close that Nnamdi Azikiwe, the famous Nigerian nationalist and leader of the party, assumed the position of president of the Union between 1948 and 1952. To his detractors, both the real and symbolic involvement of Azikiwe (himself an Igbo) with an organization committed to the advancement of Igbo interests compromised his reputation as a true Nigerian nationalist. NCNC leaders from other ethnic groups, especially the Yorubas, expressed concern for what some contended was the growing threat of Igbo domination of this southern nationalist party.[90] By emphasizing the NCNC's Igbo affiliations, AG leaders justified the need for a Yoruba-based party: since the Igbo State Union reinforced Igbo interests within the older NCNC, so should the Egbe provide the critical linkage between the AG and Yoruba communities. *West Africa*'s eloquent obituary for Obafemi Awolowo in 1987 effectively captured the ethno-regional calculus of power so unavoidable at the time:

> To have been a Nigerian in the era before independence, and immediately after, meant that there was little choice but to operate from a regional, ethnic power base. This was Awo's lesson from Azikiwe, his alter ego, with whom he was locked in an epic struggle of love-hate, permanently foiling each other but needing each other, dooming each other by their very divisions, two buds on the single stem of nationalism.[91]

It was the regional basis of decolonization, especially the expansion of the electoral process, that provoked the need to consolidate the ties between the AG and the Egbe. AG leaders insisted that their new party must integrate its mission with the Egbe so that the latter could carry the message of the AG into the local communities.[92] At the fifth meeting of the AG, held on 8 August 1950, Bode Thomas (the "reform-minded" delegate who, as we noted earlier, cautioned against the direct involvement of obas in politics the following year) underscored the need to enlist the support of obas and chiefs for mass mobilization. The party leadership formally agreed that the AG should be made the political wing of the Egbe in Yoruba towns. In addition, they pledged their cooperation with the Edo Union, another powerful ethnic organization in the region, in which the Oba of Benin, Oba Akenzua II, and his chiefs had assumed a dominant role.[93]

At the inaugural conference of the AG (in Owo, 26–29 April 1951), Awolowo was elected president of the party, while notables such as M. A. Ajasin, Gaius Obaseki, W. A. Mowarin, and Arthur Prest became vice-presidents. Bode Thomas was elected general-secretary while Anthony Enahoro, an Ishan who soon became prominent in regional politics, and S. O. Sonibare became assistant secretaries. S. O. Ighodaro, another non-Yoruba member, was elected treasurer and M. A. Ogun became the party's publicity and propaganda secretary. S. T. Oredein was elected administrative secretary; M. E. R. Okorodudu and S. L. Akintola, editor of the *Daily Service*, became the party's legal advisors.

Two months later, the party achieved a milestone in its bid to seize control of the regional government in Ibadan. In June, Egbe leaders and prominent obas pledged their support to the AG. The decision of the traditional rulers was announced by two distinguished patrons of the Egbe, and preeminent Yoruba obas, the Ooni and the Alaafin. The AG subsequently won the majority of seats in the regional election of September 1951.[94] Political mobilization in the Western Provinces thus operated mainly through a pan-Yoruba ethnic alliance dominated by regional politicians, obas, baales, and other community leaders in the various Yoruba hometowns.[95] As in the case of the NCNC in the east, and the NPC in the north, it was a pan-ethnic discourse, deployed in the competitive context of the federation and the regions, that was critical for political success. As interests crystalized along ethno-regional lines, the *Egbe Omo Oduduwa* allowed for an effective political collaboration between pioneering politicians,"paramount rulers" and grassroots leaders, laying the foundation for a regional political party in turn. In reaction to political developments in Nigeria as a whole, and to the need of Yoruba commercial and bureaucratic elites to mobilize protection and support, the AG, led by Awolowo, was able to take power in the West. A strong pan-Yoruba ideology was the basis of its legitimacy and appeal; an evolving pan-Yoruba identity was key to mass mobilization and support.

4

THE POLITICS OF DECOLONIZATION

A major dimension of Nigerian decolonization was the struggle of "traditional" and "modern" elites for state power at the local, regional and federal levels of government. For the politicians who subsequently controlled each of the dominant regional parties, the Action Group (AG) in the west, the National Council of Nigerian Citizens (NCNC)[1] in the east, and the Northern People's Congress (NPC) in the north, chieftaincy structures were vital to the initial strategies of legitimation which sustained regional power configurations during decolonization. In addition to these indigenous modes of political legitimacy, the inheritors of state power also emphasized the importance of education and modern skills that traditional rulers generally lacked. The processes of political institutionalization that emerged during this period thus involved a strategy of mobilization that sought to reconcile antecedent structures with the pressing demands of the modern state project.[2] In major towns of the old Oyo Province, especially Ibadan and Oyo, conflicting local interests were reconfigured in response to the reform policies of the new AG regional government.[3] The AG's reforms were thus challenged by conservative obas, chiefs, elders and other local leaders who now sought refuge from the formidable regional opposition party, the NCNC. These two regional parties provided the organizational nexus around which elite alliances and competition were organized. While the AG provided the institutional medium through which the Yoruba commercial and bureaucratic elite tended to mobilize support, the NCNC emerged as the party of disaffected politicians, obas, chiefs and community leaders. Claiming to be the custodian of local values and aspirations within rapidly fading native

69

authority structures, traditional title-holders featured prominently in the conflicts that ensued.[4]

The politics of decolonization in the old Oyo Province, and especially in its principal city, Ibadan, must be understood in the historical context of precolonial notions of traditional authorities, the political configurations that resulted from indirect rule, and the colonial reforms of the 1930s and the 1940s. Specifically, it continued to reflect the thorny questions of indigenous law and local governance, issues taken up again by the Yoruba politicians who rose to power in the 1950s. The case of Oyo, featuring the celebrated Alaafin affair of the 1950s, is particularly illuminating. Drawing from earlier analyses and new primary materials, this tragic episode in twentieth-century Yoruba history shows how the modern reconstruction of a pre-eminent Yoruba crown defined neotraditional ideologies of resistance for particular local interests during this important period of transition.

The Lyttleton Constitution

In the previous chapter we showed how the Macpherson Constitution attempted to forge a compromise between competing regional political interests of modern and traditional elites in the initial stages of decolonization in 1951. Not surprisingly, the first year of the Constitution witnessed major conflicts between the national and regional governments. Constitutional crisis in the Eastern Region and riots in the Northern city of Kano in 1953 heightened the general insecurity of the period.[5] To resolve these problems regional politicians and British officials met in London in 1953, and again in Lagos early in the following year, to work out a new constitution for Nigeria. The level of representation of the various parties at the conference was proportional to their electoral performance in 1951. Of the twenty Nigerian delegates at the conference, the NPC had five, while its main regional adversary, the Northern Elements Progressive Union (NEPU) had one; likewise, the AG provided five delegates from the Western Region, and the regional opposition, the NCNC, was granted only one. The Eastern Region was represented by four representatives from the NCNC, and two from the minority Nigerian Independence Party (NIP). Significantly, this constitutional conference, unlike the 1951 conference, reserved no specific representation for Nigeria's traditional rulers.

The document that emerged from the conferences of 1953–1954 resulted in the Lyttleton Constitution of 1954.[6] Unlike the 1951 Constitution, it provided for a bicameral legislature at the federal level. An upper house, the Senate, was composed of twelve representatives from each region, appointed by the regional governors. In the case of Lagos, the federal capital, two representatives were appointed by the Governor-General, while the Oba of Lagos and his chiefs elected one representative. The popularly elected House of Representatives consisted of 320 members from the Regions, with the North comprising the highest proportion of its membership. Unlike the Macpherson Constitution, emirs and obas of the Northern and Western Regions were denied the power to elect members to this house. Significantly, the constitution gave considerable autonomy and control over resources to the regional governments. As Larry Diamond notes:

> As the regions become the primary centers of power and wealth in Nigeria, the struggle between their ruling parties for socioeconomic resources came to dominate Nigerian politics. This struggle was manifested in repeated political conflicts over issues [such] as the timing of self-government, revenue allocation, and the NPC's effort to purge Southerners from the Northern bureaucracy and economy. But most of all, it was evinced in electoral competition.[7]

The Lyttleton Constitution also provided for bicameral legislatures, consisting of a House of Chiefs and a House of Assembly at the regional level. In comparison to the preceding constitution however, the House of Chiefs' authority was significantly curtailed. In the Eastern and Western Regions, the House of Chiefs could delay money bills only for one month, and other bills for a year, after which the House of Assembly could override the veto. The legislative powers of the Northern Region House of Chiefs, on the other hand, was in many ways comparable to that of the House of Assembly.[8] Furthermore, the emirs' authority in the North was enhanced by their presence in the regional executive; as many as four of the eleven cabinet ministers were drawn from the House of Chiefs. In the Eastern and Western Regions, in contrast, no more than three members of the House of Chiefs were allowed to serve on the regional executive council.[9]

Thus, in keeping with the established trend, the Lyttleton Constitution further marginalized Yoruba obas from formal political authority. Now under the firm control of Western-educated elites, the AG government's reform policies posed the regional authorities against powerful obas and chiefs in Ibadan and Oyo who had just recently been devastated by the NA reforms. The following case studies of native court and local government reforms in Ibadan and Oyo reveal the political ferment that accompanied regional government policies during this period.

The Politics of Native Court Reforms

The cases of the Butcher and Hayley reform commissions discussed in the previous chapter highlighted the conflict that local government reforms could cause in a city as complex as Ibadan. The AG's attempts to reorganize the Ibadan native authority (NA), implementing local government and native court reforms formulated by the colonial administration in the early 1950s, brought the regional authorities into direct conflict with the chiefs and mogajis.

Evolving partisan alignments also played a critical role. We have already discussed how the alliance between AG leaders, elders in the *Egbe Omo Oduduwa*, and obas was in part responsible for the success of the AG in the 1951 regional elections, only two years after the party's formation. Since neither the AG nor the NCNC, however, was able to dominate the Ibadan elections, local government and native court reforms proved to be more contentious here than in most Yoruba towns. The situation in Ibadan was further complicated by the reforms of previous decades. By advocating comprehensive local government reforms, Commissioner Butcher had opened a Pandora's box. Even the Christian elites, who had called for local government reforms in the 1920s and 1930s, had managed to score only a minor victory, since influential Oshun politicians such as S. L. Akintola and J. O. Adigun, now prominent AG leaders, had secured the separation of their division from the Ibadan NA. Moreover, by supporting the rights of native settlers to land ownership and local government representation, AG leaders had alienated powerful political interests in Ibadan. Indeed, most AG politicians in Ibadan, as notable Ijebus, Egbas, Ijeshas, Ekitis and Oyos, were active leaders of the much-hated Native Settlers' Union. Thus, the outcome of Butcher's reforms, especially the new constitutional rights granted native settlers and the Oshun separatists, encouraged dissident groups of the 1930s and 1940s to form an alliance against forces they now considered inimical to the collective interest of Ibadan natives. For example, powerful local groups such as the IPU, the Ibadan Citizen's Committee (ICC), the Ibadan Welfare Association, the Maiyegun League and the *Egbe Omo Ibile* that had confronted each other in the preceding conflict came together to form an umbrella organization, the United Front Committee, in March 1951. The bitter conflict that had resulted in the Butcher reforms could not, however, be easily forgotten; as the regional election of 1951 approached, the tenuous coalitions promptly disintegrated.

During this period of political ferment, a new breed of politicians emerged to displace the older IPU representatives from their prominent position in city politics. Unlike the relatively elitist IPU, this new group was made up of an assortment of politicians from various social backgrounds, with close ties to chiefs, mogajis, and other local leaders. Adegoke Adelabu, the most prominent of these younger politicians, soon emerged as Ibadan's political boss, combining a colorful personality and a populist identification with the city's impoverished masses. Along with contemporaries such as A. M. A. Akinloye and S. O. Lanlehin, Adelabu's popularity was initially based on what local leaders saw as a deep commitment to Ibadan communal interests. Some of these politicians had previous connections with the two major parties of the region: Akinloye and Lanlehin, for example, were prominent in the early activities of the Ibadan branch of the AG in May 1951. Adelabu had publicly embraced the NCNC early in the same year.[10]

These prominent native sons, however, soon realized the limits placed on their potential influence in the two major parties, where other influential politicians, most of them native settlers, had assumed leadership roles. Thus, in order to fully harness the populist temper of Ibadan, they decided to create a party dedicated solely to local interests. The appropriately named Ibadan People's Party (IPP) was founded at Mapo Hall in June, with Akinloye as president and Adelabu as vice-president.[11] In alliance with the *Egbe Omo Ibile*, and with the blessing of the Olubadan and the chiefs, the party scored a major victory in the regional elections of September 1951, sending all six of its candidates—Akinloye, Adelabu, Aboderin, Lanlehin, Akinbiyi and Akinyemi—to the Western Region House of Assembly. Subsequently, however, amid political maneuvering between the major parties and local communal-based groups, five of the new IPP legislators declared their support for the AG. Adelabu alone embraced the NCNC, a step that would later prove crucial not only for Ibadan, but for the region as a whole. This election, in which the AG eventually won a majority, was indirect; this made it possible for the party to win over many electors in the final electoral colleges.[12] With the sudden demise of the IPP, and with the grassroots organizations that provided its foundation in disarray, the IPU, now in coalition with the Ibadan Citizen's Committee (ICC), again seized control of local politics. In the NA Council election later that year, the IPU-ICC (in alliance with the AG), recorded an impressive performance, and in February 1952, by virtue of its control of a majority in the assembly, it elected all thirty-nine councillors to the council.[13] Since this victory was largely due to the absence of an effective opposition, the electoral success of the IPU-ICC was also short-lived.

These processes of political alliance and schism in Ibadan had serious implications for state policy during this critical transitional phase, especially the volatile issues of "indigenous" law and local government reforms. In August 1950, at a time when regional and local parties were in their infancy, the governor of the Western Provinces established a commission of inquiry to investigate the provincial native courts. This did not come as a surprise, given the widely held view that the native courts were grossly inefficient and corrupt. The commission, under the chairmanship of Mr. Justice N. J. Brooke, was made up of senior colonial administrators and two distinguished Nigerians, A. Soetan, a prominent barrister, and Chief J. R. Turton, the Risawe of Ilesha. It was authorized to examine all aspects of the native court system in the Western Provinces, especially their practices and procedures, and even to repeal or amend the Native Court Ordinance.[14]

After a year of deliberation that included visits to several Yoruba towns and ethnic minority communities, the Brooke Commission presented its report to the Governor in 1951. Its findings mirrored the general feeling of both British administrators and educated elites, who, over the last decade, had called for the modernization of the native courts. The commission first acknowledged the vital role of the courts in the maintenance of law and order in local communities throughout the region. Drawing from the memorandum of the district officer of Ado Ekiti, who in his testimony had underscored the sociopolitical relevance of the courts, the commission observed that the native courts as presently constituted had a utility far wider than the performance of their purely judicial functions. In many areas the native court had formed the basis of political union by bringing chiefs and people together from village units that would otherwise have had no reason to meet. The court (concluded the report) provided one of the few public expressions of traditional authority and was a highly treasured possession of every village that had one.[15] Nevertheless, in view of serious charges of corruption and inefficiency, and in line with its critical role, the commission called for the repeal of the 1948 Native Court Ordinance, and for the introduction of a new native court bill that would consolidate its recommendations.[16] Furthermore, the commission called for the separation of the executive and judicial structures of local administration.

Now armed with literate judges, the new courts would be organized to consist of Grade C and D courts as courts of first instance for cases involving customary law, Grade B courts as courts of first instance for land matters, and a Court of Appeals for final adjudication of cases involving customary law. They would be brought under the control of a colonial administrator and a native court adviser, with regional government control further ensured by granting the Resident authority over appointment of court members.

Not surprisingly, the AG regional government enthusiastically embraced the Brooke Commission's recommendations. Leader of Government Business and Minister of Local Government and Justice, Obafemi Awolowo even decided to introduce the reforms in Ibadan before the official release of the report. This can be attributed to Ibadan chiefs' and elders' earlier resistance to local government reform, as well as the city's central role as the regional capital. After an initial meeting with AG allies in the IPU-ICC dominated NA council, Awolowo launched a campaign to discredit the existing court system. In a press conference, he claimed that the Ibadan courts had hundreds of outstanding cases and were unable to handle the volume of litigation in the city. More broadly, he charged that the courts were hindered by the chiefs' advanced age, their lack of modern skills, and their preoccupation with chieftaincy, land and lineage matters.[17]

In a memorandum to the Resident, Senior District Officer John F. Hayley took a similar line, contending that, due to multiple responsibilities in local administration, land and chieftaincy matters, the chiefs had consistently neglected the courts. Hayley claimed it was not uncommon that court proceedings were interrupted so that members could attend ceremonial functions or NA Council meetings. His most scathing attack was on the notorious Babaogun system, inherited from the nineteenth-century tributary relationship between Ibadan chiefs and the provinces. Incorporated into the colonial structure as a system of clientage, a re-invented Babaogun became a state-sanctioned system through which mogajis, acting as intermediaries, secured favorable judgements for their clients. Hayley warned:

> As long as tradition successfully dictates to reason there is little hope of rooting out the evil influence of the Babaogun operating in the Divorce Courts. . . . Their presence there is condoned and encouraged by the court members whose servants they too often are. . . . [18]

Hayley also emphasized the fact that: "court staff were usually poorly trained and unable to handle records, correspondence and accounts."[19] While making an exception of the Lands Court, headed by Chief I. B. Akinyele, the Otun Balogun and pioneering member of the IPU, Hayley blasted the administration of other courts. The Court of Appeals (which the Olubadan presided over in theory but which he seldom attended) had, he charged, earned a reputation for "masterly inactivity due to the old age of its members and their other social and political obligations."[20] The lower courts at Ojaba, administered by junior chiefs, were regarded as only marginally more efficient: the performance of these judges, too, was generally hampered by custom and their responsibilities in the NA Council. Hayley reserved the most withering criticism for the Bere Courts. He noted that the most notorious of them, the Bere I Native Court, had

> long since lost claim to any of the attributes of a court of law and has become rather a house of exchange, trading in women. Grave charges of corruption are leveled against it by the public, and its administration is non-existent. Adjournments go unrecorded, "complainants" wait for days for the hearing of their cases, and Babaoguns, often the judges' own messengers, render dubious and unwanted assistance to the litigants.[21]

All this, of course, was an integral product of British colonial policy: under indirect rule, a series of native court ordinances had sanctioned the authority of certain chiefs as custodians of Yoruba indigenous law.[22] The central problem of reconstructed indigenous law in British Africa is now widely accepted in Africanist scholarship. Richard Crook observes in the case of the Gold Coast:

> All that can be said with some certainty is that African litigants, chiefs, and elders did not arrive in court with blank minds; they helped to create the law, whatever social or political interests they may have been pursuing. The common-law tradition of the British, together with the doctrine of "judicial notice", produced a "case law" based on indigenous concepts. . . . For the British, therefore, the legitimacy and authenticity of enforcing "native law and custom" lay in its local provenance, its language and procedure, and in the fact that its rules and concepts came to be recognized as law by the courts.[23]

In the terminal years of colonial rule, however, earlier British policies were no longer the main bone of contention. Awolowo, who had been an eloquent critic of indirect rule,[24] was now as leader of the regional government more concerned to attack the vested interest of conservative chiefs in the established structures.[25] His Native Court Reform Bill gave the regional government the power to establish local and district courts, to define their jurisdiction, grade and power, and to appoint, suspend or dismiss members of the bench. Specifically, the bill required native court presidents to have a minimum level of Western education.[26] The bill also established three categories of courts. "Grade A" courts would have jurisdiction in certain criminal cases, and in civil cases relating to customary marriage, divorce, custody of children and inheritance.[27] "Grade B" courts exercised similar jurisdiction, though limited to criminal cases with a maximum penalty of six months imprisonment, or fifty pounds fine, or both. "Grade C" courts, the lowest category, were limited to cases involving civil damage not exceeding twenty-five pounds, or criminal cases involving no more than twenty-five pounds in fines or a prison term of three months, or both.[28]

The bill ended fifty years of chiefly dominance of the native courts. In February 1953, a select committee of the NA Council was formed to apply the law to Ibadan. It recommended that the Ibadan courts should be entirely separate from the local executive machinery, which meant that judges and assessors would no longer be permitted to sit as members of the NA. All the native courts in the city were reorganized,[29] and Chief Akinyele, the Otun Balogun, was named judge of the new Judicial Court of Appeal. He had been actively involved in city politics for many years, first as one of the educated councillors appointed to the NA in the celebrated years of Resident Ward-Price, then as a senior chief in the NA Council and judge of the Lands Court. By the mid-1940s, Akinyele had become one of the most distinguished personalities in Ibadan. In a memorandum to Resident Robinson supporting Akinyele's nomination as the new chief judge of the Court of Appeal, Senior District Officer Hayley noted that

> his name is synonymous with incorruptibility; his services are demanded on almost every committee that is formed, his advice sought by chief and commoner on every public issue. His term as President of the Lands Court will long be remembered for the high standard set and achieved in the administration of justice in that Court. . . . He is the elder statesman *par excellence* and the community must avail itself of his invaluable services in as wide a field as practicable.[30]

Under the Native Court Reform Bill, the Bere, Ojaba and Lands Courts were to be reorganized to consist of a single literate judge sitting with assessors in each of these courts. The new judges would receive a salary of at least 720 pounds per annum, and the new education requirement meant that they would now be selected from the ranks of the same Christian-educated elite that dominated the IPU-ICC and the NA Council.[31]

In order to gain the cooperation of the junior chiefs and mogajis, who had now lost one of their main sources of influence, Resident Robinson, acting on the advice of Akinyele and Hayley, appointed some of them as court assessors. Both British officials and the regional government felt that this strategy would blend customary ideas with the demands of a modern urban context, while at the same time promoting a smooth transition to the new judicial system.[32] Soon after his appointment as chief judge however, Chief Akinyele announced a number of reforms that further threatened the traditional power of the senior chiefs. He abolished the institution of Babaogun in the divorce courts and established a central register in which all court records would be kept. In order to dispose of the large backlog of cases, Akinyele advised the new judges to strike out cases where both parties were absent without adequate reason.[33]

Aware of the radical consequences of this policy, the Olubadan, chiefs and mogajis mounted new resistance against Akinyele's reforms which, despite the attempt to accommodate some traditional title-holders, fundamentally deprived them of their longstanding influence in the courts. Chiefs and their supporters argued that the native courts were the private domain of the Olubadan and the chiefs.[34] An alliance, drawing in all those groups that had brought charges against Chief Agbaje a few years before, was forged, mounting opposition to the court reforms on various fronts. Adelabu, the vociferous NCNC leader of the opposition in the Regional House of Assembly, had discovered a new political instrument with which to contest the impending local government elections. A man of extraordinary political acumen, Adelabu was able to mobilize these voices of discontent into The Ibadan Tax Payers Association (ITPA), in opposition to the IPU-ICC-controlled local authority and the AG regional government.[35]

At this stage of the Western Region's development, the Olubadan and most of the senior chiefs were not altogether opposed to the idea of local government reorganization. However, they did favor a more moderate reform in which they would retain a significant degree of control over local administration and chieftaincy matters. To achieve this, the Olubadan mobilized the junior chiefs and mogajis, and petitioned the British administrators, registering their opposition to the proposed reforms and suggesting a "more reasonable" method of reorganizing the courts. In a petition to Hayley, the senior chiefs suggested that the president of the Judicial Court of Appeal should confer with the Olubadan and the senior chiefs on all legal matters.[36] Furthermore, they proposed that the Olubadan recommend the appointment of judges and associate members to the Resident for his approval. Oba Igbintade requested that where literate chiefs and mogajis were not available, he should be allowed to appoint anyone he felt adequate for the position. On the issue of land, the chiefs advocated the abolition of the newly established Lands Committee, while suggesting that all land matters be resolved by the Olubadan and the chiefs.[37]

Since Hayley gave them the cold shoulder, the chiefs took their case to higher authorities. In a petition to the Chief Commissioner and the Resident (in which they referred to themselves as "loyal and relegated senior chiefs"), the Ibadan chiefs showed their objection to the AG's plans for self-government. The chiefs pleaded that

> oppression cannot be agreeable to us, we have been aware of the changes taking place in the administration of Ibadan contrary to our customary law and wishes. . . . We have been aggrieved and dissatisfied and therefore protest and disagree with the question of self-government, owing to the fact that Ibadan was a self-governed and independent state. We can no longer continue with the said new government. We have been relegated and disgraced.[38]

The senior chiefs turned their attack on their pro-reform colleague and AG supporter, Chief Akinyele, whom they accused of treachery—for accepting the position of chief judge and recommending judges without the Olubadan's consent—and of insubordination—for not paying the customary homage to Oba Igbintade. Claiming that Otun Balogun Akinyele had lost their confidence, they demanded he surrender his chieftaincy title and position as Chief Judge. Resident Robinson dismissed the charges, stating that since native court reform had the government's seal of approval, he was "not prepared to entertain any criticism of the arrangement."[39] As to the chiefs' demand that Akinyele be deposed, he advised them to settle their differences with the Otun Balogun in a "friendly spirit of co-operation." With such a response from both the Resident and Chief Commissioner, the senior chiefs took their case to the Lieutenant Governor of the Western Region. They pleaded that

> quite plainly our rights and interest have been swindled away gradually and dexterously until at present we have become aware and conscious of the fact that we have been deprived of all our powers and are left destitute of any power and influence, or any post which constitutes authority in the administration of Ibadan.[40]

The junior chiefs and mogajis mobilized the support of local organizations such as the *Egbe Omo Ibile* and the Ibadan Welfare Band of Unity, which had demonstrated in the past their popular local appeal. In March, they called on leaders of the Egbe and other organizations to "resist the evil intentions of the Ijebu-dominated AG government." Their campaign soon resulted in an alliance of neo-traditionalists within the city. In April, Adelabu provided the essential organizational umbrella through which these voices of discontent could be effectively expressed.[41] The ITPA emphasized its commitment to the "special position of chiefs" in local administration, arguing that Ibadan's "cultural and moral codes of social behavior are a noble heritage that must be preserved secure from the desecrating encroachment of shallow amateur iconoclasts."[42] As a closely knit coalition mobilized against the dominance of the AG-IPU-ICC, the association, through an NCNC platform, embraced a variety of highly sensitive issues: native court and local government reforms, the erosion of chiefly power, and the impending separation of subordinate communities from the Ibadan NA, all this amidst the deepening economic crisis produced by the cocoa swollen-shoot disease.[43]

All these issues, coupled with Ibadan's status as regional headquarters, explains the city's exceptionalism in the 1950s, and the formidable mobilization of local organizations and chiefs under the populist leadership of Adelabu. The ITPA described the IPU-ICC-controlled NA Council as the "imposition of a minority clique" on the people of Ibadan. Thus, while the evolving regional structure of the Nigerian federation had prompted the Yoruba political class to construct a relatively cohesive pan-ethnic ideology, bringing together historically diverse subgroups, in the Ibadan context chiefs and community leaders in fact saw the policies as an attack on their collective interest. They thus revived a town-based doctrine to undermine the pan-ethnic ideology that the new regional political elite was working so feverishly to cement.[44] In late 1953, Adelabu and other leaders of the ITPA formed a new local party, the *Mabolaje* (don't spoil the honor of the chiefs), to contest the March 1954 local government elections. What Adelabu and the chiefs could not achieve through petitions to British administrators they would try to achieve at the polls. With the endorsement of Olubadan Igbintade, the chiefs openly campaigned for Adelabu's Mabolaje and its grand alliance with the NCNC. On 18 March, the party crushed the AG in the election, winning fifty-six seats to the AG's dismal total of fourteen; other minor parties and independent candidates gained only eight seats.[45] Awolowo himself admitted that the AG's defeat was due to the positions that his government had taken on the chiefs.[46] Awolowo's colleague, A. M. A. Akinloye, secretary of the Ibadan Branch of the AG and Regional Minister for Agriculture and Natural Resources, claimed that his party's poor performance was due to the Olubadan's undue influence in the election. He may have been right.

At his inaugural address as chairman of the newly established Ibadan District Council, Adelabu declared: "the paramountcy of the Olubadan was inviolate, and chiefs and mogajis must take their customary places in the native scheme of things."[47] Adelabu promptly violated this pledge. The first issue he faced as chairman was the controversial native court reforms, which had been a contentious issue for almost two years. In his inaugural address, Adelabu charged that the reforms had been introduced without the consent of the people of Ibadan. Hence, he charged that the appointment of Chief Akinyele was "scandalous, objectionable and unacceptable" since power should reside with the Olubadan.[48] Adelabu later noted that

> the court reforms must be suspended forthwith in deference to duly accredited public opinion. Those who persisted in imposing unwanted and obnoxious measures on the people of Ibadan against their expressed wishes must bear full responsibility for any political damage it may entail.[49]

So, Adelabu called on the NCNC-Mabolaje-controlled council to take disciplinary action against chiefs who opposed the council's position on court reforms. Moreover, the chairman threatened to withhold the salaries of the judges and the assessors appointed under the reform.[50] It was immediately evident, however, that despite the spirited challenge of the NCNC-Mabolaje council, it would be difficult to reverse a reform that had the full support of the colonial authorities. Native court reform was, however, not the only contentious issue between Adelabu's Ibadan Council and the AG regional government. Another important issue involving the Ibadan chiefs was the Western Region Local Government Law of 1952, which came into effect in 1954.

The Politics of Local Government Reforms

In the previous section we saw how Adelabu's NCNC-Mabolaje Grand Alliance, armed with the support of chiefs and a strong emotional appeal to neotraditional doctrines, gained control of the Ibadan District Council. The 1952 Western Region Local Government Bill provides another example of confrontation between the AG Regional Government and the NCNC-Mabolaje Council in which chiefs would once again play a critical role. The 1952 Local Government Bill provided the legal platform for the AG government's reform policy in local government and administration. Introducing the bill on the floor of the House of Assembly on 16 July 1952, Awolowo underscored the significance of a comprehensive local government reform in the region:

> the evaluation of local administration has been a comparatively slow and painful process. . . . We have moved tardily from Lord Lugard's principle of Indirect Rule to Sir Donald Cameron's reinstatement of it. . . . [It] is our

duty, therefore, to aim at the erection of a new edifice much nobler in conception, more artistic in design, and more massive in structure and extent than any that has hitherto been erected or contemplated.[51]

Fashioned after the English Local Government Act of 1933, Awolowo's bill proposed a three-tier system of divisional, district and local councils. Each council would be autonomous with its own corporate identity, and would be authorized to assess taxes and rates, award contracts for public works, and employ its own staff, including a local authority police force. Their jurisdictions were clearly defined. The divisional council, the largest of the three, would exercise authority over an area coterminous with an existing administrative division; the district council would exercise authority over a substantial group of towns and villages where economic, social and historical factors had developed common bonds; and the local councils, where appropriate, would exercise jurisdiction over remote communities.[52]

The 1952 Local Government Bill also sought to counterbalance the power of traditional leaders with that of elected councillors. Unlike previous colonial NA ordinances where chiefly power dominated council affairs, it required that three quarters of the council members must be elected. This meant that no more than 25 % of the council members would be obas and chiefs. The bill, however, allowed for the appointment of "paramount rulers" with traditional suzerainty as presidents of local government councils. Yet presidency of NA councils now entailed only nominal roles as ex-officio council members. *De facto* and *de jure* leadership of the councils was transferred to elected chairmen. These provisions spelled the overwhelming subordination of chiefs to elected councillors.

Finally, the bill provided regional authorities with considerable regulatory powers over local government. First, the regional government could appoint inspectors who would evaluate the performance of the local councils, have access to all council meetings and records, and provide advice on any local matter. Second, regional authorities could amend the instrument establishing local councils, redefine their areas of jurisdiction and alter their status, functions and membership. Finally, they could dissolve local councils should they contravene important provisions of the bill.[53] This would later prove to be the regional government's most effective legal control over local authorities. In effect, this stipulation allowed the AG government to regulate the actions of local councils, including those under the control of the opposition party, as in Ibadan. The regional authority's local bill was officially passed into law by the AG-dominated Western Region House of Assembly.

This was the situation when Adelabu and his NCNC-Mabolaje Grand Alliance assumed control of the Ibadan District Council in April 1954. The council now had 93 members, 20 of whom were chiefs, including the Olubadan, and 73 councillors elected from 43 city and 30 district wards. Despite the stipulations of the law, the council used this new-found political platform to further weaken the little power the AG had left in Ibadan politics. More importantly, Adelabu used the council to undermine chiefs considered sympathetic to the AG, and simultaneously brought the institution of chieftaincy under his control. This put him at odds with independent-minded chiefs like Akinyele, who had assumed the distinguished senior title of Balogun after the death of Chief Agbaje, and was regarded as next in line for the Olubadan title. He also alienated Chief Salawu Aminu, who had been elevated to Akinyele's previous title of Otun Balogun.[54] Having had himself elected chairman of all the standing committees, including chieftaincy, Adelabu now could dominate every aspect of council affairs. The Ibadan chiefs, in turn, opposed what they considered his excessive powers. Moreover, they argued that Adelabu's obligations as regional opposition leader and NCNC federal minister prevented the committees from functioning effectively.[55] The chiefs' worst fears were realized when Adelabu excluded Balogun Akinyele, and Otun Balogun Aminu, from his chieftaincy committee in August 1954. This committee then became a weapon against pro-AG chiefs.[56]

During the preceding local elections, many chiefs had joined the alliance with Mabolaje politicians and leaders of grassroots organizations[57] over issues of jobs, contracts, taxes and the new local government reforms. Now, AG politicians stepped into the breach, embracing a minority of chiefs who were taken aback by Adelabu's aggressive stance. Complaints from these chiefs and Ibadan AG politicians led the new Minister of Local Government and Justice, F. A. Rotimi-Williams, to declare that the Ibadan Council, under the 1952 Local Government Law,

> did not have any function in respect to the selection and appointment of chiefs: consequently it could not delegate them to a committee, and the proceedings of its chieftaincy committee was *ultra vires*.[58]

Adelabu ignored this warning. Indeed, it soon became apparent that his attack on chiefs was directed not solely towards opponents of Mabolaje, but towards the institution of chieftaincy itself. In late 1954, for example, the council withheld the salaries of senior chiefs and the following year rejected a recommendation by the regional government to increase chiefs' salaries' by twenty pounds. Some chiefs also complained of Adelabu's abuse of traditional members of the council.[59]

Adelabu's most controversial action as chairman was his abortive attempt to install a new Olubadan following the death of his one-time ally, Oba Igbintade, in February 1955. Since the imposition of colonial rule, the selection of a candidate for this supreme chieftaincy title had rotated between the Baale (later Olubadan) line, and the old military line of Balogun. Because Oba Igbintade had been selected from the Olubadan line, the next oba was expected to be nominated from the Balogun line, where Adelabu's nemesis, Chief Akinyele, had recently assumed the most senior title. As the ranking chief in this line, and generally acknowledged as the most able senior chief, Akinyele was to most an ideal choice. Adelabu, of course, was opposed, although from a strictly traditional point of view, it would be an uphill task to prevent Chief Akinyele's appointment. Flouting convention, Adelabu instigated the Ashipa Balogun, the Ekerin Balogun, and the Seriki— only three of the ten senior chiefs whose duty it was to select the next Olubadan—to nominate his ally, Chief Akinyo, the Osi Balogun, bypassing both Akinyele and Aminu, the two most senior chiefs in the Balogun line.[60] The chieftaincy conflict was now thrust into party politics, with Chief Akinyo supported by Adelabu's NCNC-Mabolaje group, and Chief Akinyele, by the regional government and the Action Group. Despite Adelabu's machinations, the selection of the next oba was in the hands of the senior chiefs who, along with the Iyalode (the head of women chiefs), constituted the "kingmakers." In line with convention, six of the senior chiefs, including all those in the Olubadan line and the Iyalode, voted for Chief Akinyele. The Ashipa Balogun, the Ekerin Balogun and the Seriki, voting for Chief Akinyo, were in a clear minority. Akinyele's appointment was promptly approved by Acting Resident D. A. Murphy.[61]

Later that evening, however, a peculiar event occurred: ignoring the choice of the senior chiefs, Adelabu hurriedly installed Chief Akinyo as the Olubadan. Resident Murphy went on the air the following day to announce that Chief Akinyele's nomination was "final, irrevocable, and in accordance with the law,"[62] and that his installation as Olubadan would be on 17 February. He also declared that rumors of any other installation were false, and anyone found taking part in them would be prosecuted.[63]

Despite the council's defiance, Chief Akinyele was installed on schedule. Chief Akinyo, on the other hand, was ordered by the regional government to relinquish all claims to the Olubadan title, return the instruments of office, and make a public oath of loyalty to Olubadan Akinyele or face suspension by the governor. Akinyo immediately complied and, in a ceremony on 3 March 1955, acknowledged Akinyele as Olubadan.[64] Although Oba Akinyele and the local AG had once again triumphed, Adelabu refused to retreat. The NCNC-dominated Council still refused to rescind their recognition of Chief Akinyo, and Oba Akinyele and most other senior chiefs declined to take their Council seats.[65]

As the division between the Council and the senior chiefs widened, F. A. Rotimi-Williams, the Minister for Local Government, appointed a commission to investigate the Ibadan District Council. This commission was charged with examining allegations of abuse of power, corruption, lack of compliance with the 1952 Local Government Law, and interference with 1954/1955 tax assessment.[66] This was disturbing news for Adelabu and his allies, for, if the Council was found guilty of these charges, it could be dissolved by the regional authority and replaced with a management committee. An editorial in the *Nigerian Tribune*, a partisan AG newspaper, hailed the regional authorities' initiative:

> It is the general feeling of Ibadan today that the Ibadan District Council has abused the powers, rights and privileges conferred on it by the Local Government Law. . . . This Paper believes that the Ibadan District Council has so proved itself a failure that it deserves nothing but outright dissolution.[67]

The editor of the pro-NCNC newspaper, *The Southern Nigerian Defender*, on the other hand, saw the issue as one of abuse of power, in which the regional government was determined to subjugate Ibadan's local council. An editorial in the *Defender* countered:

> The Action Group Western Government having headache [sic] on the political belief of the Ibadan District Council is leading a mad drive to dissolve the council at all costs and to appoint an Action Group Caretaker Committee. This is taking the form of a commission of inquiry to inquire into the working [sic] of the IDC.[68]

The evidence suggests, however, that Regional Minister for Local Government Rotimi-Williams had in fact proceeded quite cautiously before taking action against Adelabu and his council. His decision to investigate had its origin in complaints by prominent chiefs dating back to the early days of the council. For example, as early as June of 1954, eight members of the council from neighboring villages petitioned Rotimi-Williams to establish a two-tiered system in order to give councillors from the rural areas a greater say in their own affairs. Three weeks later, the treasurer of the council, AG-supporter E . A. Adeyemo, accused the council of corruption and called for a commission of inquiry to investigate its affairs. In early August, the Otun Balogun, Chief Aminu, and the AG councillor, Akinade, delivered a series of complaints to Rotimi-Williams, followed weeks later by protests from Chief Akinyele (then Balogun).[69]

Despite these calls for action, Rotimi-Williams exercised restraint, and at least on one occasion publicly stated that the allegations were insufficient to justify an inquiry. By April 1955, however, the severity of the allegations prompted Rotimi-Williams to relent. His appointment of D. M. O. Akinbiyi, the town clerk of Lagos, as Sole Commissioner of the investigation only deepened the Mabolaje-NCNC's suspicion that the inquiry was in fact a political witch-hunt. Although D. M. O. Akinbiyi was not a registered member of the AG, he was son of AG legislator and Native Court Judge D. T. Akinbiyi. This made him unacceptable to the Mabolaje-NCNC-controlled council, which, in an emergency meeting on 26 April, condemned Akinbiyi's appointment. According to the resolution, the council

> considers the appointment of this obvious Action Group partisan as sole commissioner to probe into the affairs of the NCNC-controlled Ibadan District Council as a planned political inquisition at once daring, unprincipled, outrageous, indefensible and unacceptable. . . . [T]he council will boycott the Inquiry, give no voluntary deposition and only attend when subpoenaed to tell the commissioner of the council's lack of confidence in his impartiality.[70]

In retaliation against chiefs who supported the Regional Government's action, the council began investigations of its own into the activities of seven senior chiefs, alleging "subversive activities" and non-payment of tax. The Council's charges also included collaboration with the legal firm of Akinloye, Odumosu and Cole, in which Akinloye, the Ibadan branch secretary of the AG, was a partner.[71] For a council that was itself under siege, there was little time to prosecute the chiefs; the campaign against Akinbiyi did succeed, however, as the government replaced him with F. W. J. Nicholson, the Town Clerk of Abingdon Council in England, who happened to be on a lecture tour in Nigeria.

Nicholson officially opened his inquiry into the administration of the Ibadan District Council on 2 September 1955. An impressive group of southern Nigerian lawyers represented the two major parties and local groups in the investigations.[72] After twenty-seven sessions—including sixty-five petitions of evidence and exhibits given by chiefs and councillors, administrative officers, leaders of local organizations and contractors—Commissioner Nicholson identified eleven substantial failures of the District Council.

Four, he noted, were beyond redress: the administration of Ibadan's bus terminal at Ogunpa, the assessment and collection of taxes, and the unbridled patronage involving council members, their supporters, and business associates. With regard to the Ogunpa Motor Park, Nicholson observed that there was compelling evidence to suggest that Mabolaje-NCNC councillors repeatedly "demanded money from revenue collectors . . . interfered with the affairs of the motor park without the knowledge of committee; and fraudulently let sites on council land."[73] On the tax issue he concluded that, since the Mabolaje-NCNC-controlled council had packed the tax unit committee with its supporters, tax assessment and collection had been subject to fraud and nepotism. While there was no real evidence to suggest that the committee favored NCNC over AG supporters, assessment of some councillors was remarkably low.[74] Moreover, Nicholson noted that, since the previous year, 13,286 people fell from Schedule II (sliding scale) to flat-rate payers. Finally, there were irregularities in the relationship between the council and three local trading companies: Charles Allen had supplied goods above the standard price; C. L. Adepoju exercised some corrupt influence over Adelabu and other council members; from Are Brothers, the council had accepted the highest bid for prison supply. In addition, prominent councillors had obtained public contracts for their private businesses, while appointments and promotions of council staff "involved several irregularities."[75]

Despite these problems, Nicholson stated that, as a corporate body, "the council was not wholly to blame," noting that a fair assessment of the council's administration should take into account the "handicaps" inherited from the previous NA. Referring to the specific role of Adelabu, Nicholson, identifying six instances of corruption and dishonesty, concluded: "As the energy of the Chairman of the council contributed to his achievements, so his lack of integrity, his excessive interference and his domineering conduct, brought about almost all its failure."[76] To make matters worse, opponents in the regional government seemed set to carry Nicholson's findings to their logical conclusion. Amidst the uproar that followed Nicholson's report, Adelabu was forced to resign his appointment as Federal Minister of Social Services in Lagos. In Ibadan, the regional authorities further weakened Adelabu's authority by establishing a new chieftaincy committee under the Western Region Appointment and Recognition of Chiefs (Amendment) Law of 1955. The new law included within the chieftaincy committee the Olubadan, senior chiefs and five baales of district villages.[77]

For the first time since his rise to regional prominence, Adelabu's opponents had forced him into a vulnerable position, where they could inflict a fatal blow. The initial strategy was to isolate Adelabu from the NCNC-Mabolaje controlled council by calling on members to reject his leadership; this could prevent the regional authorities from dissolving the council.[78] As the wrangling intensified, Awolowo's AG government stepped in to dissolve the council on 4 March 1956. Four days later, the government appointed a provisional council, which elected Oba Akinyele its president and chairman. Thus, the Olubadan and the senior chiefs, armed with the support of the regional authority (at least for the time being), dislodged Adegoke Adelabu and the Mabolaje-NCNC council that had dominated city politics for several years.

The socialist historian Bill Freund's summation of the Adelabu saga may have been harsh, but it nevertheless captures an important aspect of Ibadan politics during this critical era of transition:

> The greatest Yoruba town, Ibadan, continued to back the NCNC under the impress of the patronage system established by its "boss", Adegoke Adelabu. Adelabu was a flamboyant and corrupt politician, fundamentally demagogic in that his vague populism was devoid of any serious social critique. He was the quintessential Nigerian politician whose following was built on a use of bread and circuses for the masses and manipulation of the petty bourgeois aspirations that stemmed from the strength of the vast bazaar network and myriad of small producers.[79]

Thus, Adelabu's council was no more than "a populist aggregation of residential, occupational, and protest organizations,"[80] incapable of formulating effective policies as far as local governance and development were concerned.

The council's dissolution, however, would prove to be a temporary victory for the AG. Mabolaje's takeover of Ibadan politics in 1954 was repeated during the federal elections in 1959, when a faction allied to (and financed) by the Northern Peoples Congress (NPC) easily defeated AG candidates in six out of seven seats. Clearly, Adelabu's popular appeal did not end with his removal from the council, nor even with his tragic death in a car crash in 1958.[81]

The Alaafin Affair

A second example of conflict was the celebrated dispute between the Alaafin of Oyo, Oba Adeniran Adeyemi II, and the AG Oyo Divisional Council. Although also a direct product of the 1952 Local Government Law, this conflict differed from the Ibadan tussle in several ways. Most striking was the pattern of political alliances: In Oyo, the AG-controlled Divisional Council had the cooperation of the regional government, while Oba Adeyemi formed an alliance with the local NCNC. What the two cases have in common grew out of the competition for the patronage dispensed by those in control of the local authority. As elsewhere, community development was based on a complex political process dominated by the interests of powerful groups and individuals, and in which reconstructed local traditions, histories, and communal doctrines were once again deployed. As in Ibadan, the Alaafin's neotraditional populism proved to be a formidable force against the political authority of both regional and local AG politicians.

The conflict between the Alaafin and the AG also reveals the tortuous strategies of the new political class—deploying both modern skills and traditional symbols, as in the formation of the *Egbe Omo Oduduwa*, to reinforce their status, while undermining the old guard, obas and chiefs. The appropriation of traditional themes was matched by the politicization of local organizations; the elaboration of pan-ethnic ideology by the intensification of communal divisions at the local level; the processes of decolonization by the struggle to incorporate indigenous structures.

Oba Adeniran Adeyemi II typified the old-style conservative Yoruba oba. The successor of Captain Ross's old ally, Alaafin Ladigbolu, he had assumed political control of Oyo Division in 1945. The early years of his reign thus coincided with a major turning point in Nigerian political development. With the introduction of parliamentary democracy and modern local government structures in the 1940s and 1950s, the Alaafin, like other paramount rulers under the Lugardian system of indirect rule, was forced to yield a significant part of his authority to elected councillors. Appointed as a sole native authority in 1945, by the early 1950s Oba Adeyemi was obliged to share power with nominated NA members, and lost even more authority when the Oyo Divisional and District Councils came under the control of elected councillors in 1952.[82]

Although Alaafin Adeyemi II lacked Western education, he nevertheless attempted to collaborate with prominent Yoruba politicians and elders to accommodate reform. In 1948 for example, he became a patron of the *Egbe Omo Oduduwa*. In 1950 he gave Sir Kofo A. Abayomi, a prominent educated elite and leader of the Egbe, the chieftaincy title of Ona-Isokun of Oyo. Oba Adeyemi hosted the Egbe's second annual general assembly, and donated 150 pounds to its endowment fund. His relationship with leaders of the AG was equally cordial, notably with Bode Thomas and Abiodun

Akerele. In 1950 he honored Thomas with the chieftaincy title of Balogun, and in the 1951 regional elections he actively supported him and Akerele in their successful bid for the house of assembly. Following the elections in 1952, Thomas was elected chairman of the Oyo Divisional NA, which had jurisdiction over Oyo town and its hinterland, while Akerele became the chairman of the Oyo Southern District NA. Both councils had been under the jurisdiction of Oba Adeyemi when he was made Alaafin in 1945.

Unfortunately, the Alaafin's cordial relations with Thomas and Akerele rapidly deteriorated. Through their power in the new council, AG councillors had steadily introduced reforms undermining the Alaafin's power. For example, the Oyo Divisional NA's native court reforms of 1952 withdrew one of the Alaafin's main sources of economic and political power by replacing the *Iwefa* chiefs (the traditional judges) with appointees of the new local authorities. Moreover, the partisanship that accompanied the elections of 1950 and 1951 and the wave of reforms implemented by the regional government encouraged senior chiefs, baales of district towns and civic groups such as the Oyo Progressive Union (OPU)—an influential town-based group dominated by Western-educated elites—to assert their claims within the new political dispensation.[83] The Alaafin was no longer legally recognized as paramount. Finally, the AG government's tax program, which introduced the ten shilling capitation tax and the four shilling education rate, together with a new system of collection, brought an end to the Alaafin's seven-year control of tax assessment and collection.[84]

The Alaafin's initial reaction was to withdraw his support from the AG and from affiliated organizations such as the *Egbe Omo Oduduwa*. Oba Adeyemi explained himself later, grousing that

> no sooner had power come into the hands of our highly sophisticated ambitious African politicians through the introduction and implementation of the new constitution, the reverse began to appear (AG domination) . . . and later, upon closer examination of their policy and method I withdraw my public support.[85]

The Alaafin backed up his words with action. In a letter declining the invitation of the Secretary of the Egbe, Sir Kofo Abayomi, to the 1952 General Assembly of the organization in Lagos, Oba Adeyemi noted an incident in which Akerele had aroused local people against him, and another in which Thomas had insulted him by addressing a meeting at Atiba Hall without formally inviting him.[86] Furthermore, Oba Adeyemi openly flouted government policies, encouraging opposition to both regional and local authorities. In early 1953, for instance, along with his son, the *Aremo*, the

"Crown Prince" of Oyo, he actively opposed the new tax policies, encouraging local people not to cooperate. It was alleged that at a meeting in the afin (the palace), the Alaafin passed a resolution opposing the government's education rates and capitation tax.[87] Oba Adeyemi resisted the government's native court reforms by establishing his own private courts in the Afin and in the residences of trusted chiefs. The Alaafin's courts soon rendered the state courts impotent, as litigants (especially those involved in matrimonial cases) preferred the quick decisions of the Alaafin's courts. The Alaafin's opponents in the AG-controlled councils further charged that Oba Adeyemi's supporters intimidated all those who opposed them. In 1950, for instance, when the Oyo Native Authority (NA) Council was formed, some councillors who disagreed with the Alaafin were allegedly attacked.[88] In another widely reported incident, in early 1953, the Chairman of the Divisional Council, Bode Thomas, charged the Aremo with aggravated assault. The Aremo was actually convicted later that year, although subsequently cleared of the charge on appeal.[89]

Not surprisingly, the AG councillors reacted against what they considered to be the Alaafin's abuse of power. An anti-Alaafin group, consisting of AG politicians and a few Oyomesi chiefs, led by the Bashorun, mounted a campaign accusing the Alaafin and the Aremo of autocracy and of flouting the law by sabotaging the regional tax, local government and native court policies. As a punitive measure, the Oyo Divisional NA reduced the Alaafin's salary by 650 pounds a year, and canceled the salary of the Aremo and several palace courtiers altogether. Later in April, an emergency meeting of the council passed a resolution rejecting Oba Adeyemi II as the Alaafin, and banishing his son, the Aremo, for posing a threat to public order.[90]

The tense political atmosphere which ensued brought the *Egbe Omo Oduduwa* into the conflict. In May, the Egbe sent a peace mission of senior obas and distinguished Yoruba elders to Oyo to mediate the conflict. AG councillors agreed to rescind the resolution rejecting the Alaafin if he was willing to accept certain conditions, including the abolition of the title of Aremo and the acceptance of the government's tax, native court and local government reforms. Leaders of the Egbe called on Oba Adeyemi to seek the advice of the Oyomesi before making important decisions, especially those pertaining to appointment of chiefs.[91] The Alaafin accepted the terms, but Oyo's political climate remained quite tense.

Two months later, the Alaafin and his supporters began another attack against the AG council. Prominent members of the Oyo Progressive Union formed the *Egbe Omo Oyo Parapo*, "the organization for the Unity of Oyo People," in August 1953. The organization, which named Alaafin Adeyemi as its patron, formed an alliance with the NCNC to advance the cause of the Alaafin. With renewed support from prominent native sons, the Alaafin gained fresh confidence, and in October he sent a letter to the council repudiating the terms of the May agreement. Moreover, in a public demonstration of his new political alliance, the Alaafin campaigned for the NCNC-*Egbe Omo Oyo Parapo* in the local government elections of 1954. The AG-controlled council acted swiftly, again rejecting Oba Adeyemi as Alaafin and demanding that the regional government depose him forthwith.[92]

The Alaafin's endorsement of the NCNC, which damped the spirit of reconciliation that had temporarily emerged, would ultimately prove fatal to Oba Adeyemi himself. Not even a suit for peace by leaders of the *Egbe Omo Oduduwa* could bring respite to the crisis now.[93] The sudden death of Bode Thomas at only thirty-four further intensified an already charged political atmosphere. Reacting to alleged celebrations of Thomas's death by the Alaafin's supporters, Awolowo's funeral eulogy was prophetic. The Premier warned his NCNC opponents: "let no evil doer imagine that he had an unrestricted field for the execution of his diabolic plans. For Bode may yet prove stronger in death than alive."[94] Sporadic outbreaks of violence between AG and Oyo-Parapo-NCNC supporters persisted throughout the spring of 1954. The wave of violence reached a peak in the riots of 5 September in Oyo and several district towns, resulting in the deaths of six people believed to be AG supporters. Many more were seriously injured, and property worth thousands of pounds was destroyed.

Predictably, Awolowo and his cabinet in Ibadan viewed this incident as an assault on the AG regional government's authority. Given the AG's vulnerability in Ibadan and Ilesha Divisions, the party could hardly afford similar challenges in another important area. A delegation of senior obas and elders, however, intervened, calling on the Premier and the Minister of Local Government to allow them as "Fathers of the Yoruba People" to find a solution to what was now an open confrontation between the government and one of Yorubaland's pre-eminent obas. A conflict of this magnitude, they feared, could undermine AG authority in Oyo Division, and bring the institution of obaship into disrepute. The emergency meeting on 6 September 1954, which included senior AG politicians, obas and leaders of the *Egbe Omo Oduduwa*, denounced the Alaafin.[95] And at the insistence of AG politicians, obas, led by the Ooni and the Alake of Egbaland, accepted the government's suspension of Oba Adeyemi as Alaafin, and his temporary exile from Oyo.

Although the immediate crisis subsided, the regional authorities' punitive measures only widened the gulf between the feuding factions in Oyo and its hinterland. Many senior chiefs and prominent Oyo natives, both at home and abroad, saw the government's stern measures as an affront to the revered institution of the Alaafin, and an insult to their hometown. This response also reflects the traditional rivalry between the Oyo and Ife crowns. Influential Oyo sons had long believed that the AG authorities favored the Ooni of Ife, Sir Adesoji Aderemi, over the Alaafin. This was only heightened by the Ooni's role in the disciplinary action taken against the Alaafin. Their concern was not unfounded. By portraying the Alaafin as a self-serving monarch, averse to progressive change, AG authorities in contrast embraced the Ooni as a model oba who was committed to the government's critical reforms. As a confirmation of Ooni Aderemi's "spiritual leadership" of Yoruba obas, and his strong alliance with AG stalwarts, the Ooni, who had participated in several constitutional conferences, was subsequently appointed to the largely ceremonial but influential position of regional governor in 1959. Prominent Oyo notables, chiefs, and leaders of local organizations also passed resolutions condemning the government's harsh position and, in some cases, volunteered to accompany the Alaafin *en masse* into exile. Some prominent Oyo AG supporters switched their loyalty to the NCNC.[96]

The Governor of Nigeria, Sir John Macpherson, accepted the recommendation of the Western Region Government to appoint a commissioner to investigate the conflict in Oyo and its district towns. He appointed Richard D. Lloyd, a senior crown counsel, as sole commissioner to investigate the causes of the conflict and to make recommendations to the government. In an inquiry which took center stage in regional politics, AG councillors in Oyo's local authorities, with the support of the regional government, alleged that in 1952 and 1953 Alaafin Adeyemi had consistently broken state laws by rejecting the regional government's native court and tax reform policies, holding illegal courts, interfering with courts and encouraging non-payment of taxes. They further accused the Alaafin of involving himself in partisan politics by establishing the *Oyo Parapo* and organizing an alliance with the NCNC. Oba Adeyemi's transgressions also included "autocracy" and creation of illegal chieftaincy titles.[97]

With the exception of the charge concerning illegal courts, all allegations against Oba Adeyemi were dismissed. Commissioner Lloyd, moreover, argued that the new men of power who dominated the councils should have shown more tolerance. Like most administrators, Lloyd pronounced the conflict as a straightforward confrontation between a modernizing elite, committed to the progressive transformation of local communities, and a reactionary traditional aristocracy, uncompromisingly opposed to change. He thus concluded that

> it seems to me that a greater degree of tolerance could have been shown by the elected councillors in the various councils, who are mainly young and educated to the older nominated members who are for the most part illiterate. They are accused of being reactionary whereas I feel that they really do not understand the procedure in the working of the new councils. . . . In looking at these events, one must bear in mind that during the last few years a revolution has taken place and is still taking place in the Western Region. The old order has changed. Former customs and habits are being replaced and cast aside by the impact of Western democracy.[98]

By laying the blame for the riots at the feet of local politicians, especially the AG councillors, Lloyd exonerated the Alaafin and recommended his return from exile. The AG government, however, felt differently; the Minister of Local Government rejected Lloyd's recommendation and officially deposed Oba Adeyemi as Alaafin by executive order in 1956. Despite Lloyd's pronouncement, a careful reading of the commissioner's report, including evidence and petitions from witnesses, suggests that the conflict was less cultural or generational than political, involving opposing factions and interest groups. As in Ibadan, this was a struggle over the power and distributive resources of the state, and over the sources and symbols of legitimacy. The Alaafin's grievances therefore became a platform for all those who felt marginalized by the new political dispensation.

This bitter conflict, coupled with the formidable opposition of the NCNC-Mabolaje-controlled Council in Ibadan, indicated to regional authorities that they needed to bring obas, baales, and other title-holders under stringent state control.[99] This control was manifested through the enactment of three important laws in quick succession, bringing local government, native courts, communal land matters and chieftaincy under regional control.[100] First, the Customary Court Law of 1957 brought the customary courts under the jurisdiction of the regional Attorney-General and the Minister of Justice. Second, on 20 June 1957 the House of Assembly enacted the Chiefs' Law, allowing the regional authorities to appoint, approve, suspend and depose chiefs.[101] Lastly, the Communal Lands Rights Law of 1958 radically altered the authority of obas, chiefs and leaders of important landowning families over communal land. It gave regional authorities power to appoint boards of trustees to manage communal land, hitherto under the protection of the "paramount rulers." This was consequently challenged in the House of Chiefs and had to be modified by the government; a compromise resulted in the appointment of obas as trustees to manage the land on behalf of the government. The overall result of these bills, however, was to shift power decisively to the regional government. The majority of obas, and many other chiefs from ethnic minority areas, now shifted their support to the dominant regional party, the AG.[102] For their part, AG politicians were pragmatic when formulating reforms. In most cases they adapted modern programs to existing indigenous structures and attitudes, and awarded patronage to supportive obas and chiefs. Concessions on both sides ensured a relatively peaceful period of transition and contained conflicts in those areas where they had occurred. This trend continued immediately after Nigeria's independence in October 1960.

5

CHIEFTAINCY AND THE CRISIS OF REGIONALISM

The preceding chapter showed how chiefly power was transformed by the political and constitutional reforms instituted during decolonization. In the tripodal federal structure, the regional parties emerged as the medium through which ethnic-based elites—projecting their own objectives as the aspiration of local communities—consolidated their political and economic fortunes. The AG had cemented its political gains in the Western Region through the propagation of a Yoruba myth of origin, the mobilization of hometown civic organizations and the implementation of an ambitious social welfare program. Regionalization thus reinforced Yoruba collective political action under the leadership of educated elites, obas, chiefs and elders.[1] A key expression of this was the regional House of Chiefs, which became an effective platform for the domination of the AG. Although it initially met with opposition in major Yoruba urban centers, notably Ibadan, Ilesha and Lagos, as well as in ethnic minority areas, this pan-Yoruba strategy sustained the domination of the Yoruba political class until the AG crisis of 1962.

A benchmark in Nigerian history, the AG crisis revealed the profound limitations of the 1960 Nigerian Independence Constitution. And within the Western Region, a combination of personal and ideological factors had complicated the Yoruba political configuration. The AG crisis thus had serious implications for the regional balance of power, undermining the cohesion of the Yoruba political class.

The National Political Context

Given the implications of this crisis for Yoruba political alignments, it is worth examining in detail the constitutional bases of political relations between the regions during the immediate post-independence period. The 1960 Independence Constitution was the direct product of a decade of innovations in Nigeria's complex federal system. In the regions, it created a bicameral system of popularly elected lower Houses of Assembly and largely ceremonial upper Houses of Chiefs. Executive authority was vested in a premier and cabinet drawn from the House of Assembly. At the national level an upper house or Senate, with nominated members, was combined with a popularly elected federal House of Representatives. Appointed from the ranks of the party that controlled the federal legislature, the prime minister and cabinet constituted the Federal Executive Committee. Finally, elaborate rules established the exclusive domains of the national government and the concurrent legislative functions of both regional and federal authorities.

Elections to the first federal House of Representatives were held in December 1959, with 312 parliamentary seats at stake. This crucial election was dominated by the major regional parties, and minor parties representing numerous communal interests. The Northern Peoples Congress (NPC) won 134 of the 174 seats from the Northern Region. The National Council of Nigerian Citizens (NCNC) won 58 of the 72 seats in the East, 21 seats in the Western Region, 8 seats in the North (in alliance with the Northern Elements Progressive Union—NEPU), and 2 seats in the Federal Territory of Lagos—89 seats overall. Despite a vigorous campaign, the performance of the Action Group (AG) was the least impressive. It won only 73 seats: 33, a majority in the Western Region, 14 seats in the East, 1 in Lagos, and—in a coalition with the United Middle Belt Congress (UMBC) and the Bornu Youth Movement (BYM)—25 seats in the North. In addition, four local and ethnic minority-based parties contested the elections in alliance with the NPC. The Igala Tribal Union won 4 seats; 1 seat each went to the Igbirra Party and the Niger Delta Congress, respectively, while Ibadan's *Mabolaje* won 6. NEPU, the nemesis of the NPC, with an ambiguous combination of Islamic populism and socialist ideology, managed to secure 8 seats. Four seats went to independents, who later shifted to the NPC and the AG. Overall, whether through its alliance with minority parties or through NEPU parliamentarians "crossing the carpet" to embrace the victorious party, the NPC gained a large plurality, with 148 of the 312 seats. Despite the attempt by the British authorities to establish democracy on an optimistic note, the campaign was marred by violence, intimidation, electoral fraud, and blatant appeals to ethnic prejudices.[2] This set the stage for the acrimonious politics that ultimately destroyed the First Republic.

The failure of any party to obtain a simple majority led to successive negotiations among party leaders. Initially, the NCNC and the AG hoped to forge a parliamentary coalition, with NCNC leader Nnamdi Azikiwe as prime minister. Their legacy of acrimonious rivalry destroyed the attempt. Thus, the NCNC looked north, to the NPC. While the two parties represented very different cultural and ideological traditions, both resented the AG's aggressive appeal to ethnic minorities in the East and North. The NPC/NCNC coalition that ensued agreed on Sir Abubakar Tafawa Balewa, the deputy NPC leader, as prime minister, while NCNC's Nnamdi Azikiwe resigned his post as party leader to become president of the Senate. Michael Okpara, premier of the Eastern Region, took over the helm of the NCNC. In the North, the regional party and government remained under the control of the Sardauna of Sokoto, Sir Ahmadu Bello. Regionalism, at least for now, had triumphed. This was complicated, however, by a structural imbalance that favored the North over the two other regions.[3] As the Western Region crisis would clearly demonstrate, this particular regional equation intensified the tendencies towards ethnic particularism and the construction of systems of spoils at all levels of government, in which corruption and patronage would prevail. The Yoruba political class was now responsible for leading the opposition in the federal parliament. Awolowo, who had resigned his post as premier of the Western Region to contest the federal elections, provided spirited leadership in this respect. S. L. Akintola, the AG deputy-leader, succeeded him as premier in the West. Under Akintola, obas and chiefs became even more ardent supporters of the AG. This chiefly endorsement of party policies was particularly evident in the Western Region House of Chiefs, until the outbreak of the AG crisis in 1962.[4]

The Consolidation of Regional Power: The Western Region House of Chiefs

As did Awolowo in the 1950s, Premier Akintola consolidated his regional base in part by appropriating the assumed legitimacy of obas and title holders in the Western House of Chiefs. He did this by promoting the status of AG allies, while isolating opponents, especially those who remained loyal to the NCNC. Prominent AG supporters were appointed ministers without portfolio in Akintola's regional government. The Olubadan, the

Osemawe of Ondo, the Oluwo of Iwo, the Awujale of Ijebuland, the Obi of Agbor and the Olu of Warri, were all appointed ministers in this way. And these appointments were no hollow ceremonial titles. Through them obas gained extensive political influence: access to the premier and other members of the regional executive, to legislators in the House of Assembly and to party officials in their local communities. More importantly, the ties guaranteed access to patronage and state resources. In turn, obas enthusiastically supported government policies in the House of Chiefs, where government bills passed with ease. An observation by an ethnic-minority ruler favorable to the NCNC, the Onogie of Ewohimi, shows the frustration this situation caused to opposition chiefs. The Onogie declared in the house that

> any bill passed in the House of Assembly surely must be blessed by this House [of Chiefs]. . . . [A]ny law passed there [House of Assembly] was sure to be blessed here. Is this a blessed House? . . . How many bills have we overthrown on the ground that they are bad for the common man?[5]

It was this loyalty to the regional government that earned the House of Chiefs the label of "a useless institution" that only rubber-stamped government bills.[6] This unabashed partisanship can best be illustrated by the dispatch with which the obas endorsed government bills in 1960–61. The 1960 Local Government Amendment Bill, for example, which was graciously presented in the House by the Olowo of Owo, the Olishua of Ishua and the Alaperu of Iperu, passed with little debate and by a clear majority. The government's bills concerning taxes, agriculture, technical and commercial education, training of medical and health personnel and the 1960–65 development plan, were all approved. The Timi of Ede's generous praise for a controversial tax bill typifies this obsequious stance:

> I have special praise for the wisdom of the Western Regional Government in the relief given to the tax payers and the tax measures proposed. . . . The obas and chiefs of this region are particularly grateful to the government for the new system being proposed.[7]

Indeed, the AG positions on all the contentious issues of the 1950s—chieftaincy, local government, and native (customary) court reforms—were now embraced by obas.[8] In 1962, for example, Minister of Justice S. O. Ighodaro, introduced a bill that sought to bring customary courts under the direct supervision of the regional chief justice, the high courts and the magistrate courts. The House of Chiefs gave its obligatory approval. Similarly, the

House of Chiefs' bill received the obas' enthusiastic endorsement, despite its giving control over the selection of members of that house to the regional authorities.[9] The 1961 amendment to the Chiefs' Law, which had granted the regional government the power to establish "competent chieftaincy authorities," was even more revealing. It brought chieftaincy institutions under even greater regulation by regional authorities than had existed before independence.[10] Despite assurances by the Minister for Chieftaincy Affairs, NCNC opposition members in the Houses of Assembly and Chiefs saw the bill as a mechanism of government intimidation of independent-minded traditional rulers.[11] Objections raised by opposition leader Remi Fani-Kayode reveal the concerns of government opponents:

> The new law may be applied by this minister to any area of his choice in the Western Region from time to time as occasion demands. In these areas, new chieftaincies can be created by persons virtually appointed by the government. . . . The law makes a caricature of the native law and customs in the region and a caricature of traditional rulers in the country . . . . The Action Group has given a stroke of death to genuine chieftaincy in the region.[12]

The Oba of Benin, Oba Akenzua II, an NCNC supporter and leader of the Mid-West Region Movement (a minority state's rights movement) also criticized the bill:

> Chieftaincy titles are traditional and as such they must not be made political. . . . The government, from time to time, has always said that it is preserving this institution. The business of the government as far as chieftaincy titles are concerned, is to recognize the chiefs, not create the titles.[13]

Generally, however, the obas' response was governed by party affiliation. Yoruba obas on the other side of the aisle, such as the Olubadan of Ibadan, the Ewi of Ado-Ekiti, the Deji of Akure, the Elekole of Ikole and the Odemo of Ishara defended the bill, which passed the House of Chiefs with a comfortable margin,[14] and the House of Assembly with a resounding majority of fifty-two votes.

The obas' endorsement of AG objectives was equally enthusiastic in the local government councils. In Mushin District Council, for example, senior chiefs served as councillors, while their junior colleagues became official party agents in the council. Sandra Barnes has noted the mutually beneficial arrangement between obas and AG politicians in the early 1960s:

> Although the chiefs carried out other functions, the relationship of many of them to the AG at this time was such that they were acting as a virtual arm of

the party. In return for their assistance party leaders and councillors . . . acted as spokesmen for the oba to the government in an ongoing struggle to gain official recognition for them. Indeed, the chiefs were beholden to community leaders for their continued existence and support, and they became their clients.[15]

This happy relationship was short-lived, however, as the alliance between obas and AG politicians was suddenly interrupted by the AG crisis of April 1962. This conflict set the stage for the fall of the First Republic in January 1966. It also entailed a major shift in Yoruba political alignments that had profound implications for local chieftaincy institutions.

The AG Crisis: Regional Power and National Opposition

The early months of 1962 were a period of political consolidation for the Yoruba political class.[16] Indeed, the 1960 regional and local elections had further diminished NCNC representation in both the House of Assembly and in local government councils. This success was confirmed when the AG gained control over the former NCNC stronghold of Ibadan in the local government council elections of August 1961.[17] The AG also improved its standing in ethnic minority areas, winning 46 % of Edo, Urhobo and Ishan votes in the regional election of 1960. Ironically, it was during this period of electoral triumph that the AG suffered the setback that ultimately led to its demise in Nigerian politics.

The AG's predicament can partly be attributed to the frustration suffered by most opposition parties in postcolonial African states.[18] As leader of the federal opposition, Awolowo had led a spirited challenge to the policies of the NPC/NCNC federal government. He considered the federal government to be both reactionary and inept, unable to confront Nigeria's pressing sociopolitical and economic problems. For Awolowo, it was the responsibility of the federal opposition to rally the voices of discontent in all three regions under what he considered the progressive AG banner. Drawing from a proposal of the National Reconstruction Committee (a special committee set up by the Federal Executive Council of the AG), the AG leadership issued a radical new manifesto in December 1961. In foreign policy matters, the party's Federal Executive Committee abandoned the moderate pro-Western position, for which it had campaigned in 1959, for the radical concept of "non-alignment." This perspective became a rallying cry to radical nationalists in the Zikist National Vanguard, the Pan-African Youth Movement, the Nigerian Youth Congress and the Nigerian Trade

Union Congress.[19] Furthermore, a new principle of democratic socialism became the party's blueprint for economic and social policies in the post-Independence era. This declaration, which was considerably more radical than the celebrated social welfare programs of the Western Region Government in the 1950s, endorsed a comprehensive national program of universal primary education, medical care and the establishment of a minimum wage.[20]

The new path favored radical intellectuals, such as Sam Ikoku, AG leader in the Eastern Region, and Ayo Okusaga, education minister in Awolowo's regional government in the 1950s.[21] Although, part of a left wing minority within the AG, these men, for strategic reasons, had endorsed the ideological perspective of Fabian socialism and welfare state capitalism that dominated the party in the 1950s.[22] Apart from Awolowo, prominent Yoruba leaders such as Abiodun Akerele and Rotimi-Williams, non-Yoruba party stalwarts like Anthony Enahoro, Alfred O. Rewane and his brother O. N. Rewane, and Northern allies Ibrahim Imam, Joseph S. Tarka and Patrick Dokotri tended to share these ideological perspectives.

Awolowo's new shift in favor of the radicals alienated the more conservative politicians, obas, businessman and civil servants who had been influential at the regional level. Insisting on a party platform that would continue to mesh with AG domination of local state apparatus, many AG politicians harbored strong regionalist sentiments that ran counter to the new radicalism of the AG Federal Executive Committee. More importantly, prominent "conservatives" such as regional Premier Akintola and party secretary Ayo Rosiji favored an accommodationist strategy towards the ruling NPC/NCNC federal coalition. Many were uncomfortable with the idea that the regional party, which had been a bastion of power and class dominance would now provide a platform for disaffected ethnic minorities, poor peasants and workers in both the North and South.[23]

As the division between the "conservatives" and the "radicals" widened, the relationship between Awolowo and Akintola deteriorated as well. Akintola increasingly brought state institutions under his personal control, adopting policies and taking decisions independent of Awolowo and the AG's federal executive.[24] In March 1960, for instance, a new tax bill exempted women from income tax and reduced the flat rate by nearly 50%; later, in January 1961, Akintola cut the price of cocoa, the Western Region's major source of foreign exchange earnings, without consulting Awolowo or even the regional Minister of Agriculture, Chief Akin-Deko (an Awolowo confidant). Finally, while excluding Awolowo loyalists from state affairs, Akintola increasingly surrounded himself with trusted allies, appointing them to important positions as cabinet ministers and heads of statutory corporations.[25]

Larry Diamond has noted the ideological implications of these tensions:

> If we may assume that Chief Awolowo had developed by 1962 a real moral and ideological commitment to a leftist program, so it is also clear that Chief Akintola, and the businessmen and traditional leaders around him, felt strongly opposed to this program and genuinely threatened by it. . . . Chief Akintola and his allies were most disturbed by the avowed determination of the Awolowo faction to dismantle the system of rewards that had made politics in Nigeria such a lucrative and cherished calling. Thus, the intensification of this objective, with the call for sharp austerity measures on Western Region politicians, occasioned one of the most acrimonious debates between the two factions. That debate was one of many indications of the class component in the conflict.[26]

The federal opposition's new anti-regionalist stance also threatened the NPC and NCNC interests in their home regions as well; it was regional power that underlay their control of the federal government, not to speak of the Eastern and Northern governments.[27]

The stage was set for a confrontation between AG leader Awolowo and Premier Akintola. The opening salvo was fired at the 8th Annual AG Congress, held in Jos in February 1962. Awolowo's historic presidential speech formally opened the ideological debates. In a frontal attack on Akintola and fellow conservatives, Awolowo declared:

> If we would be candid with ourselves, we must admit . . . that our party has now within the ranks of its leadership and followership a number of real and dangerous contradictions. They are only just growing or rearing their heads; other are already waxing strong.[28]

Outnumbered by "progressives," conservatives unsuccessfully called for the postponement of the elections to the Federal Executive Committee.[29] Although Akintola was re-elected deputy leader, supporters of his such as Ayo Rosiji and A. M. A. Akinloye were relieved of their positions in the party executive. Awolowo and his followers dominated the election; Awolowo retained his position as president and national leader while Igbo radical Sam Ikoku was elected secretary-general in place of Rosiji. Anthony Enahoro, the Ishan AG spokesman for foreign affairs in the federal parliament and Ibrahim Imam, leader of the Bornu Youth Movement (BYM) in the Northern House of Assembly, were both elected vice-presidents; Rotimi-Williams was elected legal adviser in place of Akinloye.[30] This resounding left-wing victory sealed any remaining "conservatives" hopes for determining the party's course of action. Moreover, the election of prominent ethnic-minority politicians to important national executive positions indicated that the AG would not abandon its objective of vigorously contesting elections in the home regions of the NPC and the NCNC. To rub salt on the wound, the conference humiliated "conservatives" by passing an amendment granting more power to the party leader and the executive committee on regional government and party matters. A critical amendment to the party manifesto gave Awolowo as party president the power to call for executive action against any party official whom he considered a threat to the party. Confronted with this new threat to his authority as premier, Akintola and his supporters withdrew from the Jos Conference and returned to Ibadan.

Evoking his newly acquired power as president, Awolowo called a meeting of the party's Federal Executive Committee at his home in Ikenne. He called on AG legislators in the regional House of Assembly to reject Akintola and elect a new premier. Akintola responded by calling for a vote of confidence in the House of Assembly. Yoruba obas and elders in the *Egbe Omo Oduduwa* intervened to avert a confrontation between the two AG leaders, admonishing them to call off any meetings while they, as "father of the Yoruba people," secured an amicable solution to the crisis. Several peace initiatives undertaken by obas and elders, however, failed to achieve the desired objectives.[31]

At a meeting of the Western Region Executive Council on 19 May 1962, Awolowo accused Akintola of maladministration, gross indiscipline and anti-party activities, and immediately called for the premier's resignation. The following day, the AG Federal Executive Committee unanimously voted to remove Akintola as deputy leader and premier of the Western Region. This initial step towards eliminating Akintola was completed when a majority of AG members in the House of Assembly signed a petition calling on the governor, Oba Aderemi, to dismiss the premier. When he did, D. S. Adegbenro, the Egba Minister of Local Government, was appointed premier in Akintola's place. Challenging the constitutionality of his dismissal, Akintola protested to Prime Minister Abubakar Tafawa Balewa, and filed a motion in the courts. The few supporters he had left in the House of Assembly disrupted two parliamentary sessions following Adegbenro's appointment as premier. The political impasse in the House prompted Balewa to exercise his constitutional prerogative by calling on the federal parliament to declare a state of emergency in the region. Despite pleas by obas for an internal solution to the dispute, the NPC/NCNC controlled federal legislature dissolved the Western Region House of Assembly. In accordance with the Emergency Act of March 1961, Balewa appointed his Minister for Health, the Egba physician M. A. Majekodunmi, as administrator of the Western Region. Majekodunmi was given the power to nominate commissioners in place of ministers, give executive orders and take charge of the local government and the Nigerian police force in the region. He appointed fourteen commissioners, which included Dr. Omololu Olunloyo (a young University College–Ibadan lecturer, who later became prominent in regional politics) as Commissioner for Economic Planning; O. Esan (a senior official in the Ibadan District Council in the 1950s) was appointed Commissioner of Labor; and Chief E. A. Adeyemo (a prominent Ibadan chief who became Olubadan in the late 1980s) was appointed Commissioner for Local Government.[32]

The dissolution of a Yoruba-dominated regional government by their opponents naturally deepened the Yoruba elite's suspicions of the federal coalition government. Furthermore, despite their ambivalence about the increasing radicalism of the AG Federal Executive Committee, Yoruba obas, chiefs and party elders now had more to fear from what they saw as an attack by a Hausa-Fulani- and Igbo-dominated federal government.[33] Indeed, the despatch with which the NPC/NCNC-coalition government dissolved the Western Region House of Assembly indicated that the radicalism of AG intellectuals was less threatening than the prospect of an Hausa-Fulani- and Igbo-led federal government directing Yoruba political affairs. Balewa's declaration of an emergency thus created a feeling of vulnerability among Yorubas of diverse community and class backgrounds.[34] Moreover, a decade of relative prosperity, coupled with the remarkable improvement in both the quality of life of millions of Yorubas and the economic fortunes of the commercial and bureaucratic elite had all combined to give Awolowo a special status and prestige; his enviable record as premier in the 1950s had made him the pre-eminent leader of the Yorubas as a whole. These accomplishments, along with the now precarious position of the Yoruba political class, prompted obas and other community leaders to reaffirm their loyalty to the beleaguered Awolowo.[35] A high-profile meeting of obas called by the Regional Administrator Majekodunmi was a clear indication of the obas' allegiance during this period. After the obligatory salutations and assurances not to "injure the honored institution of chieftaincy," Majekodunmi warned:

> Obas and chiefs must decide for themselves the extent to which they can legitimately play an active role in party political strife. By this I do not mean cooperation with the government of the day, which is a duty enjoined upon

all loyal citizens; what I mean is active partisanship at election and other times.[36]

In an attempt to co-opt their support, Majekodunmi appointed six obas ministers without portfolio.

During the emergency, however, political events turned drastically against Awolowo and his supporters. Conversely, Akintola, who along with Ayo Rosiji had formed a new party, the United People's Party (UPP), saw his fortunes rise. In a three-to-one decision in July 1962, the Supreme Court ruled that Akintola's removal as premier by the governor, without a House of Assembly vote, was illegal.[37] Awolowo's attempt to redress this decision at the Privy Council was overridden in the federal Parliament by an *ex post facto* law that abolished Privy Council appeals in Nigeria. Even more serious for Awolowo and his supporters, AG members in the regional House and the federal Parliament defected *en masse*, casting their support for what seemed like the next winning coalition, of Akintola's UPP with the NCNC. With only twenty-one of the original seventy-five opposition members remaining in Parliament by December 1962, Balewa withdrew recognition from the AG as the official federal opposition.

A Region in Crisis

The obas' position in this period was determined to a large extent by the partisan realignment that emerged after the emergency period. In what can best be described as a shrewd political maneuver, the new UPP formed a coalition government with Yoruba NCNC in the Western Region in January 1963. Akintola once again took control of the Western Region; without any regional election, he was "installed" premier. Remi Fani-Kayode, the former opposition leader in the House of Assembly, was appointed Deputy Premier and Minister of Local Government; Sir Odeleye Fadahunsi, Ijesha NCNC elder statesman, replaced the Ooni as governor. Although critics questioned the propriety of this governing coalition, calling instead for fresh elections, Akintola and Fani-Kayode, with the support of their new allies, Prime Minister Balewa, NPC leader Sir Ahmadu Bello, and NCNC leader Michael Okpara, were determined to maintain the new coalition. The UPP/NCNC/NPC alliance thus forced the AG into the unfamiliar status of official opposition in the Western Region itself.

Three other developments further complicated the situation in the West. First, the subordination of the UPP to its new allies in the federal coalition government undermined the prestige of Akintola and his associates among an already disillusioned Yoruba elite. Second, regional politics was irreversibly transformed by a new desire of Yoruba NCNC parliamentarians to purse a different path from their allies in the East. This would ultimately lead to the demise of the NCNC in Yoruba politics. Finally, policy disagreements between the NPC and NCNC leaders eventually led to the disintegration of the federal coalition that had been established in 1960. In the embattled Western Region, this had profound implications for the major regional parties, the UPP, the AG and the NCNC.

We have already shown how the political objectives of regionalists like Akintola led to the formation of a new party, the UPP. In the political context of the Western Region, the UPP in part represented those who felt that the destiny of the Yoruba elite would best be served by conceding political control in the North and East to the respective dominant regional parties, the NPC and the NCNC. By forming a governing alliance, the Yoruba NCNC and UPP leaders indicated that their main objective was to seize control of state institutions at the regional level.[38] This alliance was based on an expedient strategy in which Yoruba UPP and NCNC politicians assumed the position of junior partners with the NPC/NCNC federal government. At least with specific reference to the national NCNC, this alliance was most profoundly expressed in Akintola's willingness to accept the carving out of a Mid-West Region from the West.[39] To fully share in the federal government's "system of rewards" as Post and Vickers have described it, Yoruba coalition leaders sought to consolidate power at home.

Akintola's new regional government initially attempted to achieve this through the reconstruction of a pan-Yoruba doctrine as in the earlier days of the AG. Government leaders floated the idea of establishing a new party, the *Yoruba Parapo* (Yoruba league), but when this project failed, they settled for the next best thing by forming a new pan-ethnic cultural group, the *Egbe Omo Yoruba*, which was founded on a similar ethnic model as the *Egbe Omo Oduduwa*.[40] Like the pan-Yoruba organization of old, obas and chiefs were appointed patrons of the new Egbe. However, the popularity of Awolowo throughout the region (millions of Yorubas saw Awolowo as martyred to appease the non-Yoruba dominated federal government) rendered the new Egbe ineffective when compared to the *Egbe Omo Oduduwa* in its earlier years.[41] Indeed, the status of Awolowo—which assumed near-mythic proportions following his imprisonment—led to a popular perception that Akintola and his associates had selfishly betrayed the Yoruba cause.[42] Yoruba solidarity now took on an even more distinctively populist dimension in which rich and poor, literate and illiterate, rural and urban united to question the legitimacy of the new coalition government. A creative wave of war songs, *ewi* (Yoruba poems) and slogans exalted Awolowo and his followers as incorruptible, progressive and devoted native sons, and derided their opponents in the coalition government as reactionary, corrupt politicians who had "sold out" to the Hausa-Fulani oligarchy. Popular resistance precipitated a political tidal wave that the regional government was simply unable to overcome. Once again, the conflict exposed the "hometown" foundations of Yoruba politics, as Akintola and his predominantly Oyo and Oshun Yoruba supporters sought to isolate Awolowo's Ijebu stronghold (Awolowo was a native of Ikenne in Ijebu Remo Division), exploiting the historical rivalries among Yoruba subgroups. As did Adelabu in Ibadan in the 1950s, Akintola attempted to use these divisions exacerbated by the nineteenth-century wars as a strategy of political mobilization against Ijebu resistance. Funso Afolayan notes the significance of this for contemporary Yoruba politics:

> The memory of the nineteenth century division and inter-group rivalry threatened to undermine the influence of the Yoruba in twentieth century Nigerian politics. It made them vulnerable to the scheming of the leaders of groups from the North and East of the country who time and again have successfully attempted to sustain their hegemony by allying together, driving the Yoruba to a permanent position of opposition.[43]

This time, however, the communal strategy backfired. With the exception of Akintola's hometown of Ogbomosho, where the premier, as the pre-eminent native son, enjoyed widespread support, AG loyalists emerged as forces of unity crosscutting Yoruba subgroups such as the Oyo, Oshun, Ekiti, Ijesha, Egba and Ijebu. As we shall soon observe, the sub-ethnic dimension of the conflict was no doubt more sharply drawn in the non-Oyo areas of Ijebu, Egba and Ekiti, where Akintola clearly failed to attract popular support. Even in Oyo and Oshun, Akintola's problem was compounded by his inability to translate the support of prominent native sons into more broad-based popular appeal. This was not for want of trying: prominent UPP politicians sought to explain the conflict in sub-ethnic terms, dismissing Awolowo as the stereotypical Ijebu who had stubbornly rejected the "time honored Yoruba value" of compromise, reconciliation and comradarie. This shows the limitations of the hometown concept as an immutable feature of Yoruba collective political action. Hometown and pan-ethnic feelings were both crucial to any political strategy; it was the political environment, however, that ultimately determined political allegiance in the post-emergence period. The limitations of mass mobilization through such communal appeals account, in fact, for the authoritarian measures adopted by the UPP/NCNC coalition government in order to retain power.

Since most obas and chiefs—especially those from Ekiti, Egba, Egbado and Ijebu Divisions—retained their loyalty to the AG, the regional authority revised the laws in order to control the chiefs. For example, they reorganized the House of Chiefs, giving the regional authorities sweeping powers to appoint, suspend and dismiss obas and chiefs from the upper house.[44] This amendment provided an important legal mechanism through which the UPP/NCNC coalition government silenced AG sympathizers among obas and title holders. Regional authorities promptly replaced AG loyalists such as the Otun of Ikorodu, the Apesin of Itoku and the Odemo of Ishara; obas favorably disposed to the new administration were appointed in their place.[45]

The government's most effective instrument of chieftaincy control was, however, the newly constituted local authorities. In April 1963, the House of Assembly passed an amendment to the local government law that permanently replaced elected councillors with management committees.[46] Another amendment, later that year, granted the government power to appoint new members of the management committees.[47] By October, the regional authorities had replaced 111 of 135 councils with management committees, and had nominated their supporters to serve on chieftaincy committees.[48]

Similarly, the regional authorities used the customary courts and other state institutions as agencies of local political control. Under section 5 of the customary court law, the courts had been placed under the control of a Judicial Review Commission and the regional Chief Justice. Control was now transferred to a government-appointed Local Government Service Board. This new body could appoint, dismiss and discipline customary court judges in all local government areas. This law also repealed Majekodunmi's restrictions on customary courts. Customary court grades A, B, and C were once again given jurisdiction over statutory criminal offenses.[49] These provisions became instruments of local political domination until the fall of the First Republic in January 1966.

The Limits of Regionalism

If the regional coalition between the UPP and the Western wing of the NCNC prospered, the federal alliance between the NPC and the national

NCNC declined. The reasons for the disintegration of the four-year federal coalition government are complex and cannot be fully discussed here. More importantly, for our purposes, are the factors that shaped political alignments in the West.

Control over state agencies, whether regional or federal, became critical during this period of political uncertainty. Akintola's coalition government had to demonstrate to its new allies in the national government that it had effective control over the Western Region. Of the three dominant parties, it was only the NPC, with its grip on both the Northern Region and the federal government, that retained its political pre-eminence. By contrast, the NCNC—despite its control over the Eastern Region—faltered in its core constituencies in the Mid-West and West. And as shown earlier, the AG had suffered major setbacks in early 1962, and no longer figured as a viable opposition in the federal Parliament or the Western House of Assembly. While the AG and NCNC floundered in political misfortune, the NPC, by late 1963, had allied itself with Akintola's UPP. NPC leaders saw Akintola as a more reliable ally than NCNC leader Michael Okpara. Post and Vickers have noted that the controversial 1962 and 1964 national censuses were among a long list of issues which strained the relationship between the two federal allies. Having inflated the figures in their own regions, NCNC leaders in the East and Mid-West then contested the national figures, claiming that they had been grossly inflated in favor of the North.[50]

The national NCNC's mounting problems were compounded when Akintola, with the encouragement of his new allies in the NPC, announced the formation of a new political party, the Nigerian National Democratic Party (NNDP) in March 1964. This represented a merger of the UPP and a minor party, the Southern People's Congress (SPC), along with a number of Yoruba representatives of the NCNC. After Deputy Premier Fani-Kayode declared his support for the new party, many NCNC legislators in the House of Assembly switched to the NNDP as well. With the NCNC reduced from 29 members to a mere 7, the NNDP secured a majority of 60 members in the House. The AG retained its opposition status with only 27 seats.[51] Akintola's move effectively killed the NCNC in Yoruba politics. As the 1964 federal elections approached, Akintola renewed his alliance with the NPC; the NNDP, NPC and several minor parties united to contest the elections under the banner of the Nigerian National Alliance (NNA). The NNA was opposed by an unexpected alliance between the rump NCNC and their old AG adversaries, now called the United Progressive Grand Alliance (UPGA).

Unlike some other notable groups, the NNDP leadership was well aware that the ultimate test of credibility would be the impending federal and regional elections of 1964 and 1965. NNDP government stalwarts in the West were thus bent on using local officials, courts and other state resources to assure a favorable result. Pro-NNDP obas and chiefs enjoyed a sudden rise in fortune, receiving patronage and promises of public infra-structure for their towns. They repaid the favor by awarding chieftaincy titles to prominent NNDP allies, in the hope that this would enhance these politicians' status among the electorate. While some obas, baales and chiefs were discreet in their support of the NNDP, transmitting the "good intentions" of the party to local clients, others openly campaigned for the party as the elections approached. Institutions under the direct control of the regional government, such as local constabularies, the customary courts and the local government councils, were used to suppress obas or commu-nity leaders who opposed the NNDP. The local management committees were most reliable in this respect. Indeed, after the formation of the NNDP, Akintola's government had further purged the committees of members sus-pected of remaining loyal to the beleaguered AG. The Mushin Manage-ment Committee, for instance, charged with "corruption and malfeasance," was dissolved in 1964. The new committee, chosen for its loyalty to the NNDP, lacked any real local connection. Barnes notes:

> Four of the members had served on the preceding 1963 committee, but otherwise all entrenched local leadership was absent from its roster. The com-mittee included several relatively affluent entrepreneurs who were not previ-ously prominent in political affairs, and the chairman was better known in municipal Lagos than in Mushin. Public resentment against the outsider appointees was strong, and in ensuing months the house of the new chair-man was burned. The committee lasted for eight months.[52]

Similarly, in Ibadan, councillors became notorious agents of the regional authorities, no longer responsive to communal aspirations and needs.[53]

Effective local resistance in many communities —such as Ikeja, Ibadan, Oyo, Ijebu and Ekiti Divisions—prompted NNDP agents to assume even more extreme measures during the elections. Opposition operated partly through chieftaincy structures, which retained a certain autonomy and where the AG influence could still be felt. Chieftaincy thus became an "alterna-tive source of power and legitimacy" for all those who were shut out of the formal state structures at the local government level.[54] Again, in Mushin, AG played an important role in the advisory councils of the chieftaincy committees, where they had previously acted as patrons of local chiefs.

Such local structures were often connected to powerful clientelist networks; if they had previously served as effective "organizations of competition," they quickly became "organizations of rebellion" as the crisis intensified.[55] In contrast, the new NNDP Mushin Management Committee was brought under close government control; councillors enthusiastically responded, openly campaigning for the NNDP in the elections of 1964 and 1965.[56] Regional newspapers such as the *Daily Sketch* and *Nigerian Tribune* covered the ways in which NNDP councillors abandoned their duties to become pro-government agents during the elections. The Management Committees of Owo District, Ibadan City, Oyo Central and Iseyin were notable examples in this respect.[57] As Nigerian political scientist Alex Gboyega notes:

> Far from local government becoming an instrument of self-realization for the community, it became the instrument for the waging of personal feuds. This development rendered local government councils, at best, suspect—a far from satisfactory image for an institution whose growth and strength is dependent on communal support.[58]

And whenever management committees failed to achieve the desired objectives, regional authorities were quick to punish their members. They dissolved the Mushin Management Committee, for instance, for failing to secure victory and quell disturbances during the elections in 1964.[59]

The regional government also brought the customary courts (the old NA native courts) under partisan sway. With extensive civil and criminal powers granted by the Minister of Local Government, pro-NNDP customary court judges brought trumped-up charges of theft, libel, assault, tax evasion, and conspiracy against AG sympathizers. AG politicians were soon busy defending these charges, undermining the party's ability to mount a credible opposition in the legislature. Moreover, since judges (mostly baales and title holders) were often poorly paid, the customary courts increasingly became an avenue for supplementing their paltry salaries with payoffs and "dash."[60]

This cynical use of local institutions had far-reaching implications for chiefly power throughout the region. Obas and chiefs who collaborated with the management committees were showered with state recognition and patronage, while those who maintained their loyalty to the AG were consistently persecuted. The Ooni of Ife, Sir Adesoji Aderemi, was one of the first obas to be subjected to the Management Committee's reprisals. As regional governor, the Ooni had approved Akintola's dismissal as premier, and had confronted Deputy-Premier Fani-Kayode in a major conflict in the 1950s. His conflict with Fani-Kayode can be traced to the rivalry between two AG factions in Ife town. This pitted the old guard, the *Erinjogunola*, led by the Ooni, against the populist *Talaka Parapo* (commoners' organization), led by Remi Fani-Kayode, the charismatic son of a prominent Ife Protestant minister. This conflict, which ended with Fani-Kayode's defection to the NCNC in 1959, was connected to Fani-Kayode's nomination as AG representative to the federal Parliament, over the Ooni's son, Adedapo, in the mid-1950s. The rivalry between the *Erinjogunola* and *Talaka Parapo* factions continued until the 1959 elections when Fani-Kayode lost his seat to Michael Omisade, who had been endorsed by the Ooni.[61]

It was in the context of such local political divisions, specifically the longstanding rivalry between the Ooni and Fani-Kayode, that the Ife Divisional Caretaker Committee attempted to sack Oba Aderemi. At an emergency session in August 1964, the committee unanimously passed a resolution:

> This council prays the regional government that as Sir Adesoji Aderemi no longer enjoys the confidence of the peoples of the Ife division, and as the said Sir Adesoji Aderemi has betrayed the trust vested in him by God and the people and in the interest of peace, order, good government, and tranquility in the division, and as the said Sir Adesoji Aderemi now constitutes a grave danger to the peace of the realm that he be removed from office of Ooni of Ife by the regional government under Section 22 (1) of the Chief's Law without further delay and that he be confined to a safe area in the region in the interest of peace, order, and good government.[62]

The Management Committee also charged the Ooni with corruption. This referred to a controversial commercial venture involving the state-owned Ife Forest Reserve and the Aderawo Company, a logging company in which Sir Aderemi had a significant financial interest.[63] Despite the legal details of the case, the Ooni's reflective stance, the increasingly conciliatory attitude of Premier Akintola and Deputy Premier Fani-Kayode, and the wise counsel of senior obas and elders prevented a major confrontation. The Ife court forced the Ooni to surrender his controlling interest in the Forest Reserve and pay the local authority all profits made by the company since March 1963.[64] In return, and in a public show of support for the regional government, Oba Aderemi embraced his old adversary Fani-Kayode and conferred on him the distinguished title of Balogun of Ife.

NNDP authorities were less compromising in Ijebu Division, where Awolowo, as the leading native son, enjoyed extraordinary prestige. The NNDP's heavy-handedness should not be surprising given the fierce resistance of Ijebu townspeople to the regional and local authorities. The predicament of the Akarigbo of Ijebu Remo, Oba M. S. Awolesi II, was typical of the Ijebu obas' plight during this period. In the first of two resolutions calling on the regional authorities to depose Oba Awolesi, the Offin (Shagamu) Management Committee accused the oba of "encouraging riots, lawlessness, confusion, and bloodshed" in the Ijebu towns of Shagamu, Iperu, Ogere and Ode-Remo during the campaign tour of the UPGA leader, Michael Okpara, in June 1964.[65] Charging that Oba Awolesi had lost the confidence of the local ruling houses, chiefs and townspeople, the Management Committee passed a second resolution calling for the Oba's resignation.[66] It was the timely intervention of the *Egbe Omo Olofin*, a Yoruba solidarity group formed to mediate the wave of conflicts between NNDP politicians and their opponents, that prevented the regional authorities from approving the resolution. Led by prominent Yoruba elders—such as the former NCNC politician, H. O. Davies, Sir Adetokunbo Ademola, Chief Justice of Nigeria, Dr. Akinola Maja, the former president of the *Egbe Omo Oduduwa*, and Dr. Majekodunmi, regional administrator during the emergency—the *Egbe* successfully pleaded the case of the Akarigbo to the regional authorities.

Although the government agreed not to depose Oba Awolesi outright, it nevertheless endorsed the Offin Management Committee's decision to humiliate the Oba by reducing his salary to only a penny per annum.[67] Later that year, the outspoken Odemo of Ishara, Oba Akinsanya, another Ijebu AG loyalist, suffered a similar fate when the same local authority reduced his salary too, to a penny per year. Indeed, by October 1964 the regional government itself had adopted this strategy: it suspended the salaries of the Olowo of Owo-Ijebu, the Balufe of Ijebu-Ife, and the Ladelepo of Odo Ladelepo, all junior obas from Ijebu East Central District Council, for alleged "subversive and disloyal activities detrimental to the progress of the council and interest of the Western Region Government."[68]

Similarly, in the northern Yoruba region, NNDP authorities endorsed the recommendation of the Iseyin Management Committee and deposed the Aseyin, Oba Raji Adebowale. The deposed oba was banished to Okitipupa District, and replaced by a reliable NNDP supporter, Mustapha Oyebola, who openly campaigned for the party in the 1964 election.[69] Other obas were suspended for supporting the AG during the elections. In Ikare, for instance, the Olukare, Oba Amusa Momoh, was suspended for six months in July 1964, for allegedly allowing local AG politicians to hold a meeting in his palace.[70] Deputy-Premier Fani-Kayode—who as NCNC opposition leader between 1960 and 1962 had defended chieftaincy institutions against Akintola's AG government—was now defensive about the government's attacks. He was questioned in the House of Chiefs about the way pro-AG obas were being treated by the NNDP committees. He responded that

> the Minister of Local Government has nothing to do with the reduction of oba's and chief's salaries. Each council is aware of its financial background and it is the council which fixes or agrees on how much its obas should earn. Whenever we see that there is any misunderstanding at all between the oba and the local government council the government always plays the part of peacemaker in these matters.[71]

This evasive response typified the regional government's double-talk on chieftaincy matters during the election campaigns. Its strategy for dealing with AG obas was to have them pressured by its local agents, while maintaining a stance of official neutrality. Since resistance to the NNDP was widespread the regional government could project itself as a benevolent arbiter, simply brokering settlements between management committees dominated by the NNDP and chastised obas.

The regional authorities were also able to bid for the support of obas and chiefs through their control over public resources and patronage. In many instances, they increased the salaries and benefits of obas who supported the regional government. For example, Minister for Agriculture Z. A. Opaleye announced such an increase during a visit to the Egbado Local Government Area in September 1964.[72] In May, the Ife District Council had increased obas' salaries in the local government jurisdiction by more than 300 %.[73] Moreover, obas who had openly supported the NNDP authorities—such as the Olowo of Owo, Sir Olateru; the Olubadan of Ibadan, Oba Aminu; the Oluwo of Iwo, Oba Abimbola; and the Elekole of Ikole, Oba Adeleye—were appointed ministers without portfolio in 1964 and 1965.[74]

The confrontations between pro-AG obas and the regional government do not mean that the NNDP was completely rejected in Yoruba communities. A minority of elders, politicians, obas and wealthy businessmen, disillusioned with the radicalism of the AG Federal Executive Committee, supported the regional authorities; some obas, derisively referred to by opponents as "NNDP organizing secretaries," openly sanctioned regional government policies in the House of Chiefs. The Alaba of Ajagba, for instance, reminded the opposition of the role of the House under previous governments:

> It is really our duty to support the government of the day, the ruling party, and this we shall continue to do. We have done so for the AG when it was in

power in this region. We have also done so for the NCNC when it was in a coalition government with the UPP. At the time, the NCNC praised the obas and chiefs of this region for doing their duty. Now that the NCNC is no more the ruler of the region, the obas have become politicians . . . . We are going to support the government in power. It is clear that as the fathers of all, it is our duty to support the party in power.[75]

As the campaign intensified, pro-NNDP obas became more vocal in their support. During NNA (NNDP) campaign tours to Yoruba towns, sympathetic obas such as the Olowo of Owo, Sir Olateru, and the Alake of Abeokuta, Oba Gbadebo II, ignored local disaffection by publicly embracing the NNDP. A quote attributed to the Olowo—during Akintola's tour of Owo in June 1964—illustrates his special relationship with the NNDP. Despite strong anti-NNDP sentiments among his townspeople, the Olowo announced that

he was one of the leading Yoruba obas who commissioned Chief Akintola to negotiate at the appropriate quarters for the participation of Yorubas in the federal government . . . . It was to the pride of the obas and the people of the West that Yorubas are now adequately represented in the new federal government, unlike the past.[76]

In the federal election campaign of July, the Olowo openly observed that, since the regional authorities retained exclusive control over patronage and the distributive resources of the state, obas "interested in the welfare of their people should always back the government of the day."[77] Similarly, several regional newspapers accounts reported the special ties between the Alake and NNDP leaders during the campaign.[78] During a campaign visit by the premier to the Egba and Egbado Divisions in June 1965, the Alake used his ties to the NNDP government to solicit favorable policies for Abeokuta. The Oba called on Akintola

to influence the extension of the nursing school in the town, to complete the sugar factory already embarked upon by the regional government and to establish a leper colony in Egbaland . . . and to bring about the merger of the two divisional councils and name it Egba Central Council.[79]

Other obas saw the correlation between providing electoral support to the regional government and gaining access to public resources and patronage. The Ewi of Ado-Ekiti, Oba Aladesanmi, the senior oba in Ekiti Division, impressed on townspeople that "nobody ever lost anything by supporting the government of the day. . . . [T]he support for the government of the day is the key to social and economic progress."[80] In the northern Yoruba town of Ede in Oshun Division, senior chiefs openly pledged their support to Akintola's party, "praying that his party might win the forthcoming election to the Western Nigerian house of assembly with an overwhelming majority."[81]

Even obas who had earlier embraced the AG had come to realize the costly price of antagonizing the party in power, and now offered at least tacit support. At an NNA launching attended by Prime Minister Balewa as well as Premier Akintola, pro-NNDP obas such as the Alaafin, the Olowo, the Oba of Badagry, and the Olubadan, mingled with former opposition obas such as the Ooni and the Akarigbo. All the obas thanked the Prime Minister for his "commitment to Nigerian unity and support for Yoruba communities."[82] And in an atmosphere reported to have been one of exhilarating fanfare, prominent obas welcomed NPC leader Sir Ahmadu Bello to an NNA rally in Ibadan in May 1965. A regional newspaper recorded the obas' praise:

> We are happy that our people are now partners in the federal government. We pray that God may continue to bless you [the NPC leader], to bless the Prime Minister, and to bless the federation. . . . We congratulate our son, Chief S.L. Akintola, Premier of the West and the Are Onakakanfo of Yorubaland. We owe a lot to his patience, his tact, his humility, and his deep love for his people and Nigeria. We have every confidence in him and his leadership.[83]

The obas' attempt to enhance the government's popularity, while winning official recognition for themselves, was also accomplished through conferral of chieftaincy titles on NNDP leaders during the campaigns. NNDP politicians, in turn, acquired the titles with the hope of gaining local acceptance, legitimacy and prestige. Akintola emerged as the most titled man in Nigeria by the end of 1964, with chieftaincy titles from all divisions of the region. In October, he was installed 13th Are-Ona-Kakanfo (generalissimo of the realm) by the Alaafin of Oyo, Oba Gbadegesin Ladigbolu II. This important precolonial Oyo military title was conferred with great pomp and ceremony. It aimed to represent Akintola as a modern-day warrior, fighting tirelessly to safeguard Yoruba interests in the Nigerian federation.[84]

But as in the sub-ethnic identity project, the strategy of title-giving failed to confer local legitimacy on NNDP leaders. Despite Akintola's many titles, and the visibility of obas in NNDP public events, AG politicians still retained popularity among townspeople throughout the region. Indeed, opposition to NNDP rule often ran so deep that obas who openly supported the party became the targets of their local communities. In May 1964, for example, the executive committee of the Ijebu-Mushin Majeobaje Society, an organization affiliated with the local branch of the AG, publicly warned the oba of the town, Oba Oloko, against fraternizing with the NNDP.[85] In Ijebu-Remo, UPGA leaders resisted the appointment of NNDP supporters as customary court judges;[86] and in Mushin, where they had been excluded from local government institutions since the emergency, opposition politicians consolidated their political ties to local chiefs and notables. They regularly met in secret to discuss how to promote the party locally. And when a junior oba in the Mushin community of Idi-Olowo defected to the NNDP, the chiefs and other community leaders ostracized him, and named a regent in his place.[87] Abeokuta and Owo were other AG strongholds where, as discussed earlier, the Alake and the Olowo nevertheless threw their support to the NNDP. In the former, community leaders declared a policy of nonfraternization with the Alake in June 1 1964. In Owo, Michael Ajasin, a prominent AG native son, succeeded in mobilizing townspeople against the Olowo. In disturbances following the rigged election of 1965, the Oba was attacked and had to flee the town with his family. We will see in the next chapter how the Olowo, rejected by chiefs and elders, was later sacked by a military government.[88] Finally, in Oshun Division, where the NNDP had its strongest support, members of the Oshun Ifelodun AG Youth Association consistently attacked pro-NNDP chiefs. This influential group also accused NNDP Management Committees of corruption, maladministration, arbitrary tax assessment and intimidation of UPGA supporters during the 1964 election campaign.[89]

The massively rigged federal election of 1964, won by the NNA, set the stage for the Western Region election of the following year. Reacting to the vocal opposition of UPGA (AG) supporters (who dominated the media, educational institutions, the modern professions and grassroots elements such as artisans, women traders, peasants and even chiefs) Akintola and his supporters tightened their grip. NNDP agents in the federal police force, the local sanitation task force, the courts, the management committees, the Regional Electoral Commission and many other state agencies blatantly rigged the elections and intimidated opponents.[90] At one point Akintola informed his allies, the NPC leader Sir Ahmadu Bello and Prime Minister Balewa, that his party had gained fifteen uncontested legislative seats and was within striking distance of regaining control of the regional government. This announcement triggered political violence in every division of the region, especially in Ijebu, Egba, Egbado, Ife, Ilesha, Oyo and even Oshun. Obas and other pro-NNDP community leaders were now the targets of irate crowds.[91] Afraid for their safety, many fled with their families to safe hideouts in other towns. In Ilesha, Peel reports "a corrupt, unpopular and brutal ruling party dominated local government." Following the 1965 elections, "popular anger boiled over so that, for two weeks in January 1966, a systematic series of attacks was made on the houses of the hated ruling politicians."[92]

As the wave of violence continued in the West a faction of the military carried out the first Nigerian *coup d'etat*. On the night of 15 January 1966, Major Kaduna Nzeogwu and other military dissidents struck, killing Prime Minister Balewa, NPC Leader and Northern Premier Ahmadu Bello, the Western Premier Akintola, the Federal Finance Minister, Festus Okotie-Eboh, and some senior army officers. This brought the tragic saga of party politics in the Western Region to a temporary halt; it soon provided the impetus for an even greater crisis that would engulf the entire country. The next chapter, which examines the changing roles of traditional rulers under the military regimes of Generals Ironsi and Gowon, provides the first of three analyses of how chieftaincy structures adapted to contrasting styles of military governance.

6

MILITARY RULE: CHIEFTAINCY, REGIONALISM, AND GRASSROOTS POLITICS

After six years of persistent political instability, many Nigerians, especially Southerners, welcomed military rule. By the time of the January coup, some Western development experts were even suggesting that military regimes were quite capable of leading the modernization process in Third-World states.[1] Although this perspective was later repudiated by radical scholars, and more emphatically by the developments of the last three decades, its fundamental assumptions remain significant in African studies even to this day. As critical segments of the ethno-regional elites, Nigeria's military cliques were shaped not only by the norms of the officer corps but by entrenched communal sentiments as well. And these sociopolitical characteristics operated in a real-world context of conflicting local and national identities and events. In short, while military regimes have distinctive qualities, they still reflect the sociopolitical character of the ethno-regions and classes from which they are drawn.[2]

Thus, military regimes in African states cannot be reduced to a duality of "modernizing" and "traditionalizing" projects.[3] Rather, they operate in the context of communal and regional sociopolitical networks, involving such diverse elements as traditional rulers, politicians, civil servants and businessmen. Within the prevailing logic of ethno-regional power arrangements, military regimes, especially in periods of crisis, look to traditional rulers, elders, politicians and other local powerbrokers as intermediaries and sources of support. Given the complexities of Nigerian history and society, the concept of neotraditional corporatism—referring to the complex interaction between military regimes and structures of society — may be of use. Political scientist Pearl Robinson's trenchant analysis of neotraditional corporatism in Niger provides a conceptual perspective that applies to the dynamic interaction between military rule, regionalism, chieftaincy and local politics in Nigeria as well. In this context of military rule, neotraditional corporatism

> is a mode of governance associated with conditions found in many preindustrial, aid-dependent states. Its operation links civilian technocrats in an alliance with military officers who run the state apparatus with the advice of aid donor bureaucrats and the assistance of an embryonic entrepreneurial bourgeoisie. To buttress the system, neotraditional authority, historically constructed by either the colonial or the postcolonial state, is manipulated by contemporary political actors for the purpose of regime legitimation. Such authority is distinct from, but draws upon, the traditional legitimacy of cultural values and behavioral norms associated with particular ethnic, regional, or religious identities. . . . From its inception, the regime sought to associate itself with traditional legitimacy by cultivating ties with Islamic officials and customary chiefs. When the corporatist modes of participation and policy making were grafted on to the preexisting structure of legitimation, the outcome was neotraditional corporatism.[4]

Nigeria's military regimes can be seen as representing a variant of neotraditional corporatism, heavily colored by ethno-regional preoccupations and disputes.

This chapter looks at the civil/military alliances that underlay the Ironsi and Gowon regimes, highlighting the important role of communal leaders and structures in all the regions. During a period of deepening crisis, chieftaincy structures in Yorubaland, as elsewhere in Nigeria, were embraced by the new military administrators for the purpose of legitimation and control. The analysis also reveals limitations of the military's strategies of neotraditional corporatism. I argue that the apparent failure of Nigeria's first military regime (of Major General Aguiyi-Ironsi) in fact demonstrates the shortcoming of this strategy of military rule. In response to this failure, Lt. Colonel (later General) Yakubu Gowon, adopted a more conventional corporatism, drawing on regional politicians and senior civil servants for support.

This strategy, however, should not be mistaken for a repudiation of neotraditional corporatism. Rather, it will be argued that Gowon, too, embraced regional and communal centers of power. The Yoruba conflicts explored in this chapter will show how aspects of neotraditional corporatism were woven into local networks of power relations by various state military regimes. In fact, these case studies reveal that the crisis of political legitimacy witnessed by the federal military government was also reflected in the military government of the West. Tensions between the national and regional government concerns, along with the contending sociopolitical forces within them, show the massive incongruities between the Nigerian state and its diverse communities. Since influential traditional rulers and chiefs were co-opted as intermediaries of federal and state military regimes, chieftaincy structures witnessed further strain during this first decade of military rule. These important issues were initially experienced in the pre-Civil War national crisis that transformed the national and regional balance of power. During this crisis, national attention shifted away from the West to the Northern and the Eastern Regions, where the violent coup of January 1966 had far-reaching implications.

The National Political Context

Following the crisis that engulfed Nigeria after the January 1966 coup, the succeeding regime of Major General Aguiyi-Ironsi relied on traditional rulers to help restore stability in the North. During Ironsi's short tenure as head of the national government, prominent traditional rulers (especially emirs in the North) were called upon to bridge the gulf between competing regional interests and the military regime itself. The dismal failure of this policy—that sought to co-opt traditional rulers as intermediaries with the grassroots—reveals the limits of neotraditional corporatism as a viable response to Nigeria's deepening crisis. This challenges the widely held assumption that African indigenous political institutions are *ipso facto* effective intermediaries between holders of state power and the people. Having dismissed the regional politicians as corrupt, and confronted with a deepening crisis in the North, Ironsi embraced the emirs as the sole embodiments of Northern interests. We will discuss, first, the limitations of this style of civil/military rule and second, the impact of Gowon's more expansive strategy of military governance for Yoruba political alignments from 1967 to 1975.

After assuming leadership of Nigeria, Ironsi appointed military governors in the four regions of the federation. Lt. Colonel Odumegwu Ojukwu, son of a prominent Igbo businessman, was appointed to the East; Major Hassan Katsina, son of the Emir of Katsina, to the North; Lt. Colonel F. Adekunle Fajuyi and Major David Ejoor to the West and Mid-West respectively. The highest ranking Yoruba army officer, Brigadier Babafemi Ogundipe, became Chief of Staff Supreme Headquarters; a thirty three year-old Christian from the Angas minority in the North, Lt. Colonel Yakubu Gowon, was appointed Chief of Army Staff.

Initially, the new regime enjoyed the goodwill of most Nigerians. Even the Northern emirs and their people, who had lost their two pre-eminent politicians in the January coup, felt obliged to cooperate with the regime despite the seemingly sectarian coup of Major Kaduna Nzeogwu and his associates.[5] This lukewarm endorsement was, however, short-lived, as Ironsi, himself an Igbo, embraced political decisions that rekindled Northern anxiety. As far as Northern leaders and military officers were concerned, Ironsi's first transgression was his sluggishness in bringing the leaders of the January coup to justice, despite the decision of the Supreme Military Council (SMC) to proceed with their trial in May 1966. When May rolled around, Ironsi postponed the trial indefinitely. To Northern elites, especially in the military, this delay seemed to confirm that the January coup was an Igbo conspiracy to dominate Nigeria. In addition, Ironsi surrounded himself with a clique of Igbo advisors. During his seven months as Head of State, federal government policies were shaped by trusted Igbo friends—Francis Nwokedi, for instance, a former Permanent Secretary in the Ministry of Foreign Affairs. Ironsi appointed Nwokedi sole commissioner of the ill-fated commission charged with unifying Nigeria's administrative services. Another trusted friend, Gabriel Onyike, replaced T. O. Elias as Attorney General; and another eminent Igbo, economist Pius Okigbo, was appointed chief economic adviser to the federal government.[6]

More importantly, Ironsi's regime was plagued by ill-conceived policies that further aroused Northern suspicion. Contrary to the advice of the SMC, he promoted twenty one army officers, eighteen of whom were Igbos, to the rank of Lieutenant Colonel. It was, however, Ironsi's Decree No. 34, which dissolved Nigeria's federal structure, and established a unitary system of government, that proved to be the fatal miscalculation.[7] The dissolution of the regional structure and the establishment of a provincial system forced emirs, as new regional intermediaries, into the center-stage of national politics. In the upper North, the dominant political class feared that the abolition of Nigeria's federal structure would expose their region to takeover by the more advanced South. In only a matter of days, the decree sparked waves of violence in several Northern cities, notably Kano, Kaduna, Zaria, Jos and Bukuru.[8] As the riots intensified, mutinous crowds turned their rage against vulnerable Igbo minorities in the North; in Kano alone, over a hundred Igbos were brutally killed in only a few days. Afraid for their lives, many Igbos fled the North for the Eastern Region.

The federal military authorities responded to the violence by soliciting the assistance of emirs and chiefs. Having denounced regional politicians, Ironsi embraced the emirs as communicators of his good intentions to Northern elites and townspeople.[9] Ironsi also instructed the four military governors to regularly discuss important state policies with traditional rulers in their provinces. The most critical of these dialogues were those following the May riots, held between the governor of the Northern Provinces, Major Katsina, and the Northern emirs. So special was their relationship that Katsina replaced Native Authority councillors with the nominees of traditional rulers.[10]

Emirs in turn discharged their role as intermediaries with great confidence. For example, in June, after many private deliberations with Governor Katsina, the Sultan of Sokoto, Sir Abubakar III, submitted a bold memorandum to Ironsi.[11] It demanded the repeal of Decree 34, contending that the only constitutional revision that would be acceptable to the Northern Provinces must reflect the popular will.[12] Acting on instructions from Lagos, Katsina twice summoned the emirs to the regional capital in Kaduna for consultation, where he assured them that their recommendations would be considered carefully by the federal authorities.[13] In a special address to emirs at Lugard Hall, Kaduna, in June, Major Katsina declared that:

> When I assumed duty as military governor my first official action was to visit all the provinces in order to meet the chiefs and discuss with them the broad outline of our plans. I then informed you all that no permanent changes would be adopted without consultation with you and the people. We are still keeping to our word. The future constitution of Nigeria and the administrative machinery of government are by no means settled. . . . It is the duty of all leaders of opinion, particularly our chiefs, to enlighten the public about their civic responsibilities. They should know the opportunities which are now open to them if they bring their intelligence to bear on the problems facing us and produce constructive proposals in the search of a better life for all of us.[14]

And in another important meeting with the emirs only two weeks later, in which he declared that the FMC had granted emirs and district heads a wide range of state functions in legal matters, education and economic development, Katsina concluded:

> Representatives of chiefs from all the groups of provinces will also go to Lagos from time to time for the purpose of giving advice to the National Military Government on national issues. I intend that the first Conference in Kaduna will take place toward the end of September. In the meantime I want the present meeting to appoint a number of committees which can meet from time to time and make recommendations to you on various subjects before you advise me.[15]

No doubt the emirs were impressed with their rising influence in the corridors of power. Despite the persistence of Northern discontent, the rapprochement encouraged the emirs to soften their approach and even embrace the regime. While all this had little positive effect on Northern communities as a whole, Sultan Abubakar took it upon himself to convey the regime's sentiments to the people of the Northern Provinces:

> I wish therefore to assure you on behalf of my brother emirs and chiefs that there is no longer any cause for fear or anxieties. I am also pleased to inform you that committees of chiefs have from the first day of our meeting been appointed in order to advise government on matters of policy on the various important aspects affecting the well-being of the community. I assure you that we emirs and chiefs will never subscribe to any decision which is not aimed at the common good of all. I also assure you that the military government have no intention whatsoever of imposing a permanent pattern of government or administration for the benefit of a particular section of the country.[16]

This dialogue led Ironsi to convene a national conference of traditional rulers in Ibadan on 28 and 29 July 1966. Twenty-four prominent regional traditional rulers represented the provinces at the meeting, charged with finding viable solutions to Nigeria's crisis.[17] As fate would have it, Major General Ironsi could only attend the first day of the conference, when he reminded the traditional rulers of their exalted position in the administration.[18] After a state dinner in his honor, Ironsi and his host, Governor Fajuyi, were abducted and killed. The counter-coup, led by Northern officers, claimed the lives of many other Igbo officers as well.

Ironsi's short and tragic rule reveals the limitations of a neotraditionalist strategy that failed to articulate the deep divisions among the dominant ethno-regional political classes. Thus, Dudley observed that Ironsi's dialogue with traditional rulers was "a mark not only of his isolation from the populace, but also of his unrealistic assessment of the changes which had taken place in society."[19]

The counter-coup of 29 July 1966, which catapulted Chief of Army Staff Lt. Colonel Gowon to power, channeled the political course of Nigeria in yet another direction. As the crisis intensified, Gowon abandoned Ironsi's strategy of working through chiefs. For Gowon, the situation required a more comprehensive approach, integrating the efforts of a broad-based coalition of regional powerbrokers.[20] Thus, in the first few years of his administration, Gowon hardly consulted with traditional rulers—apart from some obligatory salutations especially to the Sultan and the emirs. The affairs of state thus revolved around an alliance among military administrators loyal to Gowon, senior civil servants and prominent politicians (now recognized again as important regional spokesmen). Gowon appointed politicians from the First Republic as commissioners in his Federal Executive Council and as heads of federal statutory corporations, and encouraged their participation as regional "leaders of thought" in various federal government peace initiatives.[21] The rehabilitation of the politicians cemented old alliances, encouraged new networks of power, and revived the fortunes of Obafemi Awolowo and other AG politicians who had been effectively relegated to the sidelines since the Action Group (AG) crisis of 1962.

The reemergence of the old AG stalwarts in both regional and federal politics illustrates Gowon's strategy of military governance. The Yoruba response to local, regional and national issues was conditioned by the persistent tripodal force of regionalism, the legacy of Yoruba political conflicts, and the regional pressures that ultimately resulted in the Civil War. Recognizing the central place of regionalism in the crisis, Gowon released Awolowo and his former associate, Anthony Enahoro, from prison in August 1966.[22] Predictably, Awolowo was chosen by obas and elders to lead the Yoruba delegation to the critical "leaders of thought" conferences, inaugurated by the Federal Military Government (FMG) to recommend solutions to the political crisis. To the dismay of his opponents, especially former NNDP politicians, the obas also gave Awolowo the important title of *Asiwaju* (leader) of the Yorubas. This title raised his status over that of his late adversary, S. L. Akintola, who only two years before, had been given the leading military title of Are-Ona Kankanfo by the Alaafin.

Awolowo himself was to acknowledge the political significance of the title:

What the title achieved for me is obvious: it identified a reality I personify. For the first time since Oduduwa (the legendary progenitor of the Yorubas), the Yorubas have a leader! I regard myself as an effective Asiwaju of Nigeria.[23]

Unlike most honorary titles, this one—because of the charisma of its bearer—carried with it the real influence of a modern-day Asiwaju of the Yoruba. Apart from recognizing his leadership of the Yoruba delegation, Gowon, for strategic reasons, embraced him as his most notable civilian confidant; he appointed Awolowo Federal Commissioner for Finance and Vice-Chairman of the Federal Executive Council in 1967. While this appointment enhanced Gowon's popularity among the Yorubas, Awolowo used his powerful position to influence the policies of the Western State Government.

While the AG crisis had provided the enduring basis for Yoruba political realignment, it was Awolowo's reemergence on the political scene that consolidated Yoruba collective political action in the Gowon years. This was reinforced by the persistence of regional power relations at the federal level, and the prominence of politicians in state military governments. By using their growing influence in the Western State Executive Committees, Yoruba politicians further entrenched the pre-existing partisanship under three successive state military regimes—Governors Fajuyi, Adebayo and Rotimi. Analysis of these issues, entangled in a web of political struggles among state officials, regional politicians and local powerbrokers, reveals the stress on chieftaincy institutions during this period.

Resolving Old Political Scores in Yoruba Towns

Regional conditions and policies varied after the January coup. While Governor Katsina was busy mediating the conflicts between Northern emirs and the Ironsi regime, his counterpart in the Western Provinces, Colonel Adekunle Fajuyi, was dismantling the vestiges of local control established by the previous civilian government. Fajuyi terminated the appointments of members of statutory authorities,[24] and then revoked the appointment of the regional constabulary councils. The functions of the NNDP appointees were subsequently transferred to new local government advisers and senior officers of the Nigerian Police Force.[25] Governor Fajuyi's most important policy decision, however, was the dissolution of the management committees created by the NNDP.[26]

Fajuyi's term as governor, however brief, was also a time of reckoning for those obas who, contrary to the expressed wishes of the populace, had actively supported Akintola's NNDP government.[27] We will recall the case of the Olowo of Owo, Sir Olateru Olagbegi, who had embraced Akintola's government despite the opposition of influential Owo politicians and elders. During the governor's visit to Ondo Province in May, thousands of demonstrators demanded the removal of Sir Olateru.[28] Back in Ibadan, Governor Fajuyi suspended the Olowo for six months. While announcing this decision, J. M. Buckley, Permanent Secretary in the Ministry of Local Government and Justice, noted

> the deep disaffection and great resentment shown towards the oba by the majority of his own people, who by letters, telegrams, and personal representation have demonstrated during the past few months that they do not want him to continue as their ruler.[29]

The six-month suspension brought little respite to the dispute; two years later, in 1969, Fajuyi's successor, Colonel Adebayo, formally deposed the Olowo.[30]

For the former Aseyin of Iseyin, Oba Raji Adebowale, military intervention proved to be a blessing. Deposed by the NNDP government in December 1963 for alleged loyalty to the AG, his three-year-old deposition order was now revoked by Fajuyi.[31] This was the misfortune, in turn, of the NNDP-appointed Aseyin, Oba Mustapha Oyebola. In 1968, Governor Adebayo once again carried his predecessor's policy to its logical conclusion, instituting a commission of inquiry to investigate the circumstances responsible for the removal of Adebowale as Aseyin.[32] The panel was unequivocal. It condemned the UPP/NCNC-controlled local management committee for illegally deposing Adebowale, and repealed the provision through which Oba Oyebola had been appointed in 1964.[33] Other obas, who had openly supported the NNDP government against the expressed wishes of their townspeople, were more fortunate, narrowly surviving agitations against them. In March 1966, for example, the people of Ishua in Akoko Division, led by the local tax payers' association, petitioned Governor Fajuyi to depose the Olisua of Ishua, Oba Adesunloye, whom they accused of "using his connections to promote his own interests."[34] And in Ikun in Ekiti Division, another taxpayers' association passed "a vote of no confidence" against the Onikun, Oba Awojobi. Following waves of disturbances, the oba was forced to seek refuge in Ibadan.[35] He was later reinstated as Onikun after he promised to "change his ways."[36]

Peasant Resistance and Chieftaincy Politics in Yoruba Towns

The *Agbekoya* crisis is an illustration of the intensity of the crisis of governance during Nigeria's first era of military rule. While the national crisis discussed above reveals the lack of viable institutional connections between federal, regional and local sectors of power, this peasant rebellion in Yoruba communities demonstrates the limitations of neotraditional corporatism in the context of grassroots governance. As we saw in Ironsi's strategy of military rule, Governor Adebayo's solution of mediating Nigeria's most notable peasant resistance—the Agbekoya rebellion—with the support of obas, chiefs, baales and other community leaders, proved a complete failure. Just as the national crisis was derived from deeply rooted structural and historical problems, with their ethno-regional and class implications, so was the Agbekoya rebellion an expression of the profound contradictions in Yoruba social relations. Thus, these severe problems cannot be resolved by merely projecting obas and communal powerbrokers as intermediaries with local communities.

The Agbekoya rebellion reflected the ongoing resistance of Nigerian peasants to the appropriation of rural surplus by the state.[37] Many studies have highlighted the imaginative response of rural producers to market forces and local needs that sustained the colonial and postcolonial Nigerian economy.[38] The eminent political sociologist Gavin Williams provides examples:

> Hausa farmers intensified production on manured lands; they relied on cattle from transhumant pastoralists to provide manure, as well as their own small stock. Igbos use mulches to intensify cultivation of compounds close to their home. Some areas emerged as specializing in production of relatively high-value crops such as yams, cowpeas, or rice for distant markets.[39]

Yoruba producers, specifically, responded to colonial policies and the demands of foreign commercial interests by becoming specialized cocoa farmers and agricultural wage laborers.[40] Thus, whether producing for export markets or for local consumption, rural dwellers consistently "renewed the cooperative ideology of domestic production within individual households."[41]

This case study of the Agbekoya peasant rebellion of 1968-69 not only reveals a gulf between the holders of state power and rural producers, but also underscores the increasing tension between competing local interests of chiefs, baales, councillors, wealthy farmers, traders, and the masses of the rural poor. As the Civil War raged in southeastern Nigeria,[42] Yoruba rural dwellers rebelled against the Western State Military Government in September 1968. Widely known as the Agbekoya rebellion (peasants resist abject poverty), the disturbances—which started as agitations in Oyo town and rural Ibadan Division—soon escalated into protracted confrontation between local communities and state officials throughout the region. This expressed the reaction of rural dwellers to government economic policies which, despite high inflation and a massive drop in the price of cocoa, had significantly raised taxes and reduced the provision of infrastructure. These conditions had their worst effects, of course, on the rural and urban poor. In what can best be described as spontaneous reactions, resistance move- ments organized themselves on an unprecedented scale. They were initially directed against tax increases, especially the state government's flat tax of six pounds levied on everyone whose income was below fifty pounds a year, and a substantial increase in water rates imposed by the Western State Wa- ter Corporation.

Local people also opposed a variety of new tax levies introduced by both the state and federal governments. These taxes included a state gov- ernment development levy of seven shillings and six pence per person, an income tax on self-employed women whose annual salary exceeded 100 pounds, and a five percent national reconstruction levy imposed by the Federal Government on all Nigerian households to remedy the devastation of the Civil War in 1968.[43] As Peel notes, the rebellion was caused by

> the depressed state of the rural economy (especially in the older cocoa-grow- ing area of Western Yorubaland, where trees were old and yields declining), made worse by the financial impositions of the civil war. The most novel feature of the disturbances was their region-wide character . . . but there was also a greater tendency than before to look beyond this local level to regional or national determinants of their condition.[44]

Dissatisfaction with the performance of local authorities were also cited as a major reason for the Agbekoya crisis. In many areas, local govern- ment officials collected exorbitant rates for which they were seldom ac- countable. Clearly, the sole administrator system, introduced as part of Governor Fajuyi's reform in 1966, had proved profoundly inadequate.[45] Even if they had been committed to their responsibilities, sole administra- tors were confronted with daunting tasks, as they had to supervise many communities without qualified personnel and sufficient resources. It was therefore the cumulative impact of state policies in a period of economic crisis that prompted the anger of the rural and urban poor in 1968.

A critical analysis of this crisis must also discuss the objective material conditions of the Yoruba poor in relations to important local leaders such as obas and chiefs, politicians and state functionaries. Because of their status in local communities, obas and local chiefs were drawn into the crisis as it unfolded. Those who embraced unpopular state policies without due consideration for local aspirations came under severe attack. Conversely, obas and chiefs who distanced themselves from state agents were accorded due respect and were occasionally called upon to participate in negotiations between Agbekoya leaders and the government. And in a few cases, where chiefs themselves had been disenchanted with specific policies, they secretly instigated opposition to the state.

Ibadan Division, where major Agbekoya riots occurred, witnessed the fiercest resistance. Before the initial outbreak of riots in 1968, rural communities from Ibadan South District Council Area had called on Governor Adebayo to reduce the flat tax from six pounds to thirty shillings; they also expressed dissatisfaction with the performance of their local authorities. When their requests fell on deaf ears, protesters marched on the city, carrying juju charms, dane guns and other weapons, demanding an audience with the Olubadan.[46] As tension mounted and confrontation between the farmers and government forces seemed inevitable, Governor Adebayo undertook an official tour of Ibadan provincial communities. Meeting with irate rural crowds in Akanran, Idi-Ayunre and Olode, he had no comforting news for them; he simply called for calm and admonished them to pay their taxes.[47] Failing to realize that this agitation was a formidable mass resistance, with cohesive populist doctrines that cut across communal and demographic lines, he dismissed it as no more than the handiwork of malcontents and disgruntled politicians.[48] Not surprisingly, the governor's message failed to achieve its desired effect. Later in the month, Agbekoya riots at Mapo resulted in the death of many protesters. In December, irate crowds directed their anger against the much-hated tax collectors, councillors and baales who had expressed little sympathy for their cause. Afraid for their lives, local officials and notables fled for safe haven in the city.[49] By the end of December 1968, rural dwellers had not only expelled councillors and tax collectors from their communities, but had also succeeded in preventing tax collection. An uneasy calm reigned as Agbekoya leaders, in the absence of state officials and chiefs, assumed control over many communities.[50]

In reaction to the disturbance, which had by now expanded to Egba, Ijebu, Oshun, and Oyo Divisions, the government appointed a High Court Judge, Mr. Justice E. O. Ayoola, as sole commissioner to investigate the causes of the riots and make recommendations to the state authorities. After two months of investigation, Commissioner Ayoola's report identified both economic and political causes of the riots. Although Ayoola underscored the extreme economic conditions of the poor, he still ignored the Agbekoya's demands for a significant reduction in taxes. In accordance with Ayoola's recommendations, Governor Adebayo announced a number of minor policy changes, which included a new flat rate tax of three pounds and five shilling. This fell far short of Agbekoya's demands.[51] Adebayo's response to Agbekoya's renewed opposition was to adopt a military solution to the crisis; he dispatched the police and the army to crush the rebellion once and for all. Confrontations between armed policemen and rural dwellers in July resulted in the death of many civilians in Moniya, Ogunmakin, Olorunda and Akanran.[52] Farmers' groups retaliated by attacking councillors, baales and chiefs who remained behind in the villages. For several months Agbekoya leaders retained control over rural communities. In Ibadan itself a mob stormed the federal prison in September 1969, releasing over 450 prisoners. The political impasse that ensued encouraged influential regional politicians, most notably Awolowo, to wade into the crisis.[53]

The entry of politicians into the conflict forced obas, chiefs and community leaders to embrace the partisanship that arose as a consequence of the AG crisis. Embracing the cause of the Agbekoya, Awolowo called for another inquiry and met with Agbekoya leaders in Akanran in early October.[54] By obtaining the trust of Agbekoya leaders such as Tafa Adeoye and Folarin Idowu, Awolowo not only undermined Adebayo's authority, but also out-maneuvered political opponents such as Mojeed Agbaje who had enjoyed the confidence of the farmers at the beginning of the crisis.[55] With the weight of the federal authorities behind him, Awolowo forced the Western State Military Government to concede most of the Agbekoya's demands. Governor Adebayo reduced the flat tax rate to two pounds a year; other rates, such as motor park and market fees, were temporarily suspended. With regard to local administration, Adebayo relieved local government officials of their duties and promised to investigate their assets. With the exception of those charged with murder, amnesty was granted to Agbekoya members detained during the crisis.[56] This forced agreement with Agbekoya leaders thrust a wedge between Awolowo and the governor. In only a few weeks, Awolowo had wandered into Adebayo's domain and emerged triumphant.[57] Governor Adebayo also realized that some members of the Western State Executive Committee were less loyal to him than to their political mentor, Awolowo. Former AG politicians such as D. S. Adegbenro,

Bola Ige, Bisi Onabanjo and Michael Omisade, though members of the State Executive Committee, maintained their loyalty to Awolowo.

The position of the Olubadan and the Ibadan chiefs was delicate throughout the crisis. Before the outbreak of the disturbances, Agbekoya leaders embraced Ibadan's traditional leaders, hoping they would help advance the cause of the rural poor. It was clear by December 1968, however, that several chiefs had swung their support to the government.[58] Thus, while Adebayo encountered increasing opposition, the chiefs suffered a rapid decline in popularity. In Beer's view:

> The 1968–1969 riots imposed great strain on all chieftaincy institutions in Ibadan; the role of the Olubadan and his senior chiefs was no less criticized by farmers for what appeared to be their pronounced lack of sympathy for Agbekoya demands.[59]

Rural baales, who served as the unofficial mouthpiece of state officials, were particularly vulnerable to Agbekoya attacks. Appointed as party agents by the NNDP regional authorities, baales were widely resented by local people. A memorandum submitted by a farmers' organization to Commissioner Ayoola, for instance, revealed that

> the politicians created new baales for practically every village and they are nothing more than glorified party organizing secretaries who have saddled the councils with the responsibility of maintaining them and paying their salaries. Most of these baales were not appointed by the villages but by the various party constituency leaders.[60]

By the end of July 1969, many rural communities—notably Akanran, Araromi, Akufo, Ijaiye, Okereku and Moniya—had gotten rid of their baales and chiefs who were forced to flee to the city. In their absence, Agbekoya leaders assumed leadership roles previously performed by the ousted chiefs. They settled disputes, imposed tolls on motorists and charged opponents re-entry fees. In Akanran, the prestige of the charismatic Agbekoya leader, Tafa Adeoye, exceeded that of the baale many months after the disturbances.[61] Yoruba rural producers thus had their own indigenous intellectuals—like Steven Feierman's peasant intellectuals in Tanzania,[62]—who had a profound knowledge about the past, the exploitation of the poor and the rapid changes that had taken place in the larger society. At least in the short term, these leaders effectively negotiated with military administrators, chiefs and politicians by the end of the rebellion.

In Egba Division, Agbekoya agitation was shaped by a specific division. In Abeokuta and provincial communities, the political animosity between the Alake, Oba Gbadebo (an NNDP supporter) and the former AG leader, D. S. Adegbenro, divided the leadership of the town along partisan lines. This conflict was played out in the District Council which had become a political arm of AG sympathizers. Oba Gbadebo avoided the council—where Adegbenro had predominant influence—by establishing a nonstatutory advisory body consisting of allies from the banned NNDP.[63]

Unlike the case in Ibadan and Abeokuta, where chiefs had simply responded to prevailing political forces, *Parakoyi* market chiefs in Egba provincial towns actually led the opposition against taxes. With the earlier implementation of market by-laws, which brought community markets under local government control, Parakoyi chiefs had lost their traditional power as custodians of local markets. The outbreak of the Agbekoya rebellion encouraged disgruntled Parakoyi chiefs—in Egba Owode and Egba Obafemi in November—to mobilize local traders against the military government's hawkers and squatters fees.[64] Parakoyi chiefs also instigated local opposition against tax payment, market supervisors, customary court judges and public health inspectors.[65]

In Ijebu Division, on the other hand, obas and baales tended to support government policies, and were subjected to violent attacks. In November, peasants in Ishara directed their wrath against the Odemo, Oba Samuel Akinsanya, who allegedly supported the government's aggressive tax collection policy. Following allegations that the Orimolusi had supported police repression of tax evaders in Ijebu Igbo, an anti-government mob attacked the oba's palace in December 1968, injuring members of his family and destroying properties. Further north, in Ogbomosho, the hometown of late Premier Akintola, the Shoun, Oba Olajide Laoye, his wife, and five of his chiefs were murdered in what seems to have been a well-planned assault in July 1969. The Shoun was killed by a mob led by the *Tapamose* (a society formed two years earlier to advance the interest of farmers) and a local branch of the Agbekoya following rumors that he had collaborated with the police after the government's resumption of tax raids in September.[66]

The Agbekoya crisis was on the whole a tragic tale, in which obas and chiefs lost credibility with their people for their roles as intermediaries of unpopular government policies. Thus, while Nigeria's rural communities have historically responded to the demands of both global and domestic markets, the Agbekoya case reveals that peasants are also capable of resisting exploitation from the state.[67] Indeed, the damaging consequences of an extractive state on rural production has been well documented by studies of African agrarian systems.[68] While devising imaginative strategies to evade state regulation, Agbekoya, like most other rural eruptions in sub-Saharan African, confronted state agencies when regulations became particularly repressive.[69]

The struggles between state and society in postcolonial Nigeria points to the impact of these rural eruptions for political legitimacy at the local level.[70] Chiefly authority came under severe pressure from rural resistance in a period of economic crisis. The Agbekoya movement indicates that the interests of chiefs, though often seen as in tune with local aspirations, can be at odds with those of the community. When this occurs, the prestige of obas and chiefs suffers considerably. As noted in earlier chapters on colonial rule in Oyo Province, and party politics in the Western Region, the consequences of the Agbekoya rebellion reveal a major contradiction: that traditional rulers are expected to advance the cause of the holders of state power, while at the same time drawing their legitimacy from townspeople. When these interests are blatantly at odds, the status of traditional rulers and their viability as an institution are at risk.

The Military's Local Government Reform in Yoruba Towns

A major consequence of the Agbekoya rebellion was the introduction of a comprehensive review of local government administration by Adebayo's successor, Brigadier Oluwole Rotimi, in 1972. Following the recommendation of a review panel —chaired by an oba, the Elekole of Ikole—Rotimi adopted the council manager system. This system revolved around three major branches, the area committee, the management committee and the council manager, the last assuming the position of chief executive officer of the new local authority.[71] The thirty-member appointed area committees provided a critical link between the communities and the local government council, and were charged with the responsibility for community development and local administration.[72] The management committees consisted of representatives from each area of the region. Obas and chiefs were completely excluded from performing any executive roles within local government administration. Members of the review committee contended that this would insulate traditional rulers from the acrimonious party politics of the preceding years of parliamentary democracy.[73] The panel further argued that membership in political institutions such as the House of Chiefs and local councils had trapped many traditional rulers in bitter partisan politics, thus putting considerable strain on chieftaincy institutions. Obas however, would constitute chieftaincy committees and could advise the area committees on critical matters affecting their local communities. The panel also granted senior obas the power to remain in the position of ceremonial presidents of their respective local authorities.[74] In fact, while the panel was still deliberating, a new Chiefs' Law gave chieftaincy committees exclusive authority over important chieftaincy matters, especially those relating to the appointment, promotion and discipline of traditional rulers.[75] Unlike previous years, when the local government councils served as the link between the chieftaincy committees and the state authorities, the Local Government Review Committee required that recommendations of chieftaincy committees be forwarded through the divisional officers to the state ministry of local government and chieftaincy affairs.[76] However, by giving the state government the sole authority to regulate chieftaincy, the review committee failed to provide any effective structural solution to the serious problems of chieftaincy; members of the State Executive Committee, notably civilian politicians, were deeply involved in chieftaincy politics. Yet, despite their formal exclusion from authority, individual obas were still favorably positioned to influence major policy decisions at the local level.[77] Beyond their direct involvement in the statutory chieftaincy committees, advisory duties in management committees, along with their extensive social networks and prestige, obas retained considerable influence in local administration.[78]

To the government officials involved, the edict was the comprehensive local government reform that the people of the state had longed for. In an outburst of enthusiasm, state officials contended that, since members of the new local authorities were educated professionals, the authorities would be well positioned to tackle the crisis of local governance. As demonstrated by previous cases of local government reforms, the assumption that formal qualifications and professional experience would resolve the crisis of local governance was naive. In reality, only a few of such well-educated councillors possessed real knowledge of the communities where they were assigned.[79] And as far as obas and baales were concerned, the 1972 local government reform was rather vague. Presumably motivated by a desire to insulate traditional rulers from the political feuds of earlier years, and mindful of the military government's inclination to exclude the "exalted fathers of all the people" from the indignities of administrative deliberations, the panel's refusal to incorporate chieftaincy into the local government executive was not surprising; it only confirmed what had by then become the norm in Yoruba communities. What was significant, however, was the panel's decision to grant obas extensive powers in the chieftaincy committees. This gave obas exclusive control over these most politicized institutions in local communities. This ambiguity clearly underscores the dilemma faced by the holders of state power in constructing a practical administrative role for chiefs.

The failed state and federal initiatives of the Ironsi and Gowon years were grafted on prevailing ethno-regional arrangements in which chieftaincy—assumed to be the instrument of grassroots legitimacy—was co-opted as intermediary between military regimes and local communities. Excessively expressed in Ironsi's regime, this project proved a complete failure: corporatist regimes with neotraditional proclivities were no viable alternatives to imaginative sociopolitical and economic policies and programs. The complex character of the Nigerian state and society as expressed in the pre-Civil War national crisis, the failure of superficial local government reforms, and the Agbekoya rebellion all attest to the limitations of regional and local networks of power as viable agencies of civil/military rule.

7

MILITARY REFORMS: THE RATIONALIZATION OF CHIEFTAINCY STRUCTURES

The Mohammed/Obasanjo regime was the most innovative of Nigeria's postcolonial governments. As part of its transfer program to civilian rule in October 1979, it initiated comprehensive political and economic reforms. These had a profound effect on local politics and on the status of traditional title-holders throughout Nigeria. Fueled by the windfall from petroleum revenues and by the stability of the post–Civil War years, the federal initiatives encouraged state military governments to introduce reforms of their own. Exploring the far-reaching implications of these reforms for Yoruba social formation and chieftaincy politics, this chapter will show how particular federal and state government policies further complicated local politics in Oyo State.[1]

Despite military rule, the liberalism which underpinned the objectives of the Mohammed/Obasanjo regime inspired important political debates. Indeed, it was this vision that led to the abrupt end of General Gowon's regime, as dissidents within his government accused him of abuse of power. Despite Gowon's initial popularity—especially for his policy of rehabilitating the war-torn Eastern states after 1971—he failed to effectively address the widening gap between the Nigerian state and society, growing class and communal divisions, and rising popular expectations. All these factors prompted the military coup of July 1975, toppling Gowon while he was attending an Organization Of African Unity (OAU) summit meeting in Addis Ababa.

Two members of his ruling council—Brigadier (later General) Murtala Mohammed, who succeeded Gowon as head of the Federal Military Government (FMG) and as Commander in Chief of the Armed Forces, and Brigadier (later General) Olusegun Obasanjo, the Chief of Staff Supreme Headquarters—assumed the political leadership of the federal government. Once in power, the new regime broadened the scope and depth of political activity so that military governance could more effectively accommodate an expansive political space, and the increasingly complex socio-economic conditions of the oil boom years.[2] Not even the assassination of General Mohammed in February 1976 (in a failed coup attempt by dissidents) distracted the FMG from its objectives. Mohammed's vision of progressive change was faithfully executed by his successor, General Obasanjo, who succeeded as head of state.

The first political objective of the Mohammed/Obasanjo regime was to confront the prevailing problem of regionalism by broadening the federal system. By creating seven new states in 1977, Obasanjo actually strengthened the national government at the expense of regional centers of power. State officials contended that, given the turbulence of previous decades, a stronger national government was needed to contain the fault lines of ethno-regionalism.[3] To confront the endemic problem of local governance, the FMG formulated Nigeria's first comprehensive national policy for local government, the *1976 Guidelines for Local Government Reforms*.

The Mohammed/Obasanjo administration also made good its commitment to foster a transition to civilian rule, appointing a fifty-member constitution-drafting committee under the chairmanship of the distinguished barrister, Rotimi-Williams. Furthermore, General Obasanjo established two national development panels, chaired by economists H. M. O. Onitiri and Michael Omolayole, to recommend policies that would address the deepening problems of urbanization and rural poverty.[4] The Onitiri and Omolayole Commissions, in turn, recommended the establishment of a Land Use Panel to make recommendations on a national land tenure policy. It was this panel's work that subsequently led to the Land Use Decree of 1978. Inevitably, these military attempts to rationalize governance had serious implications for the configuration of state power.[5] The regional alliances between military administrators, politicians and senior state functionaries that emerged as a consequence had serious implications for chieftaincy structures during this period of political transition. While these military reforms formally eroded the authority of traditional rulers, Nigeria's prevailing ethno-regional configuration further entrenched chiefly power. The implications of these important issues for local, regional, and national politics are the subject of the following case studies.

A Comprehensive Local Government Reform

Unlike previous initiatives, the 1976 reforms established a uniform system of local government throughout Nigeria. The military authorities, for the first time, considered local government to be worthy of a coherent national policy. In addition to providing the foundations for a transition to civilian rule, the architects of the 1976 *Local Government Guidelines* held that local government institutions, if properly organized, would be potential instruments of economic and political development.[6] Recognized by the FMG as the third tier of government, local authorities were empowered to perform specific functions such as providing basic social services, regulating commercial enterprises and levying and collecting taxes and rates.[7] This was the military administration's initial response to the endemic crisis of local governance,[8] and a first step towards the creation of new democratic institutions at all levels of government. Although they extolled the virtue of local autonomy and participatory democracy, the *Guidelines* would in fact subject local authorities to the control of the state military (and later civilian) governors. The control of the state government was specifically ensured through government-appointed inspectors directly responsible to the state governor and empowered to recommend the dissolution of local authorities considered corrupt or inefficient.[9] Thus, in practice, the policy strengthened the center at the expense of local political aspirations.

In keeping with the prevailing condition, this national policy excluded traditional rulers from the executive functions of local authorities. The FMG contended that this was because it needed to insulate "the exalted fathers" from the bitter partisan conflicts that had bedeviled electoral politics in the previous parliamentary era.[10] Regardless of this reasoning, this provision did not sit well with traditional rulers—who by this time were consolidating their ties to regional allies in anticipation of the transition to democratic rule. The sentiments expressed by a popular oba, the Odemo of Ishara, Oba Akinsanya, were symptomatic. Declaring that he was "never out of politics," the Odemo publicly dismissed the FMG's decision to exclude obas from local executive affairs:

> What else is more than politics when government speaks to the people through the obas and the people talk to the government through the same channels.

. . . Obas must follow the taste of the people on party politics—as experience had shown obas who refuse to toe the line of their people had often fallen into trouble.[11]

The *Guidelines*, like many preceding reforms, underscored the dilemma of chieftaincy in contemporary politics. Traditional rulers are expected to endorse state policies, while at the same time shunning party political activities. Clearly, the line separating local governance and partisanship is in reality a very thin one. As critical components of entrenched regional and local interests, traditional rulers are destined to walk a tight rope between the demands posed by the holders of state power and those of local constituencies.

Even Obafemi Awolowo, the progressive who, as premier of the Western Region, had mounted a cautious offensive against conservative obas, took a dim view of the proposed exclusion of traditional rulers from local governance. Speaking to an audience (that included emirs) at the convocation of the Ahmadu Bello University, Zaria, in 1976, Awolowo remarked:

> Local government is by its very name and nature intended to be local, and traditional rulers are more versed in local affairs than elected absentee councillors who visit home only when meetings are held. . . . Since the traditional rulers live permanently among the people and are involved in the day-to-day problems of the people, some arrangement ought to have been made to make them participate in the decision-making activities of the local government councils.[12]

These public debates were interrupted by the obligatory invitation of traditional rulers to Lagos and the state capitals for consultations with the head of state, members of the Supreme Military Council and state military governors. For example, at a special address of the head of state to Nigeria's traditional rulers in July, Obasanjo declared that

> It is not the intention of the federal government to destroy the organic unity of traditional local authority. . . . Your Highnesses, your roles as fathers, elders, and advisers of your people in our local government system cannot and will not be supplanted.[13]

Similarly, the chief of staff, General Shehu Yar' Adua, himself from the Katsina aristocracy, later observed that the "reforms should not be construed as an attempt at reducing or abolishing the traditional functions of our emirs, obas, and chiefs."[14] Despite lingering misgivings, traditional rulers, as they had done in the past, put a positive public face on the reform, claiming in one important instance that the *Guidelines* had "great merit" and may provide the "framework for development at the local level."[15] The *Guidelines* did grant traditional rulers a voice in chieftaincy and customary matters, at least, and responsibility for mobilizing local communities for economic development.[16]

Following these assurances, Obasanjo instructed the state governors to proceed with the implementation of the reforms. In Oyo State, the military governor, Brigadier David Jemibewon, launched the reform with great fanfare, adapting it to the "unique conditions of the state." Made up of elected and nominated councillors, twenty-one local authorities would operate a multipurpose local government system in the state.[17] Senior obas with historical "claims of suzerainty" over minor communities however, were appointed presidents of fifteen traditional councils.

The Oyo State Chieftaincy Reform

As part of the Oyo State government's strategy of rationalizing local politics, Governor Jemibewon implemented comprehensive chieftaincy reform between 1976 and 1978. Proponents of reform had argued that decades of acrimonious partisan politics had deepened local divisions, and intensified struggles over claims to major titles in Yoruba towns. As in the colonial period, hierarchies of "paramount rulers" of "metropolitan" towns and subordinate minor obas of provincial communities still provided the framework through which these struggles occurred.

Jemibewon's chieftaincy policy was partly prompted by the public conflicts among Oyo State obas for the right to wear beaded crowns. These conflicts could be traced back to the earlier system of indirect rule which gave legal approval to varying degrees of seniority among obas. Emphasizing its impact on the Ooni's prestige during colonial rule, Law contends that:

> The principal importance of the dynastic link with Ile-Ife lay in the fact that descent from a son or grandson of Oduduwa was considered necessary to validate a king's claim to the right to wear an *ade*, or crown with a beaded fringe. In 1903 this principle was given official recognition by the British authorities, who brought the Ooni, or king, of Ife to Lagos to give judgement on the claim of the Elepe of Sagamu, a minor Ijebu ruler, to wear an *ade*: the Ooni gave a list of twenty-one kings with the right to wear *ade*, not including the Elepe.[18]

Sanctioned by the colonial state as symbols of traditional authority, beaded crowns (*ade*) thus assumed new significance among obas, chiefs and hometown elites. Once again, re-constructed histories, traditions and mythologies—rigidly interpreted as legitimate Yoruba traditional political authority—reverberated in contemporary local politics. Nigerian historian A. I. Asiwaju contends that "the conferral of the title of oba in colonial Oyo Province (as opposed to the title of baale) on the Olubadan of Ibadan, the Ataoja of Oshogbo, the Olukare of Ikare, the Onimeko of Imeko, the Baale of Awaiye, and the Onilua of Ilua, neatly correlated with administrative re-organization . . . and the accelerated rates of claims to beaded crowns." Thus, the contemporary legitimacy of obaship was reinforced by the historically prestigious symbols of the beaded crowns.[19]

As Yoruba towns confronted rapid social change during decolonization, beaded crowns assumed even deeper political meaning among obas and local elites. Asiwaju further notes that

> [T]he beaded crown was seen as a mark of promotion of the head-chief whose advancement within the traditional context was expected to keep pace with the physical growth of the town in which he was the head. This mental attitude was not new in itself as instances seem to have existed in the pre-European period in which former vassal head chiefs seek to wear a crown to reflect the growing importance of their bids. . . . Reference is made here to the informal institution of patronage whereby Yoruba oba, who traditionally possess the right to the original beaded crowns commissioned new crowns allegedly on receipt of 'gifts' from many an aspirant.[20]

Indeed, these claims and counter-claims dominated much of the struggle for status and prestige by obas; having convened many expert committees, various colonial and post-colonial regimes had in fact sanctioned the proliferation of beaded crowns. For instance, the number of Yoruba crowned heads had increased from the "original" seven recorded in 1897 by Samuel Johnson, Yorubaland's pre-eminent local historian, to twenty-one in 1903, and forty-one in 1966.[21]

The problem of beaded crowns erupted again during the initial implementation of Obasanjo's local government reforms in the mid-1970s. In Ibadan, agitation arose for the Olubadan to wear a beaded crown. This was reminiscent of the early 1930s, when Christian elites, Muslim traders and leaders of civic groups successfully demanded the title of Olubadan—oba of Ibadan—(for the erstwhile Baale) from Resident Ward-Price. Again, it was the persistent pressure of native Ibadan elites that forced Governor Jemibewon to grant the Olubadan the right to wear a beaded crown. This influence of Western-educated elites in chieftaincy issues reflected long-established and widespread trends. Thus, in the colonial period the actions of Lagos-based hometown elite groups, the Olosi Native Improvement Society, the Ijesha Patriotic Union, and the Egbado Union, were critical to the Olosi stool, the Owa of Ilesha, and the Olubara quest for beaded crowns.[22]

A second epicenter of agitation was in Ogbomosho, Premier Akintola's hometown, where, in the late 1960s, the Agbekoya rebellion had been particularly violent. Although the underlying issues were similar to Ibadan, the Ogbomosho situation was complicated by the Alaafin's claim of "traditional" suzerainty over the area. In opposition to Alaafin Adeyemi's objection, Ogbomosho elites had publicly called on the state government to grant the Shoun, Oba Oyewumi, permission to wear a beaded crown. But as in many other cases, this controversy between the Alaafin and the Shoun had its origins in the indirect rule system, where provincial obas such as the Ataoja of Oshogbo had successfully campaigned for a beaded crown in 1947. Thus, to justify their position, Ogbomosho's oba, chiefs and elites drew from these earlier precedents.[23] After consultation with senior obas, including the Alaafin, Governor Jemibewon eventually granted Oba Oyewumi permission to wear a beaded crown. As in Ibadan, historical claims to this royal insignia were in doubt;[24] political expediency once again prevailed. But these developments were not limited to Ibadan and Ogbomosho. Indeed, Nigeria's leading newspaper, the *Daily Times*, recorded sixty-seven Oyo State obas as *oba alade* by the end of Jemibewon's tenure as governor.[25]

It was, however, the intractable disputes over chieftaincy itself dating back to the early colonial period, and complicated by the bitter partisanship of the years of parliamentary democracy, that prompted Governor Jemibewon to introduce the chieftaincy reform of 1976. Despite previous laws regulating chieftaincy, Governor Jemibewon was struck by the number of chieftaincy disputes and allegations of abuse of power. Jemibewon recalls the severity of this problem in his memoirs:

> I found that there were a number of chieftaincy tussles whose solution appeared to have defied all attempts by previous administrations. I also found that the number of recognized chieftaincy titles in the former Western state was so large and the problems associated with them were so complex and multifarious that attempts to tackle these problems were absorbing a disproportionate share of the time of my administration. As a matter of fact, I soon discovered that previous military administrations in the state had devoted nothing less than 85 percent of their time at executive council meetings solely to chieftaincy matters.[26]

Thus, Jemibewon appointed a chieftaincy review commission, under the chairmanship of Mr. Justice Adenekan Ademola, to investigate the customary and legal basis of chieftaincy disputes.[27] After seven months of deliberations on fifty-three disputed titles, the commission confirmed the government's worst fears:[28] made under the heavy sway of partisan politics, chieftaincy declarations had failed to conform with the relevant customary and legal requirements.[29] The declarations had often been tailored to suit the wishes of influential royal lineages, reigning obas, dignitaries and elite interest groups.[30]

The commission urged Jemibewon to establish a state registry of heads of ruling lineages and potential title candidates. Moreover, it called on the state governor to assume direct control over chieftaincy matters, assisted by a permanent secretary and senior administrative staff. Finally, the Ademola Commission advised Jemibewon to introduce a chieftaincy code of conduct.[31] With the exception of the last proposal, which some officials considered insulting to obas, the government promptly implemented the commission's recommendations.[32] Chieftaincy issues were transferred from the Ministry of Local Government, where they had been administered for nearly thirty years, to the direct control of the governor and his staff.

A National Land Reform Policy in Oyo State

The second national policy of the Obasanjo administration that had profound effect on chieftaincy institutions was the Land Use Decree of 1978. It had its most significant impact in the southern states, where the claim had been made that, in keeping with custom, traditional rulers held communal land in trust for local people. In the old Western Region, despite a series of land reform measures implemented by previous governments, land disputes remained common. The 1957 Land Tenure Act, for example, introduced by the AG government, caused serious discord among state officials, land speculators, obas and title-holders. Before discussing the impact of the 1978 decree, we should recall how colonial authorities had interpreted the role of Yoruba obas and baales in customary land tenure. The indirect rule system had reinforced the power base of Yoruba "paramount rulers," legitimating and reinforcing the claim of obas over the control and distribution of communal land. Indeed, the Yoruba maxim, *oba lo ni ile* (the oba is the owner of the land), was interpreted literally (and conveniently) by some obas and their subordinates as an indication of the wide authority of the oba under the customary land tenure system.[33] And British administrators, especially in the early colonial period, regarded some "paramount rulers" as "trustee-administrators or custodians of community lands."[34] Thus, senior obas such as the Alaafin, the Ooni, the Owa, the Awujale, the Alake and the Ewi, as "paramount" titleholders of major hometowns, derived considerable wealth and power from parcels designated as communal lands in their NA jurisdictions. As these parcels became more valuable, largely because of their growing commercial value, conflicts over land control intensified.[35] In these struggles, obas and powerful descent groups successfully out-maneuvered competitors by claiming the custodial rights over communal land, and assumed considerable power over its allocation. Thus, despite historical and regional variations, control over land, like the collection of taxes and the adjudication of civil and criminal cases, became another instrument through which "paramount rulers" rewarded allies and denied resources to adversaries.[36] The colonial interpretation of land tenure actually had little historical basis. Sara Berry's remarks on nineteenth-century Ife are instructive:

> Ife is an ancient kingdom, unlike Ibadan which was founded only c.1830, and it might seem therefore that the Ooni and chiefs derive their land-holdings and authority over other families' land-holdings from the age and stability of the traditional political system in Ife. Evidence, however, does not wholly support such a hypothesis. Life in Ife was thoroughly disrupted during the nineteenth-century wars, largely by groups of Oyo refugees who settled at Ife but did not get along very well with the local inhabitance. . . . [I]t seems unlikely that the Ooni exercised much stability over any but his immediate followers, or that he effectively controlled the use or disposition of Ife land.[37]

Berry's assessment suggests that British rule advanced the Ooni's power over communal land. The Ooni's authority, however, was achieved at the expense of competing local interests such as farmers, strangers, hunters, chiefs and the important landowning families that had exercised considerable influence over land during the previous century.[38] Colonial Ibadan was also the scene of intense struggles over land tenure as these various elements—now including Muslim traders and educated Christians as well—contested the various colonial policies on land.[39] The Ibadan NA refused to recognize a colonial ordinance which provided for land sale, granting rights of occupancy. By the 1920s, land struggles between educated "native settlers" and chiefs had already become a common political problem. For example, in one high profile case concerning a disputed parcel of land in

Iddo gate the NA Council instigated a major agitation against two "native settlers," Doherty and Vaughan.[40] These local struggles were complicated by new competition over the legal control of land between the national Supreme Court and the NA native courts.[41] While the colonial authorities strengthened the authority of the provincial courts, educated "native settlers" and lawyers consistently called for the transfer of land cases to the English-style courts.[42] In response, concern of chiefs and prominent local sons about the growing influence of "native settlers" led to the establishment of a special NA-controlled land court in 1936.[43] Finally, armed with colonial land ordinances, "paramount rulers" such as the Alaafin and the Ooni extracted some advantage from the cash crop economy, especially during the cocoa boom years of the 1920s by levying tribute on "economic trees."[44] This would continue until the reforms of the Awolowo government in the late 1950s. Senior obas suffered further reversals during decolonization, under growing pressures from "native settlers," speculators and the rising educated elites.[45] Adewoye notes of the Ibadan case:

> In the 1930s (and indeed up to the 1960s) land claims were a major staple of legal practice, providing a basis for relatively lucrative 'specialization' by such lawyers as Ade Soetan, A. M. A. Akinloye and S. B. Adewunmi. Obafemi Awolowo, who came back to Ibadan in 1947 to set up his legal practice, considered land cases the most profitable aspect of legal practice in the city.[46]

Claiming it had a mandate to reconcile customary law with the needs of rapidly changing Yoruba towns, the AG regional government passed laws in 1957 and 1959 reversing the privileges of obas over communal land.[47] In the absence of effective enforcement, however, obas and other privileged elements succeeded in retaining *de facto* control. By the early 1970s, Nigerian intellectuals and civil servants began to complain that "traditional" land tenure hindered federal and state government development initiatives. The first major official pronouncement was by Femi Okunnu, Federal Commissioner for Works and Housing in the Gowon administration. Addressing a sympathetic audience of intellectuals, during a well-publicized seminar at the University of Ibadan in 1972, Okunnu claimed that customary land tenure systems and the rising cost of land in major cities posed a serious threat to the Gowon administration's four-year development plan. Okunnu called on social scientists to recommend a rational, effective and efficient land tenure system for the country.[48] Three years later, Nigeria's Third Development Plan of 1975–1980 noted the impact of land tenure on the Nigerian housing crisis:

Individual ownership of and speculation in urban land led to considerable and continuing increases in the price of land. . . . Moreover fraudulent land transactions and endless legal tussles over title ownership have combined to stifle housing development with significant escalation in the prices of rented accommodation.[49]

It was however, the Obasanjo regime's appointment of two special panels in 1975 that eventually led to the formulation of a national land tenure policy.[50] One was the Anti-Inflation Task Force, under the chairmanship of the economist, H. M. O. Onitiri, of the Nigerian Institute of Social and Economic Research (NISER). The task force, created during a period of severe inflationary pressure, was required to identify the causes of high inflation and recommend measures to contain the problem. The Onitiri commission noted that the high cost of living, especially in the area of housing and economic development, was directly linked to Nigeria's anachronistic land tenure systems. The commission thus recommended that:

In order to reduce the injustice that stems from the private appropriation of socially created wealth and to remove the bottleneck that land now constitutes to the development of the nation, and in particular to housing expansion and agricultural development, the task force believes that a comprehensive national policy on land needs to be put into effect as a matter of urgency.[51]

Onitiri and his associates also called on the FMG to appoint an expert panel to examine the rising cost of housing. In January 1976, General Obasanjo appointed a rent-control panel under the chairmanship of another economist, Michael Omolayole. This panel, in turn, called on the federal authorities to appoint another body of experts to formulate a national land tenure policy.[52] In April 1977, General Obasanjo created such panel under the chairmanship of Mr. Justice Chike Idigbo. Chief of Staff Major General Yar' Adua recalled at its inauguration in May that

The need for the establishment of this Panel arose from the recommendations of various commissions and panels set up to examine some aspects of the structure of our social and economic life. The problem has been foreseen and articulated in the Third Development Program. Both the Anti-Inflationary Task Force and the Rent Panel Reports identified land as one of our major bottlenecks to development efforts in the country.[53]

The panel's efforts led to the formulation of a comprehensive land reform, the Land Use Decree of 1 April 1978. This historic document declared that from 1 April: "All lands comprised in the territory of each state in the federation are hereby vested in the military governor of the state and such land shall be held in trust and administered for the use and common benefit of all Nigerians."[54] The management of rural land was actually delegated to local authorities. The governors, however, retained control of urban land.[55] The decree also directed the governors to establish state Land Use and Allocation Committees that would advise the governor on all land matters, especially the management of "communal lands."[56] Thus, with a stroke of the pen, the Land Use Decree accomplished a legal revolution, abolishing the customary proprietary rights of families and individuals—and of traditional rulers—over both developed and undeveloped land. Declaring economic development, national uniformity and social equity as its goals, the decree vested all communal lands in the State Executive Committees.

An assumption of the policy was that government authorities would promote an egalitarian process of economic development in all the states. Whatever the motives, the irony gradually sank in: that military administrators (and later, career politicians and their associates in business and government), without effective legal constraints, had been granted custodial rights over Nigeria's most vital natural resource. Thus, although the decree was shrouded in what Paul Francis aptly referred to as "a rhetoric of equality, justice and universal rights for the masses of Nigeria," it soon became a medium of expropriation for particular class interest.[57]

The promulgation of the decree in Oyo State sparked a confrontation between obas and the state military governor, Brigadier David Jemibewon. Barely a week later, Sir Adesoji Aderemi, Ooni of Ife and Chairman of the Council of Chiefs, rallied opposition to the land reform. On April 7, he called an informal meeting of the state Council of Chiefs at his Onireke residence in Ibadan. Attended by twelve senior obas, the forum condemned the reforms and vowed to challenge their implementation.[58] The obas then directed their anger at the federal authorities. Following a highly publicized emergency meeting on April 10, the obas argued that the new land reform was an affront to cherished Yoruba values.[59] At a press conference, Sir Adesoji urged the FMG to reverse its decision, claiming that "to put land under the control of local and state authorities was to expose it to political patronage and partisan politics."[60] With the confidence of an aged Yoruba father making an important request from a son, Sir Adesoji called directly on the Head of State to grant obas control over communal land. And the deputy chairman of the council, Alaafin Adeyemi, described the decree as "an invitation to chaos, in which both obas and local communities have much to lose."[61] He added, however, that the obas' opposition should not be taken as "a confrontation with the government but rather an expression of the wishes of the people over a government policy."[62]

Infuriated with the obas' public opposition, Governor Jemibewon condemned the criticism as antithetical to "the conscience of the people."[63] Indeed, to counter the obas' resistance, government propagandists presented the decree as an egalitarian alternative to the anachronistic traditional and colonial arrangement, whereby obas and their wealthy allies profited from their control of land.[64] In a National Television (NTV) program, Jemibewon reminded the obas that "the government is greater than any individual." He claimed that, as custodians of communal lands

> obas abused this privilege because money accruing from land was only available for the use of obas and members of their family. . . . In the past obas held land in trust for the people. What the federal government has done now is to ensure that the state government holds land in trust for the same people. This is a very progressive approach; an achievement over the previous one.[65]

The following day, Jemibewon embarked on a tour of local communities, touting the decree's virtues and condemning the opposition of the obas. In Ibadan, where the Olubadan, Oba D. T. Akinbiyi, had distanced himself from his brother obas,[66] Governor Jemibewon met with support from the Olubadan and the chiefs. At Iyanna Ofa, in the Lagelu Local Government Council Area, Jemibewon called on townspeople to give maximum support to what he packaged as an egalitarian policy.[67] Jemibewon then took his campaign through seven major towns in Oshun and Oyo Divisions. While addressing the Ataoja (the oba), chiefs and community leaders in Oshogbo, he announced that the implementation of the decree would mean the abolition of *isakole*, the much-resented customary leasehold in which tenant farmers paid tribute to landlords in cash or in kind. In Ogbomosho, Ejigbo, Iwo, Shaki, Ede and Igbeti cheering crowds gave the governor a rousing welcome.[68]

Confronted with the governor's popularity, obas reversed themselves, assuring Jemibewon of their cooperation. At Ogbomosho, the Shoun and the chiefs pledged their full support to the decree. And in neighboring Ede, the Timi declared that chiefs and townspeople were committed to the land reform. Later at Ejigbo, the Elejigbo, the oba, assured Jemibewon of his town's cooperation with the government.[69] Finally, on April 13, the governor carried his campaign to Ile-Ife, the "domain" of the Ooni, Sir Adesoji. It was Sir Adesoji who had earlier mobilized state obas against the decree. In an address to Ife chiefs and community leaders, Jemibewon claimed that his government enjoyed overwhelming support of "all the presidents of the traditional councils, local government council chairmen, farmers, market-women, student bodies, various other organizations, and the masses of the people" in all twenty-one local government areas of the state.[70] The governor's triumphant tour forced the Council of Chiefs to reverse their earlier decision. In a communique signed by the deputy-chairman, the Alaafin, the obas declared that "after reasoned consideration of the objectives of the decree, and in view of the more detailed explanation offered by the governor, traditional rulers in Oyo State have agreed to support the government."[71] The communique, however, requested a proper place for obas in the new policy, demanding that

> Parcels of land which come under the administration of rulers, chiefs, established families and others in various quarters and compounds, would need to be administered in such a way as to involve these people to ensure respect for their traditional position.[72]

Rather than alienating local groups, especially the rural poor, that seemed to favor the abolition of *isakole*, the obas reluctantly embraced the government's reform. State authorities reciprocated by including the obas in the implementation of the decree. The Ooni, the Alaafin, the Olubadan and the Orangun of Ila were all appointed to the state Land Use and Allocation Committee, which advised the governor on land matters, especially the allocation of communal land. Obas were also appointed chairmen of the Land Use Allocation Sub-Committee in the thirteen towns of "urban" rank.[73]

Jemibewon's reform, however, fell far short of its objectives. Rather than promote equity, the new system immediately became a source of elite accumulation—even before the transfer of power to civilians in October 1979. Apart from the initial confrontation between obas and the state, the reform encountered the usual problems of implementation of government policies in communities where modern state agencies were still weak. Furthermore, as in earlier land reforms, the 1978 Decree revealed the difficulty of reconciling the conflicting claims of class interests and long-established family and communal rights. Formulating a uniform land policy was one thing; implementing it in a context of ambiguous land-tenure practices and a rapidly changing economy was another. These problems were exacerbated by an entrenched legacy of conflicts dating back to the colonial period, concerning multiple overlapping claims to land. Two important issues immediately became apparent. First, although a major objective of the decree was to counteract the growing problem of urban land speculation, the implementation of the policy in Oyo as in other states was such that speculation and multiple land ownership remained serious problems. In fact, fraudulent sales of land, especially in urban areas, increased after 1978. Second, rural tenants and landowners soon recognized the inability of the federal and state authorities' to enforce the new decree. In many cases, they simply continued to observe the customary system of land tenure, which remained more reliable for the parties involved.[74] As Francis concluded: "The persistence of traditional practice in the face of state directives is not due to irrational inertia but rather, to perceived mutual advantage, the need for security, and a rational assessment of long term interests."[75] In those sections of the state where state officials were able to exert direct influence—especially in urban areas—the decree rapidly degenerated into a legal mechanism through which officials dismissed the statutory rights of the poor.[76] The beneficiaries, as before, were politicians, civil servants, and land speculators—along with military officers—who could now combine formal legal procedures with the informal networks through which they had controlled land in the past.

The 1979 Nigerian Constitution: Chieftaincy and Regionalism

The 1979 Presidential Constitution was, of course, the most important initiative in the military administration's transition to civilian rule. It was also designed to respond to the sociopolitical problems that had plagued Nigeria for over two decades. In September 1975, the FMG had appointed a fifty-member Constitution Drafting Committee (CDC). Under the chairmanship of renowned barrister and former AG politician Rotimi-Williams, it was comprised of two representatives from each of the nineteen states, along with distinguished legal personalities and scholars.[77] At its inaugural meeting in October, the Head of State, General Mohammed, provided comprehensive guidelines for the committee's deliberations. Mohammed stated that the FMG would not compromise the prevailing federal structure, would only accept political parties that were national in character and would preserve an independent judiciary. Mindful of the disastrous failures of the previous parliamentary system, Mohammed insisted on a presidential system of government in which the president and vice-president would be popularly elected, have clearly defined powers and draw their legitimacy from all the states of the federation.[78] Finally, General Mohammed called on the committee to draft a constitution which would eliminate the

> cut-throat political competition of the past, create consensus politics based on a community of all interests rather than the interest of sections of the

country and establish the principle of public accountability for all leaders of public office.[79]

The military's transition program thus confronted the winner-take-all attitude of First Republic politicians, whose acrimonious political struggles had brought down the fragile federal structure in 1966. State officials now argued that previous attempts at liberal democracy had been undermined by the narrow interests of regional elites, who had ignored the construction of a viable "democratic political culture" and the promotion of civic values.[80] The constitutional deliberations would therefore seek to transcend the deep ethno-regional, communal, religious and class divisions that had undercut parliamentary democracy during the First Republic.[81] Significantly, Mohammed's preamble made no mention of traditional rulers.

The Constitution Drafting Committee produced a constitution that ushered in civilian rule on October 1, 1979.[82] Following the directives of the FMG, and despite political pressures from powerful titleholders, traditional rulers, for the first time in Nigeria's constitutional history, were formally excluded from the affairs of state. In the CDC's subcommittee on legislative and executive matters, a powerful minority had in fact campaigned for the creation of houses of chiefs in all the nineteen states. Rejecting the proposal, the committee observed that it would

> greatly increase the cost of administration to have a house of chiefs in every state. Were we to recommend a house of chiefs, it would lead to a proliferation of chiefs who have no traditional authority.[83]

The subcommittee, however, did give traditional rulers advisory functions in the state executive councils through the pre-existing institution of the state councils of chiefs. Councils of chiefs could advise governors on local matters such as customary law and chieftaincy affairs.[84] State governors would control these bodies, however, by retaining the power to appoint or dismiss members of the council of chiefs.[85] Similarly, senior traditional rulers were given advisory functions in the federal government through the National Council of State.[86] And, since traditional leaders remained the embodiment of local ideologies and communal identities, this constitutional rebuff did not eliminate the political significance of traditional rulers and title-holders in the post-military era.

The power of local doctrines and cultures, with which indigenous structures and incumbents were so critically linked, was most profoundly expressed in the constitutional debates over state recognition of Sharia (the

Muslim code of religious law).[87] The emotional debate over Sharia brought not only the Northern emirs, but also Islamic clerics into the deliberations of the CDC. With regard to Nigeria's perennial North/South divisions, Sharia became a new political vehicle for the articulation of regional power. By accepting the recommendation of its judiciary subcommittee, which proposed the creation of a Federal Sharia Court of Appeal in the Northern states, the CDC bowed to the formidable campaign mounted by Northern politicians, emirs and clerics, for the incorporation of Islamic law into the national legal system.[88]

In this controversy, which subsequently assumed deeper significance in Nigerian politics, a coalition of Northern leaders demanded that Islamic jurisprudence should enjoy the same authority as the secular, English-derived civil and criminal law. This became a defining issue for particular emirate elements, most notably traditional title-holders and clerics. Christian groups contested such claims. Christian minorities in the Northern states contended that they would be adversely affected, and that this would further undermine the stability of the federation. Opponents also pointed to the need for state neutrality, in a country bedeviled with acrimonious religious, ethno-regional and communal conflicts. Obviously, they failed to convince the CDC.

Despite the show of Northern solidarity, and the radical rhetoric of Islamists, Sharia was fundamentally a marriage of convenience, bringing together emirate elites of quite different ideological persuasions. "Fundamentalist" clerics led by charismatic Islamic scholar Abubakar Gumi, for example, were also challenging the *Masu Sarautas'* (the emirate's aristocracy's) legitimacy, claiming that it was an integral component of a corrupt political class. This was even more important since emirs drew their legitimacy from the unorthodox Sufi Tarika, while Gumi and his followers belonged to an influential minority of orthodox Muslims who had emerged as a formidable force in emirate society.[89]

And so we see the far-reaching ramifications of these comprehensive reforms on chieftaincy structures and social formations in Nigeria as a whole, and in Oyo State in particular. Their consequences are conditioned by the communal doctrines of chieftaincy, the impact of indirect rule, and the configuration of ethno-regional power relations that emerged during the decolonization process. The trend of marginalizing chieftaincy from the affairs of state, while conversely entrenching chiefly power within regional political alliances, was even more apparent after the withdrawal of the Obasanjo regime in October 1979.

8

THE POLITICIANS' INTERREGNUM

Party formation during Nigeria's Second Republic (the second experiment with constitutional democracy, between 1979 and 1983) continued to reflect the entrenched ethno-regionalism and class interests that had surfaced during the era of decolonization. In the Yoruba states this was reflected in the formation of a Yoruba-dominated party, the Unity Party of Nigeria (UPN) in 1979, a process that, in the states of Oyo, Ogun, Ondo, Lagos and, to a lesser extent, Kwara, was further complicated by the realignments that followed the AG crisis of 1962–66. And despite a decade of military reforms, chieftaincy structures also continued to be prominent. Electoral politics by now thus reflected the entrenched politics of regionalism and statism, reinforced by the corporatist style of military rule.

The electoral politics of the Second Republic, we will argue, further consolidated elite power around dominant ethno-regional blocs. The articulation of elite interests through communal and neotraditional ideologies circumvented the limited constitutional reforms imposed by the preceding military regime. After analyzing national and regional political trends, this chapter will return again to the case of Oyo State, confirming the persistence of chieftaincy structures in local and regional politics, reinforced by the propagation of communal doctrines drawn from reconstructed histories, myths, and neotraditional themes. Once again, we can see how the struggle for state power intensified divisions along inter-ethnic and intra-ethnic lines. In Yoruba communities this entailed the persistent manipulation of historic hometown identities, as well as the pan-ethnic political consciousness created during the decolonization process. These alternative interpretations of communal hierarchies and identities informed, indeed permeated, Nigerian politics after 1979.

The Political Context

The constitution which ushered in the Second Republic affirmed the Obasanjo regime's commitment to both federalism and democracy. It vested executive authority in the president of the federation and the nineteen state governors. In a bid to undercut regional power centers, however, the constitution reinforced federal authority at the expense of the states.[1] Legislative powers were vested in a National Assembly of 95 senators (5 members from each of the states) and a 450-member House of Representatives elected on a proportional basis. A House of Assembly was created in each state. Finally, federal and state courts were authorized to interpret laws passed by state legislatures; laws passed by the House of Representatives were subjected only to the federal courts.

The 1979 Constitution thus strengthened an executive presidency within the federal context. But if this was indeed to rationalize federal institutions, it ignored the endemic social contradictions that had plagued Nigeria's diverse communities; it failed to reconceptualize the meaning of governance as expression of the collective good.[2] Democratic institutions thus fell short of the military's rhetoric of progressive change; electoral politics promptly degenerated into the usual horse-trading among regionally based elites. The democratic transition even reinforced the prevailing culture of ethno-regional aggrandizement, encouraged the propagation of communal doctrines, and intensified an already corrosive patrimonial political culture.[3] Richard Joseph has captured this situation with the Weberian concept of prebendalism. In such a system,

> the offices of state are allocated and then exploited as benefices by the office holders [and such practices are] legitimated by a set of political norms according to which the appropriation of such offices is not just an act of individual greed or ambition but concurrently the satisfaction of the short term objectives of a sub-set of the general population.[4]

By the late 1970s, the neopatrimonial system had been progressively embedded in the psyche of Nigeria's regional elites—and to a lesser extent the society at large—for well over three decades. The *modus operandi* of ethno-regional elites was thus to use state agencies as instruments for personal wealth and aggrandizement. The state, in turn, was now held captive by

Table 8-1

Senatorial Election Results, 1979

States	Registered voters	Total votes cast	No. of votes for the political parties				
			GNPP	UPN	NPN	PRP	NPP
Anambra		942,616	12,882	10,932	200,171	19,521	699,157
Bauchi		708,322	188,799	28,959	323,417	127,205	39,868
Bendel		667,721	38,322	316,511	250,194	2,017	60,639
Benue		470,359	46,452	14,925	332,967	2,473	73,524
Borno		516,638	278,352	22,145	184,633	31,508	—
Cross River		603,966	163,953	78,479	310,011	—	51,523
Gongola		600,597	223,121	124,507	203,226	30,708	19,035
Imo		1,016,668	101,184	9,481	145,507	9,978	750,518
Kaduna		1,059,027	232,924	85,094	400,888	278,314	61,807
Kano		946,713	35,530	13,831	233,985	663,367	—
Kwara		406,867	28,874	124,547	248,530	1,950	2,966
Lagos		534,092	14,480	428,578	35,730	2,556	52,748
Niger		319,401	71,498	13,860	275,697	8,139	207
Ogun		461,954	3,078	405,047	53,099	—	730
Ondo		562,375	4,855	501,491	49,612	—	6,417
Oyo		1,010,244	11,292	787,687	200,372	2,497	8,397
Plateau		434,998	21,287	19,624	154,792	19,017	220,278
Rivers		317,889	47,185	20,164	163,463	1,024	86,053
Sokoto		901,768	317,806	34,145	511,562	38,255	—
Total	48,633,782	12,532,195	1,841,854	3,040,006	4,227,756	1,238,712	2,133,867
Percentage		25.7	14.69	24.25	34.13	9.88	17.02

Table 8-2

House of Representatives Election Results, 1979

States	Registered voters	Total votes cast	No. of votes for the political parties				
			GNPP	UPN	NPN	PRP	NPP
Anambra		1,108,771	33,944	18,535	253,979	14,954	787,359
Bauchi		807,210	196,967	27,049	481,581	68,531	33,082
Bendel		903,140	30,420	371,033	426,859	2,167	72,661
Benue		513,359	59,538	13,728	353,551	6,971	79,571
Borno		736,327	390,365	31,558	260,762	46,202	7,440
Cross River		729,667	157,975	94,443	388,354	3,066	85,829
Gongola		668,381	237,548	142,326	231,126	29,973	27,408
Imo		1,162,689	103,993	16,585	223,456	14,128	804,254
Kaduna		1,256,780	253,536	87,947	497,931	362,001	55,365
Kano		1,045,154	26,378	10,804	235,489	772,483	—
Kwara		340,692	33,024	138,359	167,737	841	731
Lagos		595,149	5,703	528,629	56,559	3,186	1,072
Niger		299,712	60,597	13,003	212,944	9,900	3,268
Ogun		612,454	1,841	557,316	53,297	—	—
Ondo		824,759	2,569	755,696	55,688	1,008	9,798
Oyo		1,011,233	10,579	790,580	199,972	3,090	7,012
Plateau		584,167	53,329	22,693	190,562	18,447	299,136
Rivers		491,264	36,480	25,542	287,575	4,314	117,293
Sokoto		1,250,647	455,268	25,757	748,262	21,390	—
Total	48,633,782	14,941,555	2,170,054	3,691,553	5,325,684	1,382,712	2,391,279
Percentage		31.0	14.52	24.57	35.64	9.25	16.00

Table 8-3

Gubernatorial Election Results, 1979

States	Registered voters	Total votes cast	No. of votes for the political parties					
			GNPP	UPN	NPN	PRP	NPP	
Anambra	1,016,065		21,136	6,735	187,388	28,790	772,061	
Bauchi	821,028		208,845	25,624	438,016	132,766	18,777	
Bendel	767,288		—	386,758	279,599	5,844	57,756	
Benue	536,367		23,947	12,323	404,438	9,021	88,290	
Borno	697,948		385,340	19,507	45,560	40,480	6,605	
Cross River	710,536		159,592	80,863	428,089	—	46,615	
Gongola	650,775		309,775	72,982	225,310	15,973	26,715	
Imo	1,094,303		59,163	7,400	122,331	20,500	881,499	
Kaduna	1,242,090		129,580	—	551,252	560,605	—	
Kano	1,151,240		14,804	8,568	218,751	909,118	—	
Kwara	362,643			174,415	188,228			
Lagos	685,875		4,049	559,070	45,572	3,335	67,594	
Niger	335,202		65,822	10,448	248,463	10,469	—	
Ogun	687,504		—	643,229	44,275	—	—	
Ondo	1,062,985		—	1,007,491	48,975	—	6,485	
Oyo	1,134,680		7,306	955,138	163,460	—	5,527	
Plateau	585,588		19,220	10,294	174,708	17,526	412,112	
Rivers	805,330		7,406	6,227	619,575	2,388	169,594	
Sokoto	1,383,508		422,381	—	768,618	33,042	—	
Total	48,633,782	15,730,895	1,838,366	3,987,072	5,402,746	1,789,857	2,559,630	
Percentage		32.35	11.69	25.35	34.34	11.38	16.27	

Table 8-4
Presidential Election Results, 1979

States	Registered voters	Total votes cast	Turn-out (%)	No. of votes for the political parties									
				GNPP		UPN		NPN		PRP		NPP	
				No.	%	No.	%	No.	%	No.	%	No.	%
Anambra	2,606,663	1,209,038	46.38	20,228	1.67	9,063	0.75	163,164	13.50	14,500	1.20	1,002,083	82.88
Bauchi	2,096,162	998,683	47.64	154,218	16.44	29,960	3.00	623,989	62.48	143,202	14.34	47,314	4.74
Bendel	2,400,174	669,511	27.89	8,242	1.20	356,381	53.20	242,320	36.20	4,939	0.70	57,629	8.60
Benue	1,636,371	538,879	32.93	42,993	7.97	13,864	2.57	411,648	76.38	7,277	1.35	63,097	11.77
Borno	2,945,925	710,968	24.13	384,278	54.04	23,885	3.35	246,778	34.71	46,385	6.52	9,642	1.35
Cross River	2,464,184	661,103	26.83	100,105	15.04	77,775	11.76	425,815	64.40	6,737	1.01	50,671	7.66
Gongola	2,308,355	639,138	27.69	217,914	34.09	138,561	21.67	327,057	35.52	27,750	4.34	27,856	4.35
Imo	3,490,484	1,153,355	33.04	34,616	3.00	7,335	0.64	101,516	8.80	10,252	0.59	999,636	84.69
Kaduna	3,455,047	1,382,712	40.02	190,936	14.00	92,382	7.00	596,302	43.00	437,771	31.00	65,321	5.00
Kano	5,266,598	1,195,136	22.87	18,482	1.54	14,973	1.23	243,423	19.94	932,803	76.41	11,081	0.91
Kwara	1,108,029	354,605	32.00	20,251	5.71	140,006	37.48	190,142	53.62	2,376	0.67	1,830	0.52
Lagos	1,829,369	828,414	45.28	3,943	0.48	681,762	82.30	59,515	7.18	3,874	0.47	79,320	9.57
Niger	1,051,160	383,347	36.47	63,273	16.60	14,155	3.67	287,072	74.88	14,555	3.77	45,292	1.11
Ogun	1,663,608	744,668	44.76	3,974	0.53	689,655	92.61	46,358	6.23	2,338	0.31	2,343	0.32
Ondo	2,573,960	1,384,788	53.80	3,561	0.26	1,294,666	94.50	57,361	4.19	2,500	0.18	11,572	0.86
Oyo	4,534,779	1,396,547	30.80	8,029	0.57	1,197,883	85.78	177,999	12.75	4,804	0.32	7,732	0.55
Plateau	1,748,868	548,405	31.36	37,400	6.82	29,029	5.29	190,458	34.72	21,852	3.98	269,666	49.70
Rivers	1,675,934	687,951	41.05	15,025	2.18	71,194	10.33	499,840	72.65	3,312	0.46	98,574	14.35
Sokoto	3,818,094	1,348,697	35.32	359,021	26.61	34,102	2.52	898,094	66.58	44,977	3.33	12,503	0.92
Total	48,633,782	16,846,633		1,686,489		4,916,651		5,688,857		1,732,113		2,133,867	
Percentage			34.64		10.01		29.18		33.77		10.28		16.75

regional political classes devoted largely to unbridled patronage. In a sort of vicious circle, the system's obsessive focus on regional power relations heightened the salience of communal doctrines that, in turn, either reinforced or challenged major ethno-regional centers of power.

In this communally competitive setting, traditional rulers and titleholders were once again key elements in political parties and alliances. Under intense centrifugal pressures, regional politicians embraced indigenous political institutions as the local symbols and custodians of ethno-regional interests. As was the case during the First Republic, traditional rulers who supported the dominant federal party instead of their ruling state party (when the two were not the same) were persecuted by state authorities. When these problems occurred, federal party officials tried to protect their local allies as best they could. But since state executive committees retained statutory authority over chieftaincy matters, the federal government's interventions were usually limited by law.

"National" Political Parties: Forging Old and New Alliances

Political parties in Nigeria's Second Republic had their roots in the political alignments of the earlier parliamentary regime. Aware of the deep divisions between and within the major regions, and hoping to undermine alternative centers of power, succeeding military regimes had curtailed party politics at the local level. The Ironsi regime, for instance, after the January 1966 coup, had banned the organizations that had traditionally dominated Nigerian postwar politics. The regime's Decree 33 of 1966 abolished eight political associations, and later that year Ironsi's successor, Yakubu Gowon, proscribed another twenty-six cultural groups suspected of clandestine political ties. Successive national and state military administrations upheld these decrees during the next thirteen years of military rule.[5] Despite these legal constraints on party activities, neither former politicians nor new aspirants were deterred; they simply went underground in preparation for the eventual return to democratic civilian rule.[6] Partisanship remained embedded in ethno-regional groups and organizations.

The persistence of these groups in regional and national politics had been prefigured in the crisis preceding the Civil War. The Gowon administration's peace initiatives included an embrace of regional powerbrokers as "leaders of thought"[7] (see chapter 5); ethnic-based politicians could thus reconstitute the old political alliances of the independence period. Encouraged by the temporary character of military intervention, politicians formed regionally based coalitions in anticipation of civilian rule. In the West, one such association was the Committee of Friends, which rallied Action Group (AG) loyalists under the leadership of Obafemi Awolowo. It was rooted in the political realignments that followed the AG crisis of 1962; this, in turn, mobilized support for the new Yoruba political party, the Unity Party of Nigeria (UPN), in 1979. Bola Ige, one of its most dedicated members, had served as AG publicity secretary during the crisis of 1962–66; he was elected UPN governor of Oyo State in 1979. Three other important Committee members and AG politicians—Lateef Jakande, Bisi Onabanjo and Michael Ajasin—became UPN governors of Lagos, Ogun and Ondo States respectively.

A number of other stalwarts of the Committee of Friends had gone on to influential positions under various state and federal military regimes in the 1960s and 1970s. These included D. S. Adegbenro, acting leader of the AG 1963–1966; Michael Omisade, a well-known Ife politician; J. S. Olawoyin, the political boss of Offa in Kwara State; and the renowned economist, Sam Aluko. Awolowo himself, as Federal Commissioner for Finance and Vice-Chairman of the Federal Executive Council in the Gowon administration from 1967 to 1971, held the highest post given to a civilian during the period. Indeed, Ige, Onabanjo, Omisade and Adegbenro were all civilian commissioners in the Western State Military Government of Major General Adeyinka Adebayo. All of these men used their influential position in the state executive to advance AG interests in sensitive regional issues such as the appointment of the Alaafin of Oyo (at issue in 1968–72) and the Agbekoya crisis of 1973 (see chapter 6). And other group members, Aluko and Tajudeen Idris, served with Ige on the Mohammed/ Obasanjo Constitution Drafting Committee (CDC) from 1975 to 1977.[8]

Other southern political blocs, similarly rooted in the politics of the First Republic, were also reconstituting their power base in the late 1970s. In the southwest and southeast, respectively, the Progressives of Lagos and the Progressives of Eastern Nigeria formed an alliance that reflected what was left of the proscribed NCNC coalition of the old Western, Mid-Western and Eastern Regions.[9] The Lagos and Eastern Progressives merged in May 1978 to form the Committee for National Unity and Progress (CNUP). This coalition later became the Southern wing of the Nigerian People's Party (NPP).[10] Like the Committee of Friends, these organizations merged the experience of an older generation of party leaders with the political aspirations of a new cohort of influential Igbo (and a minority of Yoruba) businessmen and civil servants. The CNUP, however—unlike the Committee of Friends, where Obafemi Awolowo was the towering figure—lacked a charismatic leading figure. Nnamdi Azikiwe, who had enjoyed a comparable status in the NCNC, initially had misgivings about returning to party politics. However, and despite the objection of a formidable Northern ally, the Kanuri political stalwart, Waziri Ibrahim—Azikiwe did later join the NPP, becoming its presidential candidate in 1979.[11] Ibrahim went on to form a separate party, the Great Nigerian People's Party (GNPP).

In the Northern states, too, pre-existing political associations were to provide an organizational base for the construction of parties in 1978. Most prominent of these was the National Movement, precursor to the National Party of Nigeria (NPN), which was to win the federal elections of 1979 and 1983. Although the NPN later embraced a diverse coalition of regional and class interests, few doubt its descent from the former Northern Peoples Congress (NPC), and from the political traditions set down by the Sardauna of Sokoto, Sir Ahmadu Bello.[12] The National Movement reflected an alliance of powerful emirs with a younger generation of influential northern civil servants and businessmen[13] that had emerged during the military era. Although the movement was a formidable alliance of old and new guards from major emirate towns, it also incorporated prominent Yoruba, Igbo and Edo politicians, as well as prominent ethnic minorities.[14] Southern members of the coalition fell into two major groups. One was made up of prominent politicians drawn from the Igbo, the Edo of Bendel State, and ethnic minorities of the Niger delta area. The other consisted of former Yoruba NNDP politicians, who retreated to the safety of their former alliance with the NPC.[15] Among these were A. M. A. Akinloye, the native-Ibadan AG regional minister of the 1950s who turned to the NNDP during the AG crisis of 1962–1966, and Remi Fani-Kayode, the charismatic NNDP deputy-premier of the First Republic. Thanks to a carefully crafted regional "zoning" regulation, Akinloye was elected national chairman of the NPN in 1978. Another prominent Ibadan native, Richard Akinjide, a successful barrister and Tafawa Balewa's Federal Minister of Education, ran unsuccessfully for the Oyo State governorship in 1979; he was then appointed Attorney-General and Minister for Justice by NPN President Shehu Shagari.

Finally, drawing from the radical traditions of the Northern Elements Progressive Union (NEPU), Northern socialists led by political newcomers Abubakar Rimi, Balarabe Musa, and Bala Usman formed the Second Republic's only socialist party, the People's Redemption Party (PRP). Former NEPU leader Mallam Aminu Kano was later elected party leader, following a frustrating membership in the National Movement. The PRP became the vehicle through which Northern Nigeria's deepening social contradictions were expressed.[16] As we shall see, its radicalism had profound consequences for the Northern power structure, especially the traditional aristocracy, during the Second Republic.[17]

These ethno-regional organizations provided the foundation on which the major Second Republic parties were subsequently established. With the exception of the PRP's commitment to a socialist ideology (and, to a lesser extent, the Committee of Friends' embrace of social democratic principles), the parties were ensconced in the familiar ethno-regional calculations that had dominated national politics since the regionalization process of 1951. Three months after the lifting of the ban on party politics (21 September, 1978), numerous parties were launched. Most were no more than local cliques with little regional, not to speak of national appeal; in the end, nineteen applied for registration with the Federal Electoral Commission (FEDECO).[18] Of these, only five met the FMG's guidelines to contest the 1979 election. These were the NPN, the NPP, the GNPP, the PRP, and the UPN. A sixth party—the Nigerian Advance Party (NAP), under the leadership of Lagos barrister Tunji Braithwaite—was not registered until 1982.

As we shall observe, the underlying characteristics of these parties, the principles of political mobilization that they reflected, were to have severe consequences for Nigeria's democratic transition. Political scientist Ian Shapiro has noted the implications of such alignments for fragile states:

> In reality, political parties, trades unions, business organizations, churches, and the military contain various fissures that may be more or less latent. As the political terrain begins to shift during a transition, these fissures come under pressure of various kinds, and different players try to exploit them. The effects, while often impossible to predict, can be massively consequential for democracy's future.[19]

In the Nigerian case, these fissures and alliances had been gradually shaped by the mounting political competition of the colonial and postcolonial period. As in the past, the consolidation of elite power through the political parties operated through the appropriation of myths and neotraditional themes, and the mobilization of followers along ethno-regional and communal lines.

The UPN: Chieftaincy Politics and Communal Identities

The Unity Party of Nigeria (UPN), like its precursor, the AG, drew the bulk of its support from the Yoruba states of Lagos, Oyo, Ogun and Ondo, which it won in the 1979 elections. It also prevailed in the largely Edo, Itsekiri and Urhobo areas of Bendel state, where the party won both the gubernatorial and legislative elections.[20] The UPN also emerged as a strong legislative opposition in Gongola and Kwara states. Predictably, given the bitter political legacy of the previous electoral era, the party met with complete failure in the Igbo states of Anambra and Imo, and in the Northern states of Bauchi, Kano, Niger, Plateau and Sokoto.[21]

The UPN's successes and failures revolved around the imposing personality of Awolowo, who, when the party was formally launched on 22 September 1978, emerged as the most prominent and controversial politician in Nigeria. Both allies and opponents gave considerable thought to Awolowo's influence. UPN victories in Lagos, Oyo, Ogun, Ondo and Bendel states can be attributed to Awolowo's personal popularity and the strategy he devised for the party. Richard Joseph observes that UPN political strategies were "abstractions of Awolowo," constructed with the assistance of trusted allies who had proven their loyalty since the AG crisis. The party's organizational structure and its manifesto reflected Awolowo's vision and superior administrative skills, already evident in the 1950s when he was head of government business in the Western Region. The UPN's hierarchical structure extended downwards from Awolowo, the personification of the party, to trusted lieutenants in each of the nineteen states and, finally, to younger activists who enthusiastically espoused the leader's ideals at the local level.[22]

Under the firm control of a man as popular as Awolowo, the party had little need to commit itself on the sensitive issue of chieftaincy. Its strategy in the formative months of 1978 and 1979 thus differed significantly from that pursued by its predecessor, the AG, in the early 1950s. While the AG had relied heavily on the obas' patronage in the earlier pan-Yoruba cultural organization, the *Egbe Omo Oduduwa*, by 1978 the UPN had effectively consolidated its regional power base. Reliance on such an ethnic-based cultural organization had become unnecessary. Nonetheless, pan-ethnic themes still featured significantly in Yoruba politics. For example, the deployment of a pan-Yoruba doctrine had progressed from the quasi-institutional platform of the earlier Egbe to various political slogans, such as the popular Yoruba saying in the 1979 election campaigns: *Ti wa ni tiwa*, meaning "what is ours, is definitely ours."

The fact that an ethnic strategy no longer focused on chieftaincy institutions can also be attributed to the generation gap between Awolowo and the younger obas, most of whom were appointed in the 1970s. As head of the regional government in the 1950s, Awolowo had dealt directly with the previous generation of obas. For example, he was premier during the conflict between the AG and Alaafin Adeyemi II (father of Oba Lamidi Adeyemi III), which eventually led to the deposition of the former in 1956. Given the Yorubas' deference to age, most obas held the elder statesman in high esteem, and Awolowo himself, who had assumed the title of Asiwaju (leader of the Yorubas), was careful not to antagonize them. It was left to the UPN state governors who had direct access to state executive powers to perform such tasks, usually with the approval of their leader.

Despite Awolowo's popularity, chieftaincy was still critical for the UPN. Awolowo himself had noted, during the 1979 elections, that while towns-people might reject an individual oba, they remained respectful of the in-stitution of obaship. In a vague reference to chieftaincy he said that "a good politician, as the representative of the people, should support any institu-tion which is respected by the people."[23] Like the AG before it, the UPN, in the five states it eventually controlled, promoted the status of coopera-tive obas while undermining those it considered recalcitrant. The party's success, however, depended on more substantive issues that reinforced the prevailing Yoruba political consciousness.

The UPN staked its claim to legitimacy among the Yorubas on three major themes: a social democratic ideology, Awolowo's undisputed leader-ship, and a loosely defined pan-Yoruba doctrine. Ethnic cohesiveness, in turn, was reinforced by Nigeria's entrenched ethno-regionalism, the domi-nant personality of Awolowo, and the support of obas, local elders and the Yoruba commercial and bureaucratic elites. And, as in the AG's formative years, party leaders projected the institution of obaship—and, more spe-cifically, the myth of Oduduwa—as the ultimate expression of a pan-eth-nic (Yoruba) identity. De-emphasizing the Yoruba crisis of the nineteenth century, the AG strategy had embraced Ile-Ife as the central symbol of Yoruba ethnic cohesion: Ile-Ife, the site of the formation of the *Egbe Omo Oduduwa*, the appointment of Ooni Aderemi as the first indigenous gover-nor of the Western Region, and the establishment of a regional university. As we shall see this strategy also enhanced the prestige of the incumbent Ooni of Ife at the expense of Oyo's Alaafin. In any case, this welding of a reconstructed past to more recent political developments helped secure Yoruba support for the UPN. As Dudley observes, the UPN, with some justification, could be taken as a re-creation of the AG; in 1979 it won more than 80 % of the votes in the states that formed the Western Region in 1959.[24]

Adopting broad electoral strategies is one thing. Administering a re-gion with a long history of communal conflicts is quite another. Oyo State during the Second Republic provides a case in point. Competing elite interests were expressed in rival versions of neotraditional themes, deployed in favor of, or in opposition to, the state government. Like other UPN leaders, Bola Ige—Oyo State governor between 1979 and 1982—attempted to consolidate the UPN's gains through pan-ethnic ideological appeals. As in the past, however, the loose mythological construction of a pan-Yoruba identity actually favored the interests of certain individuals or groups at the expense of others, giving rise to new schisms and alliances.

With these problems in mind, Governor Ige made efforts both to demonstrate his respect for the institution of obaship and to unify the obas under UPN leadership. In an address delivered to the State Council of Chiefs in October 1980, for example, he stated that his government "will enhance the dignity and honor of the institution of obaship. . . . because to do so is not only in keeping with the history of the Yoruba people, but also enlisting your co-operation in the implementation of my government's political, social and economic program."[25] After announcing a new package of salaries and benefits for obas and baales, state authorities admonished them to support government policies in their communities.[26]

As in the First Republic, UPN politicians elevated allies, while undermining opponents who favored the opposition NPN. The relations between the new Ooni of Ife, Oba Sijuade II, and the Alaafin of Oyo, Oba Lamidi Adeyemi III, vividly illustrates this common trend. In this episode, interpretations of hierarchical relationships were again evoked to further modern political objectives. Less than a year after his gubernatorial victory, in September 1980, Ige appointed the Ooni permanent chairman of the Oyo State Council of Chiefs.[27] Indeed, while announcing the government's approval of the Ooni-elect, Deputy-Governor Sunday Afolabi had declared that state chairmanship of the Council of Chiefs would automatically accompany the Ooni's coronation. These policies were based on the presumed seniority of the Ooni among all Yoruba obas,[28] drawn from the myth of Oduduwa as founder of the Yoruba nation.

By tying Yoruba ethnic unity to the Ile-Ife crown, state policy embraced a popular but contentious mythology. Arguments for the special status of the Ile-Ife crown had been common at least since colonial times. Commenting on Ooni Aderemi's earlier claims to pre-eminence, Law notes:

> The position of Ile-Ife as the acknowledged cradle of all the royal dynasties of the surrounding kingdoms would seem to imply a special, paramount status for the Ooni of Ife, the occupant of the ancestral throne. This was certainly the view of the Oonis themselves. Aderemi, the present Ooni of Ife

(colonial era), claims that when Oduduwa, shortly before his death, bestowed crowns on his sons, he first crowned his eldest son as Ooni of Ife, and ordered his other sons, the founders of the other kingdoms, to show filial obedience to their eldest brother. In consequence, according to Aderemi, the Ooni is still regarded by his younger brothers as their father.[29]

But when Ooni Aderemi informed Ekiti obas of his "paternal" status during a visit to Ekiti towns in 1936, Ekiti obas repudiated the claim, contending that "just as the Ooni was on the throne of his father, so also were they on the thrones of theirs."[30] However, it was the claims made by several Alaafins that provided the most consistent opposition to the Ooni's claims to pre-eminence.[31] Predictably, this historical rivalry was seized upon by pro-Alaafin politicians opposed to the UPN.

The policy thus revived the traditional rivalry between the Ile-Ife and Oyo crowns.[32] In the pro-UPN newspaper the *Daily Sketch*, local Ife historians led by the Odole Atobase of Ile-Ife, Chief M. A. Fabunmi, defended the state government's policy. "According to tradition," Fabunmi wrote, "the position of the Ooni of Ife *vis-à-vis* all other obas in Yorubaland is that of a father."[33] Conversely, drawing support from the opposition party, the NPN, Oyo hometown elites formed the Oyo Traditional Defense Committee, with Chief Raji Badmus, the Orunto of Oyo, as chairman. The committee refuted the government's claims in the pro-NPN newspaper, the *National Concord*. In one rejoinder, Chief Badmus dismissed Chief Fabunmi's argument as an expression of "political fanaticism and subservience to wealth."[34]

Despite the press debate the state government remained resolute, appointing the Ooni of Ife as permanent chairman of the Council of Chiefs. And it also threw the gauntlet to the opposition. At an emergency meeting of the Council, Governor Ige warned that "any oba having ambition or any oba who wants to involve himself in politics, any politics, is welcome to do so. . . . [W]e will take such obas on."[35] Ige further cautioned that,

> When the tiger treads softly, as you our fathers say, it is not because he is afraid. . . . [A]ny oba who is flexing his muscles for a fight does not know this government. . . . [I]t is the state government and not such traditional rulers that will choose the time, place, weapon and pattern of the fight, the battle and the war.[36]

Two weeks later a majority of the Council objected to the state government's policy. They declared that as direct descendants of Oduduwa, it is our duty which should not be taken away from us, to select our own chairman from among the ranks. . . . [T]he statement of government policy on it should reflect our unanimous choice duly presented to government and such choice will form a proper basis for governmental ratification. . . . We finally request that until this is done by us the government should avoid anything that could lead to any misunderstanding.[37]

Despite these objections, the state government stood firm. The Ooni remained the permanent chairman until January 1987 when a state military government dissolved the council.

In another attempt to promote the Ooni's prestige, state authorities declared in March 1981 that in his capacity of supreme "paramount ruler", the Ooni had the right to perform the coronation of Prince Tijani Abimbola Oyedokun as the Okere of Shaki. Shaki, however, was located in the Ifedapo Local Government Area, traditionally an Oyo provincial town. The Alaafin's supporters thus argued that it was Oba Adeyemi who had a legitimate claim to perform this rite. Opposition politicians also pointed to state chieftaincy law, which recognized the Alaafin as the consenting authority of the Okere of Shaki Chieftaincy, the approving authority in the appointment of the Okere-elect, the chairman of the Ifedapo Local Government Chieftaincy Committee and the president of the Traditional Council for Oyo North and South (where Shaki town is located). These statutory regulations, however, had little impact on state policy.[38]

These struggles were linked to another important conflict in Oyo town—a protracted dispute between Oba Adeyemi and the *Ashipa*, a senior Oyomesi chief. The origin of this conflict is rather complicated, and cannot be fully discussed here. What is relevant for our purposes is that it too became an instrument of partisanship, drawing the attention of prominent Oyo UPN and NPN functionaries. The conflict thus became a channel through which influential hometown elites, whether resident or nonresident, mobilized local support.[39]

The situation in Ilesha was quite different. There, the UPN had suffered a controversial defeat in 1983. When the Owa of Ilesha, Oba Aromolaran, then switched support to the NPN, he put himself at odds with Ijesha chiefs and elites who remained loyal to the UPN. The claim has been made that it was this that prompted the voluntary exile of the Owa in the early 1980s.[40] These stories of ambivalence and conflict in Oyo State, however, should not obscure the generally amicable relations between the UPN government and the obas. For example, the UPN was very close to the Ataoja of Oshogbo, Oba Matanmi, and to the Eleruwa of Eruwa, Oba

Gbojumola, whom Governor Ige appointed commissioner without portfolio and his special advisor in October 1980.

In other UPN-controlled states of Lagos, Ogun, Ondo and Bendel, obas were also under pressure to promote the interests of the ruling party. Obas who cooperated were once again rewarded with state recognition and occasionally with patronage. Conversely, obas that embraced the NPN were either ignored or persecuted. In Lagos state, UPN Governor Lateef Jakande appointed an ally, the Onisolo of Isolo, a relatively minor oba, as chairman of the state Council of Chiefs. This displaced the Oba of Lagos, Oba Oyekan, who in the First Republic was a well-known figure in the NCNC. The Ogun State government took more stringent measures against uncooperative chiefs. The Awujale of Ijebuland, Oba Adetona, encountered the disapproval of the UPN Ogun State authorities, presumable because of his pro-NPN stance. The Awujale observed in December 1979 that

> my experience in the membership of the council [of chiefs] was that of a political organ to rubber-stamp government plans to depose any oba or chief. Of course, any advice from us that did not agree with the wishes of the government of the day was always ignored.[41]

In fact, Oba Adetona was at the center of a confrontation with officials of the Ijebu-Ode UPN in 1981. The issue which brought the conflict to a head was the oba's alleged cancellation of the *Agemo* and *Obirin Ojowu* festivals in July 1981. Party leaders who opposed the Awujale contend that the Oba's decision was taken because the festivals provided townspeople with a critical forum through which they could express their opposition.[42]

UPN chieftaincy policies in Ondo and Bendel were generally more conciliatory, since most obas kept a safe distance from the opposition NPN. In an attempt to consolidate his government's control on traditional rulers, Governor Ajasin gave several minor obas, particularly those in Ekiti Division, the right to wear beaded crowns, a symbol of authority usually reserved for senior obas. In Bendel State, Governor Ambrose Alli appointed the influential Oba of Benin, Omo N'Oba Erediauwa, as special adviser to the state government. The case of the Oba of Benin provides a good example of a major traditional ruler whose influence with the UPN authority grew out of his special ties with the dominant bureaucratic and commercial elite, as well as from his unquestionable popularity with Benin chiefs, elders, elites and townspeople.[43]

In the UPN-controlled states, therefore, obas, like their counterparts elsewhere, reinforced the power base of the dominant ethno-party elite.

Obas who opposed the UPN had to contend with maneuvers that undermined their local influence. The political context of patronage, power and status in which the obas had functioned in the 1950s and 1960s had intensified, given the impact of the "petrol dollar" in the 1980s. Electoral politics further reinforced a clientelist structure through which obas projected their influence as intermediaries and brokers. As P. J. Dixon aptly notes, the Yoruba oba operates as

> the center of a distributive network of whatever 'resources' he has control over and struggles to place himself in a position to distribute patronage.[44]

Popular expectations were also a factor here: townspeople did regard their obas as critical links to social services, development projects, and other formulation of favorable policies. Regional comparisons reveal striking parallels with the Yoruba case, and, more importantly, bring out the implications of the configuration of power by dominant ethno-regional political elites in the Second Republic.

The Neotraditional Foundations of the NPN

Cooperation between traditional rulers and politicians was equally crucial in the formation of the National Party of Nigeria (NPN) in 1978 and 1979. As discussed earlier, the NPN was a loose coalition of the Northern Islamic aristocracy, former NPC partisans, Northern bureaucratic and commercial elites, and some Southern allies from the First Republic, who opposed the UPN or the NPP in their home states.[45] Despite this complex network of alliances, the NPN was firmly anchored to the *Masu Sarauta*, the Hausa-Fulani emirate structure. It is significant that the party was formed when emirs and other regional dignitaries assembled in Sokoto to celebrate the fortieth anniversary of Sir Abubakar III as the Sultan of Sokoto and Sarkin Musulmi.[46] Furthermore, prominent title-holders, such as Ibrahim Dasuki, Baraden Sokoto (later Sultan), and Shehu Malami, Sarkin Sudan of Wurno, played critical roles in the formative months before the 1979 elections. The Makaman Bida, one of the emirates' most important traditional chiefs and trusted adviser of the Sardauna of Sokoto, was also elected grand patron of the party in 1978. *West Africa's* editor, David Williams, who had referred to the Makaman "as a tough traditionalist," underscored his crucial role in Shehu Shagari's nomination as presidential candidate in 1979.[47] It is equally noteworthy that emirs and chiefs were charged with the task of solving conflicts among party leaders during the preceding months. The Madaki of Kano, Shehu Ahmed, for example, was one of many prominent title-holders who periodically intervened in NPN disputes.[48] While traditional rulers were not expected to play active roles in election campaigns, they were nevertheless encouraged to give their quiet approval to NPN candidates. In an insider account of the NPN, senior party official Uba Ahmed showed how NPN campaigns, conversely, were crafted to accommodate traditional authorities:

> candidates (especially presidential and gubernatorial) were ingeniously encouraged by the party to make the traditional rulers their station of first call on all electoral tours. And branch leaders made it a point to be on, as much as possible at the best terms with local traditional institutions and leadership.[49]

Once in control of state power, NPN governors and officials underscored the traditional rulers' role in the preservation of political stability and the maintenance of law and order. It was not unusual, for example, for Shehu Shagari—in his official capacity as president of the federation and as the Turakin in the Sultan's court—to pay courtesy calls on senior emirs, obas, obongs and obis; indeed, some of these visits led to the conferral of prestigious national awards on local potentates. In one important case Shagari conferred the Commander of the Federal Republic of Nigeria (Nigeria's highest award) on the Oba of Benin. He used the occasion to remind traditional rulers of their special role:

> Traditional rulers have a significant role to play in promoting and sustaining national harmony among the diverse people of this country. As the repository of traditional values, we shall always count on their understanding and co-operation. We shall certainly draw from their rich experience and collective wisdom. In the past, traditional rulers have played decisive roles by rendering wise counsel in time of need. It is my hope that as we move forward in our new constitutional evolution, they will continue to play constructive roles in ensuring the success of the new administration by joining hands with all the governments of the federation to promote the welfare of our people and sustain our democratic institutions.[50]

These comments were followed by a declaration of policy: Shagari announced that if re-elected, his government would undertake a constitutional review in order to grant statutory powers to traditional rulers.[51] This pledge, however, was pre-empted by the military coup of 1 January 1984.

Thus, like the UPN in the Yoruba states, the viability of the NPN, especially in its formative years, depended on the political alliances that dominated Nigerian politics in the First Republic. In the upper North, this legacy was based on the formidable alliance between the *Masu Sarauta* and a commercial and bureaucratic elite who had consolidated power through the domination of state agencies under military rule. This formidable regional alliance became a winning coalition when it embraced Southern allies who, largely because of the deep divisions of the past, rejected the dominant ethno-regional parties in their states.

The PRP, NPP and GNPP States

As would be expected from a socialist party in a region that combines entrenched quasi-feudal traditions with the populist resistance of Hausa *talakawa* commoners,[52] the Peoples' Redemption Party (PRP) mounted a fierce assault against the emirate structure and their modern allies who controlled federal and state bureaucracies. Dismissing the *Masu Sarauta* (the Islamic aristocracy) as feudalistic and anachronistic, PRP governors Abubakar Rimi of Kano State and Balarabe Musa of Kaduna State used the full weight of their office to challenge what northern radicals had long considered the excesses of the emirate structure from 1979 to 1983.[53] A seminar in 1980 organized by the Kaduna State Council for Arts and Culture (a Kaduna State government agency) typifies the perspective of the PRP. In the typical rhetoric of the Nigerian left, the council declared that emirs and chiefs,

> by virtue of their being members of the ruling bourgeoisie, are no longer traditional. These so-called traditional rulers are nothing more than a category of capitalist exploiters of the peasantry. . . . In addition, as an integral part of the bourgeoisie, these so-called traditional authorities have outlived their usefulness and should cease to exist as a separate protected sub-class.[54]

Once in power, the PRP governors attempted to withdraw the privileges of emirs and district heads. In Kaduna State, Governor Musa, who had to govern with a NPN-controlled state legislature, struck a temporary blow to emirate authority by abolishing the feudal *jangali* and *haraji* taxes in 1980. The PRP was divided on ideological grounds by the end of 1980,[55] and was confronted by formidable NPN opposition in the House of Assembly. Musa's assault on the emirate structure was thus short-lived, and he was impeached in 1981. Since Abubakar Rimi governed with a PRP-controlled legislature, his attack on the emirs, most notably the pro-NPN Emir of Kano, Alhaji Ado Bayero, was more effective. The animosity between

Rimi and Emir Ado Bayero in 1980 and 1981 deserves a brief discussion here. Armed with executive authority, Rimi relieved Emir Bayero of some of his powers as Kano State's pre-eminent traditional ruler, and undermined the hierarchical structure through which Alhaji Bayero maintained control over subordinate emirs, districts heads, chiefs, Islamic clerics and so on. And when the emir opposed these policies, Rimi took even greater punitive measures against Alhaji Bayero, banning all the customary greetings that district heads and chiefs would offer to the Emir of Kano during important Muslim festivals such as Sallah.[56] NPN opposition politicians in the state legislature jumped to the Emir's defense, condemning the government's action as "provocative and obnoxious." Rimi countered, claiming his actions reflected "the philosophy of the PRP and the 1979 Constitution."[57] In 1981, furthermore, without consulting senior emirs, Rimi appointed several district heads as first-class chiefs. This was the last straw. A wave of riots that claimed many lives (including one of Rimi's trusted aides, Bala Mohammed) erupted in Kano City. Confronted with a major crisis, Rimi abandoned his initial attempt to discipline the emir. Here we see the limits of sheer electoral success; despite his apparent popularity among the talakawa, Rimi seemed to have underestimated the powerful local network at the disposal of the Emir.

The radical PRP policies in Kaduna and Kano states should not, however, be mistaken for an all-out attack by socialists state officials against conservative aristocrats. PRP politicians could better be seen as reluctant to embrace traditional leaders, of whom radicals within the party were strongly critical. This ambiguity was apparent in the PRP's manifesto, which acknowledged "natural rulers with a social conscience" to be legitimate leaders of talakawa commoners that the party defined as "the salt of the earth and the driving force of history." Moreover, despite their radical opposition to the Masu Sarauta, and their conflict with more conservative elements in the PRP, such as party president Aminu Kano, Governors Musa and Rimi were also devoted Muslims; they recognized liberating aspects of their religion, and were mindful of the dangers of applying a straightforward socialist ideology to the complex social, political and religious conditions of the emirates. Indeed, Mallam Aminu Kano's popularity in Kano stemmed from his superior understanding of these complexities.[58] His distinguished thirty-year career exemplified both a genuine commitment to the talakawa, and occasional embrace of individual emirs, chiefs and Islamic leaders.[59] As Northern Elements Progressive Union (NEPU) leader, Mallam Aminu had once defended an earlier Emir of Kano, Alhaji Sanussi, when he was persecuted by Premier Ahmadu Bello.[60]

The GNPP—which controlled two Northern states, Gongola and Bornu—lacked a coherent policy towards emirs and chiefs. Nevertheless, it mounted a vigorous campaign against individual emirs who favored the opposition NPN, while seeking to bring chieftaincy institutions under its firm control. In Bornu State for instance, Governor Mohammed Gomi transferred the emirs' power to appoint district heads to state local authorities. Events in Bade Emirate immediately after the 1979 elections show how intense partisanship complicated state policy in Bornu. Gomi's decision to overrule the selection of a pro-NPN candidate, Yerima Saleh, as the Mai of Bade, and appoint in his place his brother, a GNPP sympathizer, led to riots which claimed many lives. Although a 1980 court decision reinstated Yerima Saleh as emir, Gomi carved a new emirate, Jakusko, out of Bade Emirate, appointing his favorite candidate there as emir. It was not until the NPN victory in 1983 that a new state government would relegate Jakusko to district status, demoting the GNPP emir to district head.[61]

In the Igbo states of Anambra and Imo, finally, where military rule had consolidated a new generation of Igbo leaders after the Biafran War, aspiring politicians also sought the blessings of influential chiefs in the 1979 election campaigns. Politicians from the two major parties, the NPP and the NPN, sought the endorsement of traditional rulers and chiefs. Chiefs took full advantage of their revived status as local powerbrokers, throwing their support to allies who would reward them in turn.[62] Governors Jim Nwobodo and Sam Mbakwe, for instance, promoted the status of supportive chiefs, and the overall importance of chieftaincy was reflected in the NPP's creation of ministries of chieftaincy affairs, and the appointment of a special adviser on chieftaincy matters to the Imo state governor in 1980.[63] Conversely, opposition chiefs were penalized: in Anambra, Nwobodo removed the Obi of Onitsha as chairman of the state Council of Chiefs, presumably for his pro-NPN stance; and in Imo state, Mbakwe replaced eight uncooperative chiefs with pliant ones.

Finally, state functionaries in Anambra and Imo States, like their counterparts elsewhere, enhanced their status by acquiring chieftaincy titles: during and after the elections, governors, commissioners, advisers and federal and state legislators, among others, were given titles. As Ebere Nwaubani remarked:

> More than ever before, the titles became a mark of social distinction; only few still desired to remain "Messrs." It became fashionable to be addressed as "Chief (Dr.)" or "Chief (Professor)." When Ojukwu, the erstwhile Biafran head of state, returned from exile in 1982, he was quickly invested with a

chiefly title, Ikemba Nnewi, since, having lost his military rank, it was demeaning for him to be addressed as "Mister."[64]

Two case studies from Oyo will further illustrate the interaction of parties and traditional rulers,' on the one hand; and on the other, of communal divisions and local government reforms.[65] First, we will look further at the impact of chieftaincy—and particularly of chieftaincy titles—on regional configurations of power during the Second Republic.

The Political Significance of Chieftaincy Titles

We have seen how regional politicians legitimated their claims to power by participating in local chieftaincy institutions. This encouraged a convergence of regional and local interests and the emergence of a complex network of alliances among politicians, businessmen, civil servants and traditional rulers. These networks tended to be vertically structured, focusing primarily on regions and loyalties, along with the horizontal bonding of classes, ideological movements and occupational groups. In this context, chieftaincy structures provided both the organizational node and a vital medium and ingredient of elite consolidation.

Chieftaincy titles which became such important barometers of status and power[66] were conferred, ideally, as a mark of honor to persons who had lived exemplary lives, or were extraordinarily accomplished in one or another domain. Prominent Yoruba politicians such as Awolowo and Akintola helped institutionalized the practice of the acquisition of titles by politicians, businessmen and other "modern" elites (see chapters 4 and 5). Indeed, most Yoruba politicians of the decolonization era promptly shed the Western (egalitarian) prefix of "mister" for the honorific of "chief;" the younger generation of aspiring UPN and NPN politicians followed their predecessors' lead, lobbying obas for titles.

Similarly, in the northern emirates, titles reinforced the influence of politicians and other elites. It will suffice to mention only a few prominent examples in this region where title acquisition and the control of state power have gone hand in hand. Both Ahmadu Bello, as Sardauna, and Shehu Shagari, as Turakin, used their titles in the Sultan's court as leverage for positions of regional premier and president of the federation respectively. Even military officers have benefited considerably from strong emirate ties, especially after retirement. Major General Hassan Katsina, the ex-military governor of the Northern Region and the Ciroma of Katsina (a prince), unsuccessfully attempted to use his high national status to become emir after his father's death in 1981. Another senior military administrator, Major General Shehu Yar' Adua, Chief of Staff Supreme Headquarters from 1976 to 79, combined his national military status with aristocratic claims, acquiring the title of Tafida of Katsina in the early 1980s. Both his traditional and military positions were critical to the role of civilian powerbroker he carved for himself in the 1980s and 1990s. More importantly, since titleholders often held important positions in local government councils, public corporations, and state executive committees, emirs retained considerable influence despite the military reforms of the 1970s. For example, six of the fifteen Kano State Commissioners in 1978 held titles in the court of the emir of Kano alone.[67]

In the eastern states of Anambra and Imo, the "divine right" of kings was a novel idea. Nonetheless, local chiefs, whose forebears had been appointed as "warrant chiefs" by the colonial regimes, assumed the monarchical trappings of obas and emirs.[68] Like the Yoruba, the Igbo chiefs —as well as others from many southern ethnic groups such as the Ibibio, Ijaw and Efik—witnessed a proliferation of chieftaincy titles awarded to powerful native sons. In Onitsha, which had unusually centralized chieftaincy structures, pre-eminent nationalist and NPP presidential candidate Nnamdi Azikiwe led a long list of prominent Igbos who had consolidated their ties within the dominant regional political class by taking prestigious local titles. Azikiwe, the radical nationalist during decolonization, not only took the title of Owelle of Onitsha in the 1970s, but regularly performed the associated customary rites. Although radical commentators frowned at it, deriding him as Zik of Africa, Zik of Nigeria, Zik of the Eastern Region and now Zik of Onitsha,[69] his was a classic demonstration of the political elites' embrace of their "fathers' titles." Nwaubani observes that in some areas

> families of . . . the former warrant chiefs had come to be regarded as something of "royal families." . . . In some other places, the position was filled by individuals who had previously established prominence in public life: Akanu Ibiam, the governor of Eastern Nigeria in the First Republic became the *eze ogo* of Uwana; Joseph Echeruo of Umunumo, Pius Nwogo of Mbaise, and John Nwodo of Ukehe, all ministers of the Eastern Region during the same First Republic, became the chiefs of their respective communities. . . . Elsewhere, there were fierce contests, and the chieftaincy positions were mostly taken up by the "new rich," upstarts who had stumbled on wealth by any means, and desired the position to legitimize their social standing.[70]

The proliferation of titles suggested both a new mechanism of mobility, and a struggle for legitimacy among regional elites. While titles were not always effective in this regard, they did provide symbolic ties to cherished local institutions. Chieftaincy titles thus became an expression of the new focus on local politics fostered by the insecurities of the Civil War. Its dominance was further intensified by the new money derived from the oil boom of the 1970s, along with the conspicuous consumption and status rivalry which followed. Traditional rulers, as "owners" of these symbolic resources, benefitted from their conferral on political and economic allies. Thus, Barnes' description of title-giving in metropolitan Lagos is relevant throughout Nigeria. Chieftaincy titles, she says, are

> a status award unparalleled in their capacity to bring honor to the holder, and in their capacity to create a bond between those who gave them and those who receive them. Their conferral established long-standing debts. The chiefs, therefore, used their title-giving authority to bring under their sway other leaders whose gratitude would be, at least for a long time, unshakeable.[71]

These transactions gave chieftaincy a new significance and visibility throughout the federation. This was even reflected in the emergence of powerful "chieftaincy lobbies" in regional and national politics. Since the late 1970s, these lobbies have contended that, as custodians of "cherished" local values, traditional rulers and titleholders deserve formal inclusion in state affairs. In conference papers, articles and public testimonies, various politicians, state officials and intellectuals have underscored the importance of chieftaincy in governance. Prominent historian Saburi Biobaku typifies this general perspective:

> The meaningful form of leadership in most parts of Yorubaland resides in traditional chieftaincy and not in the modern form of government. . . . [T]he paradox of [the] contemporary situation lies in grassroots support and recognition, and their lack of formal political functions.[72]

The famous Yoruba businessman and politician, M. K. O. Abiola, provides another example. He acquired several prestigious titles in the 1970s and 1980s (Bashorun of Ibadan from the Olubadan, and the Are-Ona-Kakanfo from the Alaafin). In reaction to the indifference of some policy makers to traditional rulers, and the opposition of radical intellectuals who had called for the abolition of chieftaincy, he proffered this Yoruba adage: "you cannot ride an untamed horse by force; if it throws you, you will be lucky to escape with your life."[73] Abiola was implying that government officials must not ignore the formidable force of indigenous political institutions. Another influential advocate of traditional political institutions, especially the

Masu Sarauta, was Umaru Shinkafi, former Director of the National Security Organization (NSO) and a member of the Sultan's Court.[74] Retired military rulers such as Hassan Katsina, Adeyinka Adebayo, Shehu Yar' Adua and Mohammed Jega also featured prominently in the chieftaincy lobbies of the 1980s.

Chieftaincy titles provide a lens to explore the formidable political alliance between Nigeria's "modern" and "traditional" elites. Especially during the Second Republic, titles became a critical political resource, allowing political leaders to reinforce their regional power (and even their national prestige) by appropriating cherished local symbols. Title-giving also gave chieftaincy—and "traditional culture" in general—a whole new lease on life.

The Dynamics of Local Politics

A hallmark of the First Republic had been the consistent attempt of regional governments to penetrate and control local institutions and politics. In the North, the NPC had used the NA structure to crush opposition and consolidate its position in local communities; similarly, the NNDP government in the West, responding to the AG crisis, had dissolved democratically constituted local authorities at will, imposing its own management committees under tighter regional control (see chapter 4). In spite of constitutional provisions to prevent such abuse, Second Republic politicians were no less relentless in their desire to dominate local affairs. This was exacerbated by the ongoing confrontation between the NPN federal government and the twelve non-NPN states that developed after 1979.[75] As in the earlier era of electoral politics, parties in control of the state executives did their best to bring local opposition under control, dissolving representative bodies where necessary, and replacing them with more cooperative committees manned with state appointees.

The creation of new local jurisdictions was another strategy of control. The new councils were largely tailored to strengthen ruling parties and their political allies. Local councils thus proliferated, increasing from 301 to 701 between 1979 and 1981. By 1983, *West Africa* could concluded that there was no state in Nigeria which complied with constitutional provisions for democratically elected local authorities.[76] Thus, local government reforms were motivated more by power calculations than by the concerns for functional linkages between corporate structures of government and local forms of governance.[77]

Despite this tendency, it would be inaccurate to say that all local reforms during the Second Republic were motived solely by political expediency. Oyo State provides an example of this ambiguity. While the UPN's local government policies may have been politically motivated, there were also good reasons to contemplate reform. There was an endemic crisis of local governance and administration in Oyo State, marked by maladministration, communal tensions, poor communication and primitive public infrastructure. Bola Ige, the UPN state governor, felt that the local government institutions created by the military—the *1976 Local Government Guidelines*—were seriously flawed.[78] Only two months after his election as governor, Ige appointed a commission of inquiry to propose methods of reforming local government in the state. Chaired by an Ibadan High Court Judge, Mr. Justice Yekini O. Adio, the commission consisted of a University of Ibadan historian, Dr. Wale Oyemakinde, and a retired civil servant, P. P. Ladapo. A civil servant with considerable experience in local government, O. Woye, served as secretary of the commission.

The authorities thus had a strong rationale for constituting yet another commission of inquiry to look into local governance and reform. Regardless of official intentions, however, it was apparent that any meaningful local government reform, given the competitive electoral context, would revive communal struggles, drawing on collective memory and reconstructed histories and myths.

In many Oyo towns, the state's local government reform policy met with stiff resistance. Ibadan and Ile-Ife provide good examples. As we shall see in the Ibadan case, the Olubadan, senior chiefs, and local leaders of the two major parties, in a manner reminiscent of the 1940s and 1950s, mobilized grassroots organizations against the proposed reorganization of the Ibadan Municipal Government (IMG). In Ile-Ife, mindful of the bitter historical antecedents, state authorities elected to preserve the Oranmiyan Central Local Government Council as a single administrative unit, despite renewed demands by the Modakeke people for their own separate council. As in Ibadan, Modakeke's Baale and chiefs secured the support of prominent local personalities and groups in opposition to the UPN government. And in both cases NPN leaders, looking towards the 1983 elections, capitalized on the situation, siding with Ibadan and Modakeke leaders.

Case study I—Ibadan: the politics of local government reform

Ibadan politics during the Second Republic was shaped by the political alignments established in the early 1950s. Politicians of the two major parties in the area, the UPN and the NPN, along with chiefs and civic and religious leaders, embraced community-based doctrines in order to challenge the state's proposed local government policy. The UPN government attributed corruption and maladministration in Ibadan to a overly centralized municipal authority. It thus proposed a decentralized system, dividing Ibadan into several administrative units, including a greater municipal council and a number of smaller, semi-autonomous county councils.[79]

Ibadan elites were hardly convinced by Governor Ige's arguments for local government efficiency. Although a resident of Ibadan since his youth, Bola Ige was a native of the Ijesha town of Esa Oke. As in the 1950s, local leaders thus interpreted the UPN's position as a strategy of using a non-Ibadan governor to achieve the earlier AG policy—perceived by "natives" to be so damaging to Ibadan and so favorable to "native settlers"—of undermining the remaining influence of the Olubadan and the chiefs.[80]

The opposition's strategy was an old one. Educated elites and chiefs mobilized popular support by calling on women traders, farmers' groups, artisan guilds, and other local organizations to oppose the government's plans. When the Adio Commission paid a courtesy call to the Olubadan's residence to hear the chiefs' point of view, numerous representatives spoke out against the idea of decentralization.[81] Chiefs and influential personalities collaborated to articulate an Ibadan-centered doctrine evoking what they projected as a precarious past. In typical Ibadan style, memoranda and petitions flooded the commission, registering opposition to the proposed reforms, and supporting the Olubadan and the chiefs. Groups printed pamphlets that attacked the UPN government and the small group of Ibadan politicians who, having registered their support for reorganization, were seen as having "sold out" for self-serving political reasons.[82] Several groups adopted unorthodox strategies, sending out multiple memoranda and petitions, and new organizations were formed with the sole purpose of opposing decentralization.[83]

The most articulate and best organized of these was the Ibadan Committee of Concern (ICC), a diverse umbrella group formed with the specific purpose of frustrating government objectives. An alliance of both elites and commoner elements, and cutting across party lines, the ICC claimed that its sole objective was "the orderly growth and development of that geographical entity in Yorubaland formerly known as Ibadan Province." The coalition identified three major objectives. First, coalition leaders committed themselves to the promotion of the role of the Olubadan and chiefs —the custodians of cherished local values—in local governance. Second, they called for the economic and social advancement of Ibadan, and lastly, they pledged to uphold peace among local people.[84] The ICC's major focus, however, was its uncompromising attacks on the UPN government and on the small group of Ibadan politicians who had actively campaigned for the proposed reorganization of city administration.

Supporters of decentralization were grouped in the Ibadan Reform Committee. It was led by Lamidi Adesina, a UPN member of the federal legislature and columnist for the pro-UPN newspaper, the *Nigerian Tribune*. Other prominent members of the Reform Committee were the former principal of the Ibadan Grammar School and long-time supporter of Obafemi Awolowo, Archdeacon E. A. Alayande; an Ibadan-based lawyer, Layi Ogunsola; and Niyi Adelu, a member of the Oyo State legislature. These men argued that the proposed IMG reorganization would not, in fact, undermine the political status of the Olubadan and the chiefs. They contended that, as stipulated by the 1976 local government reforms, the Olubadan would retain control over "traditional" matters in the four proposed county councils. Furthermore, the federal system of revenue allocation would favor Ibadan residents in the event of the division of the IMG.[85]

Several other pro-reform politicians, especially native sons such as Lamidi Adesina, who had been accused of betrayal, were not so conciliatory. A vocal Reform Committee member, he attacked anti-reformer politicians led by Busari Adelakun of Ejioku (Ibadan Division) who at various times served as Commissioner for Local Government, Health, and Sports in the Ige administration.[86]

The fascinating political saga of Adelakun—quintessential Oyo-Yoruba populist politician in the tradition of Adelabu—captures the complex politics of local government reform. Although a member of the state executive committee, Adelakun defied his chief executive and the UPN by opposing decentralization. Adelakun's vocal opposition made him the favored son of the Olubadan, the chiefs, and other grassroots leaders. As a renegade in the UPN administration, Adelakun was isolated and blacklisted by his colleagues. In a series of propaganda pamphlets and newspaper articles, Adelakun—alias *Eru O Bodo* (fearless as the rivers)—became the central target of UPN reformers. They represented him as a betrayer of the party, adding that Adelakun, as a villager from Ejioku, had no business dabbling in city affairs. Hence the slogan *A ti oko wa ba ile je*—"the confusionist from the (bush) village who creates havoc in the city."[87] The real conflict, of course, was between Ibadan UPN and the local leaders who saw decentralization as a threat to the control still exercised by native sons over local government administration. With their passionate appeal to Ibadan communal interests, the anti-reformer coalition succeeded in mobilizing mass support by mid-1980.

It was apparent that the ICC was undermining the state government's credibility in Ibadan. Its incorporation of influential native sons and diverse political groups under the symbolic leadership of the Olubadan turned this single-issue fringe movement into a formidable opposition. As the voice of the Olubadan and chiefs, a new generation of the Ibadan intelligentsia—most notably University of Ibadan scholar Busari Adebisi and UPN State Commissioner Kunle Abass—matched their critique of the Reform Committee with an embrace of Ibadan's chieftaincy institutions and communal heritage. As one of them declaimed:

> One would like to ask these agents of instability and avowed apostles of disunity precisely who and what they set out to reform? Our age-old culture and traditions that have seen us through many years of wars and have earned Ibadan the unique prominent place among the Yorubas and Nigerians? Are we so unreformed a people that we need to be reformed by this gang of institutional destroyers?[88]

Anti-reform politicians from both parties also attacked the state government's policy in the state House of Assembly. Indeed, throughout the controversy legislators representing Ibadan and neighboring districts—including those from the governor's party, the UPN—generally subordinated party loyalty to their perception of Ibadan's collective interest. Of the twenty-eight members representing Ibadan and neighboring communities, only five favored the proposal to divide the IMG.[89] Remarks by S. B. Lawal, representative from Ibadan East 1, typified the sentiments of the anti-reform majority:

> I rise to make my contribution to the debate on the Local Government Amendment Bill and in doing so, I have to inform this honorable house that we honorable members from Ibadan have been mandated by His Highness the Olubadan of Ibadan, His chiefs, and all the citizens of Ibadan that the Ibadan Municipal Government should remain intact. Mr. Speaker, sir, if anybody has come to this honorable house to advocate the breaking up of the present Ibadan Municipal Government as we now have it, I would say right here now that he or she is not directly from Ibadan.[90]

In the end, the fierce communal resistance to decentralization achieved its aims. While the Adio Commission recommended a significant increase in local authorities (from twenty-four to fifty-three), it agreed with the anti-reform coalition that the IMG should be preserved in its existing form. Furthermore, the IMG would retain control over all territories (including rural communities) under Ibadan's jurisdiction.[91] Aware of the mass opposition to its proposal, the government reluctantly accepted the commission's recommendations on the IMG. Thus, despite the IMG's disproportionate size and reputation for administrative inefficiency, Ibadan leaders had succeeded in preventing its demise.[92]

Thirty years before, the Olubadan, chiefs and mogajis had challenged the local government and native court reforms of Awolowo's AG government, which had threatened to abolish most of their prerogatives. Then, however, the chiefs and their supporters were on the losing side. Moreover, the earlier polarization between (pro-reform) Christian educated elites, on the one hand, and (anti-reform) grassroots organizations led by populist Muslim politicians and chiefs, on the other, was no longer a factor by the early 1980s. In fact, what was left of the IPU, which had served as the voice for the Christian elite in the 1940s and 1950s, actively opposed the government reform in the early 1980s. For example, Oba D. T. Akinbiyi, a veteran AG supporter and IPU pioneer member, was the Olubadan who from 1979 to 1981 mobilized opposition to government reform. Another IPU stalwart—senior chief and renowned local historian Chief J. A. Ayorinde—was now a dedicated traditionalist who decried reform as a threat to Ibadan native pre-eminence in local administration.[93]

The subtle religious divisions of the colonial years had also disappeared by the early 1980s. Powerful local groups such as the *Egbe Omo Ibile* and the Maiyegun League, though not explicitly religious, had harbored strong populist and Islamic tendencies that appealed to the mass of (Muslim) artisans, farmers and petty traders. These groups, whose influence declined during the 1950s, had formed an alliance with the chiefs against the reform programs of the AG (backed by the IPU). By the early 1980s, Muslims had "arrived" in Ibadan politics, and were well represented on both sides of the political spectrum. They included such politicians as Lamidi Adesina, Busari Adebisi, Busari Adelakun and Kunle Abass.

The reorganization controversy revived another sensitive historical issue that had divided the city in the 1940s and 1950s—the relative status of "native settler" areas and Ibadan's old indigenous core. Since World War II, the layouts in Oke Ado, Oke Bola, Ijebu By-Pass and Ago Taylor had been referred to as "native settler" areas, in which Ijebus were prominent. They had continued to develop a distinct character, reflecting both a predominance of non-Ibadan Yorubas, especially Ijebus, Egbas and Ijeshas, and a relative prosperity, at least compared to the old central core of the city where the majority of Ibadan natives lived. Moreover, after the Western State's partition by the Obasanjo regime in 1976, Ibadan's status diminished: no longer the political headquarters of the Yoruba region, the city experienced a rapid economic decline. The anti-reformers' strategy was similar to the communal agitations of the late colonial period, when Adelabu's *Mabolaje* took up the defense of "native" rights against the pan-Yoruba policies of AG modernizers. To mobilize community support, local elites brandished traditional symbols, defended chiefly authority and appealed to Ibadan's cherished heritage. Since the controversy surrounding decentralization reflected sub-ethnic differences within Ibadan, anti-reform politicians made political capital out of the historical division between native Ibadans and the non-Ibadan Yoruba population, notably the Ijebus, the Egbas and the Ijeshas. Hence, ICC leaders projected the government reform policy as the final death knell to the prerogatives of the vulnerable "indigenous" population, finally wresting away control of the IMG.

Thus, more than any other issue during the Second Republic, the decentralization controversy had a profound impact on Ibadan. Indeed, it modified prevailing political alignments, enhancing the popularity of the opposition NPN in the election of 1983. Conversely, the state government's reform policy worked to the disadvantage of the UPN, which became the villain of the piece. While the long-term political fallout was not immediately clear, the reorganization controversy seemed to cast doubt on the disposition of the UPN state government as far as Ibadan was concerned. Opponents of the UPN, certainly were able to present the reform as an indication of an anti-Ibadan bias on the part of the administration. In fact, ICC leaders attacked the UPN state government for a perceived imbalance in the distribution of resources that they claimed worked to Ibadan's disadvantage.[94]

The opposition NPN, meanwhile, benefitted from the controversy. For Ibadan native NPN activists, who had suffered a humiliating defeat in the 1979 elections, the controversy provided a critical opportunity to undermine the local pan-ethnic base of the UPN. As early as February 1981, a UPN legislator from Ibadan, A. Adepoju, had noted the possible political cost of IMG reorganization:

> Mr. Speaker, sir, Ibadan city should remain one. As was rightly said by one honorable member of this house we do not want the National Party of Nigeria (NPN) to take advantage of what these minority people want you to do. . . . The NPN are inciting the people to divide Ibadan so that they can use it to their advantage, and we want to appeal to you Mr. Speaker, sir, that there

is no fear at all in keeping Ibadan one. We hope this house will respect the Olubadan and all the chiefs. We hope this house will respect the opinion of cultural organizations in Ibadan, the social organizations and educationists in Ibadan. All these people want is that Ibadan should not be divided.[95]

As in many Yoruba towns, sub-ethnic tensions had persisted since the UPN victory in 1979. NPN leaders in Ibadan realized that the political struggle over local government reform would revive the old division between Ibadan natives and the descendants of "native settlers," most notably the Ijebus, in local politics. Emphasizing the significance of the ancestral homeland in contemporary politics, in which sub-ethnic identities such as Egba, Ijesha, Ijebu play a critical role, David Laitin claimed that this sort of cleavage was central during the 1979 and 1983 elections in all the Yoruba states: "NPN strategists . . . worked through the ancestral city divide, hoping to recruit Oyos and Egbas in a common stand against the Ijebu Awolowo."[96]

The NPN leadership in Ibadan could thus exploit the deep disaffection from the UPN administration, projecting itself as the defender of native Ibadans against the onslaught of outsiders, the non-Ibadan Yorubas, who dominated the state executive. The presence of prominent native sons in the NPN—such as the party's national chairman A. M. A. Akinloye, and federal Attorney General Richard Akinjide—made it easy to project this concern. The NPN had been humiliated at the polls in 1979, but this strategy promised victory in 1983. Indeed, Ibadan NPN activists who had been favored by the federal government were under severe pressure to "deliver" this critical Yoruba state for the party (otherwise centered in the North). They thus courted the Olubadan and the chiefs who had been alienated by the UPN reorganization scheme. The death of Oba D. T. Akinbiyi in 1981, and the subsequent installation of Chief Oloyede Asanike as Olubadan, only lengthened the distance between the chiefs and the UPN. As Balogun, Chief Asanike had favored NPN leaders such as A. M. A. Akinloye and Dr. Omololu Olunloyo. As Olubadan, he openly embraced the Ibadan branch of the NPN.

The problems of the UPN state authorities were not limited to the fierce opposition mounted by the Oyo State branch of the NPN. The government also had to contend with the disenchantment of Ibadan politicians within its own party. Leaders of this local faction contended that Ibadan had been denied its rightful share in the distribution of state resources and patronage. By late 1981, there was a clear division in the coalition that had formed behind the UPN in Ibadan only two years earlier. So deep was the gulf between the UPN state executive and prominent Ibadan UPN leaders that the latter withdrew their support from Bola Ige in the 1983 election. In a 1982 press release the Ibadan branch of the UPN declared: "It is our candid opinion that this present administration has not adequately compensated for Ibadan's support in 1979 and after, except in verbiage. We shall not support the extension of this administration beyond 1983. Enough is enough."[97] Apart from their rejection of the governor, these politicians embraced a simple Ibadan-centered doctrine as their electoral platform. They threatened that their support for the UPN would depend on the choice of an Ibadan native son as the party's flagbearer in the 1983 gubernatorial elections.[98] Ige—a gallant political warrior and very self-assured—refused to be intimidated. He dismissed the Ibadan politicians as nothing but "novices" and "detractors."[99] In the event, the Ibadan faction would prove unable to prevent Ige's renomination. It was led by the charismatic Adelakun, who, after switching his allegiance to the NPN, was conferred with the title of Jagun by the Olubadan. UPN dissidents called on native Ibadans to disregard their political differences, and vote the UPN administration out of power by supporting a native son. Populist slogans emphasizing loyalty to the Ibadan hometown, such as *Omo wa ni - e je o se* (we want a native son for governor) and *Ibadan o se ru mo, gomina la o se* (Ibadan will no longer be slaves, we now want to be governor), became popular during the campaign. The UPN's opponents presented the 1983 elections as an Ibadan family affair in which all members should come together and support a native son, Omololu Olunloyo, the NPN gubernatorial nominee.

The emotional appeal to the hometown during the campaign was encapsulated in a slogan of brotherhood and camaraderie—*Ohun ti agbe kale o ju ija lo, ara Ibadan o ba ti ija wa - Ohun ti a gbe kale yi ju ja lo* (the current issue is more than a mere [election] tussle; we are not here for a confrontation. This election is really about our collective survival). A new home-grown consciousness reminiscent of the glorious days of Adegoke Adelabu re-emerged; indeed, the spirit of the legendary Adelabu was injected into the NPN campaign. For example, it is said that the NPN campaign was launched at the late Adelabu's residence at Oke Odo, where, to evoke the spirit of the ancestors, a cow was killed in his memory, and food was provided for party supporters who attended the ceremony.[100] The NPN campaign in Ibadan was thus "packaged" as *Oro a la jo bi* (a kith and kin affair). This communal strategy mirrors Laitin's notion of the political significance of Yoruba hometown. NPN slogans throughout the state were designed to eulogize the names of important "native sons" —such as Adelabu in Ibadan and Akintola in Ogbomosho—who at various points had mounted local opposition against the pan-Yoruba ideology of the regional political class.

The NPN candidate won the 1983 gubernatorial election in Oyo State. The evidence suggests that the victory was far from fair; electoral fraud was rife in the state and throughout Nigeria in 1983. It is significant, however, that—unlike the prolonged violence that had accompanied the AG's defeat in the rigged 1965 elections (and the prolonged violence that followed the UPN's defeat in Ondo and Oyo states in 1983)—Ibadan was relatively peaceful after 1983. This can partly be attributed to the election of a respected native son as governor.[101]

Case study II—the Ife-Modakeke crisis in historical perspective

The Adio Commission's recommendations also affected another major communal conflict in Oyo State: the old feud between Ife townspeople and the Modakeke "settler community." This dispute, which once again came to a head in the early months of 1981, pitted Ife elites against Modakeke chiefs and elders who contended that the new local government proposal was detrimental to their interest.

This conflict dated from the political strife which engulfed much of the Yoruba region in the early nineteenth century. As noted in chapter 1, it resulted in the dispersal of northern Yoruba inhabitants and the formation of new communities south of old Oyo. Major towns such as Ibadan and Abeokuta, and smaller communities such as Modakeke, emerged as a result. Despite several decades of intermarriage with the Ifes, the Modakekes' patrilineal claims were still traced to the descendants of the refugees from the eastern district of old Oyo, who after suffering a crushing defeat from the Fulani-led forces of Ilorin, moved southward to establish a small community in an area contiguous to Ile-Ife. Modakeke migrants and their descendants suffered persistent hardship at the hands of their Ife hosts. The celebrated Yoruba local historian, the Reverend Samuel Johnson, notes in his *History of the Yorubas* that the Ooni at that time, Oba Akinmoyero, subjugated the new arrivals, making them "hewers of wood and drawers of water." Under his successors, the relationship of the Ifes and Modakekes remained a "continuous chain of open hostilities,"[102] made worse by the sixteen-year war between the Ibadan and the Ekitiparapo. Since the Oyo-Modakeke supported the Ibadan and the Ife sympathized with the Ekitis, the relationship between the Ifes and the Modakekes deteriorated.

As relations worsened, the Modakeke were forced to move their farms south and west of Ile-Ife and even as far away as the southern Oshun area. It was only with colonial support that they were allowed to resettle in a special Ife quarter in 1921.[103] Indirect rule, however, further reinforced the Ooni's authority, and the Ooni's council tightened its grip over provincial communities such as Modakeke through the native authority system. During the late 1940s cocoa boom, when Ife landlords demanded *isakole* rents (traditional Yoruba leasehold payments) from Modakeke peasants, Modakeke resistance deepened. Although the native courts consolidated the claims of Ife landowning lineages over agricultural land and the lucrative cocoa crop, tenant resistance also intensified.[104] Not surprisingly, the decolonization period witnessed persistent demands for a separate local authority by Modakeke chiefs and elites.[105]

While there was a historical basis for hostility between the Ife and Modakeke, the crisis that culminated in violence in April 1981 was prompted by two major postcolonial developments. First, Modakeke chiefs and elites interpreted Obasanjo's Land Use Decree of 1978 (see chapter 7) to mean a state-sanctioned abrogation of the customary land tenure system, and thus the abolition of *isakole* rents. Second, Governor Ige's 1981 local government reform policy had provoked new Modakeke demands from the Oranmiyan Local Government Council. The Adio Commission recommended the creation of three new local authorities from the existing Oranmiyan jurisdiction, but none of these responded to Modakeke demands. Disappointed, the Modakeke leaders claimed that the commission had simply kowtowed to political pressures from influential Ife elites. The UPN state government stood by the commission on this point, even scrapping the three new jurisdictions it proposed.

Other minor incidents exacerbated tensions in Ife. The Modakeke chiefs and civic leaders, for instance, asserted their political autonomy from Ife by launching a special "town hall" and "palace" fund in December 1980. This lent new implications to the original project, the Modakeke Progressive Union's plan for a simple "community hall" and a "baale's residence." The plan, dating back to 1973, had been supported by the late Ooni, Sir Adesoji Aderemi. His successor, Oba Sijuade, however, opposed the more ambitious 1980 version of the project, which suggested a royal claim by the baale (head chief), and at least a symbolic autonomy for the Modakeke community.[106] Modakekes also found other innovative ways of expressing their desire for independence—for example, replacing old road signs which read "Modakeke-Ife" with new ones that said "Modakeke" alone.[107]

All these factors contributed to the outbreak of violence in April 1981. An independent inquiry appointed to investigate the disturbances by the state government suggested that frustrations over the local government policy prompted Modakeke leaders to present the new Ooni with a fait accompli by proceeding with the fund-raising ceremony for the Modakeke town hall and palace fund. Confronted with this challenge only a few months after his coronation, Oba Sijuade, in turn, felt it necessary to reassert control. Thus, he allegedly encouraged the divisional police to cancel the event, on the grounds that it could undermine public peace and good will.[108] When the Modakeke Development Committee ignored the police order, hostilities broke out.[109]

After the riots, Modakeke leaders criticized the Ooni's actions and appealed for an investigation.[110] They also complained that, despite their support for the party in 1979 (which the Ifes also had supported, we should add), UPN state authorities had ignored their demands for autonomy. Furthermore, they claimed that not only had no Modakekes been appointed commissioners in the state executive or to public corporation boards, but the chairman of the local board of education, A. O. Omisade, a prominent Ife politician, had discriminated against Modakeke teachers by transferring them to remote parts of the jurisdiction.[111] Finally, Modakeke leaders charged that non-Ifes had been excluded from the benefits at the local level as well. T. O. Odetola, prominent Modakeke representative, voiced these complaints in the state legislature:

> The first 13 board appointments given to the Oranmiyan Local Government during the session of this administration, the whole 13 were shared by Ife sons, nothing was given to the vast majority of Oyo groups in that area. The people from Origbo were not given. Modakeke people were not considered; people in Garage Olode were not considered also. It was not until when I cried loud that we were given one. This is one of the Ife's oppressive measures with us. It is only when we want to work, they will say Modakeke and Ife are one, but when it comes to the question of sharing the national cake, then they will say Modakekes are strangers. This is our plight in the area and this is why we are strongly agitating for our own separate local government.[112]

The conflict provided the Oyo state branch of the NPN, meanwhile, with another disgruntled community to court and represent. In fact, the commission of inquiry charged that it was the NPN's involvement in the conflict that had triggered the violence. Since January, NPN political strategists had been portraying the UPN state government as pro-Ife sympathizers opposed to the Modakeke cause. An editorial in the pro-NPN *National Concord* extended this interpretation to the April events:

Whatever may be the eventual total casualty figure of last week's disturbance in Modakeke town in Oyo state, one undisputable fact is that the unfortunate incidents could have been averted if only Governor Bola Ige and his political mentor (Chief Awolowo) were not obsessed with the ideas of imposing their pet traditional ruler beyond his domain over the people of Modakeke.[113]

After the incidents prominent NPN politicians kept up the campaign, condemning alleged UPN bias,[114] emphasizing the historical animosity between the two communities, and evoking the distinct Oyo heritage of the Modakeke. For example, Odetola declared in the state legislature that

> Modakeke has nothing in common with Ile-Ife both socially and culturally and there is no community of interest in the two communities. Modakeke has no traditional association with Ile-Ife, we have separate customs and tradition; while the Modakeke celebrate Egungun festival, the Ife celebrate Olojo festival. We even have different dialects. As close as we are, when an Oyo man is speaking, one would know that he is an Oyo man and when an Ife man is speaking, one would know that he is an Ife man. Our past association has been a marriage of convenience, there is no love lost between us. In Modakeke, we have a line of traditional chiefs which is quite different from that of Ile-Ife. This is exactly in the same form with that of Ibadan people. Modakeke has its own principal central market named after Ogunsua of Modakeke.[115]

Similarly, pamphlets containing incendiary slogans reminiscent of the agitations of the colonial era extolled the virtues and claims of the Oyo Yoruba. According to one, "Modakeke is a town, Modakeke has history, Modakeke is an Oyo-speaking people, Modakeke should be separated from Ife."[116] Another emotional pamphlet titled *Awon Oyo ti goke agba* (the Oyos are a great people) spoke of the customary *isakole* rents, which it claimed had been abolished by the federal government: *Isakole ti di ohun itan* (*Isakole* is a thing of the past); *Awon agbe lo ni ile oko won* (peasants now own their farmlands).[117] The commission of inquiry's report concluded that the NPN strategy was "intended to hurt the people's collective psyche by whipping up emotions and appealing to parochial prejudices."[118]

The conflict was also bitterly fought out in the local authority and the legislature. Modakeke councillors in the local government council petitioned the NPN federal government to intervene.[119] In Ibadan, the state capital, the NPN minority leader in the House of Assembly, Olatunji Mohammed, blamed the riots on the state authority's local government policies, and on a visit to the area by UPN leader Obafemi Awolowo earlier that month.[120] Awolowo did seem to have encouraged UPN legislators to support the state government on the Oranmiyan Central Local Government issue.[121] Thus, the commission of inquiry concluded that "pressure groups" and powerful personalities influenced the Adio Commission's decision not to create a separate council for Modakeke, an action which the panel (the commission of inquiry) claimed was "probably taken in bad faith."[122]

The violence that erupted on April 14 resulted in the loss of many lives, the injury of over a hundred people and the destruction of property worth millions of naira. More than 150 houses belonging to prominent residents, including those of Oba Sijuade, were burned down. The state government immediately called in the police, imposed a dusk-to-dawn curfew, and banned all public meetings. Meanwhile, at the government's request, six delegates from both sides signed a treaty before Commissioner of Police Umoru Omolowo, ending the civil disturbance.[123] In a radio and television broadcast on April 15 Governor Ige announced the appointment of a four-man judicial commission of inquiry under the chairmanship of Mr. Justice Kayode Ibidapo-Obe, Judge of the Ogbomosho High Court, to explore the causes of the civil disturbance and make recommendations to the state government.[124]

The Ibidapo-Obe Commission recommended that Governor Ige should amend the Local Government Law of April 1, and, in the specific case of the Oranmiyan Central Local Government Area (LGA), permit it to be divided into two. Oranmiyan Central I would include Ife localities such as Iremo and Ilane. Oranmiyan Central II would include Modakeke and several other provincial communities.[125] The Oyo State government ignored the commission's recommendations, however, and preserved the LGA in its existing form. Another riot, also resulting in the loss of many lives, occurred during the 1983 election campaign, when Ife thugs allegedly invaded Modakeke.

Politics in Nigeria's Second Republic were shaped by the alignments that had emerged during the earlier parliamentary era. Despite the military reforms to rationalize relations between powerful political interests, entrenched ethno-regionalism and class interests dominated party politics during this period. Within these political arrangements chieftaincy structures continued to reflect the communal traditions and ideologies on which the dominant regional political parties were established. In Oyo State (as well as other Yoruba states) obas, chiefs and local elders established the dominant Yoruba party, the UPN, on clearly defined ethno-regional boundaries; by the late 1970s the party had emerged as a formidable medium of political mobilization. The mass support it enjoyed at the pan-Yoruba level was not surprising, given Nigeria's entrenched ethno-regional traditions, its fragile federal structure, and the corporatist style of military rule from 1966 to 1979. Sustaining this broad-based political allegiance, however, was not always easy in Oyo State during the Second Republic.

As in the period of decolonization, when the NCNC provided an organizational node for disaffected local leaders who defined their opposition along the boundaries of the historic communal groups, the NPN, as the regional opposition, became the institutional platform for Ibadan and Modakeke chiefs, politicians and civic leaders who mobilized mass support against the UPN's local government reform policy. The politics of local government reform, with its implications for resource allocation, elite interests, and electoral support, thus once again triggered the historical fault lines of Yoruba politics: ethnic, sub-ethnic and class divisions, overlain by conflicting interpretations of local history and reconstructed notions of tradition.

The conflicts in Oyo State were not only symptomatic of the problems confronting other states, but, more importantly, reflected even a deeper crisis at the federal government level. Amidst acrimonious party feuds, abuse of state power, massive electoral fraud in the 1983 elections, and deepening economic crisis following a significant reduction in the price of petroleum, the military intervened, toppling the Second Republic on December 31, 1983. The coup, which brought General Buhari to power, ushered in another chapter of military rule in Nigeria's turbulent political history.

9

THE RETURN OF MILITARY RULE

As we have seen, chieftaincy structures are intimately connected to the problematic character of state legitimacy in Nigeria: they have endured through recurrent bouts of authoritarianism and transitions to democratic rule. As in the Mohammed/Obasanjo military administration, the post-Second Republic regimes of Generals Mohammudu Buhari and Ibrahim Babangida adopted elaborate programs to rationalize Nigeria's political and social institutions. Major military initiatives such as Buhari's local government review, and Babangida's democratic transition program were the centerpieces of the two failed regimes. This chapter will consider the lingering significance of chieftaincy structures in late-twentieth-century Nigeria, showing that, sustained by the entrenched interests of ethno-regional elites, traditional rulers played critical roles in the policy initiatives of the Buhari and Babangida regimes. Once again, the objectives of a highly politicized officer corps would interact with the obdurate realities of communal, regional and class divisions and identities.

Another Oyo case study will look at conflicting Yoruba interpretations of traditional authority, and the ways they were sustained by interlocking networks of regional and local power and influence. This account will feature the saga of the Oyo State Council of Chiefs—an institution embedded in contemporary state structures, but informed by the mythology of the Ife and Oyo crowns—as an illustration of the significance of local historical themes in contemporary Nigerian politics. This study of reconstructed notions of indigenous political authority will analyze structural transformation within the context of adaptive and resilient indigenous institutions; it will also underscore its implications for elite consolidation under military rule in Oyo State. Both Ife and Oyo, as Yorubaland's pre-eminent crowns, provided important ideological platforms on which Yoruba elites forged alliances following the fall of the Second Republic.

Neotraditionalism in the Buhari Regime

The nineteen-month military regime of General Buhari (January 1984–August 1985) stands out as one of the most controversial in Nigeria's postcolonial history. Its notoriety can be attributed to its tendencies towards abuse of human rights, authoritarian measures, unpopular policies and alienation of powerful interests.[1] A number of important national organizations, with strong followings in the South—such as the Nigerian Medical Association and the Nigerian Bar Association, along with labor unions, teachers' unions, university students and the press—had poor relations with the Buhari regime. Traditional rulers, however, embraced by the regime, provided an informal mechanism for harnessing grassroots support. This collaboration with chieftaincy (especially close in the case of the northern emirates) was openly announced by Buhari in March 1985, when he stated that his government's mission coincided with the objectives of traditional rulers. Buhari, a Fulani, regularly consulted the Sultan of Sokoto, Sir Abubakar, on matters of state.[2] He instructed his state military governors, moreover, to embrace traditional rulers as an "informal second tier of authority."[3] Furthermore, under the regime's neotraditional policy, prominent traditional leaders, such as the Emir of Kano, the Ooni of Ife, the Oba of Benin, and the Obi of Onitsha, gained new confidence, and renewed their demands for the inclusion of chieftaincy in the formal institutions of the state.[4] This *rapprochement* influenced the military regime's decision to review the *1976 Local Government Guidelines* in May 1984.[5]

On 29 May 1984, the Chief of Staff, Supreme Headquarters, Major General Tunde Idiagbon, inaugurated a twenty-member committee—under the chairmanship of the Baraden of Sokoto, Alhaji Ibrahim Dasuki[6]—to make recommendations to the federal government on local government reforms. After a year's deliberations, including strong input from influential traditional rulers, the Dasuki Committee presented its report in April 1985. Essentially, the Committee reaffirmed its commitment to the theoretical assumptions of the *1976 Local Government Guidelines*, noting that

the system of local government in the country after the 1976 Local Government Reform had more of an operational, rather than structural problem arising
directly from behavior and attitude of the persons who operate the system[7]

The Committee thus upheld the pre-existing 301 multipurpose single-tier
local authorities established under the 1976 Guidelines. It reversed the decision of several state governments who, largely for political motives, had
dissolved duly-elected local councils during the Second Republic. Moreover, the Dasuki Committee upheld the functions of local authorities as
defined by the 1976 guidelines. On the recurring subject of the role of
traditional rulers in local government administration, the committee exceeded the stipulation of the *Guidelines*, granting traditional councils (statutory groups empowered to represent the views of traditional rulers on local
affairs) the power to formulate general proposals and to advise local government councils on all social, customary and economic matters. Traditional councils would also have access to important local authority documents such as draft estimates and by-laws of the executive committee.[8] The
Buhari regime endorsed the recommendation.

By granting the traditional councils advisory powers in the executive
affairs of local authorities, and control over customary and cultural matters,
the committee now allowed traditional rulers new powers to influence local
government policy. Buhari's brief regime thus encouraged a reassertion of
chiefly power in key regions of Nigeria. Realizing the political vacuum that
often accompanied military rule, prominent traditional rulers closed ranks to
promote their precarious authority. Their growing influence was also reflected
in the critical roles they assumed in the regional consultative committees
that dominated national and regional politics over the next decade. This
newfound influence was immediately apparent in the deliberations of the
Political Bureau, constituted by Buhari's successor, General Babangida, in
1986. It was a national committee, responsible for drafting a comprehensive transition program to civilian rule. Its functioning sheds light on both
Babangida's neopatrimonial strategy of governance, and on the critical role
of traditional rulers in a national debate on the transition to democracy.

The Babangida Years: Chieftaincy and the Crisis of Democratic Transition

As noted in previous chapters, chieftaincy structures and the configurations of elite power are central themes in the discourse on citizenship and

governance in postcolonial Nigeria. These issues, with an emphasis on the normative and utilitarian attributes of indigenous structures, had dominated discussion among old guard, traditional rulers and the new intelligentsia in the Western Region in the years of parliamentary democracy. They assumed even greater significance in the elaborate dialogues mounted by "corrective" military regimes following the Nigerian Civil War.

There is a dilemma in attributing executive authority to traditional ruler in a democratic setting. This dilemma is analyzed here through General Babangida's transition program to democratic rule. Although the ill-fated transition program was to be subverted by the military leaders themselves,[9] it nevertheless provides a good illustration of the issues that had dominated public discourse for almost four decades. Thus, in the following pages, the Babangida regime's proclaimed objective (transition to democracy) provides the context for consideration of the legacy of a highly politicized military authority attempting to mediate the increasingly explosive contradictions of the Nigerian state and society. We will see that the role of traditional rulership, as it persisted through these contradictions, was inevitably marked by the politicization and the fragmentation of the military, and by its growing domination of the extractive agencies of the state. The Babangida regime—itself a product of deep structural imbalances that had intensified since decolonization—in the end only further undermined the corporate interests of Nigeria's diverse communities.

After seizing power in a "palace coup" in August 1985, General Babangida appointed a seventeen-member Political Bureau under the chairmanship of Professor Samuel Cookey, pro-chancellor of the University of Benin, to recommend a suitable democratic system for Nigeria. At the Bureau's inauguration in January 1986, Babangida called on the panel to identify the problems that had led to previous failures and to propose realistic strategies of resolving them.[10] Unlike the 1976 Constitution Drafting Committee, this was a fact-finding commission, responsible for appraising sociopolitical conditions. This call for a critical assessment of Nigerian politics brought prominent traditional rulers, along with other elements, into the ensuing debates.

Many middle-class professional organizations were growing wary of military-sponsored transition programs and debates. Traditional rulers, on the other hand, in collaboration with powerful regional interests, actively contributed to the discussions of the Political Bureau, renewing their ties with discredited Second Republic politicians.[11] The most cohesive of these groups was organized by elite elements of the ten Northern states. Dominated by proscribed NPC and NPN party bosses of the First and Second

Republics, this organization, called the Committee of Elders, attributed Nigeria's recurrent political crisis to the under-utilization of chieftaincy institutions in local and national politics. The Northern elders called for a bicameral federal legislature, consisting of a popularly elected House of Representatives and a nominated Senate. The latter would include "leaders of thought" as well as the chairmen of the state councils of chiefs. The Senate, they insisted, should have the executive power to impeach the president and a host of other high government officials on charges of abuse of power. In addition, the Northern elders called for a consultative committee of regional "leaders of thought" to confer with the president on important national policies. They also recommended bicameral legislatures for the states, matching popularly elected houses of assembly, with nominated houses of elders, consisting of ex-state governors, chief judges, grand khadis and traditional rulers. State houses of elders, they insisted, must be empowered to advise the state governors on all important political affairs.

The Northern elders then called on the Political Bureau to repeal previous national measures that had eroded chiefly power in public affairs. For example, they called for the repeal of the customary court reforms that had been imposed by the Northern Regional Government in the 1950s; in addition, they urged the Political Bureau to reverse the assault on chiefly power represented by the *1976 Local Government Guidelines* and the 1978 Land Use Decree.

Traditional rulers and other elite elements from the South (notably from the Igbo, Ibibio, Efik, Ijaw and Yoruba communities) also vigorously lobbied the Political Bureau. In one landmark gathering, in early 1987, an organization called the Eastern Solidarity Group, consisting of traditional rulers and politicians from the Eastern states of Anambra, Imo, Rivers, and Cross Rivers, resolved to "advance eastern interests." In a second demonstration of solidarity, fifty eminent Igbo leaders from Anambra and Imo States gathered in Enugu under a regional initiative called *Oha n' Eze-Igbo* (for the people and kings of Igboland) to mount a united front on important federal government policies.[12]

In the West, Yoruba obas and politicians, under the leadership of the Ooni of Ife, inaugurated a pan-ethnic association called the *Egbe Ilosiwaju Yoruba* (the Yoruba Progressive Organization) to resolve pre-existing divisions among Yoruba political factions. In two high-profile "summit meetings," obas agreed to mediate conflict among regional politicians, rally around popular regional politicians, and establish a united front on Babangida's transition program. Calling on Yoruba obas, politicians and elders to put their house in order, the Ooni of Ife in his inaugural speech urged delegates not to see politics as a do or die affair but ensure a constant display of unity of purpose despite political differences. . . . I am sure you can do it if you would bury all past misunderstandings and start afresh in brotherhood and sisterly affection to plan together your strategy of putting the Yorubas in their deserved place among our brothers in Nigeria.[13]

And in reference to specific constitutional issues before the Political Bureau, Yoruba obas and elders freely expressed their views, calling for the integration of chieftaincy structures into the state. Like the Northern elders, Yoruba obas and politicians called for a national council of traditional rulers to advise the federal government on important national issues; for state councils of chiefs to advise the state executive committees on important local issues; and for a repeal of the Land Use Decree.

The Political Bureau, however, felt differently, rejecting proposals that called for a retreat to the past.[14] Furthermore, the panel dismissed chieftaincy structures as anachronistic in Nigeria's rapidly changing communities. It argued that

> traditional rulers should have no place in government beyond the local government level where they have relevance. Furthermore, by virtue of the scope and character of the contemporary Nigerian state, it is a misnomer to designate incumbents of these institutions traditional "ruler". . . . This official designation must not accord them a rival status with the principal political officers of the Nigerian state.[15]

The Bureau's recommendations reflected the typical perspective of Nigerian intellectuals, often suspicious of traditional rulers as political threats to an already fragile state. In this view, it would be undesirable to attribute executive, legislative or juridical functions to traditional authorities; this reflects a perception that, since the imposition of colonial rule, chiefly rulers have forged alliances with the holders of state power. Such intellectuals claim that these alleged "fathers of their people" are corrosive to the political process.[16]

William Graf notes the rationale for this perspective:

> Traditional social systems are thought to impede the growth of national political system and economy, to prevent popular awareness from transcending the horizon of family, kinship group or tribes, and thus to retard the evolution of more modern, more aware, more skilled and more deploy able "citizens"—the human material needed to sustain and nurture this modernizing development strategy.[17]

Yet, as our case studies have revealed, the dichotomy of the progressive educated elite and a reactionary traditional aristocracy is a gross oversimplification.[18] Rather, chieftaincy structures are integral to configurations of power in all major sections of Nigeria.

The Babangida regime, in any case, rejected the Political Bureau's principal recommendation: the establishment of a socialist republic. Instead, claiming to moblize Nigerians for economic and political development, it endorsed the prevailing political arrangement. This embrace of the dominant strategy of civil/military governance,[19] further entrenched the power of influential traditional rulers as representatives of local and regional interests. At the same time, earlier military reforms—such as the *1976 Local Government Guidelines*, the 1978 Land Use Decree and Babangida's own transition program—had heightened the distributive struggles centered on state resources.[20] The mounting crisis of political legitimacy was coupled with dramatic economic decline, brought on by falling oil prices, foreign debts, and shortages of foreign exchange. This intensified existing disequilibria—between classes, between regions, between community-based structures and the state.[21]

Babangida's increasing neopatrimonialism[22] enhanced the presence of prominent traditional rulers in regional and national politics. In addition, having embraced the Dasuki Report as a guideline for Nigerian local government,[23] traditional rulers were steadily encouraged to participate in state-sanctioned consultative meetings at the regional level.[24]

The growing influence of traditional rulers was cemented by the Constituent Assembly's endorsement of chieftaincy institutions in 1988. This reflected the influence of traditional rulers within networks of regional powerbrokers, as well as Babangida's increasing vulnerability vis-à-vis key sectors of Nigerian opinion.[25] Indeed, it was apparent by this time that Babangida was following a line established by his predecessor Buhari, embracing Northern emirs and chiefs as the informal sector of his regime. This rapprochement was exemplified by a publicized visit in June 1988 to congratulate Sir Abubakar III on his golden jubilee as Sultan.[26] Moreover, Babangida regularly conferred with trusted Northern traditionalists. Nigeria's controversial membership in the Organization of Islamic Conference (OIC) was also seen as an attempt to placate the emirs and Islamic leaders of the North. And a spectacular neotraditional gesture of the regime was the selection of a new Sultan, following the death of Sir Abubakar. The appointment of Ibrahim Dasuki, a Babangida favorite, over Mohammed Maccido, the more conservative choice of the Sokoto kingmakers, indicated the importance of the *Masu Sarauta*—the emirate aristocracy—in the regime's political calculations.[27]

These developments reinforced the influence of chiefly rulers in the deliberations of the Constituent Assembly. The arguments of radicals such as Bala Takaya, about the contradiction of combining a constitutional republic with monarchical and chiefly institutions, were in the minority. Rather, neotraditional views, such as those expressed by Ekiti-Yoruba delegate Bamidele Olumilua, carried the day: "in my part of the world," he said, "if it does not rain in time, we go to the oba, if there is an outbreak of disease, we first consult our oba." In a vote granting traditional rulers limited powers in local government administration, traditionalists won a resounding victory, with a vote of 233 to 54.[28]

Complicated by the economic crisis and austerity measures of the 1980s, chieftaincy politics in the Babangida years thus reflected the prevailing nexus of class and ethno-regional groupings in Nigeria. As the transition program became more contentious, now shifting in the direction of narrow regional cliques, popular pressures intensified.[29] Babangida's initial policy of dialogue was steadily replaced by manipulative and repressive measures to ward off growing discontent. This only further alienated the increasingly restless professional and civic organizations such as the Academic Staff Union of Universities (ASUU), the Nigerian Bar Association (NBA), Women in Nigeria (WIN), and the Nigerian Labour Congress (NLC). As the regime restricted the political space and civil liberties of the urban citizenry, its policies were complicated by the failure of its economic liberalization program. It was clear by the late 1980s that it would be difficult to reconcile a structural adjustment program, imposed with the blessing of the International Monetary Fund (IMF), with the regime's faltering transition program.[30]

The assault on civic and professional groups only generated greater popular pressures; even the officer corps—especially Southern junior officers—seemed increasingly leery of the regime. Some resented the erosion of the prestige and professionalism of the military. The failed coup of 1990, led by a clique of Southern junior officers, shook the confidence of the regime.[31]

The transition program was anchored on one fundamental assumption. Advisers had attributed the failure of previous democratic experiments to the undue influence of the older generation of regional politicians in electoral politics, and their abuse of state and party structures as instruments of patronage. This was the rationale for the creation of only two major political parties: the Social Democratic Party (SDP)—said to be ideologically left-of-center—and the National Republican Convention (NRC) on the right. The military regime drafted the parties' manifestos, built their secretariats, funded their conventions, and regulated their activities. It also created a new electoral commission, conducted another controversial national census, and promoted community development in rural areas (through a Directorate for Food, Roads and Rural Infrastructure). It even created agencies to promote democratic values such as the Centre for Democratic Studies (CDS), and the Directorate of Mass Mobilization (MAMSER). In short, Babangida and his associates sought to impose "democracy" from the top, paradoxically compressing Nigeria's burgeoning civil society in the process. Not surprisingly, the strategy failed.

The regime's two parties rapidly degenerated into havens for the rich and powerful[32]—the same regional political class that Babangida's advisors had warned against. When the old guard made a mockery of the transition program, Babangida turned to new cohorts of hand-picked "new breed" politicians schooled in the same political environment as the older politicians, but lacking their experience. As in the past, electoral politics was perceived as a medium for accumulation, access to money determined the composition and objectives of the parties and their candidates, and electoral strategies turned on the manipulation of communal, ethno-regional and religious differences. Once again, regional powerbrokers summoned their allies among chiefly rulers to help gain grassroots support and turn out the vote. Gradually, the Babangida regime abandoned its erstwhile objective to restructure Nigeria's dysfunctional state and society.

A presidential election was eventually held in June 1993, with two wealthy regional politicians—M. K. O. Abiola, an Egba-Yoruba Muslim, and Bashir Tofa, a Hausa-Fulani businessman from Kano—as the candidates. Although Abiola won a landslide victory, the dominant military/civilian clique, increasingly centered on the North, decided to hold on to power, and after several weeks of uncertainty Babangida annulled the election. This triggered angry reactions in Yoruba towns. To stem the discontent, Babangida resorted to repressive measures; when they failed, he installed a trusted Yoruba ally, Ernest Shonekan, as head of an interim federal government. Then, in November 1993, Shonekan was pushed aside by Babangida's deputy, General Sani Abacha. And so Abacha's coup brought this costly and cynical abuse of power to an end. He suspended the civilian constitution, dismissed the politicians, and appointed military administrators in their place. Babangida's failed transition program, like the events leading to the Civil War, exposed not only the excesses of military rule, but the profound structural defects of the Nigerian state and society, especially its ethno-regional and class arrangements. These ethno-regional struggles, and the role of traditional rulers within them, can be seen in the controversy over the chairmanship of the Oyo State Council of Chiefs.

The Chairmanship of the Oyo State Council of Chiefs

While the Political Bureau was deliberating, the Oyo State Government faced a controversy over the chairmanship of the State Council of Chiefs in 1987. The major contenders for the post were the Alaafin of Oyo, Oba Olayiwola Adeyemi III, and the Ooni of Ife, Oba Sijuade Olubuse II. The dispute was an important benchmark in terms of both its immediate political consequences and its longer-term impact on Yoruba political alignments. It had been brewing since the appointment of Ooni Sijuade in 1980.

This conflict takes its impetus from the complex nature of Yoruba politics since the colonial period in the following major ways. First, the dispute was rooted in conflicting interpretations of Yoruba traditional authority, and in the partisanship that had dominated Yoruba politics since decolonization. Second, it revealed how influential obas, using neotraditional themes and modern resources, forged alliances to consolidate their positions during a period of rapid social change. Finally, it reveals the strategies adopted by a military regime to deal with a conflict which had ignited partisan feelings in a potentially volatile region of Nigeria.

The Oyo State Council of Chiefs was an appointive body set up by the Western Region Government in 1959. Like the regional House of Chiefs (see chapter 5), the Council became an instrument to advance the objectives of the regional executive. It also conferred considerable prestige on its chairman, who figured as the most senior representative of the obas of the state, holding the most prestigious statutory position of any traditional ruler, and owned respect by the regional population and its elites.

As discussed in chapter 5, obas and title-holders had been caught up in the acrimonious conflicts of the AG crisis. Given the prominence of Oyo and Oshun politicians in the NNDP, and the apparent rejection of the party in Ijebu and Egba Divisions, NNDP politicians played on these historical divisions. Obas and elders who had shifted their support to the NNDP, moreover, were rewarded with regional government patronage, while those loyal to the AG incurred official wrath.[33] This development was discomfiting to the chairman and members of the Council, now appearing as "agents" of a regional government that lacked political legitimacy.

Sir Adesoji Aderemi, the Ooni of Ife who in his capacity as governor presided over the dismissal of Premier Akintola, and who in the late 1950s clashed with Deputy Premier Fani-Kayode, was one of the obas subject to NNDP attack. The diminution in his fortunes was the gain of the Alaafin, who became the favorite of the NNDP regional authorities. They appointed him Chairman of the Council of Chiefs, where he remained until the military intervention in 1966.

This coup was an important benchmark in the rivalry between the Alaafin and the Ooni. With the ban on party politics, the state Council of Chiefs assumed greater political significance; it was the only formal institution through which obas could communicate with the new regime. In keeping with its commitment to political change, the military reversed the chieftaincy policy of the NNDP. Lieutenant Colonel Fajuyi, Governor of the Western Provinces, appointed the Ooni as the council chairman;[34] he retained the position indefinitely, becoming chairman of the Oyo State Council of Chiefs when General Mohammed created more states in 1976. Oba Aderemi retained that position until his death in 1980. The chairmanship controversy persisted, however, since both Oyo and Ife remained within the Oyo State.

Policies undertaken by various military regimes also failed to resolve the rivalry between the Oyo and Ife crowns. An investigation conducted by Brigadier Rotimi's administration in 1974 concluded that Oba Aderemi retained the chairmanship not because of the title of Ooni but, rather, because of his personal prestige among the Yoruba.[35] In 1977, Rotimi's successor, Brigadier Jemibewon, also skirted the controversy. Avoiding the seniority issue, Jemibewon simply enlarged the council. With the obas' titles arranged in alphabetical order, the Akire of Ikire (a relatively junior oba) now headed the list.[36] Thus, like Rotimi, Jemibewon side-stepped the thorny issue of succession to the chairmanship.

As in the preceding parliamentary era, the partisan politics of the Second Republic awakened the rivalry between the two Yoruba crowns. Three developments were also important here. First, the deposition of Oba Adeniran Adeyemi ll by the AG regional authorities in 1956 had remained a sore point for Oyo elites, distancing them from AG loyalists for almost three decades. Oyo notables thus commanded limited influence in the UPN during its formative years of 1978 and 1979. Second, two decades after Oba Adeyemi's deposition, prominent NNDP politicians had played a critical role in the appointment of his son, Oba Adeyemi III, as Alaafin in 1972. Oba Adeyemi III subsequently embraced the Yoruba faction of the National Party of Nigeria (NPN), which had its origins in the defunct

NNDP.[37] Finally, the old AG loyalists who dominated the UPN favored Ooni Aderemi's successor, Oba Sijuade Olubuse II, who was appointed Ooni in 1980. In September, UPN Governor Bola Ige appointed Ooni Sijuade permanent chairman of the Oyo State Council of Chiefs.[38] This preference for the Ooni revived the rivalry between the two crowns and the respective elites of their "historic" towns. Local Ife historians, asserting the supremacy of the Ife crown among Yoruba obas, defended the state government's policy in the pro-UPN *Daily Sketch* and *Nigerian Tribune*. Oyo elites, meanwhile, refuted the government's claim in the pro-NPN *National Concord*. Despite the objection of the Council of Chiefs, the UPN authorities remained resolute (see chapter 8 for details).

The controversy over the chairmanship resurfaced after the 1983 elections. With the election of an NPN candidate, Dr. Omololu Olunloyo, as state governor, the fortunes of the Alaafin improved. For several years, the new governor had been an ally of the Alaafin. As Commissioner for Local Government and Chieftaincy Affairs in Adebayo's military government, Olunloyo had openly endorsed the appointment of Oba Adeyemi III. This special relationship was confirmed when Oba Adeyemi conferred the chieftaincy title of *Osi Balogun* on the governor immediately after the 1983 elections. With regards to the chairmanship issue, "a variable mixture of political and traditional sentiments and prejudices operated at all times," the new governor said.[39] He based the theme of his first broadcast solely on the chairmanship issue, arguing that such historical and traditional considerations were secondary; the issue was basically a constitutional matter, he said, in which the state executive council reserved the right to select the chairman. Thus, he declared, his government would not recognize "a permanent chairman appointed ex-officio in title or in person"; rather, the dilemma would be resolved by rotating the chairmanship every two years. This policy, however, was overtaken by events: the military coup of December 31, 1983.

Under the new military regimes, the tenuous relationship between the two parties deteriorated, prompting the state and federal military authorities to intervene in the chairmanship controversy. Tension continued to mount, however, resulting in the outbreak of hostilities in January 1987. Ironically, these troubles coincided with renewed activity and self-assertion on the part of traditional rulers.

At this stage, it was the Ooni who seized the initiative in the quest for regional pre-eminence and national recognition, while the Alaafin resisted what he saw as a threat to his prestige. The Ooni embraced national dignitaries and men of wealth, as well as powerful traditional rulers in other regions such as the Emir of Kano, the Oba of Benin and the Obi of Onitsha. At the regional level, Oba Sijuade won the endorsement of many of his fellow obas through his extensive connections, wealth, and traditional status. His pre-eminent status was suggested by the entourage of important personalities, including other obas, who accompanied him to important national and international events. Despite his initial allegiance to the proscribed UPN, Oba Sijuade's network of influential allies included persons of diverse political affiliation, such as the leader of the proscribed UPN, Chief Awolowo; National Chairman of the banned NPN, Chief A. M. A. Akinloye; and the ex-UPN Governor of Oyo State, Chief Bola Ige. Under the leadership of the Ooni, Yoruba obas also sought to influence the direction of the national debate on Nigeria's democratic future. We will recall that it was under the Ooni's direction that regional politicians and obas presented a memorandum to the Political Bureau calling for the integration of chieftaincy structures into the machinery of state.[40] The Ooni's influence took on international dimensions when he visited Yoruba communities in the Republic of Benin, in 1985,[41] and the "Yoruba diasporic communities" of Brazil, Cuba and Trinidad, in 1987 and 1988. These trips proved a huge success in enhancing his reputation as the "spiritual father" of all those who share Yoruba culture and religion everywhere.[42]

Oba Sijuade's extensive network, however, was not limited to the usual political and economic elites. He also acquired unconventional allies at the Universities of Ife and Ibadan. At Ife, where he was revered by certain senior academics and administrators, he gave a chieftaincy title to the vice-chancellor and renowned scholar of Yoruba Language and Culture, Professor Wande Abimbola, and in turn was awarded the honorary degree of Doctor of Civil Law in January 1984.

The controversy over the state chairmanship came to a head at the Grand Assembly of Yoruba Obas, convened by the Ooni in January 1985. Attended by many obas, politicians and elders, the Grand Assembly was projected as the obas' formal response to major political developments under the military regime of General Buhari. Four senior obas were conspicuously absent: the Alaafin of Oyo and three allies, the Olubadan of Ibadan, Oba Asanike; the Owa of Ijeshaland, Oba Aromolaran; and the Shoun of Ogbomosho, Oba Oyewumi. But it was a minor incident that triggered the open hostilities between the Ooni and the Alaafin. *Sunday Concord*, a pro-Alaafin newspaper owned by the famous Yoruba philanthropist Chief M. K. O. Abiola, reported that during the conference, Oba Sijuade had referred to the absent obas as "dissidents," implying his seniority over other Yoruba obas.[43] An editorial contended that the

Grand Assembly was intended by the Ooni as a stepping-stone towards his attainment of supremacy over all other obas and traditional rulers not only in Yorubaland but also throughout Nigeria and the Black race.[44]

Following months of exchange between the two parties, the state military governor, Colonel Popoola, intervened; he warned both parties that his government would take stern measures against anyone who threatened the peace. Popoola's attempt to resolve the dispute by adopting Olunloyo's rotational strategy, however, failed to secure the support of the state Executive Council.[45]

The chairmanship controversy continued under Popoola's successor, Colonel Olurin. The open confrontation between the two obas quickly became a source of embarrassment for the federal and state authorities, and in January 1987 the governor, responding to orders from Lagos, summoned an emergency meeting in Ibadan of the state Council of Chiefs. At the meeting, Governor Olurin rebuked the obas, whom he claimed had exposed their "exalted position to ridicule" by debating sensitive issues openly in the newspapers.[46] He failed, however, to provide an acceptable solution to the dispute.

Another major conflict erupted when the Ooni summoned a meeting of the Council in January 1987. This time, the Alaafin and his supporters took legal action against the governor, the attorney-general, Oba Sijuade, and the Council of Chiefs, calling on an Ibadan high court to prevent the meeting. The motion also called on the court to nullify the chairmanship of the Ooni. The Alaafin and his allies achieved a partial victory when the court granted the *ex-parte* motion forbidding the meeting scheduled for 5 February 1987. Governor Olurin approached the Alaafin and his supporters for an out-of-court settlement, agreeing to dissolve the Council. He did so after the dissenting obas withdrew their case. But the conflict remained dormant until 1992 when the Babangida regime carved a new state, Oshun, out of Oyo State. With Ile-Ife now in Oshun State, the Alaafin and the Ooni were, for the first time since the imposition of colonial rule, in separate administrative jurisdictions.[47]

This saga, informed by conflicting traditional interpretations, was also embedded in the prevailing partisan alignments dating back to the late colonial period. Prominent leaders of the proscribed NPN played a decisive role in the tactics adopted by the Alaafin faction, while the Ooni had the support of the banned UPN.[48] The role of Chief M. K. O. Abiola deserves special comment. A Muslim from Egba Division of Ogun state, Abiola had emerged as one of Nigeria's most affluent men by the mid-1970s.[49]

Like most men of considerable wealth in Nigeria, Abiola attracted an extensive network of powerful associates within a relatively short period of time. His political allies included traditional rulers, military administrators, senior government officials, and wealthy businessmen. Abiola also maintained a high media profile, having taken several chieftaincy titles, contributing generously to religious and social causes, and frequently expressing views on controversial political issues. He had also been active in party politics: for some time he was chairman of the Ogun State branch of the banned NPN, and one of the party's most generous financial contributors.

It was Abiola who provided financial and moral support for the Alaafin, who seemed to lack the wealth of his adversary, the Ooni. In the crucial months between December 1986 and February 1987, Abiola's newspapers, the *National Concord* and the *African Concord*, trumpeted the Alaafin's cause. Presumably as a token of appreciation, Abiola was given the prestigious chieftaincy title of Bashorun of Ibadan by the Olubadan. Later that year, Abiola was given an even more distinguished title of Are-Ona-Kakanfo by the Alaafin. The role of Abiola in the chairmanship controversy reveals how conflicting notions of Yoruba traditions were infused with contemporary political issues of prestige, status and power. Abiola's involvement in the conflict was decisive in permitting the Alaafin and his allies to resist the Ooni's push for regional pre-eminence through the state council of chiefs.

The influence of Yoruba obas and local potentates—as well as counterparts in other regions—reveals the deepening crisis of the Nigerian state and society under military rule. And as the crisis of military governance intensified, further complicated by severe economic downturn, chieftaincy structures provided critical institutional and ideological rallying-points for dominant ethno-regional political alliances. It was thus in the context of entrenched ethno-regionalism that traditional rulers and local potentates struggled to influence military policies, notably Buhari's local government review and Babangida's transition program to democratic rule. The failure of Babangida's transition program not only revealed the well-known structural imbalance of Nigeria's federal system, but also demonstrated the limitations of the prevailing ethno-regional arrangements on which political alliances had been configured since the decolonization process of the 1950s.

These regional pressures, however, were reinforced by the consolidation of elite power at the local level, discussed here in the case study on the chairmanship of the Oyo State Council of Chiefs. Once again, regional elites projected conflicting interpretations of traditional authority as a strategy of consolidating regional power under military rule. These alliances reinforced the prevailing partisanship that had been established in the First Republic. Thus, the controversy which focused on the prestige of Yorubaland's pre-eminent crowns in Ile-Ife and Oyo reveals how regional elites consolidated extensive networks of political power within the prevailing political alignments.

10

CONCLUSION

The themes and cases analyzed in this book reveal the imaginative adaptation of Yoruba indigenous political structures to the processes of state formation in Nigeria since the imposition of colonial rule. Drawing on the interactions between the state and chieftaincy in the Yoruba region, this study goes beyond earlier Africanist scholarship that attributed the resilience of these indigenous structures to their enduring normative and utilitarian qualities. Yoruba chieftaincy institutions survived both the constricting forces of colonialism and the modernization programs of postcolonial regimes not only because of their adaptability, but because of their integration with emerging centers of state power, and their role in ongoing processes of stratification and class formation. These developments have entailed a complex pattern of continuity and change, as chieftaincy structures responded to the rapidly shifting sociopolitical and economic conditions of the twentieth century.

The case studies that inform this analysis thus identify chieftaincy structures as the focal point of critical discourses of continuity and social change in Yoruba communities. Linked to externally derived forces,[1] and legitimated by neotraditional themes that are integral to Nigeria's colonial and postcolonial sociopolitical settings,[2] chieftaincy structures in the twentieth century are analyzed here in terms of three interrelated themes: the distortion by indirect rule of Yoruba traditional political institutions; the competing claims between old communal identities, expressed through reconstructed histories, traditions and myths; and the role of chieftaincy structures in the ethno-regional power configurations that emerged from the decolonization process. Exploring these topics, I have argued that chief-taincy structures have not only persisted as key communal expressions, but have sustained Nigeria's dominant political arrangements, particularly in the regions and the states.

The perspective of the *longue durée*, which has been loosely adopted here, provides a fluid framework in which chieftaincy structures—along with associated legitimacy doctrines, derived from reconstructed histories, myths and symbols—are analyzed in the dynamic context of political tur-bulence and structural change.[3] This perspective is particularly salient since colonial policies themselves were grafted on contested political structures, doctrines and claims of preceding centuries. By analyzing the shifting con-tours of communal identities, I have argued that, rather than respond to a distant colonial and postcolonial state, Yoruba elites consistently deployed subjective interpretations of their past to construct structures and ideolo-gies of power. These historical continuities are not only critical to a com-prehensive exploration of the culture of politics, but are vital to the analysis of the complex interactions between modern and traditional political hier-archies.[4] Richard Joseph has noted the implication of the connections be-tween the Yoruba past and present:

> What remained unresolved throughout the *Pax Britannica*, and after a quar-ter of a century of independent government, was the absence of a stable hegemony among the Yoruba dating back to the collapse of the Oyo Empire and the subsequent statement of a new political suzerainty centered on Ibadan. That the Yoruba continue to live their history in the present is often cultur-ally magnificent but also politically catastrophic.[5]

Although shaped by modern themes that are derived from external forces—notably colonialism, the impact of world religions, Western enlightenment and modern development—these reconstructed histories were nevertheless dominated by an "indigenous timescale."[6] In the context of the colonial encounter, "indigenous" forces were decisive in shaping the direction of change, and provided critical strategies of political mobilization in twenti-eth-century Yoruba communities.

Dominant sociopolitical themes such as the historical rivalry among communities, the conflicting manifestations of colonial rule, the processes of elite formation, the enduring nature of partisanship, the underlying po-litical economy, the corporatist style of military rule and the modernizing programs of postcolonial regimes have all combined to shape chieftaincy structures throughout the last century. This analysis of chieftaincy politics thus integrates a broad sociopolitical space, emphasizing the interaction among communal identities, the persistence of indigenous political structures and the Nigerian state project since the late nineteenth century.

Even as their formal political roles eroded in the postcolonial period, Yoruba obas and potentates were still firmly embedded to interlocking networks of local and regional power. Within these configurations, they reinforced the regional networks of influence and patronage that have dominated political behavior within a fragile federal context. These ties were solidified by communal doctrines that have assumed ambiguous forms since colonial rule. The political significance of chieftaincy structures thus lie, in part, in reconstructed histories of precolonial communities, contentious mythological and traditional themes, and conflicting idioms of colonial rule. These forces subsequently crystalized in the "ethno-clientelist" political arrangements that have dominated Nigerian politics since the decolonization process of the 1950s.[7]

Deployed by ethnic powerbrokers, these neotraditional themes are effective mediums of political mobilization. They were initially appropriated by the dominant regional elites during the period of transition—especially the inter- and intra-communal competition—that followed World War II.[8] Indeed, this critical historical period was dominated by an explosion of communal doctrines as political elites began to contest for the limited resources of the emerging Nigerian state. Permeated by the structures and symbols of chieftaincy, Yoruba ideological expressions were used in "guiding actions, defining goals, interpreting the experiences of such 'power' relationships as domination and subordination, or even expressing legitimacy."[9] Preoccupied with the mobilization of local followings, communal ideologies, rooted in reconstructed pasts, served as mediums for the representations of the meaning of power—and demonstrated the power of meaning in the process.

It was thus the exigencies of colonial and postcolonial Nigerian politics that prompted communal powerbrokers to construct broad, pan-ethnic ideologies to tie together the diverse subgroups of the Yoruba. Conversely, as narrower sub-ethnic interests confronted these pan-ethnic constructs, the "partisans" of ancestral hometowns mobilized nativist opposition against competitors and intruders.[10] The persistence of these communal identities today, as focal points and resources amidst rapid social change, show how critical indigenous political structures are to the old societies now trapped in the novel confines of the modern state. These hierarchical traditional authorities are integral to social structures that are dominated by discourses of the past in the present.[11] Their legitimacy myths and doctrines are not concerned with historical analysis per se. Rather they are preoccupied with how "various narratives express, interpret and evaluate political actions and alignments."[12]

The persistence of chieftaincy structures in local and national politics is thus integral to the historical contradictions of the Nigerian state and social formation. Given the fragile, contingent character of colonial and postcolonial institutions, the Nigerian state has hardly functioned as an effective structure of governance and administration. The ethno-regional classes that have dominated Nigerian politics since decolonization have not devised a viable mechanism of governance which effectively integrates antecedent institutions into modern state structures. The converging and conflicting interests of these regional and communal alliances have thus had far-reaching implications for the persistence of authoritarian regimes, the endless recurrence of "democratic transitions," and the struggle for democracy at the local level.

The greatest significance of chieftaincy structures is thus a consolidation of elite power that draws on ethnic and communal doctrines.[13] Chieftaincy structures thrive in the context of a rentier state where ethno-regional elites seize upon state agencies to advance class and communal interests. Within this extractive, clientelist state structure,[14] chieftaincy institutions have consistently reinforced the political and economic alliances that have sustained—or undermined—fragile governing coalitions at the regional and federal levels. This preoccupation with power configurations has not only strained the relations between traditional leaders and local communities, but has also trapped chieftaincy structures in the contradictions of the wider regional and national systems.[15] The centrifugal pressures of political ethnicity, with its communal, ethno-regional, and class dimensions—in which chiefly rulers are deeply involved—have contributed significantly to the crisis of state legitimacy in Nigeria.

The ethno-regional framework of power relations, however, sustain the representation of Yoruba obas, chiefs, title-holders and local powerbrokers (and their counterparts in other regions) as legitimate reflections of local aspirations. At the same time, since the dominant political alliances have distinct strategic and extractive concerns, traditional elites are routinely drawn into conflict with local needs and aspirations. Obas and chiefs who ignored local interests have suffered considerable loss of prestige among the townspeople upon whom their legitimacy ultimately depends. Nevertheless, these local leaders continue to deploy considerable resources to secure the approval of the holders of state power, who not only dominate state agencies and resources, but ultimately regulate chieftaincy institutions themselves.[16]

The tensions between communal interests and the priorities of the holders of state power have thus put great strain on chieftaincy institutions. In the absence of any systematic incorporation of the corporate interests of local communities,[17] state officials—whether colonial administrators, military rulers, politicians or civil servants—have coopted chiefly rulers in their attempt to project mass support. As embodiments of local values and identities, absolved from direct responsibility for the affairs of the postcolonial state, obas and title-holders retain considerable influence. The complicated role of Yoruba obas and chiefs as intermediaries between state and society is both an expression of the cultural worth and the strategic role of chieftaincy institutions, and of the blocked transformation of beleaguered local communities ravaged by poverty, marginality and exploitation. The limitations of the modern state have obliged successive civilian and military regimes to seek a *modus vivendi* with traditional rulers, attempting to co-opt their assumed legitimacy and prestige.[18] Despite this intermediary role, the dilemma of chieftaincy is immediately apparent when we consider that as institutions that draw their legitimacy from conflicting interpretations of the past, postcolonial regimes have nevertheless struggled to rationalize these indigenous institutions in rapidly changing societies.[19]

Under colonial indirect rule, and despite rapid social change, obas, chiefs, and educated elites reconstructed different versions of traditions and the past to reinforce or expand their power. In the early years of colonial rule, British policies, despite local opposition, sought to elevate the Alaafin to the status of king of Oyo Province. This interpretation, however, distorted the actual political arrangements of the nineteenth century, and failed to achieve the hierarchical political order that the architects of indirect rule had anticipated. Rather, obas, chiefs and educated elites throughout the province collaborated in appropriating communal hometown doctrines and historical constructions, as well as discourse of modern development, to justify and give voice to an array of competing identities and claims.

The process of decolonization did not provide a neat break from this problematic system. It had been expected that decolonization would be the critical historical event providing a new political framework that would transcend both the traditional and the imperial arrangements of the past. Confronted with the tripodal federal structure, however, the modernizing Yoruba political class, like its counterparts elsewhere, was obliged to appeal for broad followings, reconstituting historically disparate—but culturally intelligible—communities into pan-ethnic fronts for collective action. Responding to the regionalization of power that arose during the decolonization process, along with the new demands for modern development, the process of structural transformation led to the mobilization of obas, chiefs, and baales as junior partners of a new political class that now wielded executive and legislative authority in the new structures of the state. By projecting the myth of a culturally homogeneous political community, Yoruba nationalists, in collaboration with local and traditional elites, constructed a complex ethno-regional project whose remarkable success was largely derived from the exigencies of the Nigerian state formation itself.[20] Like the local-level struggles among hometown chiefs, elders and educated elements under colonial rule, the hegemonic ideologies that were derived from the decolonization process—as expressed through communal, class, and ethno-regional mediums—were ambiguous and conflictual as well. And since these traditional claims involved contested histories, genealogies and power calculations, they alienated those excluded by the dominant political class and its legitimating ideologies. This was resisted, and it gave rise to counter myths drawn from precolonial and colonial communal themes.

The communal and ethno-regional foundations of Yoruba politics, reinforced by chieftaincy structures during the decolonization process, remained a prominent feature of electoral politics during Nigeria's failed democratic transitions. During the turbulent First Republic, the chieftaincy structures that had affirmed Yoruba elite power during decolonization now became a formidable instrument of popular resistance during a period of Yoruba political marginality. The Second Republic, which confirmed earlier political alignments, revived the linkages between chieftaincy politics and the entangled web of acrimonious partisanship. In Oyo State, along with the other Yoruba states of Lagos, Ogun, and Ondo (and to a lesser extent Kwara), the political cleavages that had emerged in the wake of the AG Crisis became effective instruments in the hands of the UPN and NPN. In these confrontations, regional politicians routinely appropriated neo-traditional themes as they consolidated old alliances or constructed new ones. Obas and chiefs were once again dragged into feuds that only deepened communal and class divisions in Yoruba towns.

Constrained by these persistent alignments, subsequent military regimes also resorted to traditional rulers, regional politicians and other local powerbrokers as intermediaries between the state and localities. The various neotraditional and corporatist strategies of governance they adopted, however, failed to confer the legitimacy for which the military and its allies had hoped. Given Nigeria's complicated sociopolitical and economic realities, along with deep regional, communal, and class divisions, traditional authorities were simply unable to provide effective central-local linkages and the moral nexus that are required.

With the notable exception of the Mohammed/Obasanjo regime, which made a spirited attempt to rationalize local government institutions within a liberal politico-economic program, Yoruba obas and their counterparts struggled to retained their importance in the ethno-regional political framework. And at the grassroots level, obas, chiefs and other titleholders fought to assert their interests, deploying competing notions of traditional authority, in an increasingly elaborate system of state patronage. In Oyo State, these local struggles were expressed through elite agitations, on behalf of their obas, for the ultimate Yoruba royal insignia, the beaded crown. Operating in a context of military-imposed land and local government reforms, and the Obasanjo regime's push for modern development, these regional and local pressures for power and prestige were further complicated by rival chiefly claims and communal tensions.

Following the demise of the Second Republic, the neopatrimonial style of military rule adopted by Generals Buhari and Babangida reinforced the ethno-regional patterns of competition and alliances. As the major military cliques became more politicized, influential traditional rulers assumed even more central roles in regional politics. And as Nigeria's social contradictions intensified, due to the economic crisis of the 1980s and the 1990s, grassroots forces assumed even greater prominence in the volatile political environment. In Oyo State, conflicting interpretations of traditional authority sought their rationales in the contentious past, while pursuing their interests through very contemporary networks of power, patronage, and prestige. These dynamics undermined new military attempts at local government reform: three decades of political regionalization, sustained by communal doctrines and identities, had by now firmly consolidated the role of chieftaincy. With the introduction of a democratic transition program in the late 1980s, Yoruba obas, mindful of the neotraditional dimensions of other regional alliances, actively engaged in constitutional debates, demanding formal recognition in state affairs. These demands achieved only limited success. Despite their formal marginalization, however, influential traditional rulers remained critical factors in the political and economic calculus of the dominant ethno-regional blocs.

Chieftaincy structures have thrived over the last century, then, not because of a particular Yoruba loyalty to tradition, but because of their integration into regional alliances of power and privilege. As our case studies suggest, chieftaincy institutions and traditions are far from sacrosanct and immutable; they are constantly reconstructed out of the living memories, interest, and structural resources of local communities.[21] In the twentieth-century Yoruba region of Oyo, certainly, they have been woven into the

expressions of communal identities, class interest, and economic prerogatives,[22] in tandem with the overall evolution of the colonial and postcolonial
Nigerian state. In this context, a particularly important change has been
the shift in legitimating concepts—from indirect rule to what we might
call democratic regionalism. The interests of regional-based political classes
have in part been formed in the vortex of external forces (world religions,
Western nationalist culture, and global capitalism, among others), and in
part by indigenous structures and identities. The complex interactions of
these forces have shaped chieftaincy politics and Yoruba collective action
throughout the twentieth century.

NOTES

Notes to Chapter 1

1. For an authoritative analysis of the complex interplay between "structures of society" and Third-World states, see Joel Migdal, *Strong Societies and Weak States: State-Society Relations and State Capacities in the Third World*, Princeton: Princeton University Press, 1988.

2. The most salient of these interrelated points is of course the imperative of mid-century decolonization. Of the numerous studies on this subject see especially David Apter's pioneering work, *Ghana in Transition*, Princeton: Princeton University Press, 1955. For an authoritative anthropological approach see Clifford Geertz, 'The Integrative Revolution: Primordial Sentiments and Civil Politics in the New States' in Clifford Geertz (ed.), *Old Societies and New States: The Quest for Modernity in Asia and Africa*, New York: Free Press, 1967.

3. For a detailed discussion see Marion Levy, 'Patterns of Modernization in Political Development', *Annals of the American Academy of Political and Social Sciences*, March 1966, pp. 29–40.

4. Lloyd Fallers, 'The Predicament of the Modern African Chief: An Instance from Uganda', *American Anthropologist*, 57, 1955, pp. 290–305. See also Lloyd Fallers, *Bantu Bureaucracy: A Study of Integration and Conflict in the Political Institution of an East African People*, Cambridge: Heffer, 1956; Lloyd Fallers (ed.), *The King's Men: Leadership and Status in Buganda on the Eve of Independence*, London: Oxford University Press, 1964.

5. For a detailed analysis see Max Weber, *Economy and Society*, Berkeley: University of California Press, 1968; see also David Betham, *The Legitimation of Power*, Atlantic Highlands, N.J.: Humanities Press, 1991. I would like to thank Kelechi Kalu for insightful comments on this subject.

6. For a succinct theoretical analysis of this perspective see S. N. Eisenstadt, 'Continuity and Reconstruction of Tradition', *Daedalus*, 102, 1973.

7. K. A. Busia, *The Position of the Chief in the Modern Political System of Ashanti*, London: Oxford University Press, 1951.

8. Lucy P. Mair, 'African Chiefs Today', Lugard Memorial Lecture for 1958, *Africa*, 28, 1958.

9. P. C. W. Gutkind, 'African Urban Chiefs: Agents of Stability or Change in African Urban Life', *Anthropologica*, 8, 1966.

10. Michael Crowder and Obaro Ikime (eds.), *West African Chiefs: Their Changing Status under Colonial Rule and Independence*, Ile-Ife: University of Ife Press, 1970.

11. See, for example, Arrighi Giovanni and John Saul, *Essays in the Political Economy of Africa*, New York: Monthly Review Press, 1973; Samir Amin, *Neo-Colonialism in West Africa*, New York: 1974; P. C. W. Gutkind and Peter Waterman (eds.), New York: Monthly Review Press, 1977.

12. For an important Africanist analysis see Michael Bratton, 'Beyond the State: Civil Society and Associational Life in Africa', *World Politics*, 41, 1985.

13. Patrick Molutsi, 'The Ruling Class and Democracy in Botswana', in John Holm and Patrick Molutsi (eds.), *Democracy in Botswana*, Athens, Ohio: Ohio University Press, 1989; see also Patrick Molutsi and John Holm, 'Developing Democracy When Civil Society Is Weak: The Case of Botswana', *African Affairs*, 89, 1990.

14. For detailed discussion see *The Republic of Uganda: Report of the Commission of Inquiry into the Local government System*, Kampala: Government Printer, 1987.

15. *The Constitution of the Republic of South Africa*, Cape Town, 1993.

16. Gerhard Mare, *Brothers Born of Warrior Blood: Politics and Ethnicity in South Africa*, Johannesburg: Raven Press, 1992; see also Gerhard Mare and Georgina Hamilton, *An Appetite for Power: Buthelezi's Inkatha and South Africa*, Johannesburg: Raven Press, 1987; Mzala, *Gatsha Buthelezi: Chief with a Double Agenda*, London: Zed Press, 1988.

17. For an authoritative study on this important subject see Peter Ekeh, 'Colonialism and the Two Publics in Africa: A Theoretical Statement', *Comparative Studies in Society and History*, 17, 1975; see also his 'Social Anthropology and Two Contrasting Uses of Tribalism in Africa', *Comparative Studies in Society and History*, 32, 1990.

18. Jean-François Bayart, *The State in Africa: The Politics of the Belly*, London: Longman, 1993.

19. I would like to thank James E. Genova for sharing his superb knowledge on the *annaliste* historians with me during our many conversations. My brief reference to this magnificent historiography has more to do with my subject matter and does not do justice to Genova's critical insight on these important works.

20. Fernand Braudel, 'Débats et histoires et sciences sociales: La longue durée', *Annales*, 4, October 1958, p. 729.

21. *Ibid*, pp. 731–35.

22. Catherine Coquery-Vidrovitch, 'Changes in African Historical Studies in France', in Christopher Fyfe (ed.), *African Studies since 1945: A Tribute to Basil Davidson*, p. 202; see also Fernand Braudel, 'Histoires et sciences sociales: La longue durée', *Annales*, 4, October 1958.

23. Bayart, *The State in Africa*, p. 31.

24. Martin Chanock, *Law, Custom and Social Order: The Colonial Experience of Malawi and Zambia*, Cambridge: Cambridge University Press, 1985.

25. Terence Ranger, 'Tradition and Travesty: Chiefs and the Administration in Makoni District, Zimbabwe, 1960–1980', *Africa*, 52, 1982, p. 20.

26. J. D. Y. Peel, *Ijesha and Nigerians: The Incorporation of a Yoruba Kingdom, 1890s–1970s*, Cambridge: Cambridge University Press, 1983.

27. David D. Laitin, *Hegemony and Culture: Politics and Religious Change among the Yoruba*, Chicago: Chicago University Press, 1986; see also Richard Gray's review article in *African Affairs*, 86, 1987, pp. 443–44.

28. For a detailed discussion see Frank A. Salamone, 'Playing at Nationalism: Nigeria, a Nation of "Ringers"', *Genève Afrique*, 30, 1, 1992.

29. Important studies on this subject include, Roland Abiodun, 'The Kingdom of Owo', in H. J. Drewal, John Pemberton and Roland Abiodun, *Yoruba: Nine Centuries of African Art and Thought*, New York: The Center for African Art, 1989; Karin Barber, *I Could Speak until Tomorrow: Oriki, Women, and the Past in a Yoruba Town*, Edinburgh University Press, 1991; Jacob K. Olupona, *Kingship, Religion and Rituals in a Nigerian Community: A Phenomenological Study of Ondo Yoruba Festivals*, Stockholm: Almquist and Wiksell, 1991; Andrew Apter, *Black Critics and Kings: The Hermeneutics of Power in Yoruba Society*, Chicago: Chicago University Press, 1992; John Pemberton and Funso S. Afolayan, *Yoruba Sacred Kingship: A Power Like That of the Gods*, Washington: Smithsonian Institution, 1996. I would like to thank Funso Afolayan for intriguing comments on this important subject.

30. See for example, Thomas Hodgkin, *African Political Parties*, Hammondsworth: Penguin, 1961; The definitive Nigerian study on this subject is Richard Sklar, *Nigerian Political Parties: Power in an Emergent African Nation*, Princeton: Princeton University Press, 1963.

31. For a good analysis of this perspective see Bryan S. Turner, *Marx and the End of Orientalism* London: George Allen and Unwin, 1978, pp. 55–56.

32. Ekeh, 'Colonialism and the Two Publics in Africa', pp. 100–101.

33. J. D. Y. Peel, 'Olaju: A Yoruba Concept of Development', *Journal of Developing Areas*, 1979.

34. African colonial historiography and earlier African anthropological studies have critically discussed the creative ways in which local communities reconstituted themselves under the disruptive influence of colonial rule. For landmark studies see P. C Lloyd, 'The Yoruba Town Today', *Sociological Review*, 1957; Thomas Hodgkin, *African Political Parties*, Hammondsworth: Penguin, 1961; Immanuel Wallerstein, 'Voluntary Associations', in James Coleman and Carl G. Rosberg (eds.), *Political Parties and National Integration in Tropical Africa*, Berkeley: University of California Press, 1966; T. O. Ranger, 'Connexions between "Primary Resistance" Movements and Modern Mass Nationalism in East and Central Africa', *Journal of African History*, 9, 1968.

35. It is important to mention, however, that Ranger anticipated some of the limitations of this thesis in his own essay on colonial Africa in *The Invention*. These critical insights were more forcefully presented in another essay titled 'The Inven-

tion of Tradition Revisited: The Case of Africa', in Terence Ranger and Olufemi Vaughan (eds.), *Legitimacy and the State in Twentieth Century Africa: Essays in Honour of A. H. M. Kirk-Greene*, London: Macmillan, 1993.

36. Eric Hobsbawn, 'Introduction: Inventing Tradition', Eric Hobsbawm and Terence Ranger (eds.), *The Invention of Tradition*, Cambridge: Cambridge University Press, 1988.

37. A. D. Smith, 'The Nation Invented, Imagined, Reconstructed', *Millennium*, 26, 1991, p. 356.

38. *Ibid*, pp. 356–58.

39. C. S. Whitaker, *The Politics of Tradition: Continuity and Change in Northern Nigeria, 1946–1966*, Princeton: Princeton University Press, 1970

40. C. S. Whitaker, 'A Dysrhythmic Process of Political Change', *World Politics*, 19, 1967, pp. 190–217.

41. S. J. Tambiah, 'The Persistence and Transformation of Tradition in Southeast Asia, with Particular Reference to Thailand', *Daedalus*, 102, 1973, p. 55.

42. Smith, 'The Nation Invented', p. 357.

43. Morris Szeftel, 'Ethnicity and Democratization in South Africa', *Review of African Political Economy*, 60, p. 190; see also Mare, *Brothers Born of Warrior Blood*.

44. Stephanie Lawson, 'The Myth of Cultural Homogeneity and Its Implications for Chiefly Power and Politics in Fiji', *Comparative Studies in Society and History*, 32, 1990.

45. Smith, 'The Nation Invented', p. 357.

46. *Ibid*, p. 357.

47. Michel-Rolph Trouillot, *Silencing the Past*, Boston: Beacon Press, 1995.

48. For a fascinating analysis drawn from African American experiences see Robin D. G. Kelly, *Race Rebels*, New York: Free Press, 1994.

49. J. D. Y. Peel, 'Making History: The Past in the Ijesha Present', *Man*, 19, 1984.

50. *Ibid*, pp. 112–13.

51. *Ibid*, p. 129.

52. Richard L. Sklar, *Nigerian Political Parties: Power in an Emergent African Nation*, Princeton: Princeton University Press, 1963.

53. Rajni Kothari, 'Tradition and Modernity Revisited', *Government and Opposition*, 3, 1968, p. 273; see also his *Footsteps into the Future: Diagnosis of the Present World and a Design for an Alternative*, New York: Free Press, 1974, pp. 118–48.

54. For a critical analysis of this important point see William Graf, *The Nigerian State: Political Economy, State, Class, and Political System in the Post-Colonial Era*, London: James Currey, 1988.

55. Jane Guyer, 'Representation without Taxation: An Essay on Democracy in Rural Nigeria, 1952–1990', Boston University, African Studies Working Papers, 1992.

56. Richard Sklar notes that this trend is indeed common throughout postcolonial Africa. He contends that "the contours" of African communities from

which chieftaincy structures inevitably draw their legitimacy "are shaped to a great extent by their origins; traditional authority persists vibrantly within them in modern forms." For detailed discussion of this fascinating analysis of the political significance of chieftaincy structures to contemporary African politics see Richard Sklar, 'The African Frontier of Political Science', in Robert Bates, V. Y. Mudimbe, and Jean O'Barr (eds.), *Africa and the Disciplines: The Contributions of Research in Africa to the Social Sciences and the Humanities*, Chicago: University of Chicago Press, 1993.

57. With over a thousand years of archaeological evidence, rich oral traditions and, in the last three centuries, written popular and academic historical accounts, the Yoruba experience is widely recognized as one of the most complex in Africa. While pre-nineteenth-century Yoruba religious, political, sociological and historical analysis is not relevant to the themes discussed in the present book, it is nevertheless useful to note a few landmark studies of the earlier Yoruba experience that have informed the scholarship on nineteenth- and twentieth-century Yoruba studies. See for example S. A. Babalola, *The Content and Form of Yoruba Ijala*, Oxford: Clarendon Press, 1966; William Bascom, *Ifa Divination: Communication between Gods and Men*, Bloomington: Indiana University Press, 1969; N. A. Fadipe, *The Sociology of the Yoruba*, Ibadan: Ibadan University Press, 1970; R. C. C. Law, *The Oyo Empire c. 1600–1836*, Oxford: Clarendon Press, 1977; Wande Abimbola, *Ifa: An Exposition of the Literary Corpus*, Ibadan: Oxford University Press, 1976; Robin Horton, 'Ancient Ife: A Reassessment', *Journal of the Historical Society of Nigeria*, 9, 1979, pp. 69–149; Ulli Beier, *Yoruba Myths*, Cambridge: Cambridge University Press, 1980; Anthony D. Buckley, *Yoruba Medicine*, Oxford: Clarendon Press, 1985. S. A. Akintoye, however, provides an authoritative analysis of the politico-military force that transformed this relatively stable experience in the nineteenth century. See his *Revolution and Power Politics in Yorubaland, 1840–1893*, London: Longman, 1971.

58. See R. C. C. Law, *The Oyo Empire, c. 1600–c. 1836*, Oxford: Clarendon Press, 1977.

59. J. D. Y. Peel, 'Inequality and Action: The Forms of Ijesha Social conflict', *Canadian Journal of African Studies*, 14, 1980.

60. *Ibid*, p. 482.

61. The supreme council consisted of seven Oyomèsi chiefs: the Bashorun, Agbakin, Samu, Alapini, Laguna, Akinikin and Ashipa.

62. P. C. Lloyd, 'Conflict Theory and Yoruba Kingdoms', in I. M. Lewis (ed.), *History and Social Anthropology*, London: Tavistock, 1968, p. 52.

63. Toyin Falola and Dare Oguntomisin, *The Military in Nineteenth Century Yoruba Politics*, Ile-Ife: University of Ife Press, p. 17.

64. Robert Smith, *Kingdoms of the Yoruba*, London: Methuen, 1976, p. 131.

65. Lloyd, 'Conflict Theory and Yoruba Kingdoms', p. 52.

66. Ann O'Hear, 'Political and Commercial Clientage in Nineteenth Century Ilorin', *African Economic History*, 15, 1986, p. 70.

67. See G. O. Oguntomisin, 'Political Change in Yorubaland in the Nineteenth Century', *Canadian Journal of African Studies*, 15, p. 229.

68. For an authoritative analysis of Ibadan's politico-military power in the nineteenth century, see Bolanle Awe, 'The Rise of Ibadan as a Yoruba Power in the Nineteenth Century', D.Phil. thesis, Oxford University, 1963.

69. Michael R. Doortmont, 'The Roots of Yoruba Historiography: Classicism, Traditionalism and Pragmatism', in Toyin Falola (ed.), *African Historiography: Essays in Honour of Ade Ajayi*, Harlow, Essex: Longman, 1993, p. 58.

70. For a critical study of this subject see G. O. Oguntomisin and Toyin Falola, 'Refugees in Yorubaland in the Nineteenth Century', *Asian and African Studies*, 21, 1987.

71. Toyin Falola, 'Slavery and Pawnship in the Yoruba Economy in the Nineteenth Century', *Slavery and Abolition*, 15, 1994, p. 241.

72. Awe, 'The Rise of Ibadan'.

73. P. C. Lloyd, 'The Political Development of Yoruba Kingdoms in the Eighteenth and Nineteenth Century ', *Royal Anthropological Institute Occasional Paper*.

74. For detailed discussions see J. F. A. Ajayi, 'Professional Warriors in Nineteenth Century Yoruba Politics', *Tarikh*, 1, 1, 1963; see also Oguntomisin, 'Political Change and Adaptation'.

75. Samuel Johnson, *The History of the Yorubas: From the Earliest Times to the Beginning of the British Protectorate*, Lagos: Church Missionary Society, 1966.

76. For a detailed discussion see Bolanle Awe, 'The Ajele System: A Study of Ibadan Imperialism in the Nineteenth Century', *Journal of the Historical Society of Nigeria*, 3, 1964.

77. Akintoye, *Revolution and Power*, p. xix.

78. George Jenkins, 'Ibadan Politics', Ph. D. dissertation, Northwestern University, 1965.

79. Bolanle Awe, 'Militarism and Economic Development in Nineteenth Century Yoruba Country: The Ibadan Example', *Journal of African History*, 14, 1973.

Notes to Chapter 2

1. Bolanle Awe, 'The Rise of Ibadan as a Yoruba Power in the Nineteenth Century', D. Phil. thesis, Oxford University, 1963.

2. Robin Law, *The Oyo Empire, c.1600–1836: A West African Imperialism in the Era of the Atlantic Slave Trade*, Oxford: Clarendon Press, 1977.

3. The following Anglo-Yoruba treaties recognized the Alaafin as the pre-eminent ruler of Yorubaland: 'the 1988 Treaty with Yoruba Chiefs', 'the 1988 Treaty with the Alaafin of Oyo', 'the 1893 Treaty with the Alaafin', 'the 1893 Treaty with Ibadan Chiefs', and 'the Treaty of Peace, Friendship and Protection between Alaafin of Oyo and the Head of Yorubaland, and H. E., G. T. Carter on behalf of H. M. The Queen, 1893'.

4. Of these local histories, the voluminous study of the Oyo Anglican minister Reverend Samuel Johnson, completed by 1898, and first published in 1922, remains most notable. The study, which is a synthesis of mid-nineteenth-century versions of oral and written accounts of Yoruba history, attributed the political preeminence in the region before the nineteenth century to the corpus of Oyo traditions. Although it recognized the spiritual significance of Ile-Ife (and the Ooni, its king), this perspective shows up Oyo (and the Alaafin, its king) as the supreme political head of the Yoruba region. For a detailed analysis see Samuel Johnson, *The History of the Yorubas: From the Earliest Times to the Beginning of the British Protectorate*, Lagos: Church Missionary Society, 1966.

5. See for example, Cornelius Adepegba, 'The Descent from Oduduwa: Claims of Superiority Among some Yoruba Traditional Rulers and the Arts of Ancient Ife', *International Journal of African Historical Studies*, 19, 1986, pp. 77–92.

6. At the time of Carter's arrival in Ibadan, chiefs were preoccupied with waging wars and had therefore failed to select a Baale, the head of civil chiefs. Hence Carter had to meet the Balogun, the leading military general and the most senior chief at the time.

7. Kemi Morgan, *Akinyele's Outline History of Ibadan*, Part Three, Ibadan: Caxton Press, p. 165.

8. *Ibid.*, p. 165.

9. *Ibid.*

10. *Ibid.*

11. For authoritative analysis see A. G. Afigbo, *The Warrant Chiefs: Indirect Rule in Southeastern Nigeria, 1891–1929*, London: Longman, 1971.

12. For a comprehensive analysis of the conquest of this vast West African territory, see Risto Marjomaa, *War on the Savannah: The Military Conquest of the Sokoto Caliphate under the Invasion of the British Empire, 1897–1903*, Helsinki: Finnish Academy of Sciences and Letters, 1997.

13. Afigbo, *The Warrant Chiefs*, especially chapter one.

14. J. A. Atanda, 'The Changing Status of the Alaafin of Oyo under Colonial Rule and Independence', in Michael Crowder and Obaro Ikime (eds.), *West African Chiefs: Their Changing Status under Colonial Rule and Independence*, Ile-Ife: University of Ife Press, 1970, p. 216.

15. J. A. Atanda, *The New Oyo Empire: Indirect Rule and Change in Southwestern Nigeria 1894–1935*, London: Longman, 1973.

16. *Ibid.*

17. For example, two prominent Christian elites, Reverend Okuseinde and Mr. Adetoun, served on the Ibadan NA council from 1903 to 1907.

18. This is the official title of the colonial administrator charged with the administration of the province.

19. George Jenkins, 'Ibadan Politics', Ph.D. Dissertation, Northwestern University, 1965.

20. *Ibid.*

21. For examples of the symbolic political role of the Alaafin in precolonial Ibadan see Morgan, *Akinyele's Outline History*, p. 162.

22. For a detailed discussion see Bolanle Awe, 'The Rise of Ibadan as a Yoruba Power'.

23. For a critical analysis of how the routines of British colonial rules reinforced myths of traditional authority, see Karen Fields, *Revival and Rebellion in Colonial Central Africa*, Princeton: Princeton University Press, 1985.

24. See Atanda, *The New Oyo Empire*, p. 134.

25. Jenkins, 'Ibadan Politics'.

26. Atanda, *The New Oyo Empire*.

27. Jenkins, 'Ibadan Politics', p. 187.

28. *Ibid.*

29. *Ibid.*, p. 87.

30. *Ibid.*

31. Organizations such as this were certainly not unique to Ibadan during this period. In Ilesha, for instance, a group of wealthy produce buyers founded the *Egbe Atunluse* (the Young Ijesha Improvement Society) to mobilize local opinion and to make representation to the colonial authorities on behalf of their towns. Its members were concerned with two major objectives. First, the organization encouraged the foundation of a local secondary school, the Ilesha Grammar School. Second, the Egbe called for an administrative reorganization that would reconstitute Ilesha as the capital of the Northeastern Province. For detailed discussion see J. D. Y. Peel, *Ijesha and the Nigerians: The Incorporation of a Yoruba Kingdom, 1890s–1970s*, Cambridge: Cambridge University Press, 1983, p. 186.

32. Gavin Williams, 'Garveyism, Akinpelu Obisesan and his Contemporaries: Ibadan 1920–1922', in Terence Ranger and Olufemi Vaughan (eds.), *Legitimacy and the State in Twentieth Century Africa: Essays in Honour of A. H. M. Kirk-Greene*, London: Macmillan Press, 1993, p. 116.

33. *Ibid.*, p. 116.

34. Oyo Provincial File (Oyo Prof.) 2/3.

35. *Ibid.*

36. *Ibid.*

37. Atanda, *The New Oyo Empire*, p. 135.

38. Jenkins, 'Ibadan Politics', p.86.

39. *Western Equatorial Africa, Diocesan Magazine*, vol. 16, (Old Issue), no. 193, July 1910, pp. 34–35.

40. For a detailed analysis of the relationship between Christian missions and the advancement of western education, see Martin Kilson, 'The Emergent Elite in Black Africa 1900–1960', in L. H. Gann and Peter Duignan (eds.), *Colonialism in Africa 1870–1960*, Cambridge: Cambridge University Press, 1970.

41. P. C. Lloyd, *Africa in Social Change*, Hammondsworth: Penguin, 1975; see especially chapter 2.

42. Morgan, *Akinyele's Outline History*, p. 164.

43. J. D. Y. Peel, *Ijesha and Nigerians*, p. 76.

44. T. G. O. Gbadamosi, *The Growth of Islam among Yoruba Muslims*, London: Longman, 1978.

45. See Sara S. Berry, *Cocoa, Customs and Socio-economic Change in Rural Western Nigeria*, Oxford: Clarendon Press, 1975.

46. Jenkins, 'Ibadan Politics', p. 19.

47. Convinced that Captain Ross's alliance with the Alaafin had encouraged stagnation, Resident Ward-Price first embraced the educated Ooni of Ife, Oba Adesoji Aderemi, as the legitimating political platform on which his reform would be based. Ife's strategic limitations, however, encouraged him to shift his attention to Ibadan as the focal point of administrative reform in the province. For a detailed discussion see Atanda, 'The Changing Status of the Alaafin', p. 218; see also H. L. Ward-Price, *Dark Subjects*, London: Jarrolds, 1939.

48. Isaac Okonjo, *British Administration in Nigeria 1900–1950: A Nigerian View*, New York: Nok Publishers, 1974, p. 233; see also Donald C. Cameron, *The Principles of Native Administration and their Application*, Lagos: Government Printer, 1934.

49. Okonjo, *British Administration in Nigeria*, p. 213.

50. 'Native Authority Ordinance of 1933', Ibadan: National Archives.

51. *Ibid.*

52. For a detailed discussion of Sir Bernard Bourdillon's service in Nigeria, see Robert D. Pearce, *Sir Bernard Bourdillon: The Biography of a Twentieth Century Colonialist*, Oxford: Kensal Press, 1987.

53. '1939 Conference of Yoruba Obas', Ibadan: National Archives.

54. Toyin Falola, *Politics and Economy in Ibadan, 1893–1945*, Lagos: Modelor, 1989, p. 252.

55. A. H. M. Kirk-Greene, *Principles of Native Administration in Nigeria*, London: Oxford University Press, 1965, p. 26.

56. N. U. Akpan, *Epitaph of Indirect Rule: A Discourse on Local Government in Africa*, London: Cassell, 1956.

57. Oyo Prof. 236.

58. Oyo Prof. 2/3; Oyo Prof. 636/647.

59. In a letter to the Secretary of the Southern Provinces on 8 December 1934, Resident Ward-Price accused Alaafin Ladigbolu of being full of his own self-importance, usually expecting government to shower favors and authority on him and being rude and patronizing. The resident also accused the Alaafin of unleashing a reign of terror, having encouraged his courtiers and wives to exercise authority arbitrarily. See Oyo Prof. 2/3; Oyo Prof. 636/647. .

60. Falola, *Politics and Economy in Ibadan*, p. 261.

61. See Atanda, *The New Oyo Empire*.

62. Oyo Prof. 236/647.

63. *Ibid.*

64. Falola, *Politics and Economy in Ibadan*, p. 243.

65. Robin Law, 'Early Yoruba Historiography', *History in Africa*, 3, 1976, pp. 76–77.

66. *Ibid.*, p.78.

67. *Ibid.*

68. N. D. Oyerinde, Ogbomosho's most prominent educated Christian, later served as secretary-general and president of the Nigerian Baptist convention (Ogbomosho's Christian missions were deeply rooted in the missionary stations established by the American Baptist Convention). He played a critical role in the translation of the Baptist Hymnal to Yoruba in the mid twentieth century. He was appointed member of the Nigerian Legislative Council by the colonial government in the early 1940s. Oyerinde was installed Otun Baale for meritorious service to the town in the 1940s. See J. A. Atanda, (ed.) *Baptist Churches in Nigeria, 1850–1950*, Ibadan: University Press Limited, 1988, pp. 128–9

69. See N.D. Oyerinde, *Iwe Itan Ogbomosho* (A History of Ogbomosho), Jos, 1934.

70. B. A. Agiri, 'Development of Local Government in Ogbomosho, 1850–1950', M. A. thesis, University of Ibadan, 1966.

71. Graham Furniss, 'Oral Culture and the Making of Meaning', *African Affairs*, 1989, pp. 274–5.

72. *Ibid.*, p. 92.

73. See Atanda, *The New Oyo Empire*; see also Jenkins, 'Ibadan Politics'.

74. Atanda, *The New Oyo Empire*, pp. 276–7.

75. Oyo Prof. 2/e, C 26/61.

76. Oyo Prof. 1/154.

77. Oyo Prof. 2/e, C. 26/61.

78. Atanda, *The New Oyo Empire*, chapter 7.

79. Oyo Prof. 1, 157, 24/223.

80. Falola, *Politics and Economy in Ibadan*, p. 262–3.

81. Kristin Mann, *Marrying Well: Marriages, Status and Social Change among the Educated Elite in Colonial Lagos*, Cambridge: Cambridge University Press, 1985, p.7.

82. Kenneth Post and George Jenkins, *Price of Liberty, Personality and Politics in Colonial Nigeria*, Cambridge: Cambridge University Press, 1973, p.27.

83. For a detailed discussion on the Egbe see Post and Jenkins, *Price of Liberty*.

84. *Ibid.*

85. Oyo Prof. 1,157, 24/223

86. *Ibid.*

Notes to Chapter 3

1. See David Fieldhouse, 'Decolonization, Development and Dependence: A Survey of Changing Attitudes', in Prosser Gifford and W. Roger Louis (eds.),

The Transfer of Power in Africa: Decolonization, 1940–1960, New Haven: Yale University Press, 1982.

2. Richard Crook, 'Decolonization, the Colonial State and Chieftaincy in the Gold Coast', *African Affairs*, 85, 1986, pp. 75–105.

3. Robert Pearce, *Turning Point in Africa: British Colonial Rule in Africa*, London: Frank Cass, 1982, p. 141.

4. Arthur Creech Jones, 'The Place of African Local Administration in Colonial Policy', *Journal of African Administration*, 1, 1947, p. 4.

5. *1947 Despatch of the Secretary of State for the Colonies to African Governors*, London: H. M. S. O., 25 February 1947.

6. Creech Jones, 'The Place of African Local Administration', p. 2.

7. Pearce, *Turning Point in Africa*, p. 150.

8. *Colonial Office Summer School on African Administration*, First Session, 18–28 August 1947, Queens College, Cambridge, p. 20.

9. Richard C. Crook, 'Legitimacy, Authority and the Transfer of Power in Ghana', *Political Studies*, 35, 1987, p. 560.

10. *Ibid.*, p. 560.

11. D. A. Low, *Eclipse of Empire*, Cambridge: Cambridge University Press, 1991.

12. Gavin Williams, 'Garveyism, Akinpelu Obisesan and his Contemporary', in Terence Ranger and Olufemi Vaughan (eds.), *Legitimacy and the State in Twentieth Century Africa*, London: Macmillan, 1993, p. 128.

13. For a detailed discussion see Sara Berry, *Fathers Work for Their Sons: Accumulation, Mobility and Class Formation in an Extended Yoruba Community*, Berkeley: University of California Press, 1985.

14. J. D. Y. Peel, 'Olaju: A Yoruba Concept of Development', *Journal of Developing Areas*, January 1979.

15. H. L. M. Butcher, *Report of the Commission of Inquiry into Allegations of Misconduct Made Against Chief Salami Agbaje, Otun-Balogun of Ibadan and Allegations of Inefficiency and Maladministration on the Part of Ibadan and District Native Authority*, Lagos: Government Printer, 1951, p. 12.

16. Ibadan Divisional Papers (Ib. Div.), 1/1, 2910.

17. *Ibid.*

18. Butcher, *Report of the Commission of Inquiry*, pp. 45–46.

19. *Ibid.*, p. 23.

20. *Ibid.*, p. 14.

21. *Ibid.*, p. 2.

22. *Ibid.*, p. 48.

23. George Jenkins, 'Ibadan Politics', Ph.D. dissertation, Northwestern University, 1965, p. 29.

24. *Ibid.*

25. Oyo Provincial Files (Oyo Prof.) 213/267.

26. Toyin Falola, *Politics and Economy in Ibadan, 1893–1945*, Lagos: Modelor, 1989, p. 267.

27. Oyo Prof. 2/2/247/81.

28. Butcher, *Report of the Commission of Inquiry*, p. 53.

29. The 1914 Native Court Ordinance.

30. Butcher, *Report of the Commission of Inquiry*, p. 54.

31. *Ibid.*, p. 54.

32. *Ibid.*

33. The term "native settlers" was a colonial category used to describe residents of Ibadan who had migrated to the city to seek a livelihood from other Yoruba towns and villages since the 1920s.

34. Abner Cohen, *Custom and Politics in Urban Africa*, London: Routledge, 1969.

35. Toyin Falola, 'Lebanese Traders in Southwestern Nigeria', *African Affairs*, 89, 1990, pp. 523–53.

36. Toyin Falola, *Politics and Economy in Ibadan*, chapter 4.

37. *Ibid.*, p. 275.

38. *Memorandum Submitted by Ibadan Native Settlers Union to the Butcher Commission of Inquiry on 3rd February 1951*, Western Nigeria Ministry of Local Government, (W.M.L.G), File No. 23950.

39. Butcher, *Report of the Commission of Inquiry*.

40. *Ibid.*, p. 54.

41. Western Nigeria Ministry of Local Government (W.M.L.G.), File No. 23950.

42. *Ibid.*

43. Ibadan Divisional Papers (Ib. Div. 1/1, 2910).

44. Ib. Div. 1/1, 2930.

45. IPU Councillor Akinpelu Obisesan had survived the campaign of the IPA and conservative chiefs in 1941. They called for Obisesan's dismissal from the NA Council 'because of his personal ambition and his making trouble over the Otun Balogun dispute'. Oyo Prof. 3/939.

46. Having refused to cooperate with the Butcher Commission and the Hayley Committee, Olubadan Igbintade was suspended from the NA by the colonial authorities. For a detailed discussion see Kenneth Post and George Jenkins, *The Price of Liberty, Personality and Politics in Colonial Nigeria*, Cambridge: Cambridge University Press, 1973.

47. *Ibid*, p. 74.

48. *Ibid.*

49. Ib. Div. 1/1 2930.

50. *Ibid.*

51. *Ibid.*

52. Oyo Prof. 1/1.

53. The 1947 Constitution was the first attempt of the colonial authorities to establish democratic institutions in all the regions and levels of government in Nigeria. The constitution was named after Sir Arthur Richards, Governor of Nigeria from 1943 to 1947.

54. A revenue allocation system based on per capita would naturally favor the North, which had recorded a higher population in the 1943 census.

55. *Proceedings of the General Conference on the Review of the Nigerian Constitution*, Lagos: Government Printer, 1950, p. 218.

56. *Ibid.*, p. 142.

57. *Ibid.*

58. *Ibid.*, p. 79.

59. *Ibid.*, p. 58.

60. Obafemi Awolowo, *Path to Nigerian Freedom*, London: Faber, 1947, p. 74.

61. *Proceedings of the General Conference*, p. 59.

62. In a twist of fate, this pronouncement later occurred in the form of a bitter conflict between the Alaafin of Oyo, Oba Adeyemi II, and the Oyo Divisional Council which Thomas presided over as chairman between 1953 and 1954. Michael Ajasin, who shared similar views, was also a strong force behind the deposition of Oba Olateru Olagbegi, the Olowo of Owo in 1966. See chapters 4, 5 and 6.

63. *Proceedings of the General Conference*, p. 148.

64. *Ibid.*

65. See A. E. Afigbo, *The Warrant Chiefs: Indirect Rule in Southeastern Nigeria 1891–1929*, London: Longman, 1971.

66. Ebere Nwaubani, 'Chieftaincy Among the Igbo: A Guest on the Center-Stage', *International Journal of African Historical Studies*, 27, 1994, p. 354.

67. Larry Diamond, 'Nigeria: The Uncivic Society and the Descent into Praetorianism', in Larry Diamond, Juan J. Linz and Seymour Lipset (eds.), *Politics in Developing Countries: Comparing Experiences with Democracy*, Boulder: Lynne Rienner, 1995, pp. 421–23.

68. For a detailed discussion of the relationship between the central and regional legislatures see Oluwole Odumoso, *The Nigerian Constitution: History and Development*, London: Sweet and Maxwell, 1963, pp. 78–79.

69. S. A. de Smith, *The New Commonwealth and Its Constitution*, London: Steven and Sons, 1964, p. 157.

70. P. C. Lloyd, 'The Yoruba Town Today', *Sociological Review*, July 1957, p. 56.

71. After the exit of southern British Cameroons from Nigeria, the party became known as the National Council of Nigerian Citizens.

72. For extensive coverage of issues and strategies of NCNC political mobilization, see *The West African Pilot* and *The Southern African Defender* (two NCNC newspapers), in the 1950s.

73. Obafemi Awolowo, *Awo: The Autobiography of Chief Obafemi Awolowo*, Cambridge: Cambridge University Press, 1960, pp. 165–66.

74. In his pioneering book, Richard Sklar identified the following as the original founders of the Egbe in London: Obafemi Awolowo, Oni Akerele, Abiodun Akerele, Ayotunde Rosiji, A. B. Oyediran, S. O. Biobaku, Akin Reis, Victor Munis,

C. O. Taiwo and Akintola Williams. See Richard Sklar, *Nigerian Political Parties: Power in an Emergent African Nation*, Princeton: Princeton University Press, 1963.

75. For a broad African example see Thomas Hodgkin, *Nationalism in Colonial Africa*, London: Muller, 1956; and for an example from colonial Somaliland, see I. M. Lewis, 'Modern Political Movements in Somaliland', *Africa*, July 1958.

76. Bryan S. Turner, *Marx and the End of Orientalism*, London: George Allen and Unwin, 1978, pp. 55–56.

77. Immanuel Wallerstein, 'A Comment on Epistemology: What is Africa', *Canadian Journal of African Studies*, 22, 1988, pp. 331–32.

78. For a detailed account of the objectives of the Egbe, see Sklar, *Nigerian Political Parties*, pp. 68–69.

79. Awolowo, *Path to Nigerian Freedom*, p. 66.

80. The Third Annual General Assembly of the Egbe in Ondo, 18–21 October, passed a resolution that declared several obas patrons of the organization. See *Nigerian Tribune*, 31 October, 1950.

81. Adeyemo Alakija Papers. Quoted from S. O. Arifalo, 'Egbe Omo Oduduwa: Structure and Strategy', *Odu: A Journal of West African Studies*, 21, 1981, p. 83.

82. *Ibid.*

83. *Ibid.*, p. 83.

84. *Daily Service*, 29 October 1951, and *Daily Service*, 27 October 1952.

85. S. O. Arifalo, 'Egbe Omo Oduduwa', p. 85.

86. *Ibid.*, p. 85.

87. Sara Berry, 'Social Institutions and Access to Resources', *Africa*, 59, 1989, p. 44.

88. For an authoritative analysis of the politics of cultural essentialism and the strategic realities of power configuration in the Nigerian nation-building project during decolonization, see Olufemi Taiwo, 'Unity in Diversity?: Obafemi Awolowo and the National Question in Nigeria', *Canadian Review of Studies in Nationalism*, 18, 1991, pp. 43–59.

89. For a detailed discussion see James Coleman, *Nigeria: Background to Nationalism*, Berkeley: University of California Press, 1958.

90. *Ibid.*, p. 341.

91. *West Africa*, 18 May 1987.

92. Minutes of the inaugural meeting of the Action Group held in Awolowo's Oke-Bola, Ibadan residence, 26 March 1950. Quoted from Sklar, *Nigerian Political Parties*, p. 103.

93. *Ibid.*, p. 102.

94. The AG victory in the 1951 election was not without controversy. The controversy over the election was further intensified as obas, elders and Egbe leaders encouraged NCNC politicians to declare their support for the Yoruba party, the AG. See Sklar, *Nigerian Political Parties*.

95. See Western Nigeria Ministry of Local Government (W.M.L.G.), File No. 23950.

Notes to Chapter 4

1. After the exit of the Cameroons from southern Nigeria, the party became known as the National Council of Nigerian Citizens.

2. Rajni Kothari, 'Tradition and Modernity Revisited', *Government and Opposition*, 3, 1968, p. 292; see also his *Footsteps into the Future: Diagnosis of the Present World and a Design for an Alternative*, New York: Free Press, 1994, pp. 118–48.

3. The authoritative studies of Richard L. Sklar on the formation of Nigerian political parties, and Kenneth Post and George Jenkins on the biography of Ibadan's indefatigable political boss, Adegoke Adelabu, are still exemplary analyses of the complex interactions between local forces and fragile national structures during decolonization. Since the subjects of historical continuities and change are central to my study, I have attempted to streamline the complex interactions between Ibadan and Oyo chieftaincy institutions, and new local, regional and federal structures in this chapter. For this reason, I combine these earlier analyses of party politics and charismatic personalities with new primary materials that underscore power configurations and the construction of neotraditional ideologies. See Richard L. Sklar, *Nigerian Political Parties: Power in an Emergent African Nation*, Princeton: Princeton University Press, 1963; see also Kenneth Post and George Jenkins, *The Price of Liberty: Personality and Politics in Colonial Nigeria*, Cambridge: Cambridge University Press, 1973.

4. For a good analysis of this point see Richard C. Crook, 'Legitimacy, Authority and the Transfer of Power in Ghana', *Political Studies*, 35, 1987, p. 552.

5. These conflicts were not unconnected to the deep incongruities between local and ethno-regional interests in all three regions of the federation. Because of the severe marginality of Eastern traditional rulers and chiefs, the conflict was more sharply drawn in that region. For detailed discussions see James Coleman, *Nigeria: Background to Nationalism*, Berkeley: University of California Press, 1958.

6. The Constitution was named after the British Secretary of State for the Colonies, Oliver Lyttleton, who presided over the London conferences.

7. Larry Diamond, 'Nigeria: The Uncivic Society and the Descent into Praetorianism', in Larry Diamond, Juan J. Linz and Seymour Martin Lipset (eds.), *Politics in Developing Countries: Comparing Experiences with Democracy*, Boulder, Co.: Lynne Rienner, 1995, p. 422.

8. See G. I. Jones, *Report of the Position, Status and Influence of Chiefs and Natural Rulers in the Eastern Region of Nigeria*, Enugu: Eastern Region Government Printer, 1957.

9. Cyrus Reed, 'The Role of Traditional Rulers in Elective Politics in Nigeria', African Studies Program, Indiana University, 1982, p. 19.

10. Post and Jenkins, *Price of Liberty*, p. 96.

11. *Ibid.*

12. See Sklar, *Nigerian Political Parties*.

13. *Ibid.*, p. 120.

14. *Report of the Native Courts: Western Provinces Commission of Inquiry*, Lagos: Government Printer, 1953, p. 1.

15. *Ibid.*, p. 45.

16. *Ibid.*, p. 43.

17. Ibadan Divisional Files (Ib. Div.), 1/1, 1109, Vol. I.

18. *Ibid.*

19. *Ibid.*; Interview with J. F. Hayley, Senior District Officer, Ibadan Division, March 1986.

20. *Ibid.*

21. *Ibid.*

22. For an authoritative analysis see Martin Channock, *Law, Custom and Social Order: The Colonial Experience of Malawi and Zambia*, Cambridge: Cambridge University Press, 1985.

23. Crook, 'Legitimacy, Authority and the Transfer of Power in Ghana', pp. 557–58.

24. Obafemi Awolowo, *Path to Nigerian Freedom*, London: Faber, 1947.

25. For Awolowo's earlier attacks on the Native Court system see chapter 3 of this book; see also Awolowo, *Path to Nigerian Freedom*.

26. *Government Proposal for the Reform of the Native Court Law in the Western Region*, Ibadan: National Archives, 1951.

27. *Ibid.*

28. *Ibid.*

29. Ib. Div., 1/1, 1109, Vol. I.

30. *Ibid.*

31. Chief D. T. Akinbiyi, former IPU member of the NA Council, was appointed president of the First Land's Court, while D. A. Falana, the sixty-four-year-old Babasale of Ibadan Christians, became the president of the Second Land's Court. Another IPU member in the NA Council, Akinpelu Obisesan, was appointed Judge of the Ojaba Grade I Court. Two of his colleagues in the NA, S. O. Osunware, a graduate of King's College in Lagos, and J. L. Ogunsola, a former student at the Ibadan Grammar School, became president of the Ojaba Court II and Bere Court II, respectively. In accordance with the new regulation separating the executive from the judiciary, Obisesan, Osunware and Ogunsola resigned their positions in the NA. IPU co-founder and Chief Akinyele's colleague in the Ward-Price era, Chief Adetoun, the Abese Olubadan, was appointed Judge of the Ojaba Court III, while L. A. Salami, the Manager of Ibadan Islamic schools, and the only non-Christian and non-IPU member among the judges, took charge of the Bere Court II. See *Nigerian Tribune*, 24 April 1953.

32. *Nigerian Tribune*, 27 April 1953.

33. Ib. Div., 1109, Vol. II.

34. Post and Jenkins, *The Price of Liberty*, pp. 169–70.

35. *Ibid.*, p. 166.

36. *Ibid.*, p. 182.

37. Ib. Div., 1/1, 2642.

38. *Ibid.*

39. *Ibid.*

40. *Ibid.*

41. Kenneth Post and George Jenkins' authoritative biography of Adegoke Adelabu provides an in-depth analysis of the limitations of charismatic leadership during decolonization. My focus in this chapter is to underscore the role of chieftaincy politics in the administrative reforms of this critical era. For a detailed analysis of Adelabu's life see Post and Jenkins, *The Price of Liberty*.

42. Adelabu papers. Quoted from Post and Jenkins, *The Price of Liberty*, p. 166.

43. For a detailed discussion of the swollen shoot crisis see Post and Jenkins, *The Price of Liberty*, p. 186.

44. See David Laitin, *Hegemony and Culture: Politics and Religious Change among the Yoruba*, Chicago: University of Chicago Press, 1986.

45. Post and Jenkins, *The Price of* Liberty, p. 174.

46. *Daily Service*, 20 March 1954.

47. Post and Jenkins, *The Price of Liberty*, p. 207.

48. *Ibid.*, p. 208.

49. *Nigerian Tribune*, 12 April 1954.

50. *Ibid.*

51. *Charter of Freedom*, Obafemi Awolowo: Minister of Local Government moving the second reading of the Western Region Local Government Bill. Ibadan, Local Government Bill, 1952, p. 4.

52. *Ibid.*, p. 119.

53. *Western Region Local Government Law, 1953*, Sections 9 and 10.

54. See Post and Jenkins, *The Price of Liberty*, p. 86.

55. *Report of Commission of Inquiry into the Administration of Ibadan District Council*, Abingdon: Abbey Press, 1956, p. 94.

56. *Ibid.*

57. Gavin Williams and Teresa Turner, 'Nigeria', in John Dunn (ed.), *West African States: Failure and Promise—A Study in Comparative Politics*, Cambridge: Cambridge University Press, 1978, p. 151.

58. Ib. Div., 1/1 3277.

59. *Ibid.*, p. 94.

60. The supporters of the Osi Balogun claimed that Balogun Akinyele, a devout Christian, had failed to observe certain rituals and festivals that accompanied his position as Balogun. These included failing to keep the "fetish," the Balogun's staff, in his house or to sacrifice to it; refusing the gifts of the Shango Priests, who represented the god of iron and fire; and refusing to receive masquerades during the annual Egungun festivals. Even if these allegations were justified, the Ashipa-Balogun, the Ekerin Balogun, and the Seriki gave no reason for their failure to nominate the next candidate in the Balogun line, Otun Balogun Aminu, a man

who had distanced himself from Adelabu and was in fact Akinyele's nominator for the Olubadan title. See Post and Jenkins, *The Price of Liberty*, p. 249.

61. *Report of the Commission of Inquiry*, p. 87.

62. *Ibid.*, p. 86.

63. On the day of the installation, however, the Ibadan District Council in an emergency meeting approved the installation of Chief Akinyo as Olubadan. It also defeated a counter-motion by opposition Councillor Akinade, which condemned the Osi Balogun's installation as irregular and unconstitutional, and called on the council to recognize Chief Akinyele. See *Report of the Commission of Inquiry*, p. 88.

64. Post and Jenkins, *The Price of Liberty*, p. 251.

65. *Ibid.*, pp. 251–56.

66. *Ibid.*

67. *Nigerian Tribune*, 19 April 1955.

68. *Southern Nigerian Defender*, 19 April 1955.

69. *Report of the Commission of Inquiry*, p. 31.

70. *Daily Times*, 27 April 1955.

71. Ib. Div., 1/1, 3277.

72. AG minority members of the council were represented by party stalwarts Ladipo Moore, Ayotunde Rosiji and J. O. Lawson; D. O. A. Oguntoye and B. O. Obisesan represented traditional members of the council; S. L. Durosaro, J. S. Gomez and Abiodun Akerele represented the Ibadan Tax Payers' Association (ITPA). For NCNC leaders in Lagos, the investigation in Ibadan posed a major political problem. Its National Executive Committee despatched five prominent lawyers— H. O. Davies, T. O. S. Benson, B. Olowofoyeku, H. U. Kaine and J. M. Udochi— to assist two Ibadan NCNC barristers, Mojeed Agbaje and E. O. Fakayode, in their defense of Adelabu and Mabolaje. For a detailed discussion see Post and Jenkins, *The Price of Liberty*.

73. *Report of the Commission of Inquiry*, p. 34.

74. *Ibid*, pp. 34–36.

75. *Ibid*, p. 35.

76. Ib. Div., 1/1 3277.

77. Minutes of The Inaugural Meeting of the Ibadan District Council Chieftaincy Committee, 9 November 1955. See Ib. Div., 1/1 3277.

78. Post and Jenkins, *The Price of Liberty*, p. 253.

79. Bill Freund, *The Making of Contemporary Africa: The Development of African Society Since 1800*, Bloomington: Indiana University Press, 1984, p. 215.

80. Richard Joseph, *Democracy and Prebendal Politics in Nigeria: The Rise and Fall of the Second Republic*, Cambridge: Cambridge University Press, 1987, p. 115.

81. See Post and Jenkins, *The Price of Liberty*, p. 358.

82. See *The Western Region Local Government Law*, Ibadan: Government Printer, 1952; see also Sklar, *Nigerian Political Parties*.

83. See *Daily Times* 3/11/54, 11/11/54, 5/9/54; *Daily Sketch* 11/11/54.

84. *Daily Sketch*, 11/11/54.

85. Oyo Prof., 1/1 55.

86. *Ibid.*

87. For a detailed account of allegations brought against the Alaafin and the Aremo by AG leaders see *Daily Times*, 11 September 1954.

88. *Ibid.*

89. *Daily Service*, 11 March 1953.

90. *Daily Service*, 30 April 1953.

91. *Daily Service*, 5 May 1953.

92. *Daily Service*, 26 October 1953; see also Sklar, *Nigerian Political Parties*.

93. *Daily Service*, 7 November 1953.

94. *Daily Times*, 24 November 1953.

95. Obas present at these meetings were the Ooni of Ife, the Alake of Egbaland, the Oba of Lagos, the Osemawe of Ondo, the Ataoja of Oshogbo, the Akarigbo of Ijebu-Remo, the Odemo of Ishara and the Alaafin of Oyo. Egbe leaders included Akintola Maja, K. Adeyo, J. A. Doherty, A. Agbaje, M. A. Okupe, Ayo Williams, G. O. Gbadamosi, O. Ojikutu, Muri Animasaun, Ajao, S. L. Akintola and Obafemi Awolowo.

96. *Daily Times*, 11 October 1954.

97. *Daily Times*, 11 September 1954.

98. *Daily Times*, 15 November 1954.

99. Peter C. Lloyd, 'Traditional Rulers', in James S. Coleman and Carl G. Rosberg (eds.), *Political Parties and National Integration in Tropical Africa*, Berkeley: University of California Press, 1953, p. 393.

100. See the Law of the Western Provinces 1957 and 1958.

101. Law of the Western Region of Nigeria, 1959, pp. 249–50. For a detailed analysis on the 1957 Chief's Law see Wale Oyemakinde, 'The Chief's Law and the Regulation of Traditional Chieftaincy in Yorubaland', *Journal of the Historical Society of Nigeria*, 9, 1977, pp. 63–74.

102. Richard Sklar notes that by 1959 the overwhelming majority of house of chiefs' members declared their support for the AG. For detailed discussion see Sklar, *Nigerian Political Parties*.

Notes to Chapter 5

1. See Obafemi Awolowo, *Freedom and Independence for Nigeria: A Statement of Policy*, Ibadan, 1958.

2. Larry Diamond, 'Nigeria: The Uncivic Society and the Descent into Praetorianism', in Larry Diamond, Juan J. Linz and Seymour Martin Lipset (eds.), *Politics in Developing Countries: Comparing Experiences with Democracy*, Boulder, Co.: Lynne Reinner, 1995, p. 423.

3. Funso Afolayan, 'Nigeria: A Political Entity and a Society', in Paul A. Beckett and Crawford Young (eds.), *Dilemmas of Democracy in Nigeria*, Rochester, N.Y: University of Rochester Press, 1997.

4. Andre F. Baptiste, 'The Relations between the Western Region and the Federal Government of Nigeria: A Study of the 1962 Emergency', M. A. thesis, University of Manchester, 1965, p. 122.

5. *Western Nigeria House of Chiefs Debates*, 4 October 1957, p. 130.

6. *Ibid.*

7. *Western Nigerian House of Chiefs Debates*, Official Report, 1960–61.

8. *Ibid.*

9. *Western Nigerian House of Chiefs Debates*, Official Report, 1962.

10. *Western Nigerian House of Assembly Debates*, Official Report, 1961, p. 32.

11. *Ibid.*

12. *Ibid.*, pp. 34–35.

13. *Western Nigerian House of Chiefs Debates*, Official Report, 1961–62, pp. 15–16.

14. *Ibid.*, pp. 13–21.

15. Sandra T. Barnes, *Patrons and Power: Creating a Political Community in Metropolitan Lagos*, Manchester: University of Manchester Press, 1968, pp. 103–4.

16. See John P. Mackintosh, 'Electoral Trends and the Tendency to a One Party System in Nigeria', *Journal of Commonwealth Political Studies*, 1, 1962.

17. The success of the AG in Ibadan can also be explained by the tragic death of Adelabu in a car accident in 1958.

18. See Mackintosh, 'Electoral Trends and the Tendency to a One Party System in Nigeria'.

19. See Larry Diamond, *Class, Ethnicity and Democracy in Nigeria: The Failure of the First Republic*, London: Macmillan Press, 1988.

20. Baptiste, 'The Relations between the Western Regions and the Federal Government of Nigeria', p. 221.

21. Other prominent AG radical intellectuals favored by this change were Victor Oyenuga, an agricultural economist; Ayo Ogunsheye, the director of extramural studies at the University College Ibadan (UCI); Dr. Sanmi Onabamiro, lecturer at the UCI; and Dr. Otegbeye, founder of the Nigerian Socialist Workers' and Farmers' Party.

22. *Ibid.*, p. 223.

23. Diamond, *Class, Ethnicity and Democracy in Nigeria*, pp. 94–95.

24. *Ibid.*

25. Mackintosh, 'Politics in Nigeria: The Action Group Crisis of 1962', *Political Studies*, June 1963, pp. 126–55.

26. Diamond, *Class, Ethnicity and Democracy in Nigeria*, p. 114.

27. Richard Sklar, 'Contradictions in the Nigerian Political System', *The Journal of Modern African Studies*, 3, 1965; see also Diamond, *Class, Ethnicity and Democracy in Nigeria*, p. 115.

28. 'Action Group Split in Jos', *West Africa*, 10 February 1962, p. 158.

29. *Ibid.*

30. *Ibid.*

31. 'Action Group Rift Patched Up', *West Africa*, 25 February 1962, p. 187.

32. See the February, March and April editions of *West Africa*.

33. *Ibid.*

34. Kenneth Post and Michael Vickers, *Structure and Conflict in Nigeria 1960–1966*, London: Heineman, 1973, p. 88; Diamond, *Class, Ethnicity and Democracy in Nigeria*, p. 126.

35. John P. Mackintosh, 'Politics in Nigeria: The Action Group Crisis of 1962', p. 453; Diamond, *Class, Ethnicity and Democracy in Nigeria*, pp. 104–5.

36. *Nigerian Tribune*, 27 June 1962.

37. Mackintosh, 'Politics in Nigeria: The Action Group Crisis of 1962', p. 139.

38. This process was enhanced by Awolowo's increasingly precarious condition. Having been implicated by the Coker Commission of Inquiry—a commission constituted by the federal coalition government to investigate the Western Region's statutory corporations earlier in the crisis—Awolowo's problems became even more severe as he was suddenly charged and subsequently convicted of treasonable felony in a shady and controversial case to overthrow the federal government. For a detailed account, see Diamond, *Class, Ethnicity and Democracy in Nigeria*, p. 104.

39. *Ibid.* p. 106; see also Akinjide Oshuntokun, *Chief S. L. A. Akintola: His Life and Times*, Ibadan: Evans Brothers, 1982.

40. Kenneth Post and Michael Vickers, *Structure and Conflict in Nigeria, 1960–1966*, London: Heinemann, 1973.

41. *Ibid.*

42. For a succinct analysis see Richard L. Sklar, 'Nigerian Politics: The Ordeal of Chief Awolowo, 1960–1965', in Gwendolen M. Carter (ed.), *Politics in Africa: Seven Cases*, New York: Harcourt, Brace and World, 1966.

43. Funso Afolayan, 'Reconstructing the Past to Reconstruct the Present: The Nineteenth Century Wars and Yoruba History', unpublished manuscript, p. 7.

44. *Supplement to the Western Nigerian Gazette*, July 1963.

45. *Supplement to the Western Nigerian Gazette*, September 1963.

46. Ironically, it was the AG regional government that first imposed management committees when it dissolved several councils for alleged corruption in the 1960s.

47. *Supplement to the Western Nigerian Gazette*, April 1963.

48. Sandra T. Barnes, *Patrons and Power: Creating a Political Community in Metropolitan Lagos*, Bloomington: Indiana University Press, 1986, p. 149.

49. *Supplement to the Western Nigerian Gazette, Extraordinary*, 26 September 1963.

50. See Post and Vickers, *Structure and Conflict in Nigeria*, p. 99.

51. The formation of the Mid-Western Region (an NCNC stronghold) also led to a significant reduction of NCNC members in the Western House of Assembly. See Post and Vickers, *Structure and Conflict in Nigeria*, p. 99.

52. Barnes, *Patrons and Power*, p. 150.

53. Alex Gboyega, 'Local Government and Political Integration in Western Nigeria', Ph. D. dissertation, University of Ibadan, 1975.

54. Barnes, *Patron and Power*, p. 154.

55. *Ibid.*

56. *Ibid.*

57. *Daily Sketch*, 24 May 1965.

58. Gboyega, 'Local Government and Political Integration', p. 90.

59. Barnes, *Patrons and Power*, p. 151.

60. Alex Gboyega, Professor of Political Science, University of Ibadan, interview, February 1987.

61. Oyeleye Oyediran, 'Political Change in a Nigerian Urban Community', Ph. D. dissertation, University of Pittsburgh, 1971.

62. Oyeleye Oyediran, 'Local Influence and Traditional Leadership: The Politics of the Ife Forest Reserve', *Odu: A Journal of West African Studies*, 7, 1972.

63. *Ibid.*

64. *Ibid.*; see also *Daily Sketch*, 12 August 1964.

65. *Daily Sketch*, 13 August 1964.

66. *Daily Sketch*, 27 August 1964.

67. *Daily Sketch*, 5 September 1964.

68. *Nigerian Tribune*, 2 November 1964.

69. *Nigerian Tribune*, 21 May 1964.

70. *Nigerian Tribune*, 22 July 1964.

71. *House of Chiefs Debate*, 1964–65, p. 260.

72. *Daily Sketch*, 30 September 1964.

73. *Minutes of a Joint Meeting of the Ife Divisional and District Council's Management Committee*, 11 November 1964.

74. *Supplement to the Western Nigerian Gazette*, March 1965.

75. *House of Chiefs Debate*, 1964–65, p. 135.

76. *Daily Sketch*, 12 June 1965.

77. *Daily Sketch*, 13 July 1964.

78. In one high-profile case, leaders of opinion such as the Anglican Bishops of Ibadan and Lagos, the Chief Imam of Ibadan, and several prominent obas, had gathered to mediate the political conflict dividing the region. A *Daily Sketch* article had criticized the NNDP leaders for insulting the distinguished peacemakers. It was reported that Oba Gbadebo took up their defense. See *Daily Sketch*, 10 June 1965.

79. *Daily Sketch*, 26 June 1965.

80. *Daily Sketch*, 31 August 1964.

81. *Daily Sketch*, 30 June 1965.

82. *Daily Sketch*, 3 November 1964.

83. *Daily Sketch*, 3 May 1965.

84. *Daily Sketch*, 24 June 1965.

85. *Nigerian Tribune*, 19 May 1964.

86. *Nigerian Tribune*, 20 June 1964.

87. Barnes, *Patrons and Power*, p. 151.

88. Following the disturbances that greeted the massively rigged election, the Olowo was forced to go into exile in December 1965. He made a futile effort to return to Owo in 1966.

89. *Nigerian Tribune*, 11 July 1964.

90. See Post and Vickers, *Structure and Conflict in Nigeria*.

91. *Daily Sketch*, 13 September 1965.

92. J. D. Y. Peel, *Ijeshas and Nigerians: The Incorporation of a Yoruba Kingdom, 1890s–1970s*, Cambridge: Cambridge University Press, 1983.

Notes to Chapter 6

1. See, for example, Lucian W. Pye, 'Armies in the Process of Political Modernization', in John J. Johnson (ed.), *The Role of the Military in Underdeveloped Countries*, Princeton: Princeton University Press, 1967, pp. 80–89; see also Samuel Huntington, *The Soldier and the State*, Cambridge: Harvard University Press, 1967.

2. Robert Price, *Society and Bureaucracy in Contemporary Ghana*, Berkeley: University of California Press, p. 208.

3. Ali A. Mazrui, 'Soldier as Traditionalizers: Military Rule and Re-Africanization of Africa', in Ali A. Mazrui (ed.), *The Warrior Tradition in Modern Africa*, Leiden: E. J. Brill, 1977.

4. Pearl T. Robinson, 'Niger: Anatomy of a Neo-Traditional Corporatist State', *Comparative Politics*, 24, 1991, p. 4.

5. Given the fact that a coup dominated by junior Igbo officers violently eliminated the Northern Regional Government and a Northern-dominated federal government, the Northern political class was wary of a military regime headed by Major General Aguiyi-Ironsi, an Igbo, who assumed leadership as Head of State and Commander in Chief of the Armed Forces.

6. B. J. Dudley, *Instability and Political Order: Politics and Crisis in Nigeria*, Ibadan: Ibadan University Press, 1970, p. 119.

7. *Broadcast to the Nation by His Excellency Major-General J. T. U. Aguiyi Ironsi, Head of the National Government and Supreme Commander of the Armed Forces on Tuesday, 24 May 1966*, Lagos: Government Printer, 1966, p. 3.

8. Ola Balogun, *The Tragic Years: Nigeria in Crisis, 1966–1970*, Benin City: Ethiope, 1973, p. 27.

9. Dudley, *Instability and Political Order*, p. 120.

10. *Ibid.*, p. 117.

11. 'Soldiers and the Sultan', *West Africa*, 11 June 1966.

12. Balogun, *Tragic Years*, p. 27.

13. 'Hassan and the Emirs', *West Africa*, 11 June 1966.

14. 'Hassan Addresses Northern Emirs and Chiefs', in A. H. M. Kirk-Greene (ed.), *Crisis and Conflict in Nigeria: A Documentary Source Book, 1966–69*, London: Oxford University Press, 1971, p. 182.

15. 'Hassan Addresses Meeting of Northern Chiefs in Kaduna', *Ibid.*, p. 189.

16. 'Addresses of the Sultan of Sokoto to the People of the North', *Ibid.*, p. 190; see also *New Nigerian*, 20 June 1966.

17. The Obi of Onitsha, the Onyeisi of Ngwaland, the Eze of Arochukwu, and the Amanyanabos of Opobo and of Kalabari were among representatives of the Eastern Provinces. Representatives of the North included the Emir of Kano, the Etsu Nupe, the Emir of Argungu, the Atta of Igala, the Emir of Bedde and the Aku Uka of Wukari. Yoruba obas were represented by the Ooni of Ife, the Alake of Abeokuta, the Awujale of Ijebuland, the Olubadan of Ibadan, the Ewi of Ado-Ekiti and the Deji of Akure. The Oba of Benin, the Olu of Warri, and the Obi of Ubulukwu represented the Mid-West, while Oba Oyekan represented the federal territory of Lagos.

18. 'Ironsi's Address to the National Conference of Traditional Rulers', Ibadan, 28 July 1966, in Kirk-Greene, *Crisis and Conflict*, p. 191.

19. Dudley, *Instability and Political Order*, p. 134.

20. *Ibid.*, pp. 136–39.

21. *Ibid.*

22. *Ibid.*

23. This statement was reproduced in the *Nigerian Guardian* of 7 June 1987 after the death of Chief Awolowo in May of the same year.

24. *Western Nigerian Gazette*, No. 12, 1966.

25. *Western Nigerian Gazette*, No. 13, 1966.

26. *Western Nigerian Gazette*, No. 1, 1966.

27. *Ibid.*

28. *Ibid.*

29. *Daily Sketch*, 13 June 1966.

30. *Gazette of the Western State of Nigeria*, No. 17, 1969.

31. *Gazette of the Western Provinces of Nigeria*, No. 48, 1966.

32. *Ibid.*

33. *Gazette of the Western State of Nigeria*, No. 14, 1968.

34. *Daily Sketch*, 2 March 1966.

35. *Daily Sketch*, 6 May 1966, and 14 May 1968.

36. *Ibid.*

37. For an authoritative analysis see Gavin Williams, 'Why Is There No Agrarian Capitalism in Nigeria?', *Journal of Historical Sociology*, 1, 1989.

38. See Sara Berry, *Cocoa, Custom and Socio-Economic Change in Rural Western Nigeria*, Oxford: Clarendon Press, 1975; see also Gavin Williams (ed.), *Nigeria: Economy and Society*, London: Rex Collings, 1975.

39. Gavin Williams, 'Primitive Accumulation: The Way to Progress?', *Development and Change*, 18, 1987.

40. A. G. Hopkins, 'African Entrepreneurship: The Relevance of History to Development Economics', *Genève Afrique*, 26, 1988, pp. 8–23.

41. Dei, 'A Ghanaian Town Revisited: Change and Continuities in Local Adaptive Strategies', *African Affairs*, 91, 1992.

42. The failure to find a solution to Nigeria's year-old national crisis led to the secession of the Eastern Provinces from the federation. The declaration of the Republic of Biafra formally led to the Nigerian Civil War of 1967–70. For a comprehensive account of the events leading to the Nigerian Civil War; see Kirk-Greene, *Crisis and Conflict in Nigeria*, Volumes I and II.

43. *Report of the Commission of Inquiry into the Civil Disturbances in Certain Parts of the Western State of Nigeria in the Month of December, 1968*, Justice E. O. Ayoola, Sole Commissioner, Ibadan: Government Printer, 1969, p. 68.

44. J. D. Y. Peel, *Ijesha and the Nigerians: The Incorporation of a Yoruba Kingdom, 1890s–1970s*, Cambridge: Cambridge University Press, 1983.

45. *Report of the Commission of Inquiry.*

46. C. E. F. Beer, *The Politics of Peasant Groups in Western Nigeria*, Ibadan: Ibadan University Press, 1976, pp. 179–80.

47. *Ibid.*, p. 180.

48. *Ibid.*

49. *Ibid.*

50. *Ibid.*

51. C. E. F. Beer and Gavin Williams, 'The Politics of the Ibadan Peasantry', in Gavin Williams (ed.), *Nigeria: Economy and Society*, p. 149.

52. *Ibid.*

53. *Ibid.*, p. 150.

54. *Ibid.*, pp. 149–50.

55. Beer, *The Politics of Peasant Groups*, p. 162.

56. *Ibid.*, p. 151.

57. *Ibid.*

58. *Ibid.*, p. 151.

59. *Ibid.*, p. 190.

60. *Memorandum from Ibadan Farmers to the Commission of Inquiry.*

61. Beer and Williams, 'The Politics of Ibadan Peasantry', pp. 154–55.

62. Steven Feierman, *Peasant Intellectuals: Anthropology and History in Tanzania*, Madison: University of Wisconsin Press, 1990.

63. *Report of the Commission of Inquiry*, p. 26.

64. *Ibid.*

65. *Ibid.*, pp. 25–27.

66. Beer, *The Report of Peasant Groups*, p. 195.

67. Michael Bratton, 'Beyond the State: Civil Society and Associational Life in Africa', *World Politics*, 41, 1989, pp. 409–11.

68. For authoritarian analyses see Gavin Williams, 'Taking the Part of Peasants: Rural Development in Nigeria and Tanzania', in Peter Gutkind and Immanuel Wallerstein (eds.), *The Political Economy of Contemporary Africa*, Beverly Hills Calif.: Sage, 1976; Joel Samoff, 'Underdevelopment and Its Grassroots in Africa', *Canadian Journal of African Studies*, 14, 1980; Frank Holmquist, 'Defending Peasant Political Space in Independent Africa', *Canadian Journal of African Studies*, 14, 1980; and Rosemary Galli, 'On Peasant Productivity: The Case of Guinea-Bissau', *Development and Change*, 18, 1987.

69. Gavin Williams, *State and Society in Nigeria*, Idanre: Afrografrika, 1980; see also Lionel Cliffe, 'The Debate on African Peasantries', *Development and Change*, 18, 1987.

70. See, for example, Robert Bates, *Markets and States in Tropical Africa: The Political Basis of Agricultural Politics*, Berkeley: University of California Press, 1981.

71. *Supplement to Western Nigeria Gazette Extraordinary*, No. 53, December 1972.

72. *An Introduction to the New Local Government Council System in the Western State of Nigeria*, Ibadan: Government Printer, 1972.

73. *Ibid*.

74. *Ibid*.

75. *Proposal for the Reorganization of Local Government in the Western State of Nigeria*, Ibadan: Government Printer, p. xxi.

76. *An Introduction to the New Local Government Council*, p. 22.

77. *Ibid*., p. 23.

78. *Ibid*.

79. Oyeleye Oyediran, 'The Chosen Few: Policy makers in the New Local Government System of Nigeria', *Quarterly Journal of Administration*, July 1974, p. 397–406.

Notes to Chapter 7

1. The twelve states of the federation were further divided into nineteen in 1976. Of these, the Western State was carved into three, namely Oyo, Ogun and Ondo. See the *Report of the Panel Investigating the Issue of the Creation of More States and Boundary Adjustments in Nigeria*, Lagos: Government Printer, 1976.

2. For critical analyses of the impact of the oil boom on Nigerian social formation, see Thomas Biersteker, *Multinationals, The State and Control of the Nigerian Economy*, Princeton: Princeton University Press, 1987; Julius Ihonvbere, *Towards a Political Economy of Nigeria: Petroleum and Politics at the (Semi) Periphery*, Aldershot: Gower, 1988.

3. To achieve this objective, the FMG appointed a special panel under the chairmanship of Mr. Justice Ayo Irikefe. See *Daily Times*, February 4, 1976.

4. The Anti-Inflation Task Force and the Rent Control Commission were chaired by economists, Drs. Onitiri and Omolayole.

5. David Goldsworthy, 'On the Structural Explanation of African Military Interventions', *Journal of Modern African Studies*, 24, 1996, p. 184; see also Timothy Shaw, *Towards a Political Economy of Africa: The Dialectics of Dependence*, London, 1985.

6. *Guidelines for Local Government Reform*, Lagos: Government Printers, 1976, p. 3.

7. The exclusive and concurrent functions of the local authorities are listed in Appendix A and B of the *Guidelines*.

8. For critical analyses see Ladipo Adamolekun, *Politics and Administration in Nigeria*, Ibadan: Spectrum, 1986; Ladipo Adamolekun and L. Roland (eds.), *The New Local Government System in Nigeria*, Ibadan: Heineman, 1978; Dele Olowu and Paul Smoke, 'Determinants of Success in African Local Governments: An Overview', *Public Administration and Development*, 12, 1992.

9. Alex Gboyega and Oyeleye Oyediran, 'Local Government and Administration', in Oyeleye Oyediran (ed.), *Nigerian Government and Politics under Military Rule 1966–1979*, London: Macmillan Press, 1979, p. 183.

10. *Guidelines*.

11. *Daily Sketch*, 7 October 1976.

12. *Daily Times*, 11 December 1976.

13. For a full text of the Head of State's address, see *Daily Times*, 8 July 1976.

14. *Guidelines*, Foreword.

15. *Daily Times*, 9 July 1976.

16. *Guidelines for Local Government Reform*. See also Keith Panter-Brick, 'The Reform of Local Government in Nigeria', Seminar paper on the Revival of Local Government, London: Commonwealth Studies, 1977, p. 2.

17. *Ibid.*, pp. 4–5.

18. R. C. C. Law, 'The Heritage of Oduduwa: Traditional History and Political Propaganda among the Yoruba', *Journal of African History*, 14, 1973, p. 211

19. Asiwaju, 'Political Motivation and Oral Historical Tradition', *Africa*, 46, 1976, p. 125.

20. *Ibid.*, p. 122

21. *Ibid.* See also Funso Afolayan, 'Reconstructing the Past to Reconstruct the Present: The Nineteenth Century Wars and Yoruba History', unpublished manuscript, 1989.

22. *Ibid.*, p. 125.

23. Asiwaju, 'Political Motivation and Oral Historical Traditions', p. 115.

24. *Ibid.*, pp. 143–44.

25. *Daily Times*, 16 May 1977.

26. David M. Jemibewon, *A Combatant in Government*, Ibadan: Heinemann, 1979, p. 141.

27. Jemibewon, *A Combatant in Government*, p. 142.

28. *Report of the Commission on Chieftaincy Declaration and Government Decision Thereon*, Ibadan: Government Printer, 1977, p. 3.

29. *Ibid.*, p. 7.

30. *Ibid.*, p. 9.

31. *Ibid.*, p. 7.

32. *Ibid.*, pp. 19–20.

33. C. K. Meek, *Land Tenure and Native Administration in Nigeria and the Cameroon*, London, Her Majesty's Stationery Office, 1957, p. 6.

34. *Ibid.*

35. J. S. Eades, *The Yoruba Today*, Cambridge: Cambridge University Press, p. 74.

36. For a detailed analysis of the position of the Yoruba oba in the customary land tenure system, see P. C. Lloyd, *Yoruba Land Law*, London: Oxford University Press, 1962, and T. O. Elias, *Nigerian Land Law and Custom*, London: Routledge and Kegan Paul, 1962.

37. Sara Berry, *Cocoa, Custom, and Socio-Economic Change in Rural Western Nigeria*, Oxford: Clarendon Press, 1975, pp. 121–22.

38. *Ibid.*, p. 122.

39. *Ibid.*, pp. 121–22.

40. Oyo Provincial Papers (Oyo prof.), 4, 5, 98.

41. *Ibid.*

42. Oyo prof. 1, 10.

43. Oyo prof. 3, 375.

44. Berry, *Cocoa, Custom and Socio-Economic Change*, pp. 120–21.

45. *Ibid.*, p. 121.

46. Omoniyi Adewoye, 'The Legal Profession in Southern Nigeria', Ph.D. dissertation, Columbia University, 1968.

47. *Gazette of Western Region of Nigeria*, 1959.

48. *Daily Sketch*, 28 November 1972.

49. Quoted from *The Report of the Anti-Inflation Task Force*, Lagos: Federal Ministry of Information, October 1975, p. 46.

50. *Ibid.*

51. *Ibid.*, pp. 46–47.

52. *Federal Military Government's Views on the Report of the Rent Panel*, Lagos: Federal Ministry of Information, 1976.

53. *Daily Times*, 27 May 1977. The speech of the chief of staff was delivered by Commodore Oduwaiye.

54. *Supplement to Official Gazette Extraordinary*, No. 14, 29 March 1978.

55. *Ibid.*

56. *Ibid.*

57. Paul Francis, 'For the Use and Common Benefit of All Nigerians: Consequences of the 1978 Land Nationalization', *Africa*, 54, 1984, p. 12.

58. *Daily Times*, 8 April 1978.

59. *Daily Times*, 11 April 1978.

60. *Punch*, 11 April 1978.

61. *Ibid.*

62. *Ibid.*

63. *Daily Sketch*, 12 April 1978.

64. *Ibid.*

65. *Daily Times*, 12 April 1978.

66. The Olubadan's lukewarm support for the oba's opposition can be explained by the system of land tenure in Ibadan, where, unlike most Yoruba towns and villages, chiefs had little control over communal land. With the exception of their erstwhile authority in the land courts, land in the city had, by the early 1950s, come under the firm control of speculators and absentee commercial farmers.

67. *Daily Times*, 12 April 1978.

68. *Daily Sketch*, 13 April 1978.

69. *Ibid.*

70. *Daily Times*, 14 April 1978.

71. *Daily Times*, 15 April 1978.

72. *Ibid.*

73. *Daily Sketch*, 12 May 1978.

74. Francis, 'For the Use and Common Benefit of all Nigerians', pp. 12–17.

75. *Ibid.*, p. 23.

76. See, for example, Peter Keohn, 'Land Allocation and Class Formation in Nigeria', *Journal of Modern African Studies*, 21, 1983.

77. Chief Awolowo, who was among the fifty members of the Constitution Drafting Committee, declined to serve on the body, thereby reducing their number to forty-nine.

78. *Report of the Constitutional Drafting Committee Containing the Draft Constitution*, Vol. 1, Lagos: Federal Ministry of Information, 1976, p. xiii.

79. *Ibid.*, p. xiii.

80. For a critical analysis see Ian Shapiro, 'Democratic Innovation: South African in Comparative Context', *World Politics*, 46, 1993, p. 126.

81. Goldsworthy, 'On the Structural Explanation of African Military Interventions', p. 185.

82. The chairman of the committee formally handed a draft copy of the constitution to General Mohammed's successor, General Obasanjo, on 14 September 1976. The document was later ratified by a Constituent Assembly in 1978.

83. *Report of the Constitution Drafting Committee Containing the Draft Constitution*, Vol. II, Lagos: Federal Ministry of Information Printing Division, p. 79.

84. *Ibid.*

85. *Ibid.*, Vol. I, p. 49.

86. *Ibid.*, Vol. I, p. 55.

87. *Ibid.*

88. For a detailed discussion see David D. Laitin, 'The Sharia Debate and the Origins of Nigeria's Second Republic', *Journal of Modern African Studies*, 20, 1982.

89. For a detailed analysis see Ibrahim Jibrin, 'Religion and Political Turbulence in Nigeria', *Journal of Modern African Studies*, 29, 1991.

Notes to Chapter 8

1. *The Constitution of the Federal Republic of Nigeria*, Lagos: Daily Times Press, 1979, p. 11.

2. Julius Ihonvbere and Olufemi Vaughan, 'Democracy and Civil Society: the Nigerian Transition Program, 1985–1993', in John A. Wiseman (ed.), *Democracy and Political Change in Sub-Saharan Africa*, London: Routledge, 1995, pp. 73–75; see also Julius Ihonvbere, *Nigeria: the Politics of Adjustment and Democracy*, New Brunswick, N.J.: Transaction Press, 1997.

3. For a detailed theoretical analysis see Rene Lemarchand, 'Political Clientelism and Ethnicity in Tropical Africa: Competing Solidarities in Nation Building', *American Political Science Review*, 66, 1972.

4. Richard A. Joseph, *Democracy and Prebendal Politics in Nigeria: The Rise and Fall of the Second Republic*, Cambridge: Cambridge University Press, 1987, p. 67.

5. Billy Dudley, *Instability and Political Order: Politics and Crisis in Nigeria*, Ibadan: University of Ibadan Press, 1973.

6. *Ibid.*

7. As we discussed earlier, prominent First Republic politicians such as Obafemi Awolowo, Anthony Enahoro, and former NPC, NEPU, and UMBC leaders led regional delegates to various peace initiatives before the outbreak of the Civil War.

8. See Tajudeen Abdulraheem, 'Politics in Nigeria's Second Republic', D.Phil. dissertation, Oxford University, 1990. I would like to thank my friend Tajudeen Abdulraheem for sharing his research materials and his outstanding insight on party politics during Nigeria's Second Republic.

9. The Lagos Progressives included the former Yoruba NCNC stalwart, Adeniran Ogunsanya. A Lagos State Commissioner for Education during the military years, he subsequently became National Chairman of the Nigerian People's Party (NPP) in 1978. Other prominent members of the group were T. O. S. Benson, Toye Coker, Kola Balogun and Femi Okunnu (the latter had served as General Gowon's Federal Commissioner for Works). The Eastern Progressives included former NCNC notables such as Mbadiwe and Dennis Osadebay, the first premier of the Mid-Western Region. These regional favorites from the old era provided leadership for an organization now mainly made up of less-experienced men—businessman Jim Nwobodo, for instance, publisher Arthur Nwankwo, and acclaimed writer Chinua Achebe.

10. Club 14 (later Club 19) led by Alhaji Waziri Ibrahim, a Kanuri businessman from Bornu State provided what later became the Northern wing of the Committee for National Unity and Solidarity (CNUS). This coalition, which was later transformed into the Nigerian People's Party (NPP), disintegrated because of

Azikiwe's entry into the party and other personal feuds between Ibrahim and party president Adeniran Ogunsanya. Ibrahim's estranged faction later formed a Northern based party, the Great Nigerian People's Party (GNPP).

11. See Abdulraheem, 'Politics in Nigeria's Second Republic.'

12. B. J. Dudley, *Political Parties in Northern Nigeria*, London: Frank Cass, 1968; and C. S. Whitaker, *The Politics of Tradition, Continuity and Change in Northern Nigeria, 1946–1966*, Princeton: Princeton University Press, 1970.

13. Nurtured by Sir Ahmadu Bello's visionary leadership, a powerful Northern commercial and bureaucratic elite had come to its own as Nigeria's most cohesive and dominant ethno-regional political class by the end of the Civil War. Its rapid rise, which is the envy of other major ethno-regional political classes, especially the Yoruba and the Igbo, is often derided as a plot of a shadowy and reactionary "mafia" to dominate the country. This is, in my view, a gross oversimplification. It is my contention here that a deeper understanding of this political class (both civilian and military) would require a critical historical analysis that incorporates nineteenth-century emirate societies and structures into the history of state formation in twentieth century Nigeria. Toyin Falola's authoritative project on the politics of religion in colonial and postcolonial Nigeria has set the pace for others to follow. For detailed analyses see Toyin Falola, *Religious Militancy and Self-Assertion: Islam and Politics in Nigeria*, London: Avebury Press, 1996; Toyin Falola and Mathew Kukah, *Religious Impact on the Nation State: The Nigerian Predicament*, London: Avebury Press, 1996; Toyin Falola, *Violence in Nigeria: The Crisis of Religious Politics and Secular Ideologies*, Rochester: Rochester University Press, 1998. See also Shehu Uthman, 'Classes, Crisis and Coup: The Demise of Shagari's Regime', *African Affairs*, 83, 1989.

14. Abdulraheem, 'Politics in Nigeria's Second Republic.'

15. Larry Diamond, 'Nigeria: The Uncivic Society and the Descent into Praetorianism', in Larry Diamond, Juan J. Linz and Seymour Martin Lipset (eds.), *Politics in Developing Countries: Comparing Experience with Democracy*, Boulder, Co.: Lynne Rienner, 1995.

16. *Ibid.*, p. 435.

17. Toyin Falola and Julius Ihonvbere, *The Rise and Fall of Nigeria's Second Republic*, London: Zed Press, 1985.

18. Chaired by a leading high court judge, Mr. Justice Ovie Whiskey, FEDECO was mandated by the Federal Military Government to establish electoral rules during Nigeria's second experiment with liberal democracy. The commission was specifically charged with the responsibility of ensuring that political parties fulfill the requirements laid down in the electoral decree of 1977.

19. Ian Shapiro, 'Democratic Innovation: South Africa in Comparative Context', *World Politics*, 46, 1993, pp. 129–30.

20. Billy Dudley, 'The Nigerian Election of 1979: The Voting Decision', *Journal of Commonwealth and Comparative Politics*, 19, 1981, p. 277.

21. *Ibid.*

22. Richard Joseph, 'Political Parties and Ideology in Nigeria', *Review of African Political Economy*, 13, 1978.

23. This statement was quoted from a compilation of Chief Awolowo's speeches in *The Nigerian Guardian*, 7 June 1987, following his death in May of the same year.

24. Dudley, 'The Nigerian Election of 1979', p. 277.

25. Collection of Speeches of Governor Bola Ige, Ibadan, Government Printer, 1982.

26. *Daily Sketch*, 5 June 1981.

27. For a detailed account see the following newspaper accounts: *Daily Sketch*, 18 September 1980; 12 December 1980; 16 December 1980; *Sunday Concord*, 2 December 1980.

28. *Daily Sketch*, 18 September 1980.

29. Robin Law, 'The Heritage of Oduduwa: Traditional History and Political Propaganda among the Yoruba', *Journal of African History*, 14, 1973, p. 212.

30. *Ibid*, p. 212; see also Robert Smith, *Yoruba Kingdoms*, London: Methuen, 1976; and A. Oguntuyi, *A Short History of Ado Ekiti*, Akure, 1957.

31. Law, 'The Heritage of Oduduwa,' p. 212.

32. Olufemi Vaughan, 'Ife and Oyo Crowns in Colonial and Postcolonial Nigerian Politics', in Simon McGrath, Charles Jedrej, Kenneth King and Jack Thompson (eds.), *Rethinking African History*, University of Edinburgh (Centre of African Studies), 1997.

33. 'Ooni of Ife: Head of Yoruba Race', *Daily Sketch*, 12 December 1980.

34. *Sunday Concord*, 2 December 1980.

35. *Daily Sketch*, 16 December 1980.

36. *Daily Sketch*, 16 December 1980.

37. *Sunday Concord*, 4 January 1981.

38. *Daily Sketch*, 8 March 1981.

39. Alex Gboyega, Professor of Political Science, University of Ibadan, interview, February, 1987.

40. *Ibid*.

41. *Daily Times*, 16 December 1979.

42. *Daily Sketch*, 18 July 1981.

43. Alex Gboyega, interview, February, 1987.

44. P. J. Dixon, 'Uneasy Lies the Head: Politics, Economics, and the Continuity of Belief among the Yoruba of Nigeria', *Comparative Studies in Society and History*, 33, 1, 1991, p. 69.

45. See Shehu Othman, 'Classes, Crisis, and Coup', p. 333.

46. David Williams, *President and Power in Nigeria: The Life of Shehu Shagari*, London: Frank Cass, 1982.

47. *Ibid*.

48. Mohammed Uba Ahmed, 'The National Party of Nigeria: Origins to Electoral Success', M.Sc. thesis, Birmingham University, 1985, p. 39.

49. *Ibid.*, p. 93.

50. Aminu Tijani and David Williams (eds.), *Shehu Shagari: My Vision of Nigeria*, London: Frank Cass, 1981.

51. *Daily Times*, 18 July 1983.

52. See Alan Feinstein, *African Revolutionary: The Life and Times of Nigeria's Aminu Kano*, New York: Times Book Company, 1973.

53. For a succinct analysis of the spread of radicalism in Northern Nigeria, see Yusuf Bala Usman, *For the Liberation of Nigeria: Essays and Lectures, 1969–1978*, London: New Beacon Books, 1979.

54. Comments on the Proceedings and resolutions from the National Seminar on Nigeria's Political Culture, Kaduna, 2–5 November 1981, p. 9.

55. For a detailed discussion of the PRP's ideological split, see Larry Diamond, 'Nigeria: The Uncivic Society', p. 435.

56. *National Concord*, 26 December 1980; see also Philip Mawhood, 'The Place of Traditional Political Authority in African Pluralism', *Civilisations*, 32–33, 1982–83, p. 226.

57. *Ibid.*

58. For a good biography of Aminu Kano see Alan Feinstein, *African Revolutionary*.

59. See Whitaker, *The Politics of Tradition*.

60. This narrative benefitted significantly from Tajudeen Abdul Raheem's, Yakubu Aliyu's, Martin Dent's and A. H. M. Kirk-Greene's superior insight of Northern Nigerian political history.

61. I would like to thank my friend Yakubu Aliyu for sharing his knowledge of this important event with me.

62. Ebere Nwanbani, 'Chieftaincy among the Igbo: A Guest on the Center-Stage', *International Journal of African Historical Studies*, 27, 1994, p. 365.

63. *Ibid.*, pp. 368–69.

64. *Ibid.*, p. 368.

65. Earlier studies on ethno-regional and local politics in Nigeria show that rapid modernization has often reinforced communal assertiveness. This development in turn led to more dangerous forms of communal conflicts in the immediate postcolonial period. For authoritative analyses see Robert Melson and Howard Wolpe, 'Modernization and the Politics of Communalism: A Theoretical Perspective', *The American Political Science Review*, 64, 1970; see also Pauline Baker, *Urbanization and Political Change: The Politics of Lagos, 1917–1967*, Berkeley: University of California Press, 1974.

66. Sandra T. Barnes, *Patrons and Power: Creating a Political Community in Metropolitan Lagos*, Bloomington: Indiana University Press, 1986.

67. Mawhood, 'The Place of Traditional Political Authority', p. 227.

68. A. G. Afigbo, *The Warrant Chiefs, Indirect Rule in Southeastern Nigeria 1891–1929*, London: Longman, 1971; see also G. I. Jones, *Report on the Position, Status, and Influence of Chiefs and Natural Rulers in the Eastern Region of Nigeria*, Enugu: Government Printer, 1957.

69. Nnamdi Azikiwe, popularly known as Zik, was derided as have fallen down the ladder from the exalted position of a great African nationalist to what some radical intellectuals, opposed to chieftaincy structures, considered the lowly position of local Igbo chief of Onitsha.

70. Nwaubani, 'Chieftaincy among the Igbo', pp. 264–55.

71. Barnes, *Patrons and Power*, p. 189.

72. Saburi Biobaku, 'Political Leadership and National Development: Traditional Leadership in Contemporary Nigeria', paper presented at the Conference on Leadership and National Development in Nigeria, Nigerian Institute of Social and Economic Research (NISER), 8–12 April 1984, pp. 8–9.

73. *Africa Confidential*, 21 May 1986.

74. *Ibid*.

75. The collective opposition of non-NPN parties against NPN domination was expressed through the failed alliance of 'progressive' governors in 1980 and 1981. For detailed discussion see Diamond, 'Nigeria: The Uncivic Society'.

76. *West Africa*, 10 January 1983.

77. Jane I. Guyer, 'Representation without Taxation, An Essay on Democracy in Rural Nigeria, 1952–1990', Boston University, African Studies Center, Working Papers, 1990.

78. Chief Bola Ige, Oyo State Governor, interview, Ibadan, February 1987.

79. Chief Bola Ige, interview, February 1987.

80. Dr. Busari Adebisi, member Ibadan Committee of Concern (ICC), interview, Ibadan, February 1987.

81. Dr. Wale Oyemakinde, member of the Commission of Inquiry, interview, Ibadan, February, 1987.

82. Dr. Busari Adebisi, interview, February 1987.

83. Dr. Busari Adebisi, interview, February 1987.

84. *Press Release of the Ibadan Committee of Concern (ICC) on the Situation Created by the Misguided Efforts to Balkanise Ibadan Municipality*, Ibadan, 1982, p. 3.

85. Proceedings of the Oyo State House of Assembly, 20 February 1981, p. 2511.

86. Others prominent opponents of the UPN government such as Richard Akinjide, Attorney-General in Shagari's federal government; Yinka Abass, former chairman of the Ibadan Management Committee; and S. Labanji Bolaji, editor of the pro-NPN newspaper, *The National Concord*, were also criticized by pro-reformers.

87. Dr. Busari Adebisi, interview, February 1987.

88. *Press Release of the Ibadan Committee of Concern*, p. 4.

89. Proceedings of the Oyo State House of Assembly, Official Report, 26 February 1981, p. 2727.

90. Proceedings of the Oyo State House of Assembly, 20 February 1981, pp. 2512–13.

91. *Ibid.*, p. 4.

92. Dr. Wale Oyemakinde, interview, February 1987.

93. Chief Ayorinde, senior Ibadan chief, interview, Ibadan, February 1987; Chief Adeyemo, senior Ibadan chief (later Olubadan), interview, Ibadan, February 1987.

94. *Press Release of the Ibadan Committee of Concern.*

95. Proceedings of the Oyo State House of Assembly, 26 February 1981, p. 2729.

96. David Laitin, *Hegemony and Culture: Politics and Religious Change among the Yoruba*, Chicago: University of Chicago Press, 1986, p. 157.

97. *Press Release from the Unity Party of Nigeria (UPN) Ibadan Branch. Nomination for Oyo State UPN Gubernatorial Candidate in 1983: Our Stand Today*, 4 April 1982, p. 6.

98. *Ibid.*

99. Dr. Busari Adebisi, interview, February 1987.

100. Dr. Busari Adebisi, interview, February 1987.

101. This case study benefitted significantly from the information provided by many individuals who were involved in some of the events discussed here. I would like to thank Chief (later Oba) J. A. Adeyemo, Chief Bola Ige, Dr. Omololu Olunloyo, Chief J. A. Ayorinde, Chief A. M. A. Akinloye, Archdeacon Alayande, Drs. Busari Adebisi, Toyin Falola, Alex Gboyega and Wale Oyemakinde for providing vital information.

102. Samuel Johnson, *The History of Yorubas: From the Earliest Times to the Beginning of the British Protectorate*, Lagos: C. M. S., 1921, p. 230.

103. *Ibid.*

104. *Report of the Judicial Commission of Inquiry into the Communal Disturbances in Oranmiyan Local Government Area of Oyo State*, Ibadan: Government Printer, 1981, p. 9. For a detailed analysis of the postwar cocoa boom and isakole disputes between Ife landlords and Modakeke tenants, see Oyeleye Oyediran, 'Modakeke in Ife: Historical Backgrounds to an Aspect of Contemporary Ife Politics', in Oyeleye Oyediran, *Essays in Local Government Administration in Nigeria*, Lagos: Project Publications, 1988.

105. *Ibid.*

106. *Report of the Judicial Commission*, p. 11.

107. *Ibid.*

108. *Ibid.*

109. *Ibid.*

110. *Ibid.*

111. Proceedings of the Oyo State House of Assembly, 15 March 1981, p. 2572.

112. *Ibid.*

113. *National Concord*, 22 April 1981.

114. *National Concord*, 12 April 1981.

115. Proceedings of the Oyo State House of Assembly, 16 May 1981.

116. *Report of the Judicial Commission of Inquiry*, p. 19.

117. *Ibid.*, p. 20.

118. *Ibid.*, pp. 19–20.

119. *Daily Sketch*, 16 April 1981.

120. *Daily Times*, 17 April 1981.

121. *Report of the Judicial Commission of Inquiry*, p. 31.

122. *Ibid.*, p. 32.

123. *Daily Times*, 22 April 1981.

124. Other members of the commission of inquiry are former Oyo State head of service M. S. Adigun, University of Ibadan Political Scientist Dr. Tunde Adeniran and commission secretary L. O. Dada.

125. *Report of the Judicial Commission of Inquiry*, pp. 38–39.

Notes to Chapter 9

1. In a poignant analysis of Nigeria's postcolonial crisis, Wole Soyinka, Nigeria's Nobel laureate in literature, goes behind the well-known human rights record of the Buhari regime to reveal a network of political alliances that further entrenched the domination of the Northern political class. See Wole Soyinka, *The Open Sore of a Continent: A Personal Narrative of the Nigerian Crisis*, New York: Oxford University Press, 1996.

2. See for example, *Africa Confidential*, 10 April 1985.

3. Dan Agbese, *Newswatch*, 8 September 1986.

4. *Africa Now*, March 1984.

5. This confidence may have prompted two prominent traditional rulers, the Emir of Kano, Alhaji Ado Bayero, and the Ooni of Ife, Oba Sijuade Olubuse II, to undertake an "official" trip to Israel in August 1984. The visit, which embarrassed the regime (given Nigeria's strong diplomatic relations with Arab states), led Buhari to take disciplinary action against the two traditional rulers. Buhari withdrew the passports of Alhaji Bayero and Oba Sijuade and confined them to their local government area for a period of six months. See *West Africa*, 27 August 1984.

6. During the time of his appointment as chairman of the Review Committee, Dasuki, who following the death of Sir Abubakar in 1988 became Sultan of Sokoto, held the senior title of Baraden in the Sultanate. The appointment of an important Northern title-holder as chairman of this national local government review committee was another example of Buhari's favorable disposition toward the dominant Northern political class. The regime's embrace of emirs benefitted Southern traditional rulers who assumed new leadership roles in regional and national issues.

7. See the *Views and Comments of the Federal Military Government on the Findings and Recommendations of the Committee on the Review of Local Government Administration in Nigeria*, Lagos: Federal Government Printer, 1985, p. 3.

8. *Ibid.*, pp. 22–25.

9. See, for a good example, Oyeleye Oyediran, 'Transitions without End: From Hope to Despair—Reflections of a Participant-Observer', in Paul A. Beckett and Crawford Young (eds.), *Dilemmas of Democracy in Nigeria*, Rochester: University of Rochester Press, 1997.

10. *Report of the Political Bureau*, Lagos: Federal Government Printer, 1986, p. 2.

11. See Olufemi Vaughan, 'Traditional Rulers and the Dilemma of Democratic Transitions in Nigeria', in Beckett and Young (eds.), *Dilemmas of Democracy*, p. 424.

12. *West Africa*, 2 July 1987.

13. *National Concord*, 7 April 1988.

14. *Report of the Political Bureau*, p. 146.

15. *Ibid.*, p. 48.

16. Richard L. Sklar, 'The African Frontier for Political Science', in Robert H. Bates, V. Y. Mudimbe, and Jean O' Barr (eds.), *Africa and the Disciplines*, Chicago: University of Chicago Press, 1993.

17. William D. Graf, *The Nigerian State: Political Economy, State, Class and Political System in the Post-Colonial Era*, London: James Currey, 1988.

18. See Arthur W. Lewis, *Politics in West Africa*, New York: Oxford University Press, 1965.

19. Richard Joseph, 'Democratization under Military Rule and Repression in Nigeria', in Beckett and Young (eds.), *Dilemmas of Democracy*, p. 144.

20. It was evident by this time that the transition program had become a complex network of patronage dominated by the military and trusted civilian advisers. Drawing on the insight of leading social scientists, Babangida established several federal agencies, notably the Directorate of Food, Roads, and Rural Infrastructure; the Constituent Assembly; the Constitution Review Conference; the National Electoral Commission; the Centre for Democratic Studies; the Directorate for Social Mobilization; the National Council for Inter-Governmental Relations; and the Movement for Mass Mobilization for Self-Reliance and Economic Recovery. These agencies provided the regime with additional sources of patronage for its rapidly growing civilian and military clients. See Oyediran 'Transition without End', in Beckett and Young (eds.), *Dilemmas of Democracy*, p. 181.

21. Goran Hyden and Donald Williams, 'A Community Model of African Politics: Illustrations from Nigeria and Tanzania', *Comparative Studies in Society and History*, 36, 1994, pp. 68–96.

22. For a succinct analysis of how the new debates on power-sharing and the federal character principle further complicated the relations among federal, state and local governments, see Rotimi Suberu, 'Federalism, Ethnicity and Regionalism in Nigeria', in Beckett and Young (eds.), *Dilemmas of Democracy*.

23. *The views of the Federal Military Government on the Findings and Recommendations of the Committee on the Review of Local Government Administration in Nigeria*, 1985.

24. Julius O. Ihonvbere and Timothy Shaw, *Illusions of Power: Nigeria in Transition*, Trenton, N.J.: Africa World Press, 1998, pp. 126–27.

25. The March 1987 religious riots in key Northern towns were a clear indication of the vulnerability of the Babangida regime in a critical sections of Nigeria. Babangida, who referred to the riots as "a civilian attempt at a coup," recognized that religion was by then another formidable expression of division in Nigeria politics. See *West Africa*, 18 June 1987.

26. Unlike his predecessor, Buhari, Babangida initially felt that powerful traditional rulers enjoyed undue influence in state affairs. This perspective is based on the regime's limited consultation with traditional rulers in the initial years of its existence. This initial ambivalence turned into a rebuff when, in March 1988, Babangida ordered all traditional rulers to inform their local government chairmen about their travel plans before venturing out of their jurisdiction. As the regime became more patrimonial, it co-opted regional powerbrokers, among whom traditional rulers were always influential. This strategy of governance stems from the growing political pressures on the regime. These pressures led to the withdrawal of the impertinent March 1988 travel directive. See *Daily Times*, 9 March 1988; *West Africa*, 21 March 1988.

27. Both the Nigerian and the foreign press argued that it was the FMG's preference for Dasuki over his more conservative rival Maccido that ultimately determined the latter's appointment as Sultan of Sokoto in 1988. See *London Guardian*, 9 November 1988; *Africa Confidential*, 18 November 1988; *New Nigeria*, 15 November 1988; *Newswatch*, 21 November 1988; *Newbreed*, 11 November 1988; *Hotline*, December 1988, and *Africa Events*, December 1988.

28. *Newswatch*, 19 December 1988.

29. I would like to thank the renowned Nigerian political scientist and pro-democracy activist, Julius Ihonvbere for sharing his outstanding knowledge of Africa's popular struggle for democracy in the 1990s. His unparalleled studies of the popular democratic struggles of the post-Cold War era are only a refreshing reminder of the need to transcend the dominant constitutional preoccupations. He is a tireless advocate of a political economy perspective that analyzes democratic pressures in the context of an expanding political terrain, the deepening crisis of the state, and Africa's marginality in the global era. For detailed analyses see Julius Ihonvbere *Nigeria: The Politics of Adjustment and Democracy*, New Brunswick, N.J.: Transaction Press, 1994; Julius Ihonvbere, *Economic Crisis, Civil Society, and Democratization: The Case of Zambia*, Trenton, N.J.: Africa World Press, 1996; Julius Ihonvbere, 'Are Things Falling Apart? The Military and the Crisis of Democratization in Nigeria', *The Journal of Modern African Studies*, 34, 1996; and Julius Ihonvbere and Timothy Shaw, *Illusions of Power: Nigeria in Transition*, Trenton, N.J.: Africa World Press, 1998. See also Julius Ihonvbere and Olufemi Vaughan, 'Democracy and Civil Society: The Nigerian Transition Programme, 1985–1993', in John A. Wiseman (ed.), *Democracy and Political Change in Sub-Saharan Africa*, London: Routledge, 1995.

30. Abdul Raufu Mustapha, 'Structural Adjustments and Agrarian Change in Nigeria', in Adebayo Olukoshi (ed.), *The Politics of Structural Adjustments in Nigeria*, London: James Currey, 1993.

31. For a succinct analysis, see Julius Ihonvbere, 'A Critical Evaluation of the Failed 1990 Coup in Nigeria', *Journal of Modern African Studies*, 29, 1991.

32. See William Reno, 'Old Brigades, Money Bags, New Breeds, and the Ironies of Reform in Nigeria', *Canadian Journal of African Studies*, 27, 1993.

33. See Alex Gboyega, 'Local Government and Political Integration in Nigeria, 1952–1972', Ph.D. dissertation, University of Ibadan.

34. See Governor Fajuyi's chieftaincy reform policy in the *Western Nigerian Gazette*, March 1966.

35. The investigation, conducted by Commissioner for Local Government and Chieftaincy Affairs, Canon J. A. Akinyemi, concluded that Sir Adesoji retained the chairmanship because of the Government's respect for him, and not on the basis of the Ooni title. *Western Nigerian Gazette*, 1974.

36. David M. Jemibewon, *A Combatant in Government*, Ibadan: Heineman, 1979, p. 127.

37. Dr. Omololu Olunloyo, Interview, Ibadan, March 1987.

38. As discussed in the previous chapter, the UPN Leader, Chief Awolowo, and Governor Bola Ige openly embraced Oba Sijuade. Showing his allegiance to the UPN, the Ooni renamed Garage Olode, a village in his 'domain', 'Awolowo', after the UPN Leader. Oba Sijuade also gave the wife of the UPN Leader, Mrs. Hannah Awolowo, the distinguished title of Yeyeoba (mother of the king) at his coronation in December 1980.

39. For a detailed discussion of Governor Olunloyo's policy, see *Obas' Council Chairmanship Tussle Resolved—Olunloyo Speaks: Text of the Broadcast in Ibadan by the Governor of Oyo State on 2nd December 1983*, Ibadan: Ministry of Home Affairs, Information and Culture, Government Printer, 1983.

40. See the *Report of the Political Bureau*, Lagos: Federal Government Printer, 1986.

41. The Ooni's international connections were first demonstrated in Nigeria when he gave chieftaincy titles to the Cuban and Benin ambassadors in 1987. For detailed example see Kole Omotoso, *Just before Dawn*, Ibadan: Spectrum, 1988.

42. The impressive itinerary of the Ooni while on a state visit to Trinidad and Tobago shows how Oba Sijuade used the exalted title of "spiritual head of the Yorubas" in a modern political environment. These trips, filled with pomp and ceremony, demonstrated the influence of the Ooni to both allies and adversaries in Nigeria. See *The One Hundred and Fiftieth Anniversary of Emancipation and the End of Apprenticeship: Itinerary for the Visit of His Royal Highness, Oba Okunade Sijuade Olubuse II, C. F. R., The Ooni of Ife*, 31 July–8 August, 1988, The Government of the Republic of Trinidad and Tobago.

43. *Sunday Concord*, 25 January 1985.

44. *Ibid.*

45. *This Week*, 9 March 1987.

46. *Ibid.*

47. The protracted rivalry between the Alaafin and the Ooni crowns was cited as one of the reasons why the Babangida administration carved out a new state, Oshun, from Oyo State in 1992. See *Daily Sketch*, 2 October 1992.

48. Former NPN stalwarts M. K. O. Abiola, Omololu Olunloyo, ex-Chief Judge of Oyo State Fakayode and Afe Babalola, a senior advocate of Nigeria, supported the Alaafin during the dispute. The Ooni's formidable legal team included supporters of the proscribed UPN G. O. K. Ajayi, a senior advocate of Nigeria, Michael Omisade, Ayo Adebanjo and Olisa Chukura. Ajayi was installed Asiwaju (leader) following the death of Chief Awolowo in May 1987.

49. Abiola's financial empire included the publication of two leading newspapers, the *National Concord*, a daily, and the *African Concord*, a weekly magazine. His vast wealth also included investments in banking and sports. Abiola was also a regional vice-president of the International Telephone and Telecommunication Corporation (ITT).

Notes to Chapter 10

1. Christopher Clapham, 'The Longue Duree of the African State', *African Affairs*, 93, 1994, p. 434.

2. Graham Furniss, 'Oral Culture and the Making of Meaning', *African Affairs*, 91, 1992, p. 275

3. For critical analyses see John A. Armstrong, *Nations before Nationalism*, Chapel Hill: University of North Carolina Press, 1982; and Anthony D. Smith, 'Ethnic Persistence and National Transformation', *British Journal of Sociology*, 35, 1884.

4. Clapham, 'The Longue Duree of the African State', pp. 20–21.

5. Richard A. Joseph, *Democracy and Prebendal Politics in Nigeria: The Rise and Fall of the Second Republic*, Cambridge: Cambridge University Press, 1987, p. 111.

6. Jean-François Bayart, *The State in Africa: The Politics of the Belly*, London: Longman, 1993.

7. See, for example, Toyin Falola, 'A Research Agenda on the Yoruba in the Nineteenth Century', *History in Africa*, 15, 1988, p. 213.

8. See, for example, Gerhard Mare, *Brothers Born of Warrior Blood: Politics and Ethnicity in South Africa*, Johannesburg, Raven Press, 1992.

9. William Arens and Ivan Karp (eds.), *Creativity of Power*, Washington D.C.: Smithsonian Institution Press, 1989, pp. xiii–xiv.

10. Myron Weiner, *Son of the Soil: Migration and Ethnic Conflict in India*, Princeton: Princeton University Press, 1978, p. 350.

11. Maurice Bloch, 'The Past and the Present in the Present', *Man*, 12, 1977, p. 289.

12. A. F. Robertson, 'Histories and Political Opposition Ahafo, Ghana', *Africa*, 43, 1973, p. 57.

13. Jane I. Guyer, 'Representation without Taxation: An Essay on Democracy in Rural Nigeria, 1952–1990', Boston University, African Studies Working Papers, 1992.

14. For authoritative analyses see Toyin Falola and Julius Ihonvbere, *The Rise and Fall of Nigeria's Second Republic*, London: Zed Press, 1985; Joseph, *Democracy and Prebendel Politics in Nigeria*.

15. Peter Ekeh, 'Social Anthropology and the Two Contrasting Uses of Tribalism in Africa', *Comparative Studies in Society and History*, 32, 1990.

16. See for example Wale Oyemakinde, 'The Chiefs Law and the Regulation of Traditional Chieftaincy in Yorubaland', *Journal of the Historical Society of Nigeria*, 9, 1977, pp. 63–74.

17. For a succinct analysis see Guyer, 'Representation without Taxation: An Essay on Democracy in Rural Nigeria, 1952–1990'.

18. For critical analysis see William Graf, *The Nigerian State: Political Economy, State, Class, and Political System in the Post-Colonial Era*, London: James Curry, 1988.

19. Ian Shapiro, 'Letter from South Africa', *Dissent*, 1994, p. 181.

20. Sara S. Berry, 'Oil and the Disappearing Peasantry: Accumulation, Differentiation and Underdevelopment in Western Nigeria', *African Economic History*, 13, 1984, p. 10.

21. Terence Ranger, 'The Invention of Tradition Revisited: The Case of Africa', in Terence Ranger and Olufemi Vaughan (eds.), *Legitimacy and the State in Twentieth Century Africa: Essays in Honour of A. H. M. Kirk-Greene*, London: Macmillan, 1993.

22. Sara Berry, *Fathers Work for Their Sons: Accumulation, Mobility and Class in an Extended Yoruba Community*, Berkeley: University of California Press, 1985.

BIBLIOGRAPHY

Primary Sources

A. Archival Materials: Nigerian National Archives, Ibadan; Rhodes House Library, Oxford; Public Records Office, London; University of Ibadan (Africana Collection).

Comments on the Proceedings and Resolutions from the National Seminar on Nigeria's Political Culture, Kaduna, 2–5 November, 1981.

Government Proposal for the Reform of the Native Court Law in the Western Region.

Ibadan Divisional Files 1109, Vols. I, II, III, and IV: Ibadan Divisional Files, 1/1, 2624. Deals with chieftaincy and native court reforms in Ibadan Division, 1951–1954.

Ibadan Divisional Files 3277 and 3280. Deals with local government reform in Ibadan, 1952–1956.

Ibadan Divisional Files 1/1, 2910. Deals with native authority reform in Ibadan Division.

Ibadan Divisional Files 1/1, 2930. Deals with native court and native authority reform in the 1940s.

Intelligence Report, Ekiti Division of Nigeria, 1943, by O. V. Lee.

Intelligence Report, Ibadan Town, December, 1938, by R. W. C. Dickinson.

Leadership in Nigeria: Reflections of a Follower; Convocation Lecture delivered by Toyin Falola at the University of Sokoto, 14 January 1987.

Memorandum Submitted by the Ibadan Native Settlers Union to the Butcher Commission of Inquiry on 3 February 1951, Western Region Ministry of Local Government, (W.M.L.G.), File 2395.

Native Administration, Memo, Lagos, 1917, by Frederick J. Lugard, 1917.

Oyo Provincial Files 1. 157. 24/223. Deals with the relations between provincial obas and chiefs.

Oyo Provincial Files 1/1. 55 and 56. Deals with the conflict between the Alaafin of Oyo and the AG Divisional Native and Regional Governments, 1952–1954.

Oyo Provincial Files 2/3, 647/236. Deals with the relations between provincial obas and chiefs.

Oyo Provincial Files 1/154. Deals with native authority reform.

Oyo Provincial Files 2/e, c. 26/61. Deals with native authority reform.

Oyo Provincial Files 213/247. Deals with native authority and native court reform.

Oyo Provincial Files 2/2/247. Deals with native authority and native court reform.

Oyo Provincial Files 3/939. Deals with native authority reform in the 1940s.

Oyo Provincial Files 4,5,98. Deals with colonial land policy.

Oyo Provincial Files 1/10. Deals with colonial land policy.

Oyo Provincial Files 3, 375. Deals with colonial land policy.

Press Release of the Ibadan Committee of Concern (ICC) on the Situation Created by Misguided Effort to Balkanise Ibadan Municipal Government, 1982.

Press Release from the Unity Party of Nigeria (UPN), Ibadan Branch. Nomination for 1983 Oyo State UPN Gubernatorial Candidate, 14 April 1982.

Private Papers of Chief J. A. Ayorinde.

Proceedings of the Conference on Leadership and National Development, Nigerian Institute of Social and Economic Research (NISER), 8–12 April 1984.

Proceedings of the First, Second, Third, and Fourth Conferences of Chiefs of the Western Provinces held in Oyo, Abeokuta, and Ibadan, 1937, 1938, 1939 and 1940.

Proceedings of the National Conference on the Role of Traditional Rulers in the Governance of Nigeria, Institute of African Studies, University of Ibadan, 11–14 September 1984.

Proceedings of the National Seminar on the Role of Traditional Rulers in Politics, University of Sokoto, 1985.

Proceedings of the Oyo State House of Assembly Debates, 1979–1983.

Proceedings of the Western Region House of Assembly Debates, 1954–1965.

Proceedings of the Western Region House of Chiefs Debates, 1954–1965.

The Evolution of Ibadan, 1811–1913, by C. H. Elgee.

Western Equatorial Africa, Diocesan Magazine, 16, 193, July 1910.

Western Nigerian Ministry of Local Government, File 109, Vols I, II, III.

Western Nigerian Ministry of Local Government, File 23950

B. Government Reports

Bourdillon, Bernard H., *Memorandum on the Future Political Development in Nigeria*, Lagos, 1939.

Butcher, H. L. M., *Report of the Commission of Inquiry into Allegations of Misconduct Made against Chief Salami Agbaje, Otun-Balogun of Ibadan, and Allegations of Inefficiency and Maladministration on the Part of Ibadan and District Native Authority*, Lagos: Government Printer, 1951.

Collection of Speeches of Governor Bola Ige, Ibadan: Government Printer, 1982.

Colonial Office Summer School on African Administration, 18–28 August 1947, Queen's College, Cambridge.

Creech Jones, Arthur, *Despatch from the Secretary of State for the Colonies to the Governors of the African Territories*, 25 February, London: HMSO, 1947.

Development in the Western Region, 1955–1960, Ibadan: Government Printer, 1960.

Federal Military Government's Views on the Report of the Rent Panel, Lagos: Federal Ministry of Information, 1976.

Government's Views and Comment on the Findings and Recommendations of the Political Bureau, Lagos: The Federal Government Printer, 1987.

Guidelines for Local Government Reform, Lagos: Federal Government Printer, 1976.

Hailey, William M., *Native Administration and Political Development in British Tropical Africa*, Nendeln: Kraus Reprint, 1979.

Jones, G. I., *Report of the Position, Status and Influence of Chiefs and Natural Rulers in the Eastern Region of Nigeria*, Enugu: Eastern Region Government Printer, 1957.

Local Government in the Western Provinces of Nigeria, Ibadan: Government Printer, 1951.

Main Guidelines—Formation of Political Parties, National Electoral Commission, Onikan, Lagos, 1989.

Native Authority Ordinances, Oyo Province and Ibadan Division, 1898–1946.

Native Court Ordinances, Oyo Province and Ibadan Division, 1898–1946.

Nicholson, E. W. J., *Report of the Commission of Inquiry into the Ibadan District Council*, Ibadan: Government Printer, 1956.

Oba's Council Chairmanship Tussle Resolved—Olunloyo Speaks; Text of the Broadcast in Ibadan by the Governor of Oyo State on 2nd December 1983, Ibadan: Ministry of Home Affairs, Information, and Culture, Government Printer, 1983.

Obileye, Adesina, O., *Report of the Internal Inquiry into the Election of the Alaafin of Oyo*, Ibadan: Government Printer, 1969.

Proceedings of the General Conference on the Review of the Nigeria Constitution, Lagos: Government Printer, 1950.

Progress Report on the Development of the Western Region of Nigeria, 1955–1960, Ibadan: Government Printer, 1960.

Report of the Commission of Inquiry into Local Government Reform in Oyo State, Ibadan: Government Printer, 1981.

Report of the Commission on Chieftaincy Declaration and Government Decision Thereon, Ibadan: Government Printer, 1977.

Report of the Constitution Drafting Committee Containing the Draft Constitution, Volumes I and II, Lagos: Federal Ministry of Information, 1976.

Report of the Judicial Commission of Inquiry into the Communal Disturbances in Oranmiyan Local Government Area of Oyo State, Ibadan: Government Printer, 1981.

Report of the Political Bureau, Lagos: Federal Government Printer, 1986.

Speech of His Excellency the Military Governor of Oyo State, Brigadier David Jemibewon, to the People of Oyo State on Tuesday 24th August 1976: Local Government Reform in the State, Ministry of Local Government and Information, Ibadan: Government Printer, 1976.

The Constitution of the Federal Republic of Nigeria, Lagos: Federal Government Printer, 3 May 1989.

The Constitution of the Federal Republic of Nigeria, Lagos: Daily Times, 1979.

The First Report of the Anti-Inflation Task Force, Lagos: Federal Government Printer, 1976.

The Nigerian Independence Constitution, Ibadan: Government Printer, 1960.

The Report of the Panel Investigating the issue of the Creation of More States and Boundary Adjustments in Nigeria, Lagos: Government Printer, 1976.

The Constitution of the Republic of South Africa, 1993.

The Republic of Uganda: Report of the Commission of Inquiry into the Local Government System, Kampala: Government Printer, 1987.

Towards Independence: Speeches and Statements of Chief Awolowo, Premier of the Western Region of Nigeria, Ibadan: Government Printer, 1958.

Views and Comments of the Federal Military Government on the Findings and the Recommendations of the Committee on the Review of Local Government Administration in Nigeria, Lagos: Federal Government Printer, 1985.

C. Interviews

Dr. Busari Adebisi, member of the Ibadan Committee of Concern (ICC), Ibadan, February 1987.

Chief J. A. Adeyemo, Otun-Olubadan, (later Olubadan), Ibadan, February 1987.

Chief A. M. A. Akinloye, Chairman of the National Party of Nigeria (NPN), London, November 1987.

The Alaafin of Oyo, Oba Adeyemi III, Oyo, Nigeria, June 1987.

Chief Obafemi Awolowo, Leader of the Action Group (AG), and Unity Party of Nigeria (UPN), Ikenne, Ogun State, February 1987.

Chief J. A. Ayorinde, Senior Chief, Ibadan, and founding member of the Ibadan Progressive Union (IPU), Ibadan, February 1987.

John F. Hayley, former District Officer, Ibadan Division, Sussex, England, March 1986.

Chief Bola Ige, Governor of Oyo State, Ibadan, October 1979–September 1983, Ibadan, February 1987.

Dr. Omololu Olunloyo, Governor of Oyo State, October 1983–December 1983, Ibadan, February 1987.

Dr. Wale Oyemakinde, Member of the Commission of Inquiry into Local Government Reform in Oyo State, Ibadan, February 1987.

Secondary Sources

A. Books

Abimbola, Wande, *Ifa: An Exposition of the Literary Corpus*, Ibadan: Oxford University Press, 1976.

Aborisade, Oladimeji (ed.), *Local Government and the Traditional Rulers in Nigeria*, Ile-Ife: University of Ife Press, 1985.

Adamolekun, Ladipo, *Politics and Administration in Nigeria*, Ibadan: Spectrum, 1986.

———, and L. Rowland, (eds.), *The New Local Government System in Nigeria*, Ibadan: Heineman, 1979.

Adedeji, Adebayo, *An Introduction to Western Nigerian: Its People, Culture and System of Government*, Ile-Ife: University of Ife Press, 1975.

Afigbo, A. G., *The Warrant Chiefs: Indirect Rule in Southeastern Nigeria, 1891–1929*, London: Longman, 1971.

Ajayi, J. F. Ade, *Christian Missions in Nigeria, 1841–1891, The Making of a New Elite*, London: Longman, 1965.

———, and Robert Smith, *Yoruba Warfare in the Nineteenth Century*, Cambridge: Cambridge University Press, 1964.

Akintoye, S. A., *Revolution and Power Politics in Yorubaland, Ibadan Expansion and the Rise of Ekitiparapo, 1840–1893*, London: Longman, 1971.

Akpan, N. U., *Epitaph to Indirect Rule: A Discourse on Local Government in Africa*, London: Cassell, 1956.

Aliyu, Abubakar Y. (ed.), *The Role of Local Government in Social, Political and Economic Development in Nigeria*, Zaria: Ahmadu Bello University, 1982.

Allen, Christopher, and Gavin Williams (eds.), *Sub-Saharan Africa*, Sociology of Developing Societies 2, London: Macmillan, 1982.

Amin, Samir, *Neo-Colonialism in West Africa*, New York: Monthly Review Press, 1977.

Apter, Andrew, *Black Critics and Kings: The Hermeneutics of Power in Yoruba Society*, Chicago: University of Chicago Press, 1992.

Apter, David E., *Ghana in Transition*, Princeton: Princeton University Press, 1955.

Armstrong, John A., *Nations before Nationalism*, Chapel Hill: University of North Carolina Press, 1982.

Arrighi, Giovanni, and John Saul, *Essays in the Political Economy of Africa*, New York: Monthly Review Press, 1973.

Asiwaju, Anthony I., *Western Yorubaland under European Rule, 1889–1945: A Comparative Analysis of French and British Colonialism*, London: Longman, 1976.

Atanda, Joseph A., *The New Oyo Empire: Indirect Rule and Change in Southeastern Western Nigeria, 1894–1934*, London: Longman, 1973.

——— (ed.), *Baptist Churches in Nigeria, 1850–1950*, Ibadan: University Press Limited, 1988.

Awolowo, Obafemi, *Awo: The Autobiography of Chief Obafemi Awolowo*, Cambridge: Cambridge University Press, 1960.

———, *Freedom and Independence for Nigeria—A Statement of Policy*, Ibadan, 1958.

———, *Path to Nigerian Freedom*, London: Faber, 1947.

———, *Voice of Reason, Voice of Courage*, Akure: Fagbamigbe, 1981.

Azikiwe, Nnamdi, *Zik: A Selection from the Speeches of Azikiwe*, Cambridge: Cambridge University Press, 1961.

Babalola, S. A., *The Content and Form of Yoruba Ijala*, Oxford: Clarendon Press, 1966.

Baker, Pauline, *Urbanization and Political Change: The Politics of Lagos, 1917–1967*, Berkeley: University of California Press, 1974.

Balogun, Ola, *The Tragic Years: Nigeria in Crisis, 1966–1970*, Benin City: Ethiope, 1973.

Barber, Karin, *I Could Speak until Tomorrow: Oriki, Women, and the Past in a Yoruba Town*, Edinburgh: Edinburgh University Press, 1991.

Barnes, Sandra, T., *Patrons and Power: Creating a Political Community in Metropolitan Lagos*, Manchester: Manchester University Press, 1968.

Bascom, William, *Ifa Divination: Communication between God and Man*, Bloomington: Indiana University Press, 1969.

Bayart, Jean-François, *The State in Africa: The Politics of the Belly*, London: Longman, 1993.

Beer, Christopher, *The Politics of Peasant Groups in Nigeria*, Ibadan: Ibadan University Press, 1976.

Beetham, David, *The Legitimation of Power*, Atlantic Highlands, N.J.: Humanities Press, 1991.

Beier, Ulli, *Yoruba Myths*, Cambridge: Cambridge University Press, 1980.

Bello, Ahmadu, *My Life*, Cambridge: Cambridge University Press, 1962.

Berry, Sara S., *Cocoa, Custom and Socio-Economic Change in Rural Western Nigeria*, Oxford: Clarendon Press, 1975.

———, *Fathers Work for Their Sons: Accumulation, Mobility, and Class Formation in an Extended Yoruba Community*, Berkeley: University of California Press, 1985.

Black, C. E., *The Dynamics of Modernization*, New York: Harper and Row.

Buckley, Anthony D., *Yoruba Medicine*, Oxford: Clarendon Press, 1985.

Busia, Kofi, *The Position of Chiefs in the Modern Political System of the Ashanti*, London: Oxford University Press, 1951.

Cameron, Donald C., *The Principles of Native Administration and Their Application*, Lagos: Government Printers, 1934.

Carter, Gwendolen M. (ed.), *Transition in Africa: Studies in Political Adaptation*, Boston: Boston University Press, 1958.

Channock, Martin, *Law, Custom, and Social Order: The Colonial Experience of Malawi and Zambia*, Cambridge: Cambridge University Press, 1985.

Cohen, Abner, *Custom and Politics in Urban Africa*, London: Routledge, 1969.

Cole, Patrick D., *Modern and Traditional Elites in the Politics of Lagos*, London: Cambridge University Press, 1965.

Coleman, James, *Nigeria: Background to Nationalism*, Berkeley: University of California Press, 1963.

———, and Gabriel A. Almond (eds.), *The Politics of the Developing Area*, Princeton: Princeton University Press, 1970.

Creech Jones, Arthur, *The Future of the African Colonies*, Nottingham: Nottingham University Press, 1951.

————, *Labour's Colonial Policy*, London: Fabian Colonial Bureau, 1947.

Crowder, Michael, *Colonial West Africa: Collected Essays*, London: Frank Cass,1978.

————, and O. Ikime (eds.), *West African Chiefs: Their Changing Status under Colonial Rule and Independence*, Ile-Ife: Ife University Press, 1970).

De Smith, S. A., *The New Commonwealth and Its Constitutions*, London: Stevens and Sons, 1964.

Diamond, Larry, *Class. Ethnicity and Democracy in Nigeria: The Failure of the First Republic*, London: Macmillan Press, 1988.

Drewal, H. J., John Pemberton, and Rowland Abiodun (eds.), *Yoruba: Nine Centuries of African Art and Thought*, New York: The Center for African Art in association with Harry N. Abrams, 1989.

Dudley, Billy, *Instability and Political Order: Politics and Crisis in Nigeria*, Ibadan: Ibadan University Press, 1973.

————, *Parties and Politics in Northern Nigeria*, London: Frank Cass, 1968.

Duignan, Peter, and L. H. Gann (eds.), *Colonialism in Africa, 1870–1960*, Cambridge: Cambridge University Press, 1973.

Eades, J. S., *The Yoruba Today*, Cambridge: Cambridge University Press, 1983.

Ekechi, Felix, *Tradition and Transformation in Eastern Nigeria: A Sociopolitical History of Owerri and Its Hinterland, 1902–1947*, Kent, Ohio: Kent State University Press, 1989.

Elias, Taslim O., *British Colonial Law: A Comparative Study of the Interaction between English and Local Law in British Dependencies*, London: Stevens, 1962.

————, *Nature of African Customary Law*, Manchester: Manchester University Press, 1956.

————, *Nigeria: The Development of Its Laws and Constitution*, London: Stevens, 1967.

————, *Nigerian Land Law and Custom*, London: Routledge and Kegan Paul, 1962.

Evans-Pritchard, E., and M. Fortes (eds.), *African Political System*, London: Oxford University Press, 1970.

Ezera, Kalu, *Constitutional Developments in Nigeria*, London: Cambridge University Press, 1964.

Fadipe, N. A., *The Sociology of the Yoruba*, Ibadan: Ibadan University Press, 1970.

Fallers, Lloyd, *Bantu Bureaucracy: A Study of Integration and Conflict in the Political Institutions of an East African People*, Cambridge: Heffer, 1956.

———— (ed.), *The King's Men: Leadership and Status in Buganda on the Eve of Independence*, London: Oxford University Press,1964.

Falola, Toyin, *Politics and Economy in Ibadan, 1893–1945*, Lagos: Modelor, 1989.

————, *Religious Militancy and Self Assertion: Islam and Politics in Nigeria*, London: Avebury Press, 1996.

————, *Violence in Nigeria: The Crisis of Religious Politics and Secular Ideologies*, Rochester: University of Rochester Press, 1998.

————, and Julius Ihonvbere, *The Rise and Fall of Nigeria's Second Republic*, London: Zed Press, 1985.

————, and Dare Oguntomisin, *The Military in Nineteenth Century Yoruba Politics*, Ile-Ife: Univeristy of Ife Press, 1982.

Feierman, Steven, *Peasant Intellectuals: Anthropology and History in Tanzania*, Madison: University of Wisconsin Press, 1990.

Field, Karen, *Revival and Rebellion in Colonial Central Africa*, Princeton: Princeton University Press, 1985.

Freund, Bill, *The Making of Contemporary Africa: The Development of African Society since 1800*, Bloomington: Indiana University Press, 1984.

Gbadamosi, T. G. O., *The Growth of Islam among the Yoruba Muslim*, London: Longman, 1978.

Gailey, Harry, *Lugard and the Abeakuta Uprising: The Demise of Egba Independence*, London: Frank Cass, 1982.

Gifford, Prosser, and W. Roger Lewis (eds.), *The Transfer of Power in Africa: Decolonization, 1940–1960*, New Haven: Yale University Press, 1982.

Graf, William, *The Nigerian State: Political Economy, State, Class, and Political System in the Postcolonial Era*, London: James Currey, 1988.

Hargreaves, John D., *The End of Colonial Rule in West Africa: Essays in Contemporary History*, London: Macmillan, 1979.

Harrell-Bond, Barbara E., Allen M. Howard, and David E. Skinner, *Community Leadership and the Transformation of Freetown 1801–1976*, The Hague: Mouton, 1978.

Hobsbawm, Eric, and Terence Ranger (eds.), *The Invention of Tradition*, Cambridge: Cambridge University Press, 1988.

Hodgkin, Thomas, *African Political Parties*, Harmondsworth: Penguin, 1961.

————, *Nationalism in Colonial Africa*, London: Muller, 1956.

Holm, John, and Patrick Molutsi (eds.), *Democracy in Botswana*, Athens: Ohio University Press, 1989.

Huntington, Samuel, *Political Order in Changing Societies*, Cambridge: Harvard University Press, 1968.

————, *The Soldier and the State*, Cambridge: Harvard University Press, 1967.

Ihonvbere, Julius, *Economic Crisis, Civil Society and Democratization: The Case of Zambia*, Trenton, N.J.: Africa World Press, 1997.

————, *Nigeria: The Politics of Adjustment and Democracy*, New Brunswick, N.J.: Transaction Press, 1994.

————, and Timothy Shaw, *Illusions of Power: Nigeria in Transition*, Trenton N.J.: Africa World Press, 1998.

Jemibewon, David M., *A Combatant in Government*, Ibadan: Heineman, 1979.

Johnson, John J. (ed.), *The Role of the Military in Underdeveloped Countries*, Princeton: Princeton University Press, 1962.

Johnson, Samuel, *The History of the Yorubas: From the Earliest Times to the Beginning of the British Protectorate*, Lagos: Church Missionary Society, 1966.

Joseph, Richard, *Democracy and Prebendal Politics in Nigeria*, Cambridge: Cambridge University Press, 1987.

Kelly, Robin, D. G, *Race Rebels*, New York: Free Press, 1994.

Killingray, David, and Richard Rathbone (eds.), *African and the Second World War*, Basingstoke: Macmillan, 1989.

Kilson, Martin, L., *Political Change in a West African State: A Study of the Modernization Process in Sierra Leone*, Cambridge: Harvard University Press, 1966.

Kirk-Greene, A. H. M., (ed.), *Africa in the Colonial Period—The Transfer of Power: The Colonial Administrator in the Age of Decolonization*, Oxford, 1979.

———, *Crisis and Conflict in Nigeria: A Documentary Source Book, 1966–1969*, London: Oxford University Press, 1971.

———, *The Principles of Native Administration in Nigeria: Selected Documents, 1900–1947*, London: Oxford University Press, 1965.

———, and O. Rimmer, *Nigeria since 1970: A Political and Economic Outline*, London: Hodder and Stoughton, 1981.

Kothari, Rajni, *Footsteps into the Future: Diagnosis of the Present World and a Design for an Alternative*, New York: Free Press, 1974.

Law, R. C. C., *The Oyo Empire, c.1600–c. 1836*, Oxford: Clarendon Press, 1977.

Lewis, Arthur, *Politics in West Africa*, New York: Oxford University Press.

Lewis, I. M. (ed.), *History and Social Anthropology*, London: Travistock, 1968.

Lloyd, P. C., *Africa in Social Change*, Harmondsworth: Penguin, 1975.

———, *The New Elite in Tropical Africa*, London: Oxford University Press, 1966.

———, *Yoruba Land Law*, London: Oxford University Press, 1962.

———, A. L. Mabogunje, and B. Awe, (eds.), *The City of Ibadan*, Cambridge: Cambridge University Press, 1967.

Low, Anthony, D., *Eclipse of Empire*, Cambridge: Cambridge University Press, 1991.

———, and Cranford Pratt, *Buganda and British Overrule 1900–1955*, London: Oxford University Press, 1960.

Lugard, Frederick D. (ed.), *The Dual Mandate in British Tropical Africa*, Edinburgh: Blackwood, 1929.

———, *Political Memoranda: Revision of Instructions to Political Officers 1913–1918*, (first published 1919), London: Frank Cass, 1970.

Mackintosh, John P., *Nigerian Government and Politics*, London: Allen and Unwin, 1966.

Mair, Lucy P., *African Kingdoms*, Oxford: Clarendon Press, 1977.

———, *Anthropology and Social Change*, London: Altilone Press, 1969.

Mann, Kristin, *Marrying Well: Marriages, Status, and Social Change among the Educated Elite in Lagos*, Cambridge: Cambridge University Press, 1985.

Mare, Gerhard, *Brothers Born of Warrior Blood: Politics and Ethnicity in South Africa*, Johannesburg: Raven Press, 1992.

———, and Georgina Hamilton, *An Appetite for Power: Buthelezi's Inkatha and South Africa*, Johannesburg: Raven Press, 1987.

Marjomaa, Risto, *War on the Savannah: The Military Collapse of the Sokoto Caliphate under the Invasion of the British Empire, 1897–1903*, Helsinki: Finnish Academy of Sciences and Letters, 1998.

Mazrui, Ali A. (ed.), *The Warrior Tradition in Modern Africa*, Leiden: E. J. Brill, 1977.

Meek, C. K., *Land Tenure and Land Administration in Nigeria and the Cameroons*, London: HMSO, 1957.

Melson, Robert, and Howard Wolpe (eds.), *Nigeria: Modernization and the Politics of Communalism*, East Lansing: Michigan State University Press, 1971.

Migdal, Joel, *Strong Societies and Weak States: State-Society Relations and State Capacities in the Third World*, Princeton: Princeton University Press, 1988.

Morgan, Kemi, *Akinyele's Outline History of Ibadan*, Parts I, II, III and IV, Ibadan: Caxton Press.

Mzala, *Gatsha Buthelezi: Chief with a Double Agenda*, London: Zed 1988.

Nicholson, I. F., *Administration of Nigeria, 1900–1960: Men, Methods and Myths*, London: Oxford University Press, 1969.

Odumosu, Oluwole I., *The Nigerian Constitution: History and Development*, London: Sweet and Maxwell, 1963.

Okonjo, I. W., *British Administration in Nigeria 1900–1950: A Nigerian View*, New York: Nok Publisher, 1974.

Olupona, Jacob K., *Kingship, Religion and Rituals in a Nigerian Community: A Phenomenological Study of Ondo Yoruba Festivals*, Stockholm: Almuist and Wiksell, 1991.

Omotoso, Kole, *Just before Dawn*, Ibadan: Spectrum, 1988.

Owusu, Maxwell, *Uses and Abuses of Political Power: A Study of Continuity and Change in the Politics of Ghana*, Chicago: Chicago University Press,1970.

Oyediran, Oyeleye, *Essay in Local Government Administration in Nigeria*, Lagos: Project Publication, 1988.

———— (ed.), *Nigerian Government and Politics under Military Rule, 1966–1979*, London: Macmillan, 1979.

———— (ed.), *The Nigerian 1979 Elections*, Lagos: Macmillan,1981.

Oyerinde, N.D., *Iwe Itan Ogbomosho*, (A History of Ogbomosho), Jos, 1934.

Paden, John P., *Ahmadu Bello, Sardauna of Sokoto: Values and Leadership in Nigeria*, Zaria: Hudahuda, 1986.

————, *Religion and Political Culture in Kano*, Berkeley: University of California Press, 1973.

Panter-Brick, S. K., (ed.), *Soldiers and Oil: The Political Transformation of Nigeria*, London: Frank Cass, 1978.

Pearce, R. D., *Sir Bernard Bourdillon: The Biography of a Twentieth Century Colonialist*, Oxford: Kensal Press, 1987.

————, *The Turning Point in Africa: British Colonial Policy, 1938–1948*, London: Frank Cass, 1982.

Peel, P. D. Y., *Ijeshas and Nigerians: The Incorporation of a Yoruba Kingdom, 1890s–1970s*, Cambridge: Cambridge University Press, 1983.

Peil, Margaret, *African Urban Society*, Chichester: John Wiley, 1984.

————, *Consensus and Conflict in African Societies: An Introduction to Sociology*, London: Longman, 1977.

Pemberton, John, and Funso Afolayan, *Yoruba Sacred Kingship: A Power Like the Gods*, Washington: Smithsonian Institution Press, 1996.

Perham, Margery F., *African and British Rule*, London: Oxford University Press, 1943.

———, *Lugard: Years of Authority, 1898–1945*, London: Collins,1960.

———, *Native Administration in Nigeria*, London: Oxford University Press, 1937.

Post, Kenneth, *The New States of Africa*, London: Penguin, 1964.

———, *The Nigerian Federal Election of 1959: Politics and Administration in a Developing Political System*, London: Oxford University Press, 1963.

———, and George Jenkins, *The Price of Liberty: Personality and Politics in Colonial Nigeria*, Cambridge: Cambridge University Press,1973.

———, and Michael Vickers, *Structure and Conflict in Nigeria, 1960–1966*, London: Heineman, 1973.

Price, Robert, *Society and Bureaucracy in Contemporary Ghana*, Berkeley: University of California Press, 1975.

Ranger, Terence, *The Invention of Tribalism in Zimbabwe*, Gweru: Mambo Press, 1985.

———, *Peasant Consciousness and Guerilla War in Zimbabwe*, Berkeley: University of California Press, 1985.

———, and Olufemi Vaughan (eds.), *Legitimacy and the State in Twentieth Century Africa: Essays in Honour of A. H. M. Kirk-Greene*, London: Macmillan Press, 1993.

Robinson, Pearl T., and Elliot P. Skinner (eds.), *Transformation and Resiliency in Africa*, Washington, D.C.: Howard University Press, 1983.

Shaw, Timothy, *Towards a Political Economy of Africa: The Dialectics of Dependence*, London, 1985.

Skinner, Elliot P., *African Urban Life: The Transformation of Ougadougou*, Princeton: Princeton University Press, 1974.

Sklar, Richard L., *Nigerian Political Parties: Power in an Emergent African Nation*, Princeton: Princeton University Press, 1963.

Smith, Robert, *Kingdom of the Yoruba*, London: Methuen, 1976.

Soyinka, Wole, *The Open Sore of a Continent: A Personal Narrative of the Nigerian Crisis*, New York: Oxford University Press, 1996.

Tijani, Aminu, and D. Williams (eds.), *Shehu Shagari—My Vision of Nigeria*, London: Frank Cass, 1981.

Trouillot, Michel-Rolph, *Silencing the Past*, Boston: Beacon Press, 1995.

Turner, Brian, *Marx and the End of Orientalism*, London: George Allen and Unwin, 1978.

Ward-Price, H. L., *Dark Subjects*, London: Jarrolds, 1939.

Weber Max, *Economy and Society*, Berkeley: University of California Press, 1968.

Welch, Claude E. (ed.), *Political Modernization: A Reader in Comparative Political Change*, Belmont: Wadsworth,1967.

Whitaker, C. S., *The Politics of Tradition: Continuity and Change in Northern Nigeria, 1946–1966*, Princeton: Princeton University Press, 1970.

Williams, David, *President and Power in Nigeria—The Life of Shehu Shagari*, London: Frank Cass, 1982.

Williams, Gavin P., *State and Society in Nigeria*, Idanre: Afroafrika, 1980.

———— (ed.), *Economy and Society in Nigeria*, London: Rex Collings, 1976.

B. Articles

Abiodun, Rowland, 'The Kingdom of Owo', in H. J. Drewal, John Pemberton, and Rowland Abiodun (eds.), *Yoruba: Nine Centuries of African Art and Thought*, New York, The Center for African Art in association with Harry N. Abrams, 1989.

Adebisi, Busari, 'The Politics of Development Control in the Nigerian City of Ibadan', *Pan African Journal*, 7, 1974.

Adejuyigbe, Omolade, 'Reorganization of Local Government in Councils in Nigeria', *Quarterly Journal of Administration*, 6, 1972.

Afolayan, Funso, 'Nigeria: A Political Entity and a Society', in Paul A. Beckett and Crawford Young (eds.), *Dilemmas of Democracy in Nigeria*, Rochester: University of Rochester Press, 1997.

Akpan, N. U., 'Have Traditional Authorities a Place in a Modern Local Government Systems?', *Journal of African Administration*, July 1955.

Ajayi, J. F. Ade, 'Professional Warriors in Nineteenth Century Yoruba Politics', *Tarikh*, 1, 1, 1963.

Aliyu, A., 'The Nature and Implications of Local Government Reform in Nigeria', *Nigerian Journal of Public Affairs*, 1978.

Amuchaezi, Elockukwu, 'Local Government and Traditional Legitimacy: Divisional Administration in the East Central State of Nigeria', *Quarterly Journal of Administration*, July 1973.

Ardener, E., 'The Notion of the Elite', *African Affairs*, 66, 1967.

Arifalo, S. O., 'Egbe Omo Oduduwa: Structure and Strategy', *Odu: A Journal of West African Studies*, January 1981.

Aronson, D. R., 'Capitalism and Culture in Ibadan Urban Development', *Urban Anthropology*, 1978.

Asiwaju, A. I., 'Political Motivation and Oral Historical Traditions in Africa', *Africa*, 46, 1976.

Awe, Bolanle, 'The Ajele System: A Study of Ibadan Imperialism in the Nieteenth Century', *Journal of the Historical Society of Nigeria*, 3, 1964.

Awolowo, Obafemi, 'The Native Administration in Nigeria', *West Africa*, 7 April 1945.

————, 'Siyanbola, Alaafin of Oyo: The King and the Man', *West Africa*, 3 March 1945.

Awopegba, Cornelius, 'The Descent of Oduduwa: Claims of Superiority among Some Yoruba Traditional Rulers and the Arts of Ancient Ife', *International Journal of African Historical Studies*, 19, 1986.

Bach, Daniel, 'Managing a Plural Society: The Boomerang Effects of Nigerian Federalism', *Journal of Commonwealth and Comparative Politics*, 27, 1989.

Bascom, W. R., 'Urbanization among the Yorubas', *American Journal of Sociology*, 60.

Berry, Sara, 'Oil and the Disappearing Peasantry: Accumulation, Differentiation and Underdevelopment in Western Nigeria', *African Economic History*, 13, 1984.

————, 'Social Institutions and Access to Resources', *Africa*, 59, 1989.

Binder, Leonard, 'National Integration and Political Development', *American Political Science Review*, September 1964.

Bratton, Michael, 'Beyond the State: Civil Society and Associational life in Africa', *World Politics*, 1989.

Braudel, Fernand, 'Débats et histoires et sciences sociales: La longue durée', *Annales*, 4, 1958.

————, 'Histoires et sciences sociales: La longue durée', *Annales*, 4, 1958.

Brown, R. E., 'Local Government in the Western Region of Nigeria 1950–1955', *Journal of African Administration*, 7, 1955.

Callaway, Barbara J., 'Local Politics in Ho and Aba', *Canadian Journal of African Studies*, 4, 1970.

————, 'Transitional Local Politics: Tradition in Local Elections in Aba, Nigeria, Keta, Ghana', *African Studies Review*, 15, 1972.

Chazan, Naomi, 'The Africanization of Political Change: Some Aspects of the Dynamics of Political Culture in Ghana and Nigeria', *African Studies Review*, 21, 1978.

Clapham, Christopher, 'The Longue of the African State', *African Affairs*, 93, 1994.

Cole, T., 'Bureaucracy in Transition: Independent Nigeria', *Public Administration*, Winter 1960.

Coleman, James, 'Local Government in Nigeria', *West Africa*, 20 December 1952.

————, 'Nigeria under the Macpherson Constitution', *World Today*, January 1953.

————, 'Yoruba Traditional Political System', *Southwestern Journal of Anthropology*, 10, 1954.

Coquery-Vidrovitch, Catherine, 'Changes in African Historical Studies in France', in Christopher Fyfe (ed.), *African Studies since 1945: A Tribute to Basil Davidson*, London: Longman, 1976.

Creech Jones, Arthur, 'The Place of African Local Administration in Colonial Policy', *Journal of African Administration*, 1, 1947.

Crook, Richard C., 'Decolonization, the Colonial State, and Chieftaincy in the Gold Coast', *African Affairs*, 85, 1986.

————, 'Legitimacy, Authority and the Transfer of Power in Ghana', *Political Studies*, 35, 1987.

Diamond, Larry, 'Nigeria: The Uncivic Society and the Descent into Praetorianism', in Larry Diamond, Juan J. Linz, and Seynour Martin Lipset (eds.), *Politics in Developing Countries: Comparing Experiences in Democracy*, Boulder: Lynne Rienner, 1995.

Doortmont, Michael R., 'The Roots of Yoruba Historiography: Classicism, Traditionalism and Pragmatism', in Toyin Falola (ed.), *African Historiography: Essays in Honour of Ade Ajayi*, Harlow, Essex: Longman, 1993.

Dudley, Billy J., 'The Nigerian Election of 1979: The Voting Decision', *Journal of Commonwealth and Comparative Politics*, 19, 1981.

Eisenstadt, S. N., 'Continuity and Reconstruction of Tradition', *Daedalus*, 102, 1973.

Ekeh, Peter, 'Colonialism and the Two Publics in Africa: A Theoretical Statement', *Comparative Studies in Society and History*, 17, 1975.

———, 'Social Anthropology and Two Contrasting Uses of Tribalism in Africa', *Comparative Studies in Society and History*, 32, 1990.

Fadahunsi, Olu, 'The Politics of Local Administration in Western Nigeria, 1958–1968', *Quarterly Journal of Administration*, January, 1977.

Fallers, Lloyd, 'The Predicament of the Modern African Chief: An Instance of Uganda', *American Anthropologist*, 57, 1955.

Falola, Toyin, 'Lebanese Traders in Southwestern Nigeria', *African Affairs*, 89, 1990.

———, 'A Research Agenda on the Yoruba in the Nineteenth Century', *History in Africa*, 15, 1988.

———, 'Slavery and Pawnship in the Yoruba Economy in the Nineteenth Century', *Slavery and Abolition*, 15, 1994.

Fieldhouse, David, 'Decolonization, Development and Dependence: A Survey of Changing Attitude', in *The Transfer of Power in Africa: Decolonization, 1940–1960*, New Haven: Yale University Press, 1982.

Fowler, H., 'Some Observation of the Western Region Local Government Law, 1952', *Journal of African Administration*, 5, 1953.

Francis, Paul, 'For the Use and Common Benefit of All Nigeria: Consequences of the 1978 Land Nationalization', *Africa*, 54, 1984.

Furniss, Graham, 'Oral Culture and the Making of Meaning', *African Affairs*, 91, 1992.

Geertz, Clifford, 'The Integrative Revolution: Primordial Sentiments and Civil Politics in the New States', in Clifford Geertz (ed.), *Old Societies and New States: The Quest for Modernity in Asia and Africa*, New York: Free Press, 1967.

Goldsworthy, David, 'On the Structural Explanation of African Military Interventions', *Journal of Modern African Studies*, 24, 1986.

Gutkind, P. C. W., 'African Urban Chiefs: Agents of Stability or Change in African Urban Life', *Anthropologica*, 8, 1966.

———, 'The Emergent African Proletariat', Montreal Center for Developing Areas Studies, Occasional paper 8, 1974.

———, 'Political Consciousness among the Urban Poor in Ibadan', *International Journal of Sociology*, Summer 1977.

Guyer, Jane, 'Representation without Taxation: An Essay on Democracy in Rural Nigeria, 1952–1990', African Studies Working Papers, Boston University, 1992.

Horton, Robin, 'Ancient Ife: A Reassessment', *Journal of the Historical Society of Nigeria*, 9, 1979.

Hobsbawm, Eric, 'Introduction: Inventing Tradition', in Eric Hobsbawm and Terence Ranger (eds.), *The Invention of Tradition*, Cambridge: Cambridge University Press, 1988.

Hopkins, A. G., 'Economic Aspects of Political Movement in the Gold Coast, 1918–1939', *Journal of African History*, 7, 1966.

Huntington, Samuel, P., 'Political Development and Political Decay', *World Politics*, 17, 1965.

Hyden, Goran, and Williams, 'A Community Model of African Politics: Illustrations from Nigeria and Tanzania', *Comparative Studies in Society and History*, 36, 1994.

Ihonvbere Julius, 'Are Things Falling Apart? The Military and the Crisis of Democratization in Nigeria', *Journal of Modern African Studies*, 34, 1996.

———, 'The "Irrelevant" State: Ethnicity and the Quest for Nationhood in Africa', *Ethnic and Racial Studies*, 17, 1994.

———, and Olufemi Vaughan, 'Democracy and Civil Society in the Nigerian Transition Programme, 1985–1993', in John A. Wiseman (ed.), *Democracy and Political Change in Sub-Saharan Africa*, London: Routledge, 1995.

Ikime, Obaro, 'Reconsidering Indirect Rule: The Nigerian Example', *Journal of the Historical Society of Nigeria*, 4, 1968.

Jackson, Gary, 'Some Approaches to the Study of Modernization', *Journal of International and Comparative Studies*, 5, 1972.

Joseph, Richard, 'Democratization under Military Rule and Repression in Nigeria', in Paul Beckett and Crawford Young (eds.), *Dilemmas of Democracy in Nigeria*, Rochester: University of Rochester Press, 1997.

———, 'Political Parties and Ideology in Nigeria', *Review of African Political Economy*, 13, 1978.

Jibrin, Ibrahim, 'Religion and Political Turbulence in Nigeria', *Journal of Modern African Studies*, 29, 1991.

Kirk-Greene, A. H. M., '"Le Roi est Mort, Vive le Roi": The Comparative Legacy of Chiefs after the Transfer of Power in British and French West Africa', in Daniel Bach (ed.), *The British and French in West Africa*, provisional title, forthcoming.

Koehn, Peter, 'State Land Allocation and Class Formation in Nigeria', *Journal of Modern African Studies*, 21, 1983.

Kothari, Rajni, 'Tradition and Modernity Revisited', *Government and Opposition*, 3, 1968.

Laitin, David D., 'The Sharia Debate and the Origins of Nigeria's Second Republic', *Journal of Modern African Studies*, 20, 1982.

Law, R. C. C., 'The Heritage of Oduduwa: Traditional History and Political Propaganda among the Yoruba', *Journal of African History*, 14, 1973.

Lawson, Stephanie, 'The Myth of Cultural Homogeneity and Its Implications for Chiefly Power and Politics in Fiji', *Comparative Studies in Society and History*, 32, 1990.

Levy, Marion, 'Patterns of Modernization and Political Development', *Annals of the American Academy of Political and Social Science*, 35, 1965.

Lloyd, P. C., 'Conflict Theory and Yoruba Kingdoms', in I. M. Lewis (ed.), *History and Social Anthropology*, London: Tavistock, 1968.

———, 'The Development of Political Parties in Western Nigeria', *American Political Science Review*, 49, 1955.

———, 'The Integration of the New Economic Classes into Local Government in Western Nigeria', *African Affairs*, 52, 1953.

———, 'The Political Development of Yoruba Kingdoms in the Eighteenth and Nineteenth Centuries', *Royal Anthropological Institute Occasional Paper*.

———, 'Traditional Rulers', in James P. Coleman and Carl G. Rosberg (eds.), *Political Parties and National Integration in Tropical Africa*, Berkeley: University of California Press, 1964.

———, 'The Yoruba Today', *Sociological Review*, 1957.

Mackintosh, John P., 'Electoral Trends and the Tendency to a One Party System in Nigeria', *Journal of Commonwealth Political Studies*, 1, 1962.

———, 'Politics in Nigeria: The Action Group Crisis of 1962', *Political Studies*, 11, 1963.

Mair, Lucy P., 'African Chiefs Today', Lugard Memorial Lecture for 1958, *Africa*, 28, 1958.

———, 'Representative Local Government as a Problem in Social Change', *Journal of African Administration*, 8, 1958.

McGrathy, F. D., 'Field Administration and Local Government in Western Nigeria', *Quarterly Journal of Administration*, 3, 1969.

Melson, Robert, and Howard Wolpe, 'Modernization and the Politics of Communalism: A Theoretical Perspective', *The American Political Science Review*, 64, 1970.

Molutsi, Patrick, 'The Ruling Class and Democracy in Botswana', in John Holm and Patrick Molutsi (eds.), *Democracy in Botswana*, Athens: Ohio University Press, 1989.

———, and John Holm, 'Developing Democracy When Civil Society Is Weak', *African Affairs*, 89, 1990.

Mustapha, Abdul Raufu, 'Structural Adjustments and Agrarian Change in Nigeria', in Adebayo Olukoshi (ed.), *The Politics of Structural Adjustment in Nigeria*, London: James Currey, 1993.

Nwaubani, Ebere, 'Chieftaincy among the Igbo: A Guest on the Center-Stage', *International Journal of the African Historical Society*, 27, 1994.

Oguntomisin, G. O., 'Political Change and Adaptation in Yorubaland in the Nineteenth Century', *Canadian Journal of African Studies*, 15, 1986.

———, and Toyin Falola, 'Refugees in Yorubaland in the Nineteenth Century', *Asian and African Studies*, 21, 1987.

O'Hear, Ann, 'Political and Commercial Clientage in Nineteenth Century Ilorin', *African Economic History*, 15, 1986.

Olayemi, O. A., 'Movements of Population from Urban to Rural Areas of Ibadan', *Genève Afrique*, 17, 1979.

Orewa, G. O., 'The Role of Traditional Rulers in Administration', *Quarterly Journal of Administration*, 1978.

Oyediran, Oyeleye, 'The Chosen Few: Policy Makers in the New Local Government System in Western Nigeria', *Quarterly Journal of Administration*, July 1974.

———, 'Local Government in Southern Nigeria: The Direction of Change', *African Review*, 4, 1974.

———, 'Local Influence and Traditional Leadership: The Politics of the Ife Forest Reserve', *Odu: A Journal of Western African Studies*, 7, 1972.

———, 'Modakeke in Ife: Historical Background to an Aspect of Contemporary Ife Politics', *Odu: A Journal of Western African Studies*, 10, 1974.

———, 'The Position of the Ooni in the Changing Political System of Ile-Ife', *Journal of the Historical Society of Nigeria*, 6, 1972.

———, 'Transitions without End: From Hope to Despair—Reflections of a Participant Observer', in Paul Beckett and Crawford Young (eds.), *Dilemmas of Democracy in Nigeria*, Rochester: University of Rochester Press, 1997.

Oyemakinde, Wale, 'The Chiefs Law and the Regulation of Traditional Chieftaincy in Yorubaland', *Journal of the Historical Society of Nigeria*, 9, 1977.

Peel, J. D. Y., 'Inequality and Action: The Forms of Ijesha Social Conflict', *Canadian Journal of African Studies*, 14, 1980.

———, 'Making History: The Past in the Ijesha Present', *Man*, 19, 1984.

———, 'Olaju: A Yoruba Concept of Development', *Journal of Development Area*, 1979.

Pye Lucian, 'Armies in the Process of Political Modernization', in *The Role of the Military in Underdeveloped Countries*, Princeton: Princeton University Press, 1967.

———, 'The Concept of Political Development', *Annals of the American Academy of Political and Social Science*, March 1965.

Ranger, Terence, 'Connexions Between "Primary Resistance" Movements and Modern Mass Nationalism in East and Central Africa', *Journal of African History*, 9, 1968.

———, 'The Invention of Tradition in Colonial Africa', in Hobsbawm, Eric, and Ranger, Terence, (eds.)., *The Invention of Tradition*, Cambridge: Cambridge University Press, 1988.

———, 'The Invention of Tradition Revisited: The Case of Africa', in *Legitimacy and the State in Twentieth Century Africa: Essays in Honour of A.H.M. Kirk-Greene*, London: Macmillan, 1993.

———, 'Tradition and Travesty: Chiefs and Administration in Makoni District, Zimbabwe, 1960–1980', *Africa*, 52, 1982.

Reed, Cyrus, 'The Role of Traditional Rulers in Elective Politics in Nigeria', African Studies Program, Indiana University, 1982.

Robinson, Pearl T., 'Niger: Anatomy of a Neo-traditional Corporatist State', *Comparative Politics*, 24, 1991.

Salamone, Frank A., 'Indirect Rule and the Reinterpretation of Tradition: Abdullahi of Yauri', *African Studies Review*, 1980.

Shapiro, Ian, 'Democratic Innovation: South Africa in Comparative Context', *World Politics*, 46, 1993.

———, 'Letter from South Africa', *Dissent*, 1994.

Sklar, Richard, 'The African Frontier for Political Science', in *Africa and the Disciples*, Robert Bates, V. Y. Mudimbe, and O'Barr (eds), Chicago: University of Chicago Press, 1993.

———, 'Contradictions in the Nigerian Political System', *The Journal of Modern African Studies*, 3, 1965.

Smith, A. D., 'Ethnic Persistence and National Integration', *British Journal of Sociology*, 35, 1984.

———, 'The Nation Invented, Imagined, Reconstructed', *Millennium*, 26, 1991.

Steward, Marjorie H., 'Tradition and a Changing Political Order: A Dispute Affecting the Chieftaincies of Kaiama and Kenu in Nigeria', *Genève Afrique*, 17, 1979.

Szeftel, Morris, 'Ethnicity and Democratization in South Africa', *Review of African Political Economy*, 60, 1990.

Tambiah, S. J., 'The Persistence and Transformation of Tradition in Southeast Asia, with Particular Reference to Thailand', *Daedalus*, 102, 1973.

Vaughan, Olufemi, 'Assessing Grassroots Politics and Community Development in Nigeria', *African Affairs*, 94, 1995.

———, 'Les Chefs traditionnels face au pouvoir politique', *Politique Africaine*, December 1988.

———, 'Chieftaincy Politics and Social Relations in Nigeria', *Journal of Commomwealth and Comparative Politics*, 29, 1991.

———, 'Communalism, Legitimation and Party Politics at the Grassroots: The Case of the Yoruba', *International Journal of Politics, Culture and Society*, 7, 1994.

———, 'Decolonization and Legitimation in Nigeria', in Terence Ranger and Olufemi Vaughan (eds.), *Legitimacy and the State in Twentieth Century Africa*, London: Macmillan Press, 1993.

———, 'Ife and Oyo in Colonial and Postcolonial Nigerian Politics', in Simon McGrath, Charles Jedrej, and Jack Thompson (eds.), *Rethinking African History*, Centre for African Studies: University of Edinburgh, 1997.

———, 'Traditional Rulers and the Dilemma of Democratic Transitions in Nigeria', in Paul Beckett and Crawford Young (eds.), *Dilemmas of Democracy in Nigeria*, Rochester: University of Rochester Press, 1997.

Wallerstein, Immanuel, 'A Comment on Epistemology: What is Africa', *Canadian Journal of African Studies*, 22, 1988.

———, 'Ethnicity and National Integration in West Africa', *Cahiers d'Etudes Africaines*, 3, 1960.

———, 'Voluntary Associations', in James Coleman and Carl Rosberg (eds.), *Political Parties and National Integration in Tropical Africa*, Berkeley: University of California Press, 1966.

Whitaker, C. S., 'A Dysrhythmic Process of Political Change', *World Politics*, 19, 1967.

Williams, Gavin, 'Garveyism, Akinpelu Obisesan and his Contemporary: Ibadan, 1920–1922', in Terence Ranger and Olufemi Vaughan (eds.), *Legitimacy and the State in Twentieth Century Africa*, London: Macmillan, 1993.

———, and Terisa Turner, 'Nigeria', in John Dunn (ed.), *West African States: Failure and Promise—A Study in Comparative Politics*, Cambridge: Cambridge University Press, 1978.

C. Newspapers

African Events
Africa Now
Africa Concord
Africa Confidential
Analyst
Daily Service
Daily Sketch
Daily Star
Daily Times
'Iwe Irohin Yoruba'
Morning Post
National Concord
New Nigeria
Newbreed
Newswatch
Nigerian Observer
Nigerian Tribune
Punch
Southern Nigerian Defender
Sunday Concord
Sunday Sketch
Sunday Times
The Nigerian Guardian
The Nigerian Economist
This Week
West Africa

D. Theses and Dissertations

Abdulraheem, Tajudeen, 'Politics in Nigeria's Second Republic', D.Phil., Oxford University, 1990.

Adewoye, Omoniyi, 'The Legal Profession in Southern Nigeria', Ph.D., Columbia University, 1968.

Agiri, B. A., 'The Development of Local Government in Ogbomosho, 1850–1950', M.A., University of Ibadan, 1966.

Ahmed, Mohammed Uba, 'The National Party of Nigeria: Origins to Electoral Success', M.S., Birmingham University, 1986.

Awe, Bolanle, 'The Rise of Ibadan as a Yoruba Power in the Nineteenth Century', D.Phil., Oxford University, 1963.

Baptiste, F. Andre, 'The Relations between the Western Region and the Federal Government of Nigeria: A Study of the 1962 Emergency', M.A., University of Manchester, 1965.

Gboyega, Alex, 'Local Government and Political Integration in Western Nigeria, 1952–1972', Ph.D., University of Ibadan, 1975.

Jenkins, George, 'Ibadan Politics', Ph.D., Northwestern University, 1965.

Lloyd, P. C., 'Local Government in Yoruba Towns: An Analysis of the Role of the Obas, Chiefs and the Elected Councillors', D.Phil., Oxford University, 1958.

Nordan, C. R., 'The Development of British Colonial Policy 1938–1947', D.Phil., Oxford University, 1976.

Oyediran, Oyeleye, 'Political Change in a Nigerian Urban Community', Ph.D., University of Pittsburgh, 1971.

Williams, Gavin P., 'The Political Sociology of Western Nigeria, 1939–1965', B.Phil., Oxford University, 1967.

INDEX

Abacha, General Sani, 202
Abasi, Bello, 42
Abasi, Okunola, Baale of Ibadan, 47
Abayomi, Kofo A., 63, 65, 89, 90
Abeokuta, 16, 27, 118, 133, 188
Abimbola, Tijani, Okere of Shaki, 169
Abimbola, Wande, 206
Abiola, M. K. O., 178, 202, 206, 207–8, 257 n. 44, 257 n. 45
Aboderin, J. O., 36, 40
Abubakar III, Sultan of Sokoto, 124, 125, 171, 195, 200
Academic Staff Union of Universities (ASUU), 201
Action Group (AG), 60, 69, 70, 73, 79, 80, 83, 85, 86, 88, 95, 96, 97–98, 113, 134, 181, 184, 185, 231 n. 94; and Alaafin affair, 88–94, 204; and alliance with NCNC, 110; crisis of, 96, 101–6, 127, 132, 155, 162, 179, 203, 215; and election campaigns of 1964 and 1965, 111–18; formation of, 53, 62–63, 66–68; in government, Western Region, 71, 78, 79, 81, 82, 84, 85, 92; loyalists organizing during military rule, 162; in opposition in Western Region, 106–9, 110; re-creation as UPN, 162, 166, 205; reemergence of members, 1966, 126–27; and Western Region House of Chiefs, 98–101

Adebayo, General Adeyinka, 128, 162, 205; and *Agbekoya* rebellion, 129, 131, 132–33
Adebisi, Busari, 183
Adebowale, Raji, Aseyin of Iseyin, 114, 128
Adegbenro, D. S., 104, 132, 134, 162
Adelabu, Adegoke, 42, 48, 73, 78–81, 83–85, 87–88, 232 n. 3, 234 n. 41; death of, 88, 237 n. 17; memory of, 187–88
Adelakun, Busari, 182, 187
Adele II, Oba of Lagos, 65
Adeleye, Elekole of Ikole, 115
Adelu, Niyi, 182
Ademola, Justice Adenekan, 145
Ademola, Sir Adetokunbo, 114
Ademola II, Alake of Egbaland, 65
Ademola Commission, 145
Adeniran Adeyemi II. *See* Adeyemi II
Adeoye, Tafa, 132, 133
Adepoju, A., 185–86
Aderemi, Sir Adesoji, Ooni of Ife, 29, 50, 59, 60, 66, 92, 117, 169, 189, 204, 226 n. 47; attempt to remove, 1964, 113; and chairmanship of Oyo State Council of Chiefs, 167–69, 204, 256 n. 34; and conflict with Fani-Kayode (1950s) 112–13; and *Egbe Omo Oduduwa*, 65, 68; and land reforms, 149, 150, 151; as Western Region governor, 93, 104, 106, 166

279

Osi baale of Ibadan, the, 24
Osi Balogun of Ibadan, the, 18, 49,
   205. *See also* Akinyo, Chief
Otun baale of Ibadan, the, 24
Otun of Ikorodu, the, 109
Owa of Ilesha, the, 25, 39, 144, 146.
   See also Aromolaran
Owo, 60, 118
Oyebola, Mustapha, Aseyin of Iseyin,
   114, 128
Oyekan, Oba of Lagos, 170
Oyemakinde, Wale, 180
Oyerinde, N. D., 38–39, 227 n. 68
Oyesile Olugbode, Baale of Ibadan, 32
Oyesina, T. L., 36
Oyewumi, Shoun of Ogbomosho,
   144, 150, 206
Oyo (Yoruba sub-group), 13, 16, 17,
   53, 72, 108, 130, 186, 191
Oyo, town of, new, 3, 16, 23, 24, 26,
   28, 31, 69, 70, 90. *See also* Ago Oja
Oyo Division, 3, 24, 26, 89, 92, 111,
   118, 131, 150
Oyo Divisional Council, 88–94
Oyo Empire, old, 13, 16, 27, 188
Oyo Kingdom, new, 16, 23
Oyo Progressive Union (OPU), 90, 91
Oyo Province, 3, 8, 16, 19, 22, 24,
   25, 26, 27, 35, 47, 69, 214;
   subdivision of, 36
Oyo State Council of Chiefs, chair-
   manship of, 194, 203–9, 256 n.
   34, 257 n. 43, 257 n. 44
Oyo-Ile, 13, 16
Oyomesi, of Oyo, the, 14, 28, 91, 169,
   222 n. 61

Parakoyi (guild of traders/market
   chiefs, Egba), 14, 134
Path to Nigerian Freedom (Awolowo),
   60
Peel, J. D. Y., 7–8, 12, 13, 33, 48, 130

People's Redemption Party (PRP),
   163–64; in government, 1979–83,
   173–74
Political Bureau, 196, 197–200, 206
Popoola, Colonel, 207
Post, Kenneth, 42, 107, 110, 232 n. 3
prebendalism, 156
Presidential Constitution (1979), 156;
   drafting of, 152–54; shortcomings
   of, 156
Prest, Arthur, 67
"progressive governors," 251 n. 75
"progressive" unions, 22
"quasi-metropoles," 23

Raji Adebowale, Aseyin of Iseyin. *See*
   Adebowale, Raji, Aseyin of Iseyin
Ranger, Terence, 7, 9
Ransome-Kuti, Rev. I. O., 63
Regional Electoral Commission, 118
revenue allocation, 59, 230 n. 54
Richards Constitution (1947), 59, 229
   n. 53
Rimi, Abubakar, 163, 173–74
riots: Kano, 1953, 70; Oyo, 1954, 92,
   94; accompanying AG's defeat,
   1965, 188; anti-Igbo, in North,
   1966, 124; Bade Emirate, 1979,
   175; Kano, 1981, 174; following
   UPN's defeat, Ondo and Oyo,
   1983, 188; religious, 1987, 255 n.
   25; after 1993 election, 202. *See
   also Agbekoya* rebellion; Ife-
   Modakeke crisis
roads, 30, 34, 41
Robinson, Pearl, 121
Robinson, Resident, 77, 79
Rosiji, Ayo, 102, 103, 106, 230 n. 74,
   235 n. 72
Ross, Captain William A., Resident of
   Oyo Province, 26–31, 34, 38, 40,
   226 n. 47

Nigerian Chiefs: Traditional Power in Modern Politics, 1890s–1990s analyzes the imaginative adaptation of indigenous political structures to the processes of state formation in Nigeria since the imposition of colonial rule in the late nineteenth century. Drawing on the interactions between the state and chieftaincy, this study shows how Nigerian chieftaincy institutions survived both the constricting forces of colonialism and the modernization programs of the postcolonial regimes. This was made possible not only because of their adaptability, but also because of their integration with emerging centers of power and their role in the ongoing processes of stratification and class formation. On the other hand, since they were linked to externally derived forces, and legitimated by neotraditional themes, chieftaincy structures were distorted by the indirect rule system and transformed by competing communal claims. Twenty detailed case studies show how chieftaincy structures became a focal point of critical discourses on continuity and social change in twentieth-century Nigeria.

Olufemi Vaughan is Associate Professor in the Department of Africana Studies and Department of History, State University of New York at Stony Brook.

Olufemi Vaughan's *Nigerian Chiefs: Traditional Power in Modern Politics, 1890s– 1990s* is an extremely fascinating study. Kings, kingship, and chieftaincy are widely interesting subjects. Who could be kings? How well are Nigerian kings faring? How frequently have their situation[s] changed? What are chieftaincy titles? Why are Nigerian educated elites, civilian and military politicians, even the most outspoken critics of traditional rulers, receiving chieftaincy titles? The book provides answers and interesting information. . . . With superior scholarship, this is the work of an expert who sets out both to inform and interest the reader, and he achieves both.

> —Akanmu G. Adebayo, Professor of History,
> Kennesaw State University

Nigerian Chiefs is an authoritative analysis of the political aspects of traditional authority in the Yoruba region of Nigeria. . . . Its publication will encourage historians and social scientists to pursue research on this important, yet neglected, subject in many African countries.

> —Richard L. Sklar, Professor Emeritus of Political Science,
> University of California at Los Angeles

In *Nigerian Chiefs: Traditional Power in Modern Politics, 1890s–1990s*, Olufemi Vaughan demonstrates how the dynamic tensions of communal and individual identities often shape social formations with implications for political and institutional development.

> —Kelechi A. Kalu, Associate Professor of Political Science,
> University of Northern Colorado